Contents

ACKNOWLEDGEMENTS

The editor and publisher would like to thank the authors and publishers of the articles reproduced in this book for their kind cooperation. The journals from which the articles have been taken are listed below.

Bulletin of Concerned Asian Scholars, Berthoud
Economic and Political Weekly, Bombay
Herald, Karachi
Journal of Contemporary Asia, Stockholm
The New York Review of Books, New York
The New Yorker, New York
Race & Class, London
Seminar, New Delhi
Viewpoint, Lahore

Fresh Perspectives on India and Pakistan

Essays on economics, politics and culture

Edited and with an Introduction by
Iqbal Khan

Bougainvillea Books
Oxford

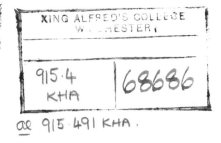
First published in Great Britain 1985
by Bougainvillea Books
68 Dene Road, Headington,
Oxford OX3 7EE

Copyright © Bougainvillea Books 1985
ISBN 0 948631 00 7

Set in Plantin
by Holywell Press Ltd., Oxford, England.
Printed by Holywell Press Ltd., Oxford, England.
Bound by J. W. Braithwaite and Son Limited, Wolverhampton, England.

For
Chinita
who brought laughter into my life

INTRODUCTION:
India and Pakistan in 1985

Iqbal Khan

1. Subcontinental Paradoxes

In 1985, thirty-eight years after their emergence as independent nations, both India and Pakistan have entered a qualitatively new phase of capitalist development and exploitation. This new phase marks a transition from what has been aptly called 'bureaucratic capitalism' to an open and unrestrained surrender to internal and external capital. In both countries, moreover, the change is being brought about under the auspices of the United States, thereby tying the two countries more closely than before to the interests of American capital and imperialism. At the same time, however, there is an important difference between the circumstances surrounding this transition in the two countries. In India the new triumph of the laissez-faire principle signifies a clearing of the way for an industrial and commercial revolution that had been gathering momentum, although haltingly and much marred by bureaucratic inefficiency and corruption, ever since the country became independent; in Pakistan, by contrast, it is a desperate (but as we shall see, largely ineffectual) attempt to ward off an impending catastrophe which in truth is being postponed only through good luck and massive foreign aid.

We will return to this important moment in the histories of India and Pakistan later in this Introduction when we discuss the nature of economic development in the two countries. What we would like to draw attention to at the moment is the complex chiaroscuro of contrasts and similarities which the economic situation referred to above manifests so dramatically, but which characterises nearly all levels of the historical experience of the two countries. As far as I know, this theme has not received the attention it deserves, yet it seems to me that an in-depth analysis of the complex contrasts and similarities that exist between India and Pakistan can prove to be very instructive. This is of course not the place to attempt such an analysis, though a few brief hints to indicate its theoretical usefulness may be in order; my main purpose is to use the theme of similarities and contrasts as a convenient framework in order to bring the present overall situation in India and Pakistan into focus.

Political systems

The most obvious contrast between India and Pakistan is of course the one that pertains to the political fortunes of the two countries. Except for the brief

1

period of eighteen months between June 1975 and January 1977 (the period of Mrs Indira Gandhi's Emergency), India has managed to sustain a secular democratic system of government on a scale unparalleled in the world. This achievement is all the more remarkable in view of the fact that India's democratic system has been nurtured under conditions usually thought to be inimical to democracy: a vast, mostly illiterate, population; an area which, although larger than the US, in most parts still has extremely poor (in some cases non-existent) means of regular communication; a great diversity of religions, sects, cultures and languages, often at war with one another; an overwhelmingly rural sector still caught in ancient social relations, customs and ways of thinking; and so on.[1] Despite all this, a democratic system has not only been established in the length and breadth of India, it has withstood some quite profound shocks, both internal and external. For example, hardly had the country the time to pull itself together after the trauma and turmoil of the Partition days when it had to face the barely concealed Pakistani invasion of Kashmir and the eventual loss of a portion of its territory to that country; then came the language riots of the fifties, which created a constitutional crisis just two years after India had proudly proclaimed its Constitution; this was followed by the Chinese invasion in 1962, the wars with Pakistan, the widespread communal riots, the Sikh challenge and the military operation against the Golden Temple, and most recently the assassination of Mrs Gandhi. Any of these crises could have provided a pretext for the suspension of the democratic order or for military intervention in the affairs of the state. However, India's democracy survived all these challenges, except once—and at the end of that inglorious episode the people of India expressed their anger against those who had deprived them of democracy—Mrs Gandhi and her Congress(I)—by inflicting a humiliating defeat on them in the elections that followed.

Equally remarkable is the fact that although the Indian National Congress and especially Jawaharlal Nehru had been passionately attached to the concept of a strongly centralised government—partly as a result of the deep fears of the 'balkanisation' of the country in the wake of Partition; partly because of an ideological confusion, itself the product of feudal social relations, which equates unity with centralisation of power and nationhood with ethnic and cultural uniformity; and partly because of the dogma that only centralisation of resources and management can carry through a programme of industrialisation and modernisation in a backward country—under popular pressure they allowed new states to be created within a space of fourteen years (1952–66) along linguistic and even religious lines. The central government, whatever authoritarian reaction it might have displayed at first to the minority nations' demands for separate homelands, did not in the end crush their aspirations by resorting to the argument that such demands would jeopardise the integrity or security of the country. In the history of nations such flexibility on the part of those who hold power is rather rare. Indeed, Indian democracy has proved resilient enough to accommodate even communist state governments within its overall system (Kerala, West Bengal, Tripura)—a fact that puts it high above the 'models' of pluralist democracy in the West. If today continuing anti-reservation and communal riots and Sikh terrorism are tearing India apart, these might indeed appear to be the result of its radical commitment to democratic and secular ideals rather than the opposite (though appearances may turn out to be deceptive, as we will see).

In Pakistan, history has taken a diametrically opposite course. The period in which Pakistan enjoyed democracy perhaps extends over a couple of years: i.e. the years between 1971 and 1973—the initial years of Zulfikar Ali Bhutto's regime. During the remaining of its thirty-eight years' history Pakistan has lived either under a provisional civilian government, which ruled without being elected (1947–54), or under despotic rule in one form or another, ranging from the populist crypto-fascist regime of Bhutto's later years to naked military dictatorship. There has been only one genuinely democratic election, in 1970, and three major attempts at framing a Constitution (in 1956, 1962 and 1973); but the country is still without a Constitution—the 1973 Constitution, the only one accepted by the people rather than imposed upon them, having first been 'suspended' by the present military regime of General Zia-ul-Haq, and then 'amended' by him in March 1985 while it remained (and remains) 'suspended'. These amendments to the 1973 Constitution have the effect of changing the balance of power in such a way that the final authority rests not in the hands of the people's representatives but in the hands of the President, who is General Zia-ul-Haq himself.

Even though General Zia has now promised to withdraw the Martial Law by the end of 1985, the notorious 'Eighth Amendment' to the Constitution, or the Indemnity Bill as it is called, which he is forcing upon a recalcitrant National Assembly and which gives a blanket validation to all Martial Law Orders, Laws, etc., including the above-mentioned amendments, and makes them unrepealable except by a 'competent authority' over and above the National Assembly, makes it quite clear that military rule will continue in Pakistan even when, and if, Martial Law is lifted. Furthermore, special tribunals are now (September 1985) being set up to 'replace' military courts which will have exclusive authority to review past sentences given by the latter and to deal with any future cases relating to 'anti-Pakistan' activities. All such cases will fall outside the jurisdiction of civil courts even after the lifting of the Martial Law. It is also believed that the government is contemplating setting up a security force on the lines of the dreaded Federal Security Force of the Bhutto era, which will be recruited from former military personnel and will be responsible for internal 'peace' and 'security'. In view of all this, there is no reason to believe that democracy is about to be given a chance in Pakistan.

4

Fresh Perspective

This sharp contrast between the political histories of the two countries naturally cries out for an explanation. India and Pakistan were carved out of the same country, why then did their political fortunes turn out to be so different? What forces led them into so totally opposite directions? The chief advantage of a comparative study of the two countries is precisely that it raises such questions. Now an important point to note is that, when studied in this perspective, an explanation of the historical processes of India and Pakistan in purely class terms, illuminating though it is, does not prove to be entirely satisfactory. This is as much true of some of the more recent, unorthodox Marxists writings which try to avoid reductionism, as it is of the older type. The exclusive concentration on the relationship between the various classes and the state in India and Pakistan, in terms of which these writings seek to understand the nature and evolution of these societies, prevents them from seeing that the state is not only the manager or arbiter of conflicting class interests, but also a cultural or ideological force, which owes its existence and efficacy, to some extent, to factors other than class interests (at least it is not linked to them in any immediate sense), and which, *within limits*, plays an independent formative role in society. In other words, an exclusively class-based analysis of the state blurs the distinction between the role the state plays *vis-a-vis* the class strucure of a society and the role it plays in its political culture. Because of this difference, states in two societies may perform the same (or similar) class roles, but generate totally different kinds of political cultures; and by doing so they may not only differently affect (i.e. reinforce or thwart) their own roles as guardians of class interests, but also—and this is particularly important—open up, or close off, certain possibilities for the development of the social formations. It seems to this writer that it is only by taking the cultural factor, as well as the class factor, into consideration that an explanation of the political contrast between India and Pakistan can be adequately given and its far reaching significance appreciated.

Political Cultures and Their Consequences

The failure of many Marxist writers to distinguish between the two aspects of the state mentioned above is of course an echo of their well-known tendency to ignore the complex dialectic between the superstructure (especially the *cultural* superstructure) and the socio-economic base, and to make no use of the former in historical and social explanation. In connection with India and Pakistan this leads to the suppression of what is one of the most important aspects of these countries' historical experience. Thus, to take a recent example, Anupum Sen in his study of the state and class formations in India is concerned to demonstrate how the state can play an autonomous role *vis-a-vis* the various classes in India:

Like the Bonapartist state, the autonomy of the state in India emerges from the fact that the power of the landlords is non-existent on the political level and the bourgeoisie is too weak; the state can claim that it is representing the interests of the small peasants and seek, on their behalf, to contain the bourgeoisie. . . .[However] the small peasant was a social force as a class-in-itself but not as a class-for-itself. That is why the state in India ... could pretend to represent their interests without, in fact, doing so.[2]

In other words, the weakness of the various classes in India is the reason why the state has become so powerful and is able to play a dominant role in relation to the classes, instead of performing a merely representative function for the most powerful of them. Now a similar thesis was formulated earlier by Hamza Alavi in relation to Pakistani state and society (though he believed that his analysis could apply to the Third World countries in general).[3] It follows that, according to this kind of analysis, the states in India and Pakistan possess essentially the same character. But if so, how can one account for the fact that democracy has survived in one country but not in the other? This question arises also in view of another similarity that existed in respect of the con-figuration of class forces at the time of Independence, viz. that despite the weakness (Sen) or equal strength (Alavi) of the two main classes (the feudal aristocracy and the bourgeoisie) the stimulus to both the Congress and the Muslim League nevertheless came primarily from the urban bourgeoisie, on whose financial support both parties depended heavily. That neither Sen or Alavi concerns himself with this issue may be because their attention is directed elsewhere, but it may also imply that for them the difference in the *political form* of the two states is either illusory or of no consequence. Both conclusions will do violence to the concrete historical experience of these societies.

An explanation of the contrasting political fortunes of India and Pakistan must take into account the role of the ideologies and cultural outlooks of the parties and leaders who played the leading role in creating these na-tions—cultures whose roots lie deep in the history of pre-independence India and particularly the complex and widely different impact Western ideas had on Hindu and Muslim elites. This is a very large subject and cannot be entered into here (though some preliminary remarks will be necessary when we discuss the economies of the two countries). What I do wish to point out, however, are the far reaching *consequences* which the difference in the political form of the states in India and Pakistan carries for the fate of these societies. For, like all bourgeois democracies, limited and merely formal though India's democracy is, the mere fact that it exists is of enormous value. Thanks to the freedom of opinion allowed by this system, there is occurring a geniune ef-florescence of knowledge and ideas—including radical ideas—in India today. The instruments of this intellectual and cultural awakening are India's numerous newspapers, magazines and journals (many of them of as high a quality as any to be found anywhere in the world), its publishing houses, its universities, and its art and cultural organisations and activities.[4] These are providing invaluable outlets for the creative energies of India's growing intelligentsia and artists (even though the quality of commercialised entertainment remains extremely poor and exploitative). This cultural phenomenon is of no mean importance: *not only is it the mainstay of Indian democracy; at its best it is promoting a modern, scientific and critical consciousness whose liberating and civilising effects have consequences that go beyond the aims of bourgeois democracy.*

In Pakistan, however, the suppression of freedoms, coupled with the belief that Pakistan was established in order to provide an independent home for (Indian) Muslim—which the self-appointed rulers of the country soon twisted into the very different idea that Pakistan was meant to be an Islamic state—has taken a heavy toll on Pakistan's cultural life. This country of 95 million people which is capable of making a nuclear bomb has few newspapers or periodicals in any field, and the readership of these, with the exception of those publications which deal with Islamic subjects or popular fiction, is exceedingly small.[5] The circulation of *Dawn*, the country's only major English language daily, has remained at its 1959 level (though the Urdu daily *Jang* claims to have increased its circulation ten-fold between 1959 and 1980). According to the World Press Encyclopaedia, in terms of newspaper readership, Pakistan ranks amongst the lowest 20 countries in the world.

Right from the beginning, with a few exceptions, conservatism and conformism have been the distinguishing features of Pakistan's publishing industry, as they have been of its intellectual life as a whole from top to bottom—and this includes also the majority of its Western-educated scholars and academics. This narrowness of outlook has been reinforced by repressive laws, which have grown progressively harsher. For example, the amended Penal Code Section 499 provides arrest without warrant and imprisonment up to 5 years, plus fine, for even mild criticism of the President. Then there are Section 124A of the Pakistan Penal Code dealing with sedition, and the Official Secrets Act and Martial Law Regulation 49 which prohibit publication of material contrary to Islam and Pakistan's ideology. Additionally, every publisher is required to pay a large sum as deposit to the government as a guarantee of good behaviour. More recently (in September) even a more draconian censorship has been imposed by the government; under this new law not only private internal and foreign mail will be heavily censored, the police has been given authority to raid bookstores and printing presses to search and destroy any literature it might consider to be anti-government or against Pakistan's ideology. A very large number of publications including works of prominent contemporary poets and writers have been banned. All this, plus the fact that publishing costs in Pakistan are very high, naturally prevents anyone except the most commercially minded and servile to engage in journalism and publishing activity.[6] Comparing the state of journalism in Pakistan with that in India, an authoritative observer was moved to write: 'It is significant that despite its common origin, the journalism of India and Pakistan has developed on divergent lines. Very few Pakistan publications display the maturity that characterises the Indian press. While three Indian papers appear in *The World's Great Dailies*, none from Pakistan has made the list.[7]

In fact the writing in the few newspapers and periodicals that are allowed to be published, including university publications, is more often than not elementary and shallow. More distressingly, it reflects a collective mind that has not been allowed to grow and has been made strongly resistant to the influence of modern, rational ways of thinking and concerns. This, to a great extent, is due to the extremely poor standards of education in Pakistan (about which more later) and particularly to the extraordinary situation that while nothing has been done to develop Urdu, the national language, so that it could carry the weight of advanced thought and literature, the teaching of English has practically been abandoned in schools and colleges as a matter of policy. The result is that the people are floundering, so to speak, in a no man's land of language, and young people go through schools and universities without acquiring any facility either in their mother-tongue or in English. But what is particularly shocking is the fact that the literacy rate in Pakistan, instead of showing any improvement, has been steadily worsening: according to recent estimates (acknowledged to be correct by no less a person than the Finance Minister, Mr Mahbub-ul-Haq) the number of literates in Pakistan amounts to little over 8%! Little wonder that there are few bookshops in the country and few books of serious nature are published: in fact, the book supply has all but dried up. According to a responsible library official there is but one book to every 63 persons in Pakistan; the total number of books in *all* the libraries of the country put together amounts to no more than a mere 6,500,000; and the per capita expenditure on books is as little as Rs0.09. This provides some measure of the extent to which long years of dictatorship have thrown Pakistan back into the Dark Ages.

Complexities of Political Behavior

The contrasting picture of the political systems of India and Pakistan that has been presented above is on the whole correct. Yet, it would be a mistake to accept it without reservation. In India's case, an uncritical acceptance of its image as even a limited bourgeois, secular democracy (even if we do not for the moment raise the question of social justice, equality, etc.) would be to ignore the autocratic—even fascist—tendencies of its government; in the case of Pakistan, a similar uncritical appraisal of the political situation there would cause us to neglect the tremendous hatred of bureaucracy and dictatorship and the desire for a democratic order which exists among Pakistani people, and which is as much a part of Pakistan's history as the brutal fact of dictatorship.

Thus (to take only the period of the past two or three years) it was the secular, liberal and democratic government of India that carried out bloodbaths in Assam and in Punjab, killing tens of thousands of its own people – and in both cases from motives that had less to do with national interest than with the interest of the ruling Congress(I) Party. The same democratic government dictatorially removed the elected chief ministers of Jammu and Kashmir and Andhra Pradesh, and tried to remove another, in Karnataka, when these ministers refused to kneel to the wishes of the Prime Minister in Delhi. Nor can it be ignored that it was the leader of the same democratic government who tried to perpetuate the rule of her family as if India were not a democratic state but a fiefdom. Again, the ruling circles of India (including persons belonging to Congress(I) high command and top members of the police and civil service hierarchy) have been indicted of planning the horrifying massacre of thousands of ordinary Sikhs in their homes in New Delhi following the assassination of Mrs Gandhi. The indictment was made in a joint report of the People's Union of Civil Liberties and the People's Union for Democratic Rights, and the evidence contained in it was further corroborated by an independent enquiry carried out by the Citizens' Commission, which was headed by a former Chief Justice of India and other respected citizens. The government has so far rejected all demands to open an investigation of the events of those days.

The strongly authoritarian and fascist reactions to national events on the part of India's rulers are neither confined to any particular government nor to a few individuals, but betray a tendency that is all too pervasive to justify any tall claims about India's democratic institutions. Thus it is estimated that even before the military operations in Assam, Punjab and Gujarat during the past two years, there had been no less than 369 military involvements in the internal affairs of the country.[8] Similarly, it is reported in the Indian daily *Hind Samachar* that between 1950 and 1984, as many as 348 Presedential Ordinances were issued by various governments—some of these ordinances having been issued even while one of the houses of parliament was in session. The frequent resort to the army and to ordinances (we are of course not counting the period of the Emergency) betrays a strong tendency on the part of India's 'democratic' governments to solve political problems through dictatorial or strong-arm methods. Moreover, is it not also true that the ruling circles of this secular democracy have consistently and systematically encouraged Hindu communalism and fundamentalism in the country, often merely to gain temporary political advantage, with the result that communal riots keep erupting in India with frightening regularity, inflicting death and destruction on thousands of poor and already enormously suffering masses?

At lower levels this propensity to resort to naked power takes equally horrible forms. Extreme police atrocities against innocent citizens, especially villagers, as well as those in police custody, are as frequent in the democratic (and Gandhian!) India as in the military-ruled Pakistan. And all this is apart from the near-fascistic tendencies in Indian society at large – tendencies which manifest themselves, to mention only one example, in the almost customary mutilation and burning alive of hundreds of helpless women and landless peasants (especially *harijans*) every year (it is reported that during 1984 – 85 over six hundred brides were burnt to death by their relatives for failure to bring dowries). Judged against this record of autocracy and brutality, any talk of India's secular democracy and culture might appear to be little more than pretentious hypocrisy.

And yet, in that same India there are now developing a forceful civil liberties movement and a radical women's movement in revolt against autocracy in all its forms, and against barbaric social customs, while Indian people at large have repeatedly revolted against the authoritarianism of the central government (the most recent example of which occurred when the people of Andhra Pradesh and Karnataka voted the chief ministers who had been victimised by Mrs Gandhi back into power in the 1985 state elections). But an equally shining example of the commitment to democracy comes from the present Prime Minister of India himself. With rare political courage and statesmanship, Rajiv Gandhi not only abandoned the near-totalitarian and confrontationalist policies of his still highly venerated mother and came to terms with reality in Assam and Punjab; he even forwent the opportunity of winning the September elections in Punjab (which was at least possible) by mounting a deliberately low-key election fight against the Akali Dal in the interest of a democratic principle of a higher order than the one that takes only numerical majority into consideration. Whatever may be said about the hollowness of India's democracy (and much remains to be said on this count) it will be vulgar in the extreme not to acknowledge that these actions of Mr Gandhi represent a triumph both for India and for democracy.

And just as in India events have time and again shown that, however delicate, the saplings of democracy and secularism are nevertheless being nourished and are growing against severe odds, so in Pakistan it was always the threat of a democratic mass upsurge against the ruling coteries that led the bureaucracy and military to intervene and impose and reimpose dictatorship in the country. Nor did Pakistani people hesitate—and again the similarity with India is striking—to rise against their most popular leader (Bhutto) in 1977 when he turned autocratic and corrupt. But perhaps the most surprising manifestation of their political maturity and innate preference for both democracy and secularism occurred in the December 1984 Referendum and the February 1985 elections to the National Assembly which followed. In the Referendum, the people were asked to vote for General Zia by voting for Islam—a diabolically cunning strategem on the part of the General whereby his victory was absolutely assured, since Pakistani people could not be expected to vote against Islam. Similarly, in the National Assembly elections, which Zia was forced to hold in order to obtain a semblance of political legitimacy for himself and his regime, he ensured his victory by first banning political parties from the elections and then by carrying out massive repression of all the opposition parties in the country.[9] Despite all this, however, and despite the intensive propaganda on behalf of Islam and General Zia to which the people had been subjected day and night for the previous eight years, the people upset all calculations of the General: the Referendum was almost totally boycotted (the official denials notwithstanding); while in the National Assembly elections all those candidates who were believed to be favoured by Zia were systematically ignored—and these included the representatives of the Jamaat-i-Islami, the most aggressive advocate for an Islamic state in Pakistan. True, *biradri* (clan) loyalties and cash offers to voters by the National Assembly hopefuls played their part in producing this result (the total amount spent on buying voters has been calculated to be in the region of one billion four hundred million rupees!) but these factors should not be allowed to minimise the element of defiance of the military regime which characterised the elections and which has indeed persisted in the National Assembly itself.

If there is any moral to be drawn from these examples it is obviously that the antithesis between a democratic India and an undemocratic Pakistan is not quite as stark as appears at first sight; the political situation in the two countries is too complex to be put into neat and preconceived categories.

The Regional Problem

Nor is this the end of the paradoxes that mark the political scene on the subcontinent. The subject cannot be left without mentioning the 'regional' problem—i.e. the problem arising from the demands of ethnic minorities for political autonomy—which can be said to have become the number one problem in both India and Pakistan. In both countries the problem is an old one, but the destinies of the problem in the two countries present yet another sharply contrasting picture. While in India, as mentioned above, the earlier regional demands were accommodated by the state, in Pakistan of course they led to tragic results. The first such demand, made by the eastern part of the country, led to a near-genocide in East Pakistan and the break-up of the country; the second time the demand arose from the Baluchistan province of West Pakistan—it was again ruthlessly crushed by Pakistani army and air force. However, what concerns us now are not the earlier events, but the more recent demands for regional autonomy: in the Indian Punjab and in Sind.

On the surface, the two problems bear strong similarities: a relatively small, culturally and geographically well-defined 'nation' (Sikhs in Punjab, Sindhis in Sind) with its own distinctive history, language and way of life has been in revolt against a majority 'nation' (Hindus in India, Punjabis in Pakistan), which dominates political power at the Centre; in both cases there is a strong feeling of discrimination and exploitation; in both cases the revolt against the central government reached such explosive proportions that it could be suppressed only by means of a ferocious military operation (in Sind during 1983–84; in Punjab in 1984). But there the similarities end; the two situations are in reality completely different.

As Shahid Kardar shows in his article in this book, Sindhis' bitter resentment against the Centre and their demand for greater political autonomy for their province has a solid objective basis. Over the years Sindhis have been subjected to systematic injustices and exploitation by every government that has come to power in Pakistan. To give just a few examples: More than one half of Pakistan's industry is located in Sind, but Sindhis do not own these and the number of Sindhis employed in these industries is insignificant; the lucrative commercial, transportation and service sector, which comprises 55% of Pakistan's GDP, is also located largely in Sind, but Sindhis do not even have a marginal share in this sector; 40% of Sind's prime agricultural land may have passed into the hands of non-Sindhis, while three-fourths of Sindhi peasants own no land at all; in 1970 out of one million workers employed in private industries in Sind, no more than one thousand were Sindhis; only 250 out of more than one thousand bank employees in the province were Sindhis; in the central government service there was only one Sindhi per thousand (note that Sindhis constitute over 43% of Pakistan's population); the Sindhi language, the second most advanced language in the country, is officially treated as if it did not exist, while Sindhi publications are subjected to extra-heavy censorship; and so on and so on.[10]

This stands in marked contrast to the situation in Punjab. As K.R. Bombwall points out in his paper 'Ethno–nationalism', Sikhs' grievances are hardly the result of injustices or discrimination against them. It should be noted that as a result of the Sikhs' earlier agitation, the state of Punjab was cut up and a new state (the present Punjab) was created in 1966 where the Sikhs constituted the majority (56% of the population). Far from being exploited, the new state has since experienced quite enviable prosperity. Moreover, the Sikhs are playing a prominent role at practically all levels of the national life. M.J. Akbar has given important statistics, which are worth quoting here:

> . . . Punjab in the 1980s began to send, alone, 60 per cent of the grain to the national food basket. Its per capita income of Rs 2,768 (all figures are 1980–81) was far above the Indian average of Rs 1,571, with only the states of Haryana and Maharashtra coming anywhere near Punjab. . . . Agriculture contributed 58.12 percent of the state's income, while employing 59.1 percent of the total work force . . . And prosperity brought other benefits.
>
> The spurt in education was reflected both in figures and in quality. The number of primary schools shot up from 7,183 in 1967–1968 to 12,384 in 1981; middle schools from 863 to 1,410; high schools from 789 to 2,158. The number of arts and science colleges rose from 71 in 1968 to 161 in 1981; there were no medical colleges in 1968, but 8 in 1981. . .

* * *

Free India has brought Sikhs prosperity outside agriculture, too. Though just under 2 percent of the population, Sikhs account for 8 percent of the total number of Central government employees; 256 (or one in every sixteen) of the 4,000 directly recruited officers in the Indian Administrative Service ... are Sikhs, as are 81 of 1,527 officers of the parallel group in the police, the Indian Police Service. More than 7.5 percent of the army is still Sikh. At the moment of writing, the President of India, Zail Singh, the Chief of the Air Force, Dilbagh Singh, and the Governmor of the Reserve Bank of India, Manmohan Singh, are Sikhs. The Sikhs have developed a major interest in trade and business with the rest of India, and one – fifth of them live and prosper outside Punjab. The other minorities in India would give an arm and leg for such statistics.[11]

Two questions naturally arise: Given the facts mentioned above, why did the Sikhs in Punjab raise the banner of revolt? And were their demands such that they could not have been accepted by the Indian government, even if that entailed drenching the Sikhs in a horrendous bloodbath? Here, we discover again a stark contrast between the Sind situation in Pakistan and the Punjab situation in India. Although so far Sindhis had been demanding a limited kind of provincial autonomy for their province within the framework of the 1973 Constitution (which General Zia 'suspended' when he overthrew Bhutto in 1977), it has now become quite clear to most Sindhis not only that that Constitution does not give them an adequate degree of political and economic control, but, more importantly, that their rights, even if accepted by the Centre, cannot be safeguarded as long as power remains in the hands of the Punjabi dominated Pakistani army. Quite understandably, therefore, a demand has now arisen for the restructuring of Pakistan as a 'confederation', which entails, among other things, a considerable reduction in the size of the state army as well as the creation of a Sindhi army. Whether or not this is possible without further breaking up Pakistan there can be little doubt that if Sind were given its due, the power structure of the country would have to be fundamentally altered.

This, however, is not the case in regard to the Punjab problem. The charter of demands known as the Anandpur Sahib's Resolution on which the Sikh political-cum-religious party, the Akali Dal, has been basing its agitation has little in it that should have become a life-and-death matter for the Indian government. True, the Charter could be interpreted by overly suspicious minds as a stepping stone towards an independent 'Khalistan'; but the facts that it has now been accepted by the Rajiv government virtually unaltered and that an agreement between the government and the Akali Dal on the Resolution was about to be finalised even in February 1984, when talks broke down under the pressure of a fundamentalist Hindu anti-minority movement, are ample proofs that such suspicions were unjustified.[12] It was Mrs Gandhi's deliberate choice to appease the Hindu communalists, whose support was essential for Congress(I), rather than the nature of the Sikhs' demands as such, which blocked any possibility of accommodation with the moderate Akali Dal and led to the escalation of violence in Punjab, the strengthening of the extremist Sikh faction under Bhindranwale, and the eventual military operation against the Golden Temple in Amritsar which the extremists had turned into an armed fortress. Moreover, there is also agreement among many investigators of the events in Punjab that the rise of Bhindranwale, who espoused the extremist demand for Khalistan, was due not to any wide support for the idea among the Sikh masses (the lower caste and class Sikhs were particularly unsympathetic), but to the machinations of Mrs Gandhi's own government, which tried by this means to divide the Sikhs in order to maintain the hold of Congress(I) on Punjab.

In short, the Punjab problem, like the problem of the Centre-State relationship in general in India, does not arise from any systematic suppression or exploitation of a minority by a deeply entrenched ruling majority, as it does in Pakistan, and as such is resolvable within the existing framework of the Indian state. No great upheaval need have occurred over the issue of greater autonomy for Punjab (or for other states). But in Pakistan the possibility of such an upheaval is built into just this relationship between the Centre and the minority provinces.

And yet, at a more fundamental level, the ethnic minorities' revolt against the state in both India and Pakistan is merely a symptom of a deeper problem, which is perhaps best characterised in cultural terms, in the sense in which 'culture' has been discussed by Ashis Nandy in his article in this book. From this point of view, the problem is not any particular arrangement between the state and the minorities, but the state itself—that is, the traditional Western state which has been transplanted onto the Indian soil. This state, as Nandy argues in his thought-provoking essay, is by its very nature coercive, no matter how many democratic trappings it might acquire. The various movements for regional autonomy (like the other liberation movements slowly ripening in India as well as Pakistan: the women's rights movement, the civil rights movement, the tribal people's rights movement, etc., etc.) point to a very different type of political order, an order constituted 'bottom upwards' to embody and protect the culture(s) of the oppressed, and one in which the political processes take the form (to use a happy phrase employed by Bombwall) of a 'daily referendum'.

Gigantic Failure

So far our portraits of India and Pakistan have revealed dramatic contrasts and similarities in practically every area, making a clear assessment of their achievements and failures a challenging—though by no means an impossible—task. It is when we ask the question 'What is the record of India and

Pakistan in solving the basic problems of their people, such as poverty, hunger, disease, illiteracy, etc., after thirty-eight years' economic planning and development?' that the picture of the two countries loses all its redeeming complexities and looks uniformly bleak. We will presently cast a bird's-eye glance at salient statistics for social services in both countries, which will give some idea of their gigantic failure in providing for even the basic needs of their people. But, first, the question obliges us to take note of the social inequalities that exist in both countries—for it is these, rather than any essential poverty or lack of development—that lie at the root of their failure.

The stark class polarisation is evident in the following figures relating to the concentration of wealth in India: the top 10% of all households own 33.6% of the country's wealth, while the top 20% possess nearly half of it (49.4%). Compared with this, the lowest 20% of households own a mere 7%.[13] Recent overall figures for Pakistan are not available, but a 'Group 83' study, published in Lahore, estimates that in 1979 the bottom 27% of rural households, or 30% of the rural population (which constitutes 70% of the total population of the country) received no more than 15% of the total rural household income; similarly, the share of the bottom 22% urban households (or 14% of the urban population) amounts to only 8% of the total urban household income.[14] The matter was put in a nutshell in a *Dawn* editorial (May 22, 1985) which noted that 'the fact is that the gap between the rich and the poor is now much wider [in Pakistan] than it was at the time of independence'.

Had these gross inequalities been an engine of capital accumulation through savings and reinvestment, and so of self-sustained development, as the capitalist doctrine claims, there might have been some slight justification for them. In the contemporary conditions of India and Pakistan, however, these inequalities have served to arrest the true developmental potential of these countries. Because the income levels of the majority are not allowed to rise, the vast internal markets remain stagnant and provide no incentive to the manufacturers. In fact, millions of rural households in Pakistan and India—those that survive on subsistence farming—even now exist entirely outside the money economy, and there is in both countries a continually growing multitude of unemployed labourers in both rural and urban areas. On the other side of the inequality divide, the greater part of the wealth of the rich is used on luxury consumption, in drug trafficking and other illegal business activities, or is exported abroad;[15] the result is that the saving rate in both countries is extremely low (in Pakistan it had declined to about 5% by 1981-82).[16] Consequently, the rich (feudal landowners and capitalists) have to be offered enormous bribes in order to get them to divert some of their wealth into productive sectors. These bribes, whether they take the form of price increases or tax-holidays, tax concessions, subsidies, etc., drain the masses of their little incomes and the treasury of it revenues, so that both India and Pakistan have to borrow massive sums of money at high interest rates to finance whatever little development efforts they undertake. All this, together with the huge expenditure on defence and bureaucracy—which, too, springs from the same structure of social inequalities—leaves precious little to be spent on raising the quality of life of the poor.[17]

But the worst form of the bribe that has to be offered to the rich is the heavy encouragement of those investment opportunities that promise high and quick profits: in other words, luxury goods and export-oriented industries, which depend on foreign technology and must be paid for by selling the country's agricultural produce. The tragic contradictions this kind of industrial development creates are immediately obvious in regard to one of the most basic necessities of life: food.

(a) Food

Thus let us note that food production in India during the past four years has been quite impressive, and with over 150 million tons in 1984-85 and now a surplus of 8 million tons has reached a record level.[18] In Pakistan, too, at least until the last two years, food production had been high. In fact, both India and Pakistan actually export food and these exports have been steadily rising, as the following figures show: The export of rice from India rose from 32,000 tons in 1970–71 to 726,000 tons in 1980–81; in the same period the export of fish more than doubled; the export of vegetables, fruits and pulses increased six times; and the export of meat, in value terms, rose from Rs30 million to Rs554 million.[19] Similarly, Pakistan in 1983-84 exported Rs8.769 billion worth of food and live animals, of which rice was, in value terms, Rs5.688 billion, fruits and vegetables Rs538 million, and fish Rs1.0007 billion.[20]

Now, let us set against all this the following facts to obtain some measure of the criminal failure of 'development' in India and Pakistan: In India, nearly half of the population (i.e. about 300 million people) lives below the official poverty line and remains hungry some parts of the year—more than a third of it remaining hungry for as much as three months or more.[21] Most of those who exist below poverty line do not get even the official minimum intake of 2,000 calories a day! In fact, according to one estimate, per capita daily consumption, for the population as a whole, has increased by only about 50 grams in the past thirty years;[22] while, according to another estimate, even as food production has risen, the net per capita availability of pulses—probably the sole source of protein for the majority of the poor who cannot afford the luxury of meat – declined from 70 grams per day in 1956 to 41 grams per day in 1983–84.[23] Nor is the situation as regards the poor any better in Pakistan. There, too, per capita consumption of cereals dropped from 160.8 kgs in 1972–73 to 155.5 kgs in 1981–82; and the proportion of the population unable to get the official minimum of 2,550 calories might be as high as 40% (though conservative estimates put it at about 33%).[24] Hunger and chronic malnutrition are thus the lot of hundreds of millions in both countries which boast of bursting granaries and high growth rates.

The picture as regards health, education, housing and sanitation is equally

16

dismal. The following figures will further indicate to what cruel extent human needs have been ignored by 'development' in the two countries and in the case of India also, alas, by 'democracy'. It must, however, be remembered that no amount of statistics can succeed in portraying the utter wretchedness of the daily lives of the masses in India and Pakistan—one has only to think of the millions who live, sleep, eat, defecate, breed children, and die on pavements and by the side of open gutters in the slums of Bombay, Calcutta and Karachi; or of those villagers—men, women and children—who, even after three decades of 'development', have never known electricity, or have to walk miles in order to get medical attention for the sick, and often even to get water to drink. But here are the statistics, which are telling enough.[25]

(b)Health (1980)

	One Physician to: as many as	One Nurse to: as many as	Total Expenditure on Health % of GNP
INDIA	*3,690 persons	*5,460 persons	n.a.
PAKISTAN	5,334 persons (and one dentist to 83,000 persons)	15,736 persons	0.59 (1979–80) 0.36 (1980–81) 0.5 (1982–)

(*These are World Bank figures for 1980-81; actual figures are most probably higher)

In addition, India 'leads' the world in blindness (on account of vitamin A deficiency), leprosy and tuberculosis. Pakistan in recent years has been hit by a typhoid epidemic; diseases like malaria—once believed to have been eliminated—keep threatening to re-appear on a large scale; and in 1985 there are estimated to be more than 1,800,000 people suffering from T.B. It is to be noted at the same time that in 1985 no less than 12,000 doctors are reported to be unemployed in Pakistan; and the huge migration of Pakistani and Indian doctors to foreign countries is well known.

(c) Education (1981)

	Primary School Enrolment (as % of relevant age group)			Secondary Enrolment (% of age group)	No. in Higher Educ. (as % of age group)	Expenditure on Educ. as %
	Male:	Female:	Total:			
INDIA	93	64	79	30	8	3.2 of GDP
PAKISTAN	73	31	56	17	2	1.7 of GNP so far; 2.2 promised for 1985–86

Thus in India about 20% of children of primary school age fail to obtain any education, while the proportion of such children in Pakistan is as high as nearly 50%. The picture at the secondary level is even more shocking: 70% of the children in this age group in India and 83% in Pakistan remain deprived of secondary education! Even these figures do not take into account the high drop-out rate and failure rate in the various examinations. For example, the drop-out rate at the primary stage alone is 50% in Pakistan and the rate increases as the children progress through the educational system; as for examination failures, the rate is 70% at the Intermediate level alone. Even so, the provision of educational facilities at the higher levels fall woefully short of the demand, as can be seen from the fact that this year in Pakistan there were 18,000 graduate candidates for university places which numbered only 2,000.

Moreover, so far no concentrated effort has been made to eliminate illiteracy in either country: in Pakistan, as noted earlier, illiteracy is actually increasing and is about to engulf the whole nation; and in India, though certainly lower than in Pakistan, the official illiteracy figure of 57% strains credence.

Nor is this all. It is of course not enough simply to enrol the children in schools; some basic physical and material conditions for learning must be provided and it must be ensured that at least certain basic standards of education are maintained in schools and colleges. As for the former, the following description of the state of affairs in India is more or less true also of Pakistan:

> Education provides an excellent example of the way in which priorities get skewed because of a focusing of attention on modernisation, on creating centres of excellence, and on bringing the communications revolution into the classroom. For the government has shown no awareness yet of the fact that more than half the five lakh primary schools in the country lack proper buildings, 40 percent have no blackboards, 70 percent have no children's books, and 80 percent have no lavatories.[26]

In both countries violence on the campus, cheating in examinations, and reliance on 'study guides' and 'keys' in place of books (especially since textbooks are simply not available or are too expensive for the students to buy or too difficult for them to read) are extremely common practices in educational institutions. But in Pakistan this 'system' has virtually replaced the normal educational process. Colleges and universities in Pakistan are kept closed for long periods, because they are the nuclei of protest against the military regime (for which reason also the government has adopted a policy of terrorising the students and teachers by means of dismissals, imprisonment, and even killings, and has frequently encouraged the fascist-religious students' organisation Islami-Jamiat-i-Tulaba to create havoc on campuses). It is also quite common for examinations to be repeatedly cancelled or for their results to be held back—the results of some of the college examinations held in 1981 and 1982 were being announced in 1985! By all accounts, education in Pakistan has virtually collapsed.

However, what has hit Pakistani education (and Pakistani intelligentsia) particularly hard over the past eight years is General Zia's Islamisation programme. Although, mercifully, the resurgence of Islamic fundamentalism has not reached the intensity it has in neighbouring Iran, it is nevertheless being injected into the educational system with considerable zeal. Indeed, it seems that for Zia and his government 'progress' in education, apart from a ritual acknowledgement of the importance of science and technology in this connection, has become entirely synonymous with its capacity to promote the Islamic way of life. Words like 'rationality', 'scientific attitude', 'critical outlook' have simply disappeared from official pronouncements on education. School textbooks are being rewritten (and rewritten by semi-literate hacks at that!) to suit the official ideology, and every attempt is being made to foster a narrowly nationalistic, in fact sectarian, mentality and sanctimonious dogmatism among the children and students at all levels. The idolisation of the Quaid-i-Azam (the founder of Pakistan) and the glorification of the Pakistan struggle and of the Muslim past (that, too, as interpreted by Sunni Muslim theologians and apologist) is fast approaching comic proportions. At the same time ancient Indian history, the Indus and Gandhara civilisations (all a precious part of Pakistan's great cultural heritage) have been tabooed as 'unholy'[27]—even the word 'India' is considered unholy and has been replaced by 'South Asia' in some history books![28]

And, yet, the irony is that this narrow sectarian and reactionary outlook that is being promoted in Pakistan through education is by no means peculiar to that country: it is equally in evidence in secular India. Since this aspect of Indian politics is generally not so well known, I shall quote at some length from a recent paper by Krishna Kumar:

> Faith in the instrumentality of education for the development of a secular society has received a serious jolt since the beginning of this decade. The jolt has come from the expression of a demand for the orientation of education in the direction of 'Indian' values. More specifically, the demand is that 'sooner rather than later we must recognise the need of duly adjusting our education to our past'. . . . The demand, which applies both to the school and higher level of education, has not been made by a fringe section of professional educators or sectarian politicians. It has been voiced by the topmost offices of the system of education, such as the Ministry of Education and the University Grants Commission . . . .

> . . . education in India has never been particularly secular or secularising. Observation and inquiry, which are directly related to a this-worldly, secular attitude, have been a low priority in the pedagogy of Indian schools and colleges. Also, patterns of authority and daily rituals

observed in schools have prevented the growth of a secular culture of education.

The current expression of the revivalist view-point on education is linked with the deepening of economic inequalities and the desperation of the elite to project a radiant identity in the midst of crisis.[29]

(d) Housing and Sanitation

The record of thirty-eight years' development in regard to the provision of housing and sanitation, too, is very similar in both countries, though conditions in India are decidedly worse than in Pakistan. In both countries during the last twenty years there has been a virtual explosion of opulent suburbs with palatial homes (some costing $1m each or more) in major cities. This has sent real estate prices skyrocketing (in Pakistan by the late 1970's real estate prices had gone up by as much as 1000 percent!) and has enormously diminished the chances of the ever-swelling lower strata of the population finding proper shelter. In India, according to a government estimate, no less than 21,300,000 new houses were needed in 1981 alone. Since such a vast number of houses is obviously not available, millions of people are forced to live in slums and on pavements, often surrounded by unspeakable squalor and filth.

Similarly, in Pakistan, in the seventies there was a shortage of 1 million houses in only urban areas. In addition, it is estimated that 116,000 houses are needed to accommodate the additional number of households created every year. Yet, the rate at which houses were being constructed in the seventies was only 3,300 per year(and the situation has hardly improved since then). The result is again that a vast multitude is forced to live in slums and *katchi abadis*, in *jhuggies* and on pavements (indeed, in both India and Pakistan quite a number of people still live in caves), with no provision for sanitation—not even for uncontaminated water. In fact, only 9.7% of the entire population of Pakistan enjoys proper sanitation and sewerage facilities; and only 26.8% of the entire population has access to clean drinking water!

Class Formations and Ideologies

Now, as mentioned earlier, this markedly similar record of India and Pakistan where the needs of the underprivileged majority are concerned, notwithstanding their contrasting political systems, is due no doubt to the fact that the social structure of both countries is based on extreme class inequalities. From this we must not conclude, however, that the nature of the class structure in the two countries is the same. Perhaps the deepest and most significant contrast between India and Pakistan lies in the differing nature of their dominant classes—a difference which goes a long way in explaining why capitalist development in the two countries is now experiencing such divergent trends.

It is well known that at the time of Partition India had a fairly developed industrial sector and that the Indian National Congress represented mainly the interests of the emerging Indian bourgeoisie. The areas that constituted Pakistan, however, had no industry to speak of and no industrial bourgeoisie, with the result that the Muslim League, which led the movement for the creation of Pakistan, was dominated, at least after 1945, by the feudal class—particularly the big landowners of the Punjab and Sind. (This was so because, even though the handful of Muslim traders and merchants who largely financed the League were in theory in a position to call the tune, they had no contact with the Muslim masses. The majority of these lived in the villages and were controlled by the landlords). The class character of the two parties was therefore quite different. What is, however, even more significant is that, as Gail Omvedt points out in her excellent article reproduced in this volume, capitalism in India at the time of Partition had already made sufficiently deep inroads in the farming sector to produce a class of rich peasants in the countryside whose wishes had to be taken into account by the policy-makers in Delhi. It was this class of rich, capitalist peasants that was the driving force behind the land reforms in India that came in the 1950s. Although these land reforms did not give land to the tiller or the landless, they did transfer land to tenants. Omvedt makes the crucially important point:

> . . . those at the head of the state knew very well that they not only had to yield to the demands of a politicized and mobilized rich peasant section who had emerged at the head of the broader agrarian masses, but also that anti-feudal land reforms and the widening of the rural home market were necessary for any real capitalist development. Thus, the five-year plans not only focused on the building up of a heavy industry, a public sector and infrastructure that included dams, roads and other forms of transportation, but also a series of land reforms and various village development programmes.

It was precisely this condition that did not exist in Pakistan in 1947. It was not simply that there was no industrial bourgeoisie—even if it had existed it would probably have collaborated with the feudal aristocracy, as the new Pakistani bourgeoisie that has since emerged actually did; and in any case would have been unable to challenge the powerful landowners even if it had wanted to, without the help of other anti-feudal classes. But such a class did not exist, as it did in India. This is the reason why the repeated attempts at land reforms in Pakistan proved hardly worth the paper they were printed on (see the article by Akmal Hussain in this book). When capitalist farming did get under way in the sixties, it further reinforced the agrarian class structure and the power of the big landowners. It is this continuing existence and power of the feudal aristocracy which has prevented the enlargement of the rural market and has also successfully repelled any attempt to tax the enormous agricultural incomes. In both ways, it has proved to be a noose around the neck of capitalist development in Pakistan.

This, however, is not the whole story. There is yet another element which differentiates the histories of India and Pakistan. Ms Omvedt, in the passage quoted above, refers to the Indian five-year plans' emphasis on 'the building up of a heavy industry, a public sector and infrastructure'. The question is: Why did the Indian government decide to build up a heavy industry or a public sector? Why did it not choose, as Pakistan did, to give practically all its attention to the building up of a consumer goods industry, and why did it not, like Pakistan, treat the idea of a public sector as if it were an evil?

We do not think a satisfactory answer to this question can be given except, again, in terms of ideology. It seems clear that at least some part was played in the formulation of those crucial economic decisions of the early days by Jawaharlal Nehru's well-known admiration for socialism (which was shared by many influential leaders in the Congress). But which class did that ideology represent? It would not be easy to find an answer to this question in terms of the generally accepted notion of a class. It certainly cannot be said to have represented the Indian bourgeoisie which was the dominant force in the Congress at the time of Independence: in fact, the goal of socialist planning was adopted by the Party in the face of opposition from the propertied and the bourgeois classes. Nearly ten years before Independence the Congress Party had appointed a National Planning Committee under the chairmanship of Nehru, which decided in favour of socialist planning for independent India. The committee included fifteen members of the Congress as well as representatives of provincial governments, princely states, and the big business. According to Nehru himself the big business was 'apprehensive and critical' of the committee and wanted the state only to 'control' the economic activity, but the committee nevertheless decided that defence and other key industries, as well as public utilities, should be state owned, while banking should be regulated and a national board shold be formed to supervise insurance. These decisions formed the basis of planning in India after Independence.[30]

The socialist ideology therefore cannot be pinned upon the Indian bourgeoisie, nor of course can it be ascribed to the more reactionary classes of Indian society. Which class did it represent, then? One cannot avoid the conclusion that it did not represent any class as such: the (mainly Hindu) intelligentsia which professed this ideology, and whose powerful representative Nehru was, cannot be dissolved into any of the dominant classes who carried forward the independence struggle. The intelligentsia and its ideology were a relatively independent force in Indian politics of that time.

To say this is not only to emphasise that ideology and culture (in the sense of intellectual or artistic culture) play a crucial role in political struggle (see P.C. Joshi's article 'Culture and Cultural Planning in India'). What we wish to point out here is that culture (in a broader sense, which of course includes intellectual culture) may play a part not merely as a reflex in the conscious realm of the material base (the mode of economic production), but may have an uneven relationship with it—sometimes lagging behind it, at others moving ahead of it. Indeed, and more radically, we wish to maintain, with Sumit Sarkar, that 'it is surely impermissible to identify the mode of production with the "economy", since it is very difficult to conceive of any system of production relations abstracted from culture, law and politics, i.e. the elements of the so-called "superstructure"', and that 'we need to move towards both a "materialist and relational concept of culture" and " a more culturally embedded analysis of the material world"'.

The socialist component in the Congress ideology was the product not so much of the industrial mode of production or the rise of the working class in India as of the impact of the Russian Revolution on a section of Hindu intellectual-politicians and, through them, on popular consciousness and culture. It was at the level of popular consciousness that radical ideas, reinforcing an already existing culture of rebellion against the everyday oppression by the upper castes, moneylenders, landowners, etc., brought India, practically over the heads of many of those intellectual-politicians themselves (particularly those at the helm of the Indian National Congress), on the brink a social revolution, from which India was 'saved' thanks to the complicity of those same intellectual-politicians with the propertied classes of India and its colonial rulers.

The history of this complex development is yet to be written, but, as Sarkar argues, the writing of such a history will necessitate taking as its guiding concept not mode of production, but culture—culture understood as a 'whole way of conflict' rather than a 'whole way of life' of Indian people. This new awareness of the significance of popular consciousness and culture for historical dynamic has important lessons for present day revolutionary movements too, as we shall see below; at any rate, it is only through such an analysis that we will adequately understand how the socialist tendency in the Congress came to play such a decisive role in determining the priorities of India's economic development at an early stage. On the other hand, and precisely because India lacked a strong industrial working class, the chief beneficiary of the preference for socialist planning turned out to be, not the workers or the masses of India, but its capitalist class.

There was, however, a much closer relationship between class and ideology in the case of the Muslim League which, as we have noted above, was dominated by the feudal landowners. Even the financially more powerful bourgeois element in the League was under the sway of the reactionary feudal *outlook*, which is not surprising since its emergence did not conflict with the existence of the landowning classes; if it had any conflict of interests it was with the Hindu merchants, moneylenders, etc. It is not that modern ideas had made no impact on the Muslim intelligentsia of old India: Sir Syed Ahmed Khan, Sir Mohammed Iqbal and others had made influential attempts to open up the Muslim mind to Western scientific and liberal ideas. However, not only were such attempts relatively weak, but because these intellectuals were financially and otherwise closely tied to the feudal aristrocracy, they invariably ended up glorifying Islam and the past rather than promoting a radical and critical consciousness. This reactionary tendency became even more pronounced when, as a reaction to Hindu communalism, the Pakistan movement gathered force and anti-Hinduism overshadowed any anti-colonial radicalism that might have been appearing in some sections of the Muslims.

The result was that the ideology of the intelligentsia which dominated the Muslim League after Partition was, on the whole, pronouncedly conservative and anti-communist. The immediate consequence was that Pakistan was placed within the orbit of American foreign policy and American capitalism without reserve. Even though the rulers of Pakistan accepted the idea of five-year plans, after an initial toying with the idea of creating a strong public sector and a heavy industry, they turned their backs resolutely against such policies because they smacked of socialism. The writer of a recent *Dawn* editorial, stung by the severe power shortages which have hit Pakistan in 1985 (and which by April had closed down 7,000 industrial units, throwing 75,000 workers out of job in the province of the Punjab alone) correctly identified the planners' 'Western-oriented' ideology as the root of the trouble:

> The policy approach of the pioneers of our economic planning was obviously overlooked by the subsequent generation of Western-oriented planners and their political mentors. The basic sectors which constitute the infrastructure for development were neglected, energy being one of them. . . . Even if the Seventh Plan target is met, it will not be sufficient to eliminate power shortage which is estimated to persist beyond the year 2000. This is the worst prospect a nation can face in the modern industrial age.[31]

Clearly, the bitter harvest of three decades of rabid anti-socialism is beginning to ripe—and not only in the economic sector. Let us take a close look at Pakistan in the middle of 1985.

2. Capitalism and Beyond

Pakistan's Economic Crisis and Political Paralysis

The present moment in Pakistan is fraught with peril, or possibilities, depending on how one looks at it. Kaiser Bengali and Khalid Nadvi have admirably telescoped the economic crisis which is developing in Pakistan in their article 'Planless in Pakistan' and shown that it is not a temporary phenomenon but a structural crisis. In the period since the article was written what might have appeared to be cracks in Pakistan's capitalist economy are now clearly signalling a general collapse of the edifice.

To the energy crisis (about which more below) is now added a water crisis due to a shortage of water in the country's three rivers on which depends 70% of Pakistan's cultivable land. In Sind the water supply by May 1985 had dwindled to a mere 40% of what was required and in both Punjab and Sind several major canals had to be closed down.[32] Drinking water, always in short supply in Sind, had simply disappeared from many areas, and in others was selling at Rs20 a tin. More important, the water shortage is anticipated to reduce agricultural production by no less than 20% – and this in a country which this year is facing an 'awesome deficit' in wheat production amounting to 2 million tons.

While the severity of the current water shortage was due to natural causes, it brought to light the scandalous neglect of the agricultural infrastructure by the various Pakistani governments. Out of a total 80.5 million hectares in Pakistan, only 29.5 million hectares is cultivable agricultural land. It is estimated that nearly 8 million hectares are wasted on account of waterlogging, approximately 30,000 hectares being lost *yearly* due to this problem. In addition some 5.7 million hectares have been rendered uncultivable due to salinity. These problems have not only continued over the years but are becoming progressively worse as time passes.

The major cause of these problems is the sorry state of the canal system. This system which was built by the British is now over a hundred years old and badly in need of repairs; yet over the past three decades virtually nothing has been done in this respect. The result is that no less than 60% of water meant for irrigation is wasted—about 40% of it wasted through seepage during transmission. On one hand, this produces water-logging and salinity leading to the huge loss of land to cultivation noted above; on the other, it produces chronic water shortages, causing vast areas to remain uncultivated.[33] In Sind no less than 88,000 sq.km. of land (i.e. 60% of the whole province) belongs to the 'arid zone', this despite the fact that, after Partition, four new barrages were built on the river Sind. Clearly the situation calls for a far greater effort to build the irrigational infrastructure than has hitherto been made.

The crisis in the energy sector is however more basic: at present the power shortage, according to Dr Mubashir Hasan, a well-known economist, has reached a 'staggering 12000 MW', while many plans for new hydel projects remain on paper and the maintenance of existing power lines is so poor that about 30% electricity is regularly lost in transmission.[34] It ought to be noted at the same time that a significant portion of the demand for energy results not from industrial activity, but from the life-style of the upper classes, dependent as it is on air-conditioners, freezers, etc., and on ostentatious waste of enormous quantities of electricity on weddings and other celebrations.

The failure to create a base for industrial development also includes the failure to promote research and technology in the country. The obvious monetary cost of this has recently been calculated by a UNESCO-sponsored study, which revealed that as much as Rs 65 billion is spent annually on the import of capital goods and raw materials for consumer goods; in addition, Rs 1 billion is paid annually by way of royalties and consulting charges to foreign firms. But the less obvious cost is even greater: even after three decades of 'industrial progress' Pakistan is not in a position to manufacture any important industrial product on its own.

One would have thought that at a moment of crisis such as this the government of Pakistan would have reconsidered its economic policies and drastically changed its course. Instead, as is clear from its 1985 Budget, the government has opted once again, and on a more liberal scale, in favour of the old recipe of pouring virtually the nation's entire revenues into the armed forces and into the pockets of the landlords and the private sector, hoping (and this hope has now become a cruel joke) that by doing so the latter will be persuaded to use their huge wealth for the country's industrial and infrastructural development. The extra resources needed for these purposes and to finance a modicum of development are then raised by (i) obtaining yet more foreign loans: Pakistan's external debt now stands at a truly crushing $19 billion, and a major portion of new loans has to be used merely to repay the interest on it! and (ii) increasing taxes on the poor (the indirect taxes now constitute over 80% of all revenues).

That this colossal mismanagement of the national economy has so far not caused a serious breakdown in Pakistan is due entirely to such adventitious factors as good weather, remittances from Pakistani workers abroad, and American interest in Pakistan. To this list must also be added the ingenuity with which Pakistani planners and financial 'wizards' can juggle figures to present a rosy picture even in dire circumstances, or conjure up illusory solutions to the country's serious problems. To some extent all governments manipulate statistics to justify their policies, but few take their nations for a ride the way Pakistani economic planners do.[35] A particularly striking example of this is the Special National Fund Bonds floated by the Pakistani government in July-August this year in the hope of covering the Rs5 billion budget deficit by 'mopping up' the great quantities of black money that exist in the country. It was jubilantly announced in September that the Bonds yielded as much as Rs17 billion. What the public was not told was that 75–90% of this money in fact came from the (nationalised) banks themselves, and to attract even the remaining sum (estimated to be about Rs2.5 billion) the black marketeers had to be offered unprecedented bribes in the form of multiple tax reductions, low interest rates, etc. When the cost of the whole exercise is calculated it may turn out that the government gave away at least as much as it received! It is believed that rather more would have been collected if the government had tightened its tax collecting machinery. Meanwhile, the greater part of the black money not only remains where it was, it has even been given government protection.

We must now place Pakistan's economic problems in a wider context. As is common knowledge, the military regime is propped up by the US, whose hold on Pakistan's 450,000-man army and economy is extraordinary. Pakistan's army is entirely dependent on American arms supply.[36] General Zia has been able to acquire this military hardware by putting Pakistan at the disposal of the CIA, which is waging a covert war against the pro–Soviet Afghanistan with the help of the Afghan refugees who have been settled in Pakistan. What the Afghan situation means for the Zia government was well put by Ayaz Amir:

> . . . the Soviet intervention in Afghanistan came almost like a Christmas present to it. Overnight its diplomatic isolation ended. Creditors reluctant to do business with what they perceived to be a shaky military government were suddenly eager to lend it assistance. The United States rushed to sign a five-year economic and military agreement. Even now, the more the CIA gets involved, the greater General Zia's leverage to demand additional aid for his government.[37]

The five–year agreement referred to above entailed economic and military aid worth $3.2 billion. In addition Pakistan's most important ministries-of Foreign Affairs, Finance and Planning-are firmly in the hands of America's men.

However, a number of contradictions are now developing which promise to alter this state of affairs profoundly. To begin with, Pakistan's continued role as a vehicle of arms and aid to Afghan guerillas has brought the danger of Russian military action against Pakistan. At the same time, there is strong resentment among the people of Pakistan, and even in some sections of the Pakistani army itself, against Afghan refugees, but even more against Zia for having turned Pakistan into a tool of American foreign policy.[38] The Zia government is thus under increasing pressure from all sides to reach an agreement with the Soviets or directly with the Karmal regime in Afghanistan. Such an agreement was virtually worked out at the fourth Geneva talks held between the Soviet and Pakistan government: agreement was reached on the three most important points, viz. the principle of 'non-interference'; the question of international guarantees; and the return of Afghan refugees. The only matter which remained contentious was how this agreement was to be practically implemented, and even this, according to Lawrence Lifschultz, a well-known political analyst, was not a big problem since the UN mediators had worked out a formula which accommodated the concerns of each side.[39]

And yet the agreement was not reached: the fifth round of Geneva talks ended inconclusively. Behind the talks' failure lies the long term US strategy for the Gulf region in which Pakistan occupies an important place. Lifschultz quoted from a 1980 study on 'Pakistan's security' prepared by the Rand Corporation:

The United States is currently building a rapid deployment force to protect Western access to oil . . . Pakistan could serve as an extremely important entrepot for an RDF moving into the . . . Gulf from the East, i.e. from Diego Garcia or the Philippines . . . Furthermore, there is the possibility that the Pakistan army could serve as a proxy force fighting in the Gulf.

The Report also maintained that Pakistani Generals would be prepared to co-operate in such a scheme, provided the US 'undertook to protect Pakistan from the consequences of such a decision'. This new US strategy, according to Lifschultz, entails a more direct confrontation with the Soviets, doing away with the need for buffer states, of the kind Afghanistan was envisaged to be had an agreement between Pakistan and Russia been signed. But the US, with an unprecedented $13.6 billion committed to the present strategy, is now not interested in peace in the region; for this new, aggressive Pentagon thrust it is necessary to keep the pot boiling.

However, there are signs that the American administration may now be contemplating a change of guard in Pakistan. General Zia, being pushed into a corner by the increasingly forceful demands by the people for an end to military rule and equally pushed by the generals' reluctance to do so, is attempting to provoke a war with India: not only has he speeded up the completion of the nuclear bomb – an extremely sore point with the Indian government, he has actually started deploying the US military hardware along Indian borders against the wishes of the US government.[40] It would not surprise anyone if the Zia regime were soon replaced by a coalition of political parties and some sort of 'democracy' restored, or a new military administration took over.

Whatever happens, however, Pakistan's economy and society will remain in a state of deep and permanent crisis. This crisis will end only when the powerful alliance of landowners, bureaucrats, the bourgeoisie, and the armed forces, which has caused history in Pakistan to become frozen, is shattered. The existing political parties are in a state of prolonged paralysis and in any case represent the ruling classes. They-including Pakistan People's Party which enjoys overwhelming mass support-are part of the problem, not the solution. It is equally futile to look to any particular exploited 'class' in Pakistan which could become an agent of revolution; no class as such is powerful enough to challenge the tight alliance of the ruling classes and groups. It is not class contradiction that can provide the dynamic for historical change in Pakistan, but the contradiction between the ethnic and regional minorities and the centre. At the moment, however, that too is being spearheaded by an interested section of the feudal class.

Nevertheless, the movement for regional autonomy can become the focus around which the oppressed strata in Pakistan can come together in a common struggle and a radical vision of the future crystallise. But this is possible only if the demand for justice raised by the provinces is appropriated by the radical activists and intellectuals who are at the moment dispersed in the women's movement, the lawyers' associations, the People's Party and the various peasant and workers' organisations. However, without a fairly prolonged and systematic cultural-political education of the political workers involved, it is difficult to see how a self-confident and visionary leadership capable of taking over state-power and accomplishing the complex tasks assigned in other societies to separate capitalist and socialist revolutions can emerge on the Pakistani scene. Failing such a development there is no prospect in Pakistan of coming about even a capitalist–industrial revolution, which is so close to the heart of Pakistan's liberal economic planners – though not actually their IMF masters.

But even if capitalist development could manage to take off, would it offer the best returns for a country like Pakistan (or India)? What is the cost of such development to the nation as a whole? To see that the benefits of capitalism—especially when it is allowed to develop on its own terms rather than as a carefully controlled accompaniment of a genuinely socialist programme of development—are highly questionable, we must turn to India, where capitalism is now experiencing its finest hour in that country's thirty-eight years' history.

India's Economic Boom and Revolutionary Prospects

In his elegantly written 1982 article 'How is India Doing?', reprinted here, Professor Sen drew attention to the upward trend in India's economy which had begun to be noticeable in the early eighties. In 1985 these trends have become strong enough to generate a miniboom in Indian economy, as the following figures clearly show:[41] food production is estimated to reach 156 million tons this year; while industrial production in the first quarter of the fiscal year 1985 had begun to show a growth rate of 7.2% – with the production of oil having risen to 29 million tons from just over 21 milion tons in 1983 and the production of coal and cement by more than 50% each during the past five years – all record fgures. At the same time there is a well-nigh explosion in the capital market – capital for new industrial projects has been growing at a rate of Rs1,000 crore (10 billion) annually for the past three years compared to less than Rs100 crore (1 billion) in earlier years. According to an analyst, the assets of hundreds of larger industrial houses in India are now counted in hundreds of thousands million rupees, when at the time of Independence even the top few were worth only Rs500 to 1000 million.[42]

This remarkable overall performance of Indian economy is, however, only the prologue to what is undoubtedly a turning point in India's economic development: the Union budget of 1985. Up until now the state held a commanding position in India's economy and controlled the activity of the private sector, ostensibly from 'socialist' motives, but in truth so as to be able to finance the huge and constantly expanding state expenditure on defence, bureaucracy and the maintenance of law and order. The 1985 budget has decisively altered this pattern in favour of private capital. On one hand, outlays for the Central Plan and public sector investment have been drastically reduced; on the other, the private sector and the wealthiest section of the propertied class have been extensively deregulated and offered extremely generous incentives. What is more, in the interest of modernisation an unprecedented opening has been provided to foreign capital. The new import-export policy allows no less than 685 new items to be imported without restriction; the most important new emphasis in this package is on automobile and electronics industries (with particular encouragement being given to electronic consumer appliances, entertainment and toys).

Conspicious by its absence in the new economic policy of the government is even the nominal concern for the 'garibi hatao' (remove poverty) programme which used to accompany earlier budgets and policies. On the contrary, there is a pronounced attempt to squeeze the poor in favour of the rich. While direct tax exemptions and other concessions have eased the economic burden of the affluent and the big business (the top 141 companies alone will save Rs33 crore or 330 million in tax), the working class and the less fortunate sections of the population are being made to foot the bill in the form of indirect taxes on a wide variety of items of daily use: within weeks of the Budget prices shot up between 5 to 19 per cent – and in some cases as much as 30%.[43] In fact, one economist estimates that except for Rs48 billion in direct taxes out of total receipts of Rs476.350 billion, most of the rest will come from the common man either through indirect taxes, profits of the state enterprises, small savings or higher prices for state services; by contrast 'a good third of all state outlays benefits the elites that number, dependent and all, no more than 5 to 10 million in all of India'.[44]

This deliberate turning of the back on the poor has come at a time when there is tremendous unemployment in the country (by the end of 1984, the number of the unemployed had risen to about 45 million and 4 million new unemployed are added every year)[45] as well as rapidly increasing landlessness among the lower strata of the peasants. Now the situation is going to get far worse on account of the reduction in public-sector outlays and as the 'modernisation' fever catches the industry. Already the drive for efficiency and the introduction of capital-intensive technology is causing labour-intensive traditional industries to shut down, leading to large scale redundancies.[46] It is to be remembered that in India, unlike the developed or the socialist countries, there is no system of welfare which can ensure the provision of at least the basic needs to the unemployed. Joblessness in India means starvation for most workers and their families who, even in normal circumstances, can barely manage to exist.

However, there is no doubt that the liberalisation of the economy that is taking place in India will boost production and the incomes of the affluent, at least in the short run. More urban families will be able to enjoy the good life, there will be more private cars, more modern homes, the fast-food joints will do an even more roaring business, and there will be a new glitter in the five-star hotels. But even if a part of the meaning of 'development' is that a country is able to stand on its own feet, technologically and industrially, then this is not going to happen. On the contrary, two of the most disturbing aspects of the economic choices made by the Rajiv government are that, one, on the excuse that Indian industry has shown no initiative in developing better technologies, the screw-driver technology of plant assembly is being encouraged in a big way;[47] and, two, a tremendous boost is being given to western life-styles and consumption patterns.

There is little doubt as to who the real beneficiary of the new economic policy will be. The policy allows Indian capitalists complete freedom and unusual incentives to enter into collaborations with foreign companies. Already by 1984 such collaborations had reached a total of 9,000, with a record number of 730 agreements (most of them with US firms) being approved in 1984 alone. However, it is not only the insatiable demand by the urban middle classes for sophisticated consumer goods which have pushed the government to open the doors further to foreign technology and capital. The pressure in fact comes from outside, arising from the needs of the western capital itself – in a state of prolonged crisis as it is due to over production and increasingly severe international competition – and from the changing strategies of the imperialist financial agencies.

In a recent article (not printed in this book) Gail Omvedt has analysed the background to these changes with reference to the huge IMF loan of $5.7 billion which India received in 1981.[48] Since that article is essential if one wishes to understand why a liberalisation trend is sweeping India, Pakistan and other Third World countries (including China), it would be useful to summarise here its main ideas.

After the war, says Ms Omvedt, the export of US capital abroad had taken two distinct forms: direct investment of private capital through the setting up of branches and subsidiaries of transnational corporations, and aid from governments or 'multi–government' agencies like the World Bank and the IMF. While the majority of the private capital went to Europe and other developed countries, public capital in the form of 'aid' went primarily to the Third World. The main reason was not that investment in the Third World was less profitable; it was rather that 'chances for exploitation were less in the sense that Third World countries often lacked infrastructure, the transport facilities, the auxiliary industries, and the "disciplined" work force needed for establishing factories, and their poverty and subsistence nature of much of their economies meant that their internal market . . . was relatively small'. In this situation public capital was necessary to build the infrastructure, so as to 'establish conditions to make private investment possible'; it was also instrumental in tying the internal investment to purchases from the aid–giving country and in helping to cover the trade deficit of Third World countries caused by the repatriation of the huge multi-national corporation profits.

Now, however, three important developments have occurred which have brought this to an end. For one thing, the harsh conditions imposed by the IMF and the World Bank on recipient countries have frequently caused what have become known as the 'IMF riots' which have led to the overthrow of pro-western governments. This development has brought these agencies into disfavour not only with the Third World governments but also with the ultra right-wing Reagan administration. More importantly, as a result of the growing financial power of the oil-exporting countries in both the IMF and the World Bank, and the increasing intransigence on the part of the Third World governments, the US government has apparently come to the conclusion that these agencies – though originally set up as arms of the US imperialism – can no longer serve its interests. Finally, says Omvedt, it is now the case that public capital in the form of 'aid' has completed its mission:

> Infrastructural facilities including transport, power, etc., and basic industries have been built in most major Third World countries. With the spread of capitalist relations in agriculture, peasants have been torn out of a subsistence economy and transformed into wage labourers; production for and buying from the market has become almost universal and so 'home markets', though still fragile, are increasing – markets that are opportunities for Nestlés as for locally produced coffee powder. For the most part the governments now in power are not only firmly committed to maintaining a capitalist economy with the imperialist framework, the state administrations that have been built up can themselves carry out functions required to make private investment safe and profitable.

In other words, the stage is set for private US and World capital to enter in a big way, though, as we noted earlier in this Introduction, socialist ideas played a more important part in laying the infrastructure for capitalist development than did the imperialist ideology. Little wonder that with the passing of Indira Gandhi who, whatever her failings, was not quite so pliable to US pressures, and the election of a rather inexperienced Rajiv Gandhi, there was unusual excitement in the chambers of power of US imperialism. One observer noted that between November 1984 and March 1985 seven US senators (four of them democrats), a Congressman, a former Secretary of State and a former Chairman of the Senate Foreign Relations Committee, sixty presidents, vice-presidents or senior executives of multinational corporations, and two dozen academicians had visited India. The American contingent that attended Mrs Gandhi's funeral had four former ambassadors to India, and each of them had discussions with officials in the Indian government and with friends in political parties and the intellectual community to explore how Indo-US relations could be improved. Secretary of State George Schultz who led the team of mourners, later despatched Henry Kissinger to Delhi to prepare the 'philosophical ground' for a possible shift in America's Asia policy.

When asked by an interviewer what the Indian government should do to improve Indo-US relations, Kissinger replied: '. . . there must be something on which Indians and Americans can work together – economic and scientific projects. That would create a body of people on both sides that at least knew each other . . . it is strange how little systematic contact there is. I'm part of a group in which leading Europeans and Americans from the private sector meet once a year. The same exists with Japan. It does not exist with India. The advantage of these private groups is not that they can make policy but it means when there is a problem you can call up and say, look I don't understand this, explain it to me'. Those who have some knowledge of the past deeds of this Philosopher of Imperialism would know the poison that is containted in this sweet picture of a Friendly Society for Mutual Enlightenment.

It needs to be emphasised, however, that in making this criticism of India's new economic policy we do not imply that development in India or any other Third World country can proceed very far without assimilating at least some aspects of Western technology or the techniques of business management, industrial organization, etc., developed in capitalist countries. Even if this were possible, the development would exact such enormous sacrifices that it would defeat its own purpose: the experiences of Stalinist Russia and China's Great Leap Forward are a grim warning aginst any such course. The choice is not between the simplistic alternative: self–reliance or Western technology. The choice is, first of all, between planned and unplanned use of Western technology (and capital). As opposed to the free rein being given to foreign technology in India, a planned approach will give priority to research and development, insist that Indian workers be trained in all aspects of the desired technologies without reservation, concentrate on upgrading the existing plants, and aim at 'mastering the very process of technological adaptation, modification and innovation'. This is the kind of policy that has been adopted by China and was adopted earlier by Japan[49] – though there is much even in China's policy towards Western capitalism which causes concern.

But secondly, and more fundamentally, the choice concerns the goals of development itself. Choosing a technology is not merely a matter of choosing machines and the know-how; it is also choosing, whether one likes it or not, a specific system of values, mode of living, and specific forms of social and physical environment – in short, a specific civilisation. With an uncritical acceptance of Western technology comes an uncritical acceptance of Western civilisation. In the rush for 'modernisation' and 'development' no one seems to have remembered to ask 'What *kind* of modernisation?' 'What *kind* of development?' 'Do we really want India to develop towards a deeply perverted, exploitative and dehumanising civilisation which capitalism is beginning to transplant onto our soil?'

And yet, it is not quite true that no one has raised such questions. What is so refreshing about India in the eighties is that more and more people are concerned about these matters, and one of the main purposes of this anthology is to highlight precisely this development (see the last section of the book). In fact as a result of the failure of traditional leftist theories and strategies – whether espoused by the communists or the Naxalites – alternative conceptions of revolution are appearing in India, which manifest a new understanding of the complexities of contemporary Indian society, deeply afflicted as it is by the advance of Western capitalist civilisation on one hand, and a variety of deeply rooted social and cultural oppressions on the other. Professor Joshi in his article on cultural planning in this book points out the devastating effects which capitalist development and the rapidly intensifying communications revolution are having on Indian society and culture. (His essay also provides important food for thought for those who, in their desire to smash all actual or potential institutions of repression, are likely to endorse a little too uncritically the call for individual, folkist, or regional libertainism: in a world already distorted by capitalist or feudal relations, this can be nothing but disastrous).

In the same section Peter Waterman, in his hard-headed and highly instructive essay on Indian labour, and Bharat Patankar point to the emergence of multi-dimensional struggles in India involving, besides the traditional working class, women, *harijans, adivasis,* and ethnic minorities against their particular oppressions. However, Bharat Patankar goes further and emphasises that the new types of struggle are an expression not only of the need to reshape property and power relations within the existing forms of civilisation, but of the need to reconstitute civilisation on the basis of alternative concepts of human relationships, of production, of the state, and of the relationship of men an women to nature.

This new demand for a radical democracy, which seeks to involve individuals at all levels of their social and political lives, on the one hand, and for the *quality* of life (not just in the material sense, but also in the *aesthetic* sense) on the other, finds an echo in the writings of an increasingly influential group of India intellectuals, which is represented here by Ashis Nandy-a highly original and provocative thinker. This convergence of practice and theory augurs well for revolutionary struggle in India. In so far as Pakistan is also caught in a similar web of oppressions-class, cultural, ethnic and imperialist-a parallel development in theory and practical struggle is urgently needed there, too.

NOTES

[1]There are sixteen officially recognised and 4,000 non-official languages and dialects in India; 71% of its population still lives in rural areas; and illiteracy is 57.6%.

[2]Anupum Sen, *The State, Industrialization and Class Formations in India,* Routledge & Kegan Paul, London, 1982 p 207.

[3]Hamza Alavi, 'The State in Post-Colonial Societies', New Left Review 74, 1972, and 'The State in Crisis' in Hassan Gardezi and Jamil Rashid (eds.), *Pakistan: The Roots of Dictatorship*, Zed Press, London, 1983

[4]With over 15,000 titles published annually by some 350 publishers in the country, India is the third largest producer of books in the world. In 1978, titles in English numbered 4,393; Hindi 2,179; Bengali 1030; the remaining titles were in regional languages. The diversity of subjects covered is equally impressive and includes (1978 figures): Literature, History of Literature & Literary Criticism (4,600 titles); Political Science and Political Economy (1,926); Religion (964); History (876); Philosophy and Psychology (421); Natural Science (492); Engineering and Technology (409).

In 1977, India had 929 daily newspapers, with an aggregate circulation of over 10 million; 12,371 periodicals; and 4,303 non-dailies (circulation over 10 million). In Delhi alone newspapers are published in thirteen languages, excluding English; and the four largest cities together publish over 4,000 newspapers.

An idea of the diversity of the publishing activity in this area, and the role English is playing in India's burgeoning intellectual renaissance, can be had from the following (the information pertains to 1977): No less than 2,765 newspapers and periodicals are published in English; 3289 in Hindi; 975 in Urdu; 875 in Bengali; and the remaining in other 54 languages. The newspapers reflect a great variety of political opinion: 92 newspapers were published by the various political parties in 1977, including the communist parties, the two largest of whom (CPI and CPI(M)) together had 41 newspapers.

(Sources for information on both India and Pakistan: *International Literary Market Place 1984 – 85*, R.R. Bowker Co., London 1984; *World Press Encyclopaedia*, Mansell Publishing Ltd., London, 1982).

[5]In 1980, the number of dailies published in Pakistan were 104, with an aggregate circulation of under 1 million, and 355 non-dailies. Periodicals numbered 1,145. Most of the dailies were published in Urdu; 14 in English; and 7 in Sindhi. Most of the non – fiction books published in Pakistan deal with Islamic religion or history and the history of Pakistan.

(Source as for note 4)

[6]Tribute must therefore be paid to *Herald* (Karachi) and *Viewpoint* (Lahore), and the journalists associated with these magazines, for endeavouring to keep some critical awareness alive in Pakistan in an extremely hostile environment.

[7]George Kurien, *World Press Encyclopaedia*, Mansell Publishing Ltd., London, 1982. Much of this information about Pakistani newspapers has been derived from this source.

[8]Romesh Thapar, 'Loyalty, Discipline, Treachery', *Seminar*, April 1985.

[9]The political parties were not allowed to contest the elections. On the eve of the February elections there were nearly two thousand prominent opposition leaders, activists and intellectuals in prison. Many of them have now been in prison for six or more years, and several have been brutally tortured.

[10]Taken from Feroz Ahmed, *Sind: National and Democratic Struggle*, Pakistan Democratic Forum, New York, 1984.

[11]M.J. Akbar, *India: The Siege Within: Challenges to a National Unity*, Penguin Books, London, 1985, pp 169 – 70.

[12]*Ibid*, p 198 ff.

[13]*India Today*, December 15, 1984.

[14]According to another study (M.B. Naqvi, *Dawn Economic and Business Review*, February 9–15, 1985, out of 6.25 million rural households, 126,807 households (or 1.18 million people) at the top own land in excess of 50 acres, and the biggest landowners among these (those who own 150 or more acres) constitute only 16,468 households (or 173,151 individuals). At the other end of the scale are 8.78 million people who belong to families owning land under 5 acres. However, the total land area belonging to farms under 5 acres amounts to only 7% of the total farm area, while the area belonging to farms of 50 or more acres amounts to 25% of the total area (i.e. at the top 1.18 million individuals possess 10,916,467 acres).

At the very bottom of the rural hierarchy is the class of landless labourers, which total 18,465,251.

(It should be noted, however, that according to Naqvi, the rural population of Pakistan comprises only 54% of the total, not 70% as is usually believed.

[15]In Pakistan, every year the quantity of black money (a significant proportion of which is connected with drug trade) increases by Rs8 to 10 billion. It has been estimated that in 1985 black money in Pakistan amounted to Rs180 billion. Moreover, up to Rs7 billion are sent abroad annually. *Jang*, London, January, 1985. In India black money is estimated to be Rs370 billion (21% of GDP). *The Times of India*, July 9, 1985.

[16]*World View* 1984, Pluto Press, London, p. 231.

[17]Pakistan government spends over 90% of its revenues on defence, police, administration and servicing its foreign debt, leaving little over 4% for education, health and other basic human needs (and precious little for the development of basic industries). The non-development (mostly defence and administration) expenditure has risen from Rs20 billion in 1977–78 to Rs83 billion in 1985–86!

[18]*The Economic Times*, September 18, 1985.

[19]Bharat Dogra, 'Farm Exports From a Hungry Land', *Economic and Political Weekly*, March 23, 1985.

[20]*Statistical Pocketbook of Pakistan*, Federal Bureau of Statistics, 1985.

[21]Bharat Dogra, loc.cit.

[22]*India Today*, February 15, 1985.

[23]*The Economic Times*, June 25, 1985.

[24]Shahid Kardar, 'Industrialisation for Whom?' *Viewpoint*, Lahore, March 21, 1985, and Viqar Ahmed and Rashid Amjad, 'The Management of Pakistan's Economy 1947–82, Oxford University Press, Karachi, 1984, pp 5–6.

[25]The information in this and the following two sections has been compiled from the *World Development Report, 1984*; *World View, 1984*; *India Today*, February 15, 1985; Viqar Ahmed, *op.cit.; Herald*, 1985; and *Jang*, London.

[26]*India Today*, February 15, 1985.

27 & 28. Mubarak Ali, 'Post-1947 Approach to History', *Viewpoint*, August 29, 1985.

[29]Krishna Kumar, 'Reproduction or Change? Education and Elites in India', *Economic and Political Weekly*, July 27, 1985.

[30]For a fuller account see Anupum Sen, op.cit. ch.4.

[31]*Dawn*, March 28, 1985.

[32]*Dawn Overseas Weekly*, May 16–22, 1985.

[33]*Dawn*, March 7, 1985.

[34]*Herald*, July 1985.

[35]See for example M. Ziauddin, 'How Planners Present a Rosy Picture', *Dawn*, February 2–8, 1985.

36

[36] *The Christian Science Monitor*, April 27 – May 3, 1985 reports that the 'large-scale infusion of American arms' into Pakistan included 40 F-16 fighters, M-48 A5 tanks, armoured personnel carriers, 155mm artillery guns, air-to-air missiles, and 15 radar units.

[37] *The Herald*, May 1985.

[38] *The Christian Science Monitor*, May 16 – 22, 1985.

[39] Lawrence Lifschultz, 'Afghanistan: The Choice Ahead', *The Economic and Political Weekly*, Aug 3, 1985.

[40] *Jang*, London, October 2, 1985.

[41] These figures have been derived from *Asia 1985 Yearbook*, published by *Far Eastern Economic Review*, Hong Kong, and *India Today*, March 15, 1985.

[42] N.B. Naqvi, 'Indian Economy: New Directions', *Dawn Economic and Business Review*, March 30, 1985.

[43] *India Today*, April 15, 1985. Within a mere four months following the 1985 Budget the investment level reached Rs14 billion. *The Economic Times*, Sept. 15, 1985.

[44] M.B. Naqvi, loc.cit.

[45] *Asia 1985 Yearbook*

[46] Within a few months of the Budget India has been hit by a wave of industries going 'sick', affecting hundreds of thousands of workers. One such industry is the famous art-silk industry of Surat, where production declined by 45%, causing 'acute economic distress' to 100,000 workers. *The Economic Times*, Sep 15, 1985.

[47] In this connection it is instructive to read B.M., 'Hemlock Deal: Meaningless Review' in *Economic and Political Weekly*, April 6, 1985. The writer argues that the government has approved a deal with the US firm Hemlock Semiconductors Corporation, to buy silicon technology worth Rs 7.5 crore, even though Indian technology exists in this area and is both superior to the imported one and more appropriate. The writer goes on to point out that the collaboration deal over silicon technology 'can become and will be made into a springboard at the appropriate time for staging a counter-offensive against indigenous effort not only in silicon field but in general. . . It is not the first time that things have been so managed that indigenous effort and capability have been thwarted in a variety of ways and in many fields. Fertilisers and steel are cases in point'.

[48] Gail Omvedt, 'India, IMF and Imperialism Today', *Journal of Contemporary Asia*, Vol 12, No. 4, 1982.

[49] Surendra J. Patel, 'China's Strategy for Its Technological Transformation', *Economic and Political Weekly*, March 3, 1984.

OVERVIEWS

MAKING SENSE OF PAKISTAN
(JOURNEY TO PAKISTAN)

Richard Reeves

All Pakistan was divided into three parts. Not geographically, because the country, twice the size of California, was made up of four provinces: Punjab, with a majority of the population, dominating the national life from the sophisticated city of Lahore; Sind, spreading out from and closing in on crowded Karachi; Baluchistan, the hard desert country, reaching from Iran to the beach at Gadani; and the North-West Frontier Province, including Chitral. The three parts were not ethnic, either, because there was no human race or style that you could not see in the seven hundred miles between Karachi and the Khyber Pass, and there were twenty-four languages spoken across the country. The division that struck me again and again as I travelled through Pakistan had to do with time. The question I mentally asked each man and woman I saw was: What century are you living in? The answers, I thought, would have separated them, roughly, into three groups: the people of the cities; the people of the towns and the larger villages; and the people of the small villages, the desert, the countryside. City, town, and rural. Those categories were far from perfect. If nomads in Baluchistan or peasants in the Sind were living in the Middle Ages (and many were), their views of the world might not be very different from those of men in the slums of Karachi—and, in fact, it was such peasants migrating from the land who were making new slums as mechanization and cash modernized the agriculture of the water buffalo and the wooden plow. The son of a tribal chieftain in the Khyber region might be a Stanford junior coming home to a mud-walled fortress to tell his people of the wonders of computers, or of the money to be made by converting local stores of opium into the heroin craved in San Francisco. There was a confusion of ages in a society where women hidden inside *burkas* waited to pass through metal detectors before boarding a Pakistan International Airlines 747 from Rawalpindi to Karachi. But the divisions in time seemed ciritcal to me as I tried to make some sense—Western sense, anyway—of the people and ideas sharing Pakistan.

An urbanized élite lived in the here and now. A comprehensible, mobile human veneer—people quite a bit like 'us.' Ph.D.s from Columbia and Oxford who were home to teach or to man the federal bureaucracy—perhaps even to stay. Young Air Force officers flying General Dynamics F-16s at twice the speed of sound. Newspaper editors, fervent in their commitment to Islam, groping for ideas and movements and men to mold a modern Pakistan that would be not Western and not Soviet.

First published as part of 'Journey to Pakistan' in The New Yorker, *October, 1984; subsequently in* Passage to Peshawar, *published by Simon Schuster. We are grateful to Deborah Rogers Ltd, for their kind permission to reproduce this extract.*

There were the bazaar people, the spiritual core of what middle classes there were in a society that had hardly anything or anybody between rich and poor. They looked more ancient than they were, squatting or sitting on rugs in their booths and shops, surrounded by bowls of bright spices and the gossip of street and square. In reality, they had some eduation and considerable commercial sophistication—enough to begin thinking about the politics of fundamentalist Islam or social democracy—and they lived near the fault line of modernization. Right on that line was a group that might be called 'bazaar graduates'—the low-level bureaucrats, the hotel clerks, and such, who lived in one world and worked in another, newer one.

And then there were, everywhere, 'the illiterate masses.' The phrase was a cliché—I sometimes heard it a dozen times a day of conversations with Pakistanis and foreigners living in Pakistan—but it had real and powerful meaning in a nation where, as far as I could tell, perhaps one person in twenty had ever been inside a school. For a while, they and I were living in the same space but in different times. I did not know their time. I could not imagine the thoughts of the Pathans—Aryans so handsome by Western standards that they looked like actors hired to play poor people—as they walked the Khyber Road past the Star Trek, one of the video-game parlors in Peshawar. A woman carrying twenty-eight bricks on a board on her head at the construction site next to our rented house in Islamabad—what did she imagine I was thinking when she turned and saw me staring? She pulled her veil across her face and went about her business, hod carrying. I looked away and went about mine.

So the twain did meet. East met West, West met East, the traditional and the modern fascinated and touched each other, recoiled, cohabited in a place, confused and frightened each other—that was the essence of the tension and the dreams of Pakistan. It was a clumsy ballet, the courtship and the struggle involving the old and the new. The governors of the city of Jhang, in the Punjab, paid for this half-page advertisement in a national newspaper, the *Pakistan Times*:

> Chairman and Members of Jhang Municipal Council consider themselves dutybound to appeal to the people of Jhang to pledge to keep the City Clean and be good citizens.
>
> 1. Pay the Municipal dues in time and cooperate in completing the schemes.
> 2. No cattle to be kept in the streets.
> 3. No dung is to be stuck on the walls.
> 4. No litter is to be thrown in the streets.
> 5. Not to allow children to use the drains as latrines . . .

It was just another well-meaning appeal to the illiterate masses, who, of course, couldn't read newpapers—and if they ever did, the newspaper was almost certainly not going to be the government-owned, English-language *Pakistan Times*. But the illiterate masses were like the weather, only more so:

everyone talked about them, no one did much of anything for them. But most of the people doing nothing wanted to tell the masses what was good for them and what was bad for them. The military rulers of Pakistan, the Westernized elite, the fundamentalist *maulanas,* or mullahs, and the progressive, younger Muslim intelligentsia, the Americans and the Russians and the Saudi Arabians and the Indians, and the politicians who were supposed to keep quiet under the country's martial law—they all had advice and schemes for the illiterate masses. And almost all those willing advisers were troubled and frustrated by the noncooperation of the masses and by their 'rampant materialism.' That was the second recurrent cliché in serious conversation in Pakistan. What disturbed many of those conversationalists was that when the illiterate masses were given a choice—on a rare day in Pakistan—they seemed to reject appeals for Allah and a life of pure Islamic sacrifice, or for capitalism and liberal democracy, or for state ownership and regulation. Generally, the masses seemed indifferent to the efficient and orderly procedures of one sort or another which were favored by their spiritual or intellectual or financial superiors, or the ones favored by the people who happened to be in charge of things because they had the guns. The better classes on all sides were distressed when illiterate Pakistanis who had got to Saudi Arabia and the other oil states and done the dirty work and brought home what for them were enormous amounts of money spent that cash on things like television sets and big portable stereophonic radios. And when the masses were allowed to vote—something that hadn't happended in almost six years—the majority of them had seemed unduly attracted to the slogan coined by the late (executed) Prime Minister Zulfikar Ali Bhutto: *'Roti, Kapra, aur Makan,'* meaning 'Food, Clothes, and House.'

So, with some regularity in intellectual Pakistani coversation, the masses' desire for the things that the people conducting the conversation already had for themselves became 'rampant, rampant materialism, which just can't be met with our meagre resources.' That remark was made by a young newspaper editor. 'Meagre resources,' by the way, was the third, and last, cliché that punctuated many conversations. It meant, I concluded after a while, that Pakistan did not seem to have much oil, and therefore a lot of the sweat of its people went toward making enough hard currency to buy the stuff from richer Muslims around the Persian Gulf. It would take a lot of oil—and sweat—to move a country from Bumburet to 1984.

I occasionally tried to use an American calendar to set a date for where Pakistan was—no easy job in a place where illiterate peasants hooked little transistor radios onto the horns of their water buffalo—and I usually found myself thinking that maybe the time, politically and economically, could be compared with the end of the eighteenth century in the United States. Perhaps it was sometime near the late seventeen-nineties—it it was much earlier in many ways—and the people of Pakistan were trying to do what the people of the young United States did over the next two centuries. But they had to begin that modernization without the conditioned reflexes of people who took freedom as their due. And while the new United States had been pretty much left alone by the more modern world, Pakistan would have to pick its way among the demands and entreaties of the giants of the world, the United States and the Soviet Union, and the giant of their corner of it, India. Then, there was also the crude anti-modernism of cadres of ignorant *maulanas* who did things like—this happened in the city of Gujran-wala—declaring *kafir* (we would say 'excommunicating') any members of their congregation who believed that Americans had walked on the moon.

But, with all the obstacles, the commitment to modernism was there. Not that there was much choice in a world already opened to the wonders of 747s, videocassette recorders, and antibiotics. 'Solution of the complex developmental problems of our age requires extensive and sustained application of sophisticated scientific knowledge and technological skills,' read the introduction to one section of the Sixth Plan, the latest of Pakistan's five-year development programs outlining government goals and budget priorities. 'As a poor developing country, our priority goals include, *inter alia*, provision of basic necessities like food, clothing, shelter, and health cover to the common man; increase in industrial/agricultural productivity;modernization of communications . . . meaningful progress towards attainment of these objectives cannot be achieved rapidly until effectiveness of the relevant development programmes is appropriately enhanced through regular infusion of latest technical know-how . . . The Sixth Plan makes many bold departures in its programmes an in its policy prescriptions. Its basic objective is the socio-economic emancipation of the masses.'

The plan, like every other public document in the Islamic Republic, was punctuated by inspiration from the Koran. The health section, for instance, began, 'If anyone saves a life, it shall be as though he had saved the lives of all mankind' (Koran 5:32). Interminable quoting of the Koran was in official deference to the Islamization program—a puritanical and cynical attempt to create Nizam-i-Mustafa (a 'System of the Prophet') by such Koranic exercises as banning liquor and instituting public flogging—initiated by General Muhammad Zia-ul-Haq, whose titles include Army Chief of Staff, Chief Martial Law Administrator, and President. He had as many uniforms, ranging from the leather, tinkling medals, and riding crop of an Army that had been defeated every time it took the field to the simple white cotton gown of the devout, pure, humble Muslim. Watching him for a couple of months during travels through the country in the summers of 1983 and 1984, I thought he must have had an exciting time picking his costume each morning and deciding who he was going to be that day. When Zia and I talked about modernization one afternoon, sipping tea at a reception in one of the elaborate Victorian government guesthouses that are part of the British legacy to the Indian subcontinent, he was wearing a long, form-fitting tunic, with a mandarin collar, in light-gray wool—his country's elegant formal dress. 'We are totally for modernization of the country,' he said. 'We want modernization and all the things it can bring to the masses.'

I asked, 'Is there anything you don't want that could come with modernization?'

'What we don't want is our women forced out of their privacy. That is the thing we don't want. And pop music and jazz—that kind of thing.'

I said, 'But don't modern societies need the brainpower of all their people—of women—to become truly productive? Don't you have to have women engineers and scientists, for instance?'

'We have women engineers. Islam dictates that women cannot be left out of the mainstream. Islam's respect for women is unlimited. But we are not going to force our women into the streets. We encourage women to be active within the parameters of Islam.'

There were, I learned, fewer than a hundred women engineers in Pakistan. The parameters, as they were defined by Zia and his Islamic advisers, who favored the strict, puritanical Islam of Saudi Arabia, provided that the testimony of a woman in court should have half the legal weight of a man's. In cases of rape, there had to be four male eyewitnesses to 'penetration.' Zia ordered that Pakistani women be withdrawn from international athletic competitions in which men might see their legs. That manly obsession with keeping the weaker sex weak, however, was a subject for another time. Discretion seemed to me the better part of conversation with the Chief Martial Law Administrator.

'You talk of productivity, and so do we, but any American, any Westerner, looking at Ramazan would conclude that almost nothing gets done here during that time.'

'Why do you say that?' he asked. 'Productivity is higher during Ramazan. I know that. Men work harder. It's amazing, but you can see it.'

What I had seen was a country of dazed irritable men (even in Islamabad, the Westernized capital city, women were invisible during the holy month), squabbling men stumbling into one another in the midday sun, and men curled in the shade, any bit of shade, sleeping, until a mad scramble for food began at Iftar, the feast each evening after sunset. At the moment the sun set—the time was announced in advance each day by maulanas—Pakistan stood still. Cars and trucks did not move. No people could be seen in the streets—or maybe just two or three, huddled together, squatting over a plate with a little rice.

But I did not quite have the courage to argue with a devout Chief Martial Law Administrator—and he is apparently very devout. I saved my skepticism for a converstion with a young Oxford-educated administrator in the Federal Planning Bureau, and asked him whether his bureau had made studies of the relative productivity of Pakistan when its people were going without food or water seventeen hours a day.

He laughed, and said, 'We wouldn't dare.'

The fabric of the society was being pulled out of shape by the tugs and tensions between the coming new and the going old. More people than Zia-ul-Haq wanted to have it both ways: to have the miracles of the new world but not give up the faith and the customs of the old. Without consulting the masses, I thought there did seem to be a Pakistani consensus on commitment to both currents, modernization and Islam—contradictions or not.

The great devotion of Pakistan, it seemed to me, was not so much to the dogma of the religion as to the ways of the past. Islam represented security, the known, and the country's reason for existence—as a haven created in 1947 for the Muslims of predominantly Hindu India. 'The country is nowhere near as devout as it seems or, perhaps, as the President believes it is,' I was told by Altaf Yawar, who is the foreign editor of Associated Press Pakistan, the government-owned wire service. 'Ten or fifteen per cent, maybe, of the people really believe in and practice Islam. But fifty or sixty per cent of the rest want the society to be based on the old principles, the traditional values. So the country is about eighty per cent "Islamic-thinking." Conservative.'

'What are they most conservative about?' I asked. 'What is it they really don't want changed?'

'Women,' Yawar said. 'Pakistani men are afraid that the place of women in an agricultural society can't be maintained in an industrial society—that women will have to be given more. Why was Bhutto hanged—really? How could they get away with it? Because he raised women too high.'

Maintaining the unquestioned power of men over women was, he thought, at the heart of 'Islamic thinking'—and was the principal reason that modernization was such agony for the men of Pakistan. It didn't matter what the Koran said; like the Bible, it said many things, many ways. Selection was argument; interpretation was power. The drafters of the Sixth Plan—modernized men who favored changing the status of women—such as my friend the planner from Oxford—used their own Koranic verses, like this one, at the head of the chapter on women: 'To men is allotted what they earn. And to women what they earn' (Koran 6:32). The plan continued:

> In all societies, women's development is a prerequisite for overall national development; indeed, no society can ever develop half-liberated and half-shackled.
> ... in Pakistan, today, the profile of women is simply shocking. The following cold statistics are a sad commentary on the legacy of neglect ... Female literacy is only 14 per cent ... the participation rate of women in the compensated labour force is only 5 per cent .... Less than 3 per cent of civil service jobs ... Crippling handicaps: illiteracy, constant motherhood, and the primitive organization of work.

And carrying bricks past my house. Or carrying the water in a countryside without aqueducts or pipe; around farmland and in slums, mothers and their daughters were everywhere—beasts of burden carrying water in pots on their heads, straining, but still able to pull up their veils if men passed. The women worked but were not paid; the reality was far worse than shocking statistics. The numbers were for Western consumption, prepared by Western-educated bureaucrats. Places like Washington can't run without statistical fuel, and places like Pakistan get a lot of money from Washington. So the bureaucrats made up numbers. The one being used most often was twenty-five per cent; according to the speeches and reports of the day, about twenty-five per cent of the people of the country had access to potable water, and about twenty-five per cent were literate. In reality, no one knew. Those statistics, as far as I could tell, rose gradually to that pathetic twenty-five per cent because of the government imperative to show improvement in succeeding five-year plans.

The chief dispenser of statistics in Pakistan and the principal author of the Sixth Plan was Mahbubul Haq, the Minister for Planning and Development. He came back from Washingon, where he had worked twelve years for the World Bank, ending that tenure as director of the Policy Planning and Program Review Department. He was brilliant, charming, persuasive. His office, in the Secretariat in Islamabad, could have been in Washington, except that its occupant was wearing the national costume—the same *shalwar kameez*, or knee-length light shirt and baggy pants, worn by the ship breakers at Gadani Beach.

'The national per-capita income is about three hundred dollars, compared, of course, with ten thousand, or whatever, in the United States—but that is a false comparison,' he told me. 'We are, economically, fifty years behind the West. Maybe eighty years in regard to the United States, or a little over. But it doesn't take fifty years to catch up fifty years anymore. Chronology is mixed. You have a country still fighting to control tuberculosis and malaria, but it has jet aircraft and satellite television transmission. Direct dialling. People who could never dream of such things as running water have television in their homes. And they want that. People want modernization. In the most remote villages, people are using refrigerators as closets, waiting for the day electrification gets to them. And it will. Look at the plan. In July of 1978, seven thousand six hundred and nine villages had electricity-out of forty-five thousand in the country. That was the beginning of the Fifth Plan, and now about sixteen thousand four hundred are electrified. By the end of the Sixth Plan,that number will be thirty-eight thousand nine hundred—ninety-five per cent of the rural population will be covered. In terms of catching up—before the Second World War the growth rate of the Western world was less than three per cent. Ours is over six per cent now. Yes, our population growth rate is more than three per cent, but death rates always fall before birth rates begin to, so ....

'When I left Pakistan in 1970, the malnutrition rate was thirty per cent, and the country couldn't afford to import enough grain to feed its people. I came back in 1982 expecting the same absolute poverty, expecting starvation. But the malnutrition rate was below one per cent. We were exporting grain. There was no obvious poverty, so ...'

Haq was glancing at his watch by now—a Washington technique I had not seen before in Pakistan—so . . . I asked for a copy of the Sixth Plan, and we shook hands. Outside the office, the Minister's assistant popped his head inside the next door and said, 'Give me one.' I had my copy.

I was in the roadway, blinking in the sunlight, almost walking into a donkey loaded with bricks, when I realized what had happened. The minister had slipped me pre-1971 statistics and compared them with 1982 statistics. 'When I left in 1970 ...' When he left in 1970, there was a West Pakistan and an East Pakistan, politically united but geographically separated by a thousand miles of India. In 1971, a brief civil war between West Pakistan and East Pakistan led to Indian intervention and the surrender of ninety-three thousand Pakistani troops (loyal to the West) to the Indian Army. East Pakistan seceded and became the new country of Bangladesh. East Pakistan, as it happened, was the poorest part of Pakistan, an abused stepchild, treated as a colony by the bureaucracy of West Pakistan. So . . . The country's worst malnutrition problem (and statistics) had been shifted to the new country of Bangladesh.

The grasscutters were at work around me as I walked from the Secretariat to my car. They cut the grass almost blade by blade, squatting in the Asian manner—comfortably, with their bodies almost like a backward N, their heads just above their knees and their hands in front of their feet, each man cutting away with a scythe the size of a bread knife.

Islamabad is one of the most resolutely modern cities in the world. Pakistan had no real capital city after it was hastily partitioned off from India by the British to create a Hindu country and a Muslim country when the old empire, the British Raj, ended, on August 14, 1947. The Indians had Delhi; the Pakistanis decided to build a new city, Islamabad. A city plan prepared by Constantinos Doxiadis, the Greek architect, was laid out on the barren plateau of Potwar, six hundred thousand trees were planted, and a city began to rise along wide boulevards and square corners. 'A city of airline terminals' was the caustic description of the novelist Salman Rushdie, who has family ties to Pakistan. Islamabad, with a population approaching two hundred thousand, was built on a scale strange to Westerners. Public buildings and officials' homes were about one and a half times the size they would by anyplace else. The Presidency, the word for Pakistan's White House—it is almost never used, because General Zia-ul-Haq prefers to live with his Army down the road in Rawalpindi—looked like the Kennedy Center, in Washington, covering with marble an area just about the size of a football field. From a distance, an American could hardly tell that it wasn't the Kennedy Center, for it was designed by the same architect, Edward Durell Stone.

It was easy to make fun of Islamabad. Nine miles from Rawalpindi and anyplace else in Pakistan—that was one local joke. But it was quite an achievement and had something of the sterile charm of Washington, including a main boulevard called Constitution Avenue—or, when I was there, Suspended Constitution Avenue.

Islamabad, designed so bravely to show how far Pakistan and its people had progressed, had the opposite effect on me: the water carriers and water buffalo in the streets constantly mocked its late-twentieth-century facade—its Holiday Inn and its Datsuns and its strange, sweet Coca-Cola. But the look of the late nineteenth century in the cities of India (and subsequently Pakistan) was also deceiving. Karl Marx was among many who miscalculated the patterns of modernization on the subcontinent. 'England has to fulfill a double mission in India: one destructive, the other regenerating–the annihilation of old Asiatic society, and the laying of the material foundations of Western society in Asia,' Marx wrote in 1853. 'Modern industry, resulting from the railway system, will dissolve the hereditary divisions of labour, upon which rest the Indian castes, those decisive impediments to Indian progress and power.'

That annihilation hasn't happened; the north of old British India is not yet what we would call a modern society. Nothing worked in Pakistan—or so an American found himself thinking day after day. The society had not evolved to the concept of the line. People did not line up at ticket windows or counters, or anyplace else; they just converged on the spot where the action was, avoiding one another's eyes, sliding between, under, and over backsides, frontsides, arms, shoulders, and heads, thrusting papers or money or whatever was to be taken or processed or, usually, stared at blankly before these dreaded words were spoken. 'Not here.' By displaying sufficient emotion—noise, anger, tears—you might be told where: another window. The windows of bureaucracy were small and were built at what I would call waist level. That was on my side. On the other side, the power side, they were at the level of the eyes and ears of a clerk sitting at a desk. To deal with that clerk, you had to bend to the window to be heard through the talking slot.

The society had also not evolved to the concept of the appointment. It was not only that Pakistanis might or might not be where you thought they were supposed to be at the appointed hour. It was that you regularly had conversations like this one, which I had with a Minister of the Islamic Republic:

'I would like to arrange an appointment to speak with you about the work of the Ministry.'

'Fine. I am free now. Come over, please.'

'Well, I'm afraid I can't do that right now. Perhaps this afternoon? Tomorrow? Any time this week?'

'But I don't know what I'll be doing then. Call me then. Perhaps I shall be free.'

And perhaps the stadium will be finished. On that same day, the *Muslim*, an English-language newspaper in Islamabad, ran a photograph with this caption: 'A view of the main stadium under construction in the Islamabad Sports Complex. The stadium was supposed to be completed a few years back but it is still unpredictable when it would be available to the sportsmen.'

Pakistan, in fact, did work, but it didn't work the way an American thought it should. Modernism as we define it—and so far we in the West have the exclusive franchise—is not a matter of buildings by Edward Durell Stone and television sets by Hitachi. The difference between the 'developed' and 'undeveloped' countries of the world, I thought more than a few times while fighting my way to the dispensing windows of Pakistan, was the difference between systematic and individual approaches to handling predictable situations or problems—distributing food, protecting property, re-paving roads,assigning airline seats. In Islamabad or Karachi, you did not find many planned, organized, work-saving, time-saving, sanity-saving procedures. Usually, if you had a problem you had to find someone, hire someone,or bribe someone who knew how, or was related to someone who knew how, to handle what were the routine chores of everyday life in any city anywhere. The most welcome words I heard in Karachi were 'Come with me'—a sign that I had finally found the person who knew enough to return me to my own life.

The old ways, charming or frustrating, usually depended on cheap labor—wealthy Pakistanis kept what amounted to slaves to run errands like throwing themselves at ticket windows—but such charming traditional ways don't come cheap. Food rots. In the Thar Parkar district, the government reported in July of 1983, thirty per cent of the vegetables grown were destroyed because they did not get to markets or cold storage in time. The official reason was transportation problems. When systems broke down or were never really started, both prices and corruption went up. The United Nations Industrial Development Organization studied transportation problems for the government of Pakistan and discovered that sixty per cent of the tires in the country were smuggled in, because local manufacturing systems produced on paper but not in factories.

The disorder and inefficiency, besides offending 'developed' folk like Americans, tended to offer some opportunities and temptations to any indigenous organizations with internal discipline and certain organizational skills—the Army, for instance. The military people in Pakistan and other 'developing' countries not only had guns, which have always been very helpful in taking over people against their will, but also had command structures and disciplines, communications systems, and, most important, transporations systems. Even the worst military organizations have in miniature some of the strengths of 'developed' societies. Armies have trucks, soldiers tend to follow orders. General Zia-ul-Haq, I was told more than once, managed to stay in power year after year—six years by the time I was there—because he was smart enough to use his troops to maintain reasonably efficient distribution of the necessities of the life of Pakistan's masses: wheat, cooking oil, tea, and sugar. It could be as simple as that for a while—particularly in a society where political systems were among those which had thus far not really developed. 'These people aren't ready for democracy yet. Sad, isn't it?' said Louis Dupree, an American scholar living in Peshawar. An expert on Afghanistan and the Pathans on both sides of the border, he had been driven into Pakistan, along with millions of others, by the Soviet invaders. 'Democracy is not going to work here for a long time—not what we call democracy now. Our kind of democracy wouldn't have worked in the United States in 1783. Communications were too poor. Loyalties were to regions. People weren't ready then. You and I were serving on committees and voting for things when we were seven years old. There's no history of that around here. People have to learn. It takes time to learn how to deal with things that are new.'

To adapt to new things or adapt new things to old ways—either is difficult. Maulana Fazl-ur-Rehman, the head of one of the largest congregations in Lahore, argued with me one day against American-style liberty for Pakistan. He analyzed our system this way: 'Your Constitution, which I have read, emphasizes "rights." If you buy a ticket, you have the "right" to a seat on the bus. That is fine, but we emphasize human values. Vacating that seat for an old lady is a human value. Do you understand?'

Almost. But then many things we understand, or think we do, are only almost understood or confusingly new in a place like Peshawar. That city—which has more than five hundred thousand people—is the effective capital of the Pathan nation, of fourteen million people, in Pakistan and Afghanistan; it is just south of the Khyber Pass, the doorway between the countries (Peshawar means 'Frontier Town' in Pashto), and was one of the places in the world where the new and the old bumped into each other every day. On July 1, 1983, local police confronted a new problem, automobile theft, by going around town letting the air out of car tires. That way, thieves couldn't move the cars.

How can you deal with people like that? That was our problem. Moving around the country, I felt as if I were spending half my life in the offices of P.I.A.—Pakistan International Airlines—forever confirming and reconfirming, finding the person who was willing to handle something for me. In Chitral, that had meant waiting an hour for the man who was supposed to open the padlocked ticket cabinet in the corner of a hut with a rough wooden table and three low chairs which served as the local P.I.A. office. He came, took out a knife, and pried the hinge off the cabinet, pulling out the screws with the slightest flip of the wrist. There was no key to the lock, hadn't been for years—everyone in the hut knew that except me. In the cities, they had computers in the offices. I could get out in a couple of minutes after half an hour or so of fighting the people crowded around the right desk. Computers think like us. We programmed them.

That was small comfort. So was getting telephone calls from the United States. The first one I got was from Kansas City. It sounded as if the caller were next door. But if he had been I probably wouldn't have been able to hear him.

'Did you have much trouble getting through?' I asked.

'No,' said the voice from Kansas City. 'Why would I have trouble? I just dialled the code and your number there.'

We were using new technologies to get around old ways. We could get around them completely with things like direct dialling—no more Pakistani operators—and get our business done the American way. Computers could go around them or through them, because the Raytheon terminals at P.I.A. brought their systems with them—the quickest and most logical of systems. Western systems. Western logic. That was happening all around me in Pakistan—a kind of new, electronic imperialism. Some of it had to do with the rules of internationalized commerce. Pakistan's airplanes were scheduled, maintained, and flown under international systems and in the international language, English. Money, with a language of its own, was moved and accounted for in approved international ways, which were monitored by Western institutions like the International Monetary Fund and Mahbubul Haq's alma mater, the World Bank.

There had been an inconvenient period (for us) in international dealings with this part of the world. Before the independence of British India and its partition into India and Pakistan, the outside world dealt with it through the British-trained and maddeningly British Indian Civil Service. Then, for a while after the British left, we had to deal with the locals. Now, it seemed, an imperious technical relationship, if not a technically imperial one, was being established by modern technology. Very few local people would be required to make Pakistan function relatively smoothly for world purposes.

Inside its own borders, though, and inside the minds and hearts of its people, the nation was going to have to suffer the agony of its own modernization. Perhaps it would be better for the Pakistanis and for us if that newest imperialism did isolate them—leave them alone, and give them more time and freedom to become whatever kind of modern people they finally decided they wanted to be. Maybe they could actually find a different kind of modernism. They might even—perish the thought—be able to become modern without becoming like us.

'You know nothing of us,' Abdullah Khan, a provincial commissioner, said to me one day with surly contempt. 'We are forced to study your history, but you are ignorant of ours. You think Islam is a nightmare because you are ignorant of it. You are afraid of us because of that ignorance.' Abdullah Khan, his name was, but he insisted on being called and written about as only Abdullah. He made a sort of hobby of browbeating foreigners. And he saw a lot of them in his position. As the Commissioner of Afghan Refugees for the North-West Frontier Province, he was responsible for the administration of some two hundred and eighty camps, which housed about two million men, women, and children who had fled or been driven from Afghanistan after the invasion by Soviet troops, in December of 1979. More than five hundred thousand dollars a day of Western money, channelled through the United Nations and international relief organizations, was supposed to go through Abdullah's office.

An interesting man: putting on a bit of the show, but still fundamentally different from me—and, like Maulana Fazl-ur-Rehman and General Zia, determined to maintain a gap between us. I did not doubt that he knew more about me than I knew about him. He had taught English and English literature before being admitted to the Civil Service, and then he had served as a political commissioner in tribal areas and as first secretary of the Pakistani Embassy in Saudi Arabia. He was forty-two years old, intelligent, attractive, combative, egomaniacal. He meant a great deal when he once wrote, 'For strength we must nurture our own roots. Our problems have arisen from foreign imposition. Their solution lies in tapping our inherent strength of character and culture.'

He was a fundamentalist Muslim, a zealot. There were many like him in Pakistan—probably including Zia—yet they were a minority within the ten- or fifteen-per-cent minority of 'believers' defined for me by Altaf Yawar, of Associated Press Pakistan. As he gathered from Zia, they saw themselves as pro-modern but not necessarily pro-Western. There was another group in Pakistan—smaller than the fundamentalist, I thought—who saw themselves that way. They were men like Mushahid Hussain, the young editor of the *Muslim*, who described himself as 'a progressive Muslim.' The groups parted company, though, on other issues—in fact, they despised each other—because there are more interpretations of Islam than there are of Christianity or of democracy. And all those interpretations created intellectual and political havoc in the Islamic Republic, because, as that name implied, and Abdullah asserted, 'We can't separate God from Caesar. That's something you think you can do.'

They saw the world differently; the communications gap was far less complicated than gaps in basic perceptions. Mushahid Hussain, thirty-one years old, with a master's degree in foreign affairs from Georgetown University, told me he had once considered himself part of a worldwide youth movement for liberal democracy, but no more. 'It began to change in the mid-seventies,' he said. 'There were Muslim successes. Oil—the long gas lines in America were a triumph for us. The Palestinians. The October War. Iran—a watershed in Muslim history, in world history. Khomeini told the United States and the Soviet Union both to go to hell. He was a new kind of leader in the Third World—he wasn't afraid of the Americans, he wasn't afraid of the Russians, and, most significant of all, he wasn't afraid of his own people. It wasn't like Egypt telling the Soviets to go to hell and then turning to the Americans. There was something to be proud of, and we began looking inward. We're searching for a way to restructure the social order here without looking east to the Soviet Union or west to the United States.'

'Progress'—a word we both claimed—was obviously in the eye of the beholder. 'We want schools and technology,' Hussain said. 'We don't want miniskirts.' In a report on the Kalash of the valley of Bumburet, the region's military commander, Lieutenant Colonel M. Afzal Khan, with undisguised condescension, described the housing of the people this way: 'These houses express nothing but primitive abundance, security and an enormous zest for living . . . they bear witness to a society that is still isolated in small units, where each has only himself and his own family to think of.' The Lieutenant Colonel, looking into the past, had seen us and the way we live. He could have been describing Teaneck, New Jersey. To him, societies inevitably progressed toward the large houses of his people, built for extended families of grandparents, children and grandchildren, in-laws, and a few cousins.

'Always remember, they think we are the barbarians,' said Louis Dupree. 'Their cultural heritage is heavy on the Crusades, when the Christians came killing and looting and destroying .'

Commissioner Abdullah, like other Pakistanis I met, had brought up the Crusades, saying, with what might have been a twinkle in his dark eyes, 'We fought the Christians many times. We know how to do that.' I thought about that when I left his office, walking into the sunlight and almost colliding with a band of Pathans lounging in the doorway with their Lee Enfields and Kalashnikov AK47s—the old British Army rifle and the newer Soviet semiautomatic rifle—and with bandoliers of cartridges draped over their *shalwar kameez.*

I went from Abdullah's office to a party at the home of the American consul in Peshawar. It was July 4, 1983. Inside the walled compound, under the American flag, men and women were chattng and sipping from cans of Budweiser-precious stuff, since drinking beer (outside the consulate) had been declared a heinous crime in Pakistan. Most of the hundred and forty foreigners living in Peshawar seemed to be there. Dan Rather was there, too, on videotape, reciting the CBS Evening News of the week before. Loudspeakers over the garden were lustily broadcasting 'Onward, Christian Soldiers.'

To a Christian or any other Westerner, the sight of hundreds, thousands of men (and the occasional woman) in a Ramazan daze or sleeping like children in the shade at the end of each day was Pakistan or Islam at its worst—or at its best, depending on your perspective. 'Faith, at the moment, could supply only the simple negatives that answered emotional needs,' V.S. Naipaul wrote in his book 'Among the Believers,' after travelling in Pakistan in 1980. 'No alcohol, no feminine immodesty, no interest in the banks,' and soon 'no political parties, no parliament, no dissent, no law courts.'

All that was still true in Pakistan in 1983. But there was more to it, I thought, even under military rule and in the quiet desperation of a mandated puritan revival. The zeal of the enforcers of the faith often verged on fanaticism, but the emphasis on family and on responsibility to your own seemed to me positive to the point of inspiration. So was a strain of egalitarianism in the faith − not always affirmed in daily life, but always there at least as a proclaimed and shared ideal. In the Majlis-i-Shura, or Federal Council, an appointed advisory body with the appearance but not the voting power of a parliament (an example of the impotent kind of 'National Assembly' favored by dictators everywhere), General Zia's appointees began banging on their desks in approval when an old man named Mahmod Ahmed Minto, who had been a political activist at the creation of Pakistan, rose and said, 'In the eyes of God, a tonga wallah'—a cart driver—'has the same rights and status as General Zia-ul-Haq.' (A tonga is a two-wheeled cart. 'Wallah,' a wonderful and widely used word, means something like 'handler of.' One man I saw regularly in an Islamabad bazaar was my 'Xerox wallah.') Another Majlis appointee, Khanzada Taj, jumped up after the old man and said, 'This country belongs to the people of Pakistan. The sooner it is handed over to them the better.' There was more banging on the desks.

I tried to remember moments like that, to remind myself that those ideas had as much claim on Islam and Pakistan as its puritanism and its subjugation of women – contradictory claims that gave the faith constant and vigorous intellectual ferment. And, in my own ferment over what I was seeing and hearing around me, I had to remind myself again and again that the 'subjugation' was in our eyes. That was my judgment. I was sure about what I believed about what we call 'equal rights' and 'human rights.' But 'they' were not 'us.' The man who said that best for me was another foreigner, a Belgian film-maker named Paul-Jacques Callebaut, who had travelled the world doing documentaries on dying religions. We met at the Chitral Aerodrome. His family and mine, a young woman from Michigan, and a couple of Christian missionaries from Peshawar on a short holiday seemed to be the only Westerners in town. 'There are no fanatics to me,' Callebaut said. 'I reject fanaticism. If Muslim mystics get pleasure from driving nails into themselves, that is their concern. If their women cover themselves, that is their concern. If our women wear pants to here'—he drew his hand across the point of his groin—'that is our affair.'

'Every time I read or hear about the floggings, I remind myself of what year it really is in this country and that there were years in our history when we used to put people in the stocks in the public square of the city of Boston,' said Louis Dupree, the American scholar. He also said that in his heart he considered himself a Muslim, even as he downed a cold beer in the privacy of his room at Dean's Hotel in Peshawar on a broiling Ramazan afternoon. (There were indeed floggings in village squares in Pakistan, but the imposition of Islamic punishments under Zia's Islamization decrees were more symbolic than real. The lashes of the whips were padded. There had been no amputations for thievery, up to the time I was there, because the new laws mandated that the amputations must be done surgically and no surgeon in the country had been willing to perform the operation.)

Drinking beer was not the only thing that might have made Dupree and me seem a bit strange to a tonga wallah in the Rawalpindi bazaar. Westerners keep dogs in the house – a practice that Muslims consider unsanitary. When I left Pakistan, I went to a country where the food was better but where in every town, in almost every house, there wree statues and pictures of stripped, bleeding men. Barbaric stuff to a modern tonga wallah. The representations were all of the same person, with blood dripping from a cut in his side. He was actually nailed, through the hands and feet, to crossed boards. The people in the towns would gather together once a week to eat bread and drink wine, chanting that it was the body and the blood of the man hanging from the boards. The country was France; the tonga wallah might have thought that it was quite a place and that Christianity was a religion of dark, negative superstitions.

When my wife, Cathy, who was in Pakistan to prepare a report on the status of Afghan refugees for Columbia University, visited the Majlis-i-Shura, she struck up a conversation with a young guard. He was fluent in English, and said that he had graduated from a Christian missionary college—high school in our system—in which English was the medium of instruction.

'The priests insisted on English at all times,' he said.

'Oh,' Cathy said, reacting to the word 'priest.' 'Was it a Catholic school?'

'What?'

'Was your college Catholic or Protestant?'

'I don't know.'

And most Americans don't have the vaguest notion of the difference between Sunni and Shia Muslims. That difference, though, is essential to even beginning a conversation about how Pakistan compares with Iran, or discussing the differing views of Mushahid Hussain, who is a Shia, and General Zia, who is a Sunni.

Both of us have a long way to go, the tonga wallah and I. But what was an inconvenience for me will be painful for him, because he is the one who has to figure out how to close the gap. I will not change very much—at least, not to accommodate illiterate masses. Pakistan will change to be like us in many ways; the struggle I saw going on was over how much of what they were they would give up to get some of what we have. It was sometimes very moving. One night in Lahore, a friend, a thirty-four-year-old attorney named Anwar Kamal, proudly took us to a new park in his city. Thousands of families were roaming great lawns long into the hot night, renting paddleboats and motorboats on an artificial lake, riding a miniature train – a wonderful place. When we praised it, Anwar said, 'Yes, but . . .' and began talking about his one long trip outside Pakistan. He had travelled across Europe by train and then across the United States by bus for three weeks, from New York to San Francisco.

'You have created heavens on earth,' he said in wonder as he talked of the freedom, the health, and the wealth of Europeans and Americans. 'I want us to do that for ourselves. We can do that here. I know it, and I want to be part of it.'

A few nights later, my wife and I had dinner with one of the most important spokesmen for fundamentalist Islam in Pakistan—a man whose name is an important part of his country's history, the son of a man who was talked about as America might talk about Thomas Jefferson. He and I carried on a conversation on one side of the room while the women congregated on the other; even in the most Westernized groups, men pulled me away from conversations with women. His wife would draw her veil self-consciously if I happened to look across. He told me he thought that the Islamization pronounced and promulgated daily by the Zia regime was neither sincere nor sweeping enough. More discipline and more turmoil were needed, not only to preserve real Islam but to return the faith to its basic principles. He was going to miss some of the turmoil, however. His wife was a physician (there were many women doctors in the country, because female patients ordinarily do not see male doctors), and he was going to Waco, Texas, with her next year, so that she could do advanced study at Baylor University Medical School in her specialty, dermatology.

Three thousand men – fierce-looking Afghans in dirty flowing robes and wearing turbans with the loose end hanging almost to their waists—sat cross-legged under a tin roof on a hot and dusty plain called Nasir Bagh, near Peshawar, on the morning of July 2nd. A handsome young *maulana* with a sense of drama, using gestures and inflections that reminded me of evangelists I had seen in the American Bible Belt, animatedly recited and interpreted the Koran. On cue, a wild-eyed old man in the front would leap to his feet screaming, and three thousand voices would chant *'Allahu akbar'*—'God is great.'

There was remarkable discipline in the scene. The men did not move, despite the heat that shimmered off the plain. At least, they did not move until they heard a noise, and then, one by one, they looked away from the *maulana* to stare at three jet helicopters flying in formation. A few bold ones stood to get a better look, then a few more, then many. The Holy Book could not compete with the spectacle and the sense of power as the clattering machines came lower, creating their own weather, a dust storm over the place called Mr. Nasir's Orchard, where thirty-two thousand Afghan men and women were living in tents and mud huts.

The helicopters were bringing the Secretary of State of the United States of America to a refugee camp to have his picture taken for television. That night, Americans back home—and people in a few other parts of the world—saw images of Secretary George Shultz against the background of robes, turbans, and *maulanas*, and were visually reminded that millions of Afghans had fled their country, most of them to Pakistan, rather than live under the control of invaders from the Soviet Union and of its chosen government in Kabul. 'You fight valiantly, and I want you to know,' Shultz said in English, then waited patiently while Commissioner Abdullah translated his words into Pashto, 'you do not fight alone.' Cheers. 'I come here with a simple message. We are with you.'

A *malik*, a tribal chieftain, had spoken before Shultz, pledging that the

Afghan Mujahideen, the 'fighters of the Holy War,' would resist the Russians until death, and he added, incidentally, that they were with the United States all the way in its efforts to gain control over left-wing insurgencies and governments in Central America.

'What's his name? Where is he from?' I asked Abdullah.

'I don't know,' he answered.

I persisted, asking for the name again. The Commissioner was annoyed by my insistence on things like names and dates. I was sure he thought it a debating trick Westerners used to avoid real discussion of large questions about God and man.

'What does it matter?' he said, with contempt in his voice. 'He is the man who speaks to the Americans. He knows what they want to hear. We've done this dozens of times.'

The American version of the relationship that developed between the United States and Pakistan after the Soviet Union invaded Afghanistan on December 24, 1979, was pronounced in drier language. The State Department and the Department of Defense reported to the House Foreign Affairs Committee on March 9, 1983:

> The stability and security of Pakistan contribute importantly to meeting U.S. objectives in South and Southwest Asia. As a frontline state [that is a new American cliché] resisting Soviet expansionism, Pakistan has incurred additional security responsibilities. . . . Moreover, the Pakistanis have provided refuge to the nearly three million Afghans fleeing the fighting in Afghanistan. . . . Our commitment to Pakistan's security is given both real and symbolic shape through the existence of our six – year [$3.2 billion] program of security and economic assistance and through our willingness to contribute to Pakistan's military modernization program.

That three billion two hundred million dollars—which is supplemented by about one hundred million a year in direct and indirect American aid to the Pakistani government for refugee programs, and by a little more to buy weapons and ammunition for the Mujahideen—made Pakistan the third – ranking recipient of American foreign aid. (Israel is first, and Egypt, our other client state in the Muslim world, is second.) That is a great deal of money in an economy with a gross national product of less than thirty billion dollars. But the United States didn't make such a bad deal for itself. Most of the money would be coming right back to the United States, much of it to defense contractors. Among other items of expensive hardware that Pakistan was obligated to buy were forty F-16 fighters from General Dynamics, at something like twenty million dollars each. The local estimate of how much of the American aid would be personally pocketed by the generals and bureaucrats of Pakistan's military and civil-service elites was twenty per cent.

cent. But even some of that would come back to the United States, in tuitions at Stanford and Harvard, and for land in places like Sacramento, California – one of the cities where Pakistani expatriates live in the United States.

It was a tricky business, because neither side, neither the Pakistanis nor the Americans, really trusted the other, and both sides seemed highly doubtful whether, if a crisis came—an overt Soviet move from Afthanistan into the North-West Frontier Province or Baluchistan, say—Pakistan would actually resist long or effectively. 'The volatile nature of past U.S.-Pakistani relations' was the phrase used in the State Department's briefing of Congress. That referred to the burning of the American Embassy by a mob in Islamabad back in November 1979, and to the resentment of all Pakistanis—from generals to sporadically jailed dissenters—who believed that the United States had abandoned or betrayed Pakistan in its times of greatest need, the 1965 and 1971 wars with India over territorial claims to Kashmir and the secession of East Pakistan. The United States, despite a mutual-defense-cooperation treaty with Pakistan that went back to 1959, delayed or cut off military supplies and spare parts to the Pakistan Army during those conflicts. I met very few Pakistanis who did not believe that the same thing would happen again if there was trouble with India—and almost all Pakistanis seemed to expect trouble with India.

Besides that, even the most anti-Soviet American officials—the ones who believed that any negotiations with the Russians were bargains with devils—had other doubts. For one thing, the Pakistan Army had started three wars and lost them all badly. The only people ever conquered by that impressively medalled bunch under General Zia were the people of Pakistan. For another, in the nineteen-eighties the country became the most important supply point for narcotics headed for the West; American drug officials in Islamabad told me that eighty-five per cent of the heroin in New York and Los Angeles currently came through Pakistan, usually following a route from the Khyber Pass to Karachi. And, finally, as far as American intelligence agencies could tell, or would admit, Pakistan was ready or getting ready to build an atomic bomb at a secret installation at Kahuta, in the Punjab, in violation of assurances to the United States—and of common sense, because exploding a nuclear device could lead to a fourth and final (losing) war with India. This seemed dangerous for Pakistan – which was traditionally determined to see itself as the military equal of India, even though India was almost ten times its size in every way – and embarassing for us, because American policy was to prevent proliferation of nuclear weapons. Nevertheless, the Pakistani consensus, at may levels of the society, seems to be 'If India's got it, we want it.'

So there was a volatile nature, also, to American-Pakistani relations, depending as they did on a foundation of self-interest that—on both sides—was not very solid-looking, at least to me. The United States wanted its 'frontline state,' and the Zia government wanted not only American money and expertise but the legitimacy that came with having the most powerful of democracies constantly building up the legitimacy of military rule. In American newspapers, Chief Martial Law Administrator Zia seemed to be evolving from the executioner of an elected Prime Minister—Zulfikar Ali Bhutto was hanged on April 4, 1979—to a defender of the free world and protector of refugees.

'Our personal views of human rights may be a little too esoteric in this part of the world,' said Ronald Spiers, the Amrican Ambassador to Pakistan in 1983. 'As an individual American, there are many things I would like to speak out about. But publicly, as a representative of the United States government, I don't go around lecturing people about the way we do things at home.' There was obviously some truth in that, but in making my own assessment of the permanence of our self–interested friendship with Pakistan, I couldn't help noticing that two of the three helicopters that brought Secretary of State Shultz's party to Nasir Bagh were Soviet machines. The Russians had provided materiel to the Pakistan Air Force for almost ten years after the Pakistanis concluded that we had deserted them in the 1971 war that led to East Pakistan's becoming the independent country of Bangladesh. Before that, relations between Pakistan and the United States had been very friendly; Yahya Khan, the second of the country's military dictators, had used Pakistan's close relations with its neighbor the People's Republic of China to help set up the 1972 trip of President Richard Nixon to Peking. (The strong Pakistan-China connection has survived, bonded by fear of the Soviet Union.) Pondering the ups and downs of Pakistani-American relations while driving near Peshawar one morning with a Pakistani official, I was reminded of something else. 'That's the field where Francis Gary Powers took off,' he said, pointing to an airstrip in the distance. 'Before the Russians shot down his U–2 in 1960.'

Airstrips in faraway places are the insignia of superpowers. We are everywhere, or we used to be or will be. We've moved into—and sometimes been kicked out of—about every place you can put up a plane or put up an antenna pointed toward Moscow. Hope springs eternal in official American breasts, and particularly the ones decorated with ribbons and medals. Admiral Thomas Moorer, the retired chairman of the Joint Chiefs of Staff, writing in the magazine *Strategic Review*, suggested that the United States should utilize Gwadar, in Baluchistan, as a military port to replace the Iranian military bases and facilities lost in 1979, when the fundamentalist Shia Muslim government took power. That was a profitable year for the rulers of Pakistan, because even before the Russians penetrated Afghanistan the Iranian revolution had left the United States without a geopolitical best friend in that critical area between the Soviet Union and the Persian gulf. 'There is the possibility that the Pakistan Army could serve as a proxy fighting in the Gulf . . . provided once again that the United States undertakes to protect Pakistan from the consequences of such a decision,' Frank Fukuyama, a member of the

State Department's Policy Planning Staff, said in testimony before a congressional subcommittee in 1982.

The people of Pakistan, because of the geopolitical chance that put their land along invasion routes mapped by strategists from Alexander and Genghis Khan to Leonid Brezhnev, were going to be facing the consequences of many decisions, most of which they never made.

The homes of most of the Afghan refugees were hard to see. They blended into the earth, because they were made of earth. A few of the perhaps two million women, children, and men who crossed the mountains into Pakistan lived in tents supplied by the United Nations, but by the summer of 1983 most of them had been there long enough to construct houses of earth mixed with water, buffalo dung, and a little straw.

On the roads and in the bazaars, the Afghans themselves blended into the people and the summer dust of Asia before the monsoons. There were no walls, no fences, no guards around the refugees or their camps. The image I retain of those people coming through the passes of the Hindu Kush with only what they could carry is of men and boys and water buffalo in muddy irrigation canals. The road from Peshawar to Nasir Bagh ran along a canal, and sometimes it seemed that I could not see the opposite bank because of the human beings and animals finding what coolness they could out of the bright heat.

Those people, the refugees taken in, were, if anything, even poorer than Pakistani villagers. By the summer of 1983, one out of five or one out of six people in Pakistan's North-West Frontier Province was a refugee, and there were some in Baluchistan and some in the Punjab. There had been, for all practical purposes, no trouble. Pakistan worked. Not our way, but it got by. People were generous.

Commissioner Abdullah told this story: 'About two years ago, a group of two hundred refugee families came to a village because they knew somebody there. The villagers told the refugees that they were poor, landless people who earned their livelihood either by working on a government farm or in the city. They had nothing to offer the refugees but their own houses. They literally halved their houses. If someone had two rooms, he offered one room to a refugee family and kept one for himself. It actually happened.' With great pride, he said, 'It is the way of Islam.'

The Commissioner had reason to be proud of his faith and his people. What would happen if more than six million Mexicans came into the United States between Texas and California during an invasion of their country (that would be the proportional equivalent to the Afghan migration)—would we, Christians on both sides of the Rio Grande, be as generous? The situations would not be so different; for instance, a good many Afghans were unofficially (illegally) in Pakistan's northwest before the Russians came, just as a good many Mexicans are illegally among the Mexican-Americans of the American Southwest. But the reactions might be different.

The refugees began coming in large numbers in the spring and summer of 1978, when a new Communist government in Kabul, which had taken power in a coup d'etat against other Communists, attempted to impose land reforms, and violence erupted in the countryside. Before that exodus began, perhaps half of the fourteen million or so Pathans lived on the Afghanistan side of the mountains. After three years, fewer than four million were left there. More and more families, and entire villages, crossed into Pakistan—the mountainous border is cut by more than three hundred passes, some known only to the Pathans—as successive Communist governments, all unelected, harshly increased the pressure on the countryside to live according to the new dogma of Kabul. By December of 1979, there may have been four hundred thousand Afghans in Pakistan.

Armed resistance by the Pathans against the Communists in Kabul escalated constantly—escalated so much that the Soviet Union decided to quash the local rebellions at the end of 1979. Eighty-five thousand Soviet soldiers invaded Afghanistan, beginning on that 24th December, and the Russian placed their own man, an Afghan Communist named Babrak Karmal, in power in Kabul. Within twelve months, as many as a million more Afghans fled to Pakistan, bringing stories of Soviet terror and brutality. (Smaller numbers of refugees went to Iran.) Most came across in groups of fifty or a hundred—villages or nomad clans led by their *maliks*. They brought more than two million animals with them—goats, sheep, buffalo, and camels. It was a timeless sight. The men in turbans or wool or embroidered caps and baggy pants and vests or robes like academic gowns, with bandoliers of cartridges across their chests old rifles or new machine guns on one shoulder. Their sons were dressed the same way, miniatures of their fathers. The animals and the women walked behind.

I saw Afghan women only when I travelled with my wife during her inspection of medical installations—tents set up by such organizations as the International Rescue Committee, the Red Crescent Society, and the International Red Cross. The women came to the medical tents with their children (the average refugee family had six children, in a society where surviving male children were de-facto old-age insurance), and sometimes their husbands, to what was clearly the social event of the day or the week—literally the only way to get out of the house. Even then, many of the men did not allow their women to speak to male doctors or technicians, instead reciting their wives' real or imagined symptoms.

'I would rather see them die than be corrupted by these males who call themselves doctors,' roared Malik Haji Tur Gul, scattering the women waiting at the International Rescue Committee tent in a camp called Lakhti Banda. He was an important man, a white-bearded giant who was the accepted chief of thousands of refugees. He seemed to be over seventy years old—'He looks like Noah,' said Dr. John W. Hennessey, an American in charge of International Rescue Committee medical programs, coming out of the tent—but it was impossible to know, because the Afghans do not record birthdays. The wife with him appeared to by about sixteen. It was obvious that part of his rage was at the thought that she might have to wait in line behind the other women.

Dr. Hennessey and Dr. Sayed Abdul Rahman Hashmee, himself an Afghan refugee, tried to calm the old man, explaining that there was a female physician on their team but that she was away for a short leave.

'And who are you to decide these things?' the Malik said. 'Two bulls who want to roam among the cows.' Afghan society is more fundamentally religious and traditional than Pakistani society. When Afghan women give birth to sons, there are feasts and rifle shots fired into the sky. If the baby is a girl, the event is simply not mentioned. One of the frustrations of the workers in the World Food Program and others distributing food in the camps was that they knew that the Afghan men ate first and well, and then the boys. What food was left went to the women and the girls.

Only a quarter of the people in the camps, though, were men, and a disproportionate number of those were old men, like Haji Tur Gul. Yet almost all the patients in refugee hospitals scattered around Peshawar were men between the ages of sixteen and forty. The camps served as the military bases of the Mujahideen. Thus, many of the men who had registered in the camps were actually in Afghanistan or else in the hospital. Others had never crossed the border but had sent their women and children to safety in Pakistan.

'We close our eyes to what is really going on,' said an official of the Peshawar office of the United Nations High Commissioner for Refugees, an organization obviously pledged to neutrality in such matters as civil wars and resistance movements.

It was already a long war. The Soviets, who had more than a hundred thousand troops in Afghanistan by 1984, had been in combat there for longer than they fought Germany in the Second World War. In one of the Afghan hospitals – in Avicenna Balkhi, near Nasir Bagh – there was a poster of a child's crayon drawing of Soviet troops machine-gunning rows of uniformed schoolgirls in Afghanistan in December of 1981. Tulips sprouted from the pools of blood. 'We will not be defeated by them,' Dr. Mummad Mohmand, a Kabul surgeon, who was the director of the hospital, said when he saw me looking at the poster. 'We fought the British, we fought Genghis Khan, we fought Alexander. They could not defeat us. We will not be defeated, because we will fight to the last blood of a small child.'

The refugee hospitals of Peshawar—more than a dozen of them—were there not only to treat the war wounded of Afghanistan; they were there also to impress foreigners, and particularly Americans, with the horror of Soviet tactics in Afghanistan—which included the use of small anti-personnel bombs (dropped from planes) in the shape of toys and wrist-watches. I was impressed. At the Afghan Surgical Hospital, run by Pakistan's most militant fundamentalist organization, Jamaat-i-Islami (the Islamic Party), I was not allowed to leave without going from bed to bed—forty beds. At each one, the stump of an arm or leg would be thrust at me, or a dressing would be lifted away to show a red hole that had been a face. A young man, what was left of him, held my eyes with his until I cried, as the blankets were pulled from his wasting body, most of it scar tissue from burns. The truck he had been riding on was hit by a Soviet mortar shell, and exploded into a ball of flame around him. An older man, named Abdul Kareem, who said he had been a farmer at a place called Bagh Lan, north of Kabul, proudly showed me the foot-long stumps of his legs. 'It was the poison gas, I know it,' he said, through a translator. 'A Russian threw it into the room where I was staying. Three children were killed.' He was almost certainly wrong about the gas—I could find no evidence to support the many stories that any American was quickly told about Soviet toxic weapons—because soldiers do not use poison gas where the fumes would kill or maim them, too.

'How do you know it was a Russian?' I asked.

'I know Russians,' he said, making a face. 'They have red faces. They look like monkeys.'

The maimed men around me burst into laughter. They were broken only in body—and the bodies of many of them were being patched up so they could fight another day. Sermons and readings from the Koran were broadcast from loudspeakers on the walls of what had once been a mansion with a large inner courtyard. It was Ramazan, and twenty-four of the patients were fasting. The sixteen others were being force-fed by doctors.

The Russians obviously knew what was going on in Peshawar—a city of spies—but in the summer of 1983 the situation along the Afghanistan border seemed acceptable to all concerned. The Pakistanis, the Americans, the Russians, the refugees—all had reason to be satisfied with the way things were in the far, violent land. For Pakistan, the influx of refugees meant an influx of both foreign aid and foreign sympathy. The aid included hundreds of millions of dollars a year in hard Western currencies, the coin that the world demands for everything from gasoline for running trucks to tear gas for controlling mobs—cash that was critical to a country that spoke, quite accurately, of meagre resources. But the sympathy was probably more critical to the people currently running that country—the military. General Zia was certainly one of the few military dictators around the world who were often quoted as humanitarians. 'We are looking after them'—the refugees—'ungrudgingly purely for the sake of humanitarian grounds and we will continue to do so even if the population increases,' the Chief Martial Law Administator was quoted as saying at the beginning of January, 1983, report of the United Nations High Commissioner for Refugees on the status of the Afghan refugees. 'But it is a very large burden. . . . We are a poor country but we are prepared and we are sharing with our neighbors and friends who may have perhaps less than we have.'

The refugee population gave the regime respect and legitimacy abroad, and the burden of the Afghans and the threat of the Russians probably kept Zia in power. Even his worst domestic enemies—lawyers and other Western-educated political activists—sometimes defined the situation on the frontier as a national 'emergency,' and 'emergency' has always been the favorite world of military rulers everywhere. There was one other advantage supplied by the refugees in the North-West Frontier Province. Their labor was needed in Pakistan. As poor as the country was and as low as the cost of a man's pay was, there was a labor shortage around Peshawar, because so many of the local men were working in the Gulf states as laborers in and around the oil fields. The money was much better in Saudi Arabia and the United Arab Emirates, and for the past several years Pakistanis in general—two million at any time—and Pathans in particular had been going to the oil countries to fill three-year and five-year labor conracts at wage levels many times what they could earn at home. Estimates of how much money they were sending back ranged from as low as two and a half to as high as seven and a half billion dollars a year, perhaps as much as twenty-five per cent of their country's gross national product. Under any circumstances, someone would have been need-ed to repair the roads and carry the loads of Pakistan, and it turned out to be the hundreds of thousands of Afghans coming over the mountains.

For the United States, the refugees offered the irresistible chance to embar-rass the Soviet Union on a continuing basis. All that the Afghans had to do was stand there—preferably in front of cameras—looking displaced and poor. Their plight and the pictures provided legitimate commentary on the values and the reality of the Soviet system. Even better, the Afghans weren't satisfied to shame the Russians—an endeavor of dubious prospect—but wanted to kill them. And they were doing it, although at a terrible cost. A reasonable estimate of the fatalities on each side during more than four years of Mujahi-deen rebellion might have been several hundred thousand Afghans dead, almost all civilians, and perhaps eight thousand Soviet citizens killed, almost all soldiers. The Afghans fought on, brave men; many did indeed intend to fight to the last blood of a small child. 'Why are you, who have everything, afraid of the Russians? We have nothing and we are not afraid of them,' said Dr Mohmand at his hospital for the wounded. 'Why won't you give us weapons? Answer that to me.'

'The answer is we do,' a high American official in the country at the time said when I told him of the doctor's question. 'But they want heavier weapons, stuff they probably couldn't handle. They have enough to keep this going. That's what we want—to keep this going as long as possible to make the Soviets look as bad as possible to the rest of the world.'

The Russians, for their part, seemed to think that the price was worth pay-ing. They were getting what they wanted: control over the land of Afghanistan. I couldn't be sure of all their considerations, but the reasons cer-tainly included obtaining control over Afghanistan's natural resources, setting up a military buffer zone, avoiding the embarrassment of the overthrow of a client Communist government, checking the flow of Islamic fervor into their own Asian republics, and providing themselves with an eventual path (through Baluchistan) to the warm-water ports of the Arabian Sea and the water routes of the world's oil supplies.

The Russians were patiently gaining control over one of the most uncontrollable countries on earth by depopulating it. No one had ever really conquered the fierce tribal people of Afghanistan—the British and the Russians tried for all of the nineteenth century, but the mountain snipers always drove them out—and the Soviet strategy this time seemed to be to conquer the country if not the nation. The nation—or, at least, the most difficult elements of its population—was being eliminated in one way or another. There were fifteen million Afghans when the Russians invaded. By the summer of 1983, hundreds of thousands were dead, almost three million were in Pakistan, and more than a million were in Iran.

Among those missing were the most troublesome—the tribal warriors in the camps of Pakistan, and the small educated élite of Kabul, who were scattering to richer places. There were, when the Soviets came, about twelve hundred physicians in Afghanistan, said Dr Mohmand, who had studied for five year at Texas A. & M. and had been jailed for ten months by the Communists in Kabul. He told me that there were only two hundred left, almost all of them recent medical – school graduates. He said it proudly, as proof of the unpopularity of the Soviet rule. But I drew a different meaning from his figures.

'How many Afghan doctors are there in Peshawar?' I asked.

'Between fifty and a hundred,' he said.

So nine hundred physicians, three-quarters of his country's doctors, were gone. They were in Europe or the United States—aching, perhaps, for their land and people but making new lives for themselves in places where their skills made them welcome. The same was true of Afghans in other professions and among Afghan merchants. The upper classes and upper middle classes had been driven out or had fled. Those pitifully small élites were gradually being replaced by cadres of Afghan physicians, teachers, engineers, and administrators being trained by the thousand in Moscow. There was going to be a new Afghanistan.

And for the refugees, the Afghans driven from their lands, life was better. I was told this many times—by Pakistani and Afghan doctors, by foreign and United Nations relief officials, even by refugees—before I began considering that it might be true. They were being given something, for the first time in their lives, for the first time in their history: food, medicine, education, wages.

Each day, each refugee was supposed to be provided, by the World Food Program and the United Nations High Commissioner for Refugees, with this food: five hundred grams of wheat (a little over a pound); thirty grams of edible oil; thirty grams of powdered milk; twenty grams of sugar; and three grams of tea. That would add up to about two thousand two hundred calories a day, which is also the average Pakistani intake and is just below the twenty-five hundred calories a day considered the minimum daily requirement by most Western health agencies. Each refugee was also, on paper, receiving twenty-five litres of 'potable' water each day. That, however, was impossible in a country whose water supply, but its own government's most optimistic estimates, less than twenty-five percent potable.

That, it seemed, was enough. The Pathans are hard people, still living by old codes, which include *melmesta* (hospitality to strangers), *nan awati* (asylum to fugitives or refugees), and *badal* (an eye for an eye). They have always done whatever they wanted to do, and if anyone didn't like it the Pathan response—particularly in the tribal areas—began with harsh, threatening screaming and quickly escalated to killing and blood feuds for generations.

The world relief agencies supplied the refugees with soybean oil (from the United States government) for cooking. The Afghans threw it out or sold it. They would use only ghee—butter made from buffalo milk. The UNHCR gave them kerosene from their fires. They used only wood until they had stripped the barren land of every bit of loose firewood, and then began uprooting bushes and killing trees by hacking upward from the lower branches until not enough tree was left to survive. And if their Pakistani cousins needed that wood—well, the Afghans had guns.

'They are wild men, who will end up destroying our country,' said a Pakistani sociologist, a woman with a passionate hatred of the refugees. I encountered that hatred many times in educated men and women. 'The government wants these people in order to maintain the state of emergency and to get money and sympathy from the international community. But they are terrorizing our people. After all the years it took us to persuade the Pathans in the north-west to give up their guns—in exchange for roads and the things a modern government could provide—now they are invaded by these barbarians. The Afghans are living better than the masses. Are Pakistanis being treated by American doctors? Afghans are going to destroy us, because one day they will revive the Pukhtunistan issue.'

'Puhktunistan!' is the cry for an independent Pathan nation ('Pathan,' 'Pushtun,' and 'Pukhtun' are all Westernized versions of the same sounds in the language of the frontier), which has been heard in this land over the years, and particularly in the nineteen-fifties. 'Baluchistan!' is another cry expresing another separatist dream, and until the early nineteen-seventies there was civil war in the hills of that even poorer province south of the North-West Frontier Province.

'Pakistan!' was only a separatist cry less than forty years ago. The Land of the Pure didn't exist before the nineteen-thirties, when Muslim intellectuals, led politically by Muhammad Ali Jinnah, the Quaid-i-Azam, or Great Leader, began agitating for a separate state for the Muslims of Hindu-dominated India. It was an artificial country created along a set of lines drawn in London and Delhi by the departing British rulers. Half of it, East Pakistan, disappeared in 1971, and there was always a real chance (and a real fear) that all of it could disappear—perhaps with the Punjab and the Sind becoming aligned in some way with India, and autonomous states of Pukhtunistan and Baluchistan coming into being and then, sooner or later, coming under some kind of Soviet control exercised through the new Soviet-trained cadres in Kabul.

The centrifugal forces acting on Pakistan have been many and great for a long time: four provinces in uneasy alliance; twenty-two regional languages; powerful neighbors, suspicious or hostile, in India and the Soviet Union; and, perhaps, a fierce new population, the refugees, owing allegiance to nothing modern, including the flag of the country. The one thing that united Pakistan was its religion − its original raison d'être. The bonds of Islam, which were not strong enough to hold East Pakistan and West Pakistan together, were still the only bonds. It was inevitable that the rulers of the nation, whether civilian or military, would always resort to appeals to 'Islamic socialism,' as Zulfikar Ali Bhutto did, or to 'Islamization,' as Muhammad Zia-ul-Haq was doing while I was there. There would be an Islamic Republic of Pakistan, or there would be no republic.

The holiest month in the Islamic Republic is Ramazan, Islam's holy month of fasting, and in 1983 Ramazan ended with the sighting of the beginning of a new moon on the evening of 11 July, 1983. There were cheers in the streets of Islamabad, and the lighting of dazzling displays of colored bulbs draped on public buildings, including the embassies of other Muslim countries. Great necklaces of red and green lights hung in strand upon strand, drawing crowds all through the night. *Eid-ul-Fitr*, a joyous thanksgiving holiday of feasting, gifts, and family visiting, had begun.

In Rawalpindi, President Zia-ul-Haq issued an *Eid* proclamation in the way an American President would offer a little inspiration as he lit the White House Christmas tree:

> Let us beseech him in our *Eid* prayers to grant to Muslims throughout the world the will and the wisdom to promote and strengthen bonds of brotherhood and respond to hostile challenges as a single, united people. . . . It is fitting that a period of self-denial be followed by the reward of rejoicing. But it is no less binding that the sense of enjoyment be tempered with the feeling of solicitude for the indigent . . . enable the less fortunate members of the community to make arrangements to celebrate this auspicious day . . . .
>
> We bow our heads in gratitude to the Almighty Allah that we have been able to take important steps toward the establishment of a truly Islamic order in our country . . . and banish from our midst regional, parochial, sectarian, and similar other divisive tendencies.

I had never heard of *Eid*, but I had certainly heard all that before. It was what any politician says, except that the symbols were a little different from the ones I was used to.

'This shouldn't be all that exotic to an American,' said Hamid Alvi, a Pakistani who worked in the offices of the United States Information Service in Islamabad. 'Pakistan is working out all the problems of national identity and rapid modernization that the United States worked out a hundred and fifty or a hundred and seventy – five years ago. But you were lucky enough to be able to do it in absentia from the world. There was no one around then. Pakistan is being pressured on every side, on every border. Our real problem, creating the real gaps in our society, is that you can't tell where each man stands on the scale of modernity. The trick is always how to embrace and advocate modernism without making it a rejection of the old values.'

'What are the old values;' I asked.

Alvi needed only one word: 'Islam.'

I thought then, not for the first or the last time, that what Pakistanis, sincerely or cynically, were calling Islamization—and were arguing over—was really, in the end, going to be a cover for the modernizaion of a very backward society. Pakistan was going through the stress of becoming new by talking about the old. Pakistanis had to talk in the context of the only thing they all knew: Islam. Newspapers were packed with rambling and redundant essays on 'Islam and Science' and 'Islam and Democracy'—all of them quoting the Koran, and almost all of them arguing for more and more technology and scientific education and for elections. A truck I saw near Peshawar could have been the symbol of the process. Pakistani trucks were rolling, smoking galleries of folk art, brightly decorated, like circus wagons, with paintings of landscapes, animals, and religious symbols. This one listed a litany of Islamic saints and heroes—Ali, Fatimah, Hasan, Husayn—symbolically flying on a painting of an F – 16.

The American jet, the material confirmation of Pakistan's status as a 'frontline state,' quickly became the ultimate symbol of modernism in the country. But it had to coexist with old symbolds and ritual. The pull between the new and the old has been a part of the national identity crisis that has been Pakistan's curse since its hasty founding, on 14 August, 1947. On that day, the British, well aware that the Indian subcontinent could explode with religious violence between its dominant Hindus and its minority of Muslims, carelessly divided their Indian empire into India and Pakistan. The creation of the Islamic Republic—or, to be precise, of a stubborn Muslim intransigence that made a united India seem even more impossible than the divided one—was principally the doing of Jinnah, whose impeccably tailored three-piece suits and cool, secular Anglophilia were as much a symbol of his intention to create a nation of modernism as Gandhi's simple dress was a symbol of his devotion to the old ways.

But Pakistan was created so quickly and sloppily that even Jinnah, its founder, had to migrate there. He was born in Karachi but had lived most of his life in Bombay. Decades later, Pakistanis still identified one another by whether or not they were *mohajirs*, or 'migrants,' of 1947 or descendants of the migrants. (Zia-ul-Haq, for instance, came as a twenty-three-year-old Army lieutenant fleeing the Hindu-Muslim violence of the Indian Punjab.) It was one of too many non-religious divisions for the good of the country. Next, they identified each other by region, with Punjabis set against Sindhis and Baluchis and Pathans, and by the two dozen languages spoken across the thousand miles, including Urdu, the official national language, which came from Central India with the migrants, and English, the language of Pakistani élites. Then they looked at each other on Alvi's scale of modernity, which was often a test of whether a man or a woman identified with Western or Eastern traditions. Beyond that, those drawn to the Eastern world were often divided over whether Pakistanis should identify with India or, as Muslims, with the Arabic countries across the Arabian Sea. (Some, usually Shia Muslims, wanted to identify with Iran and Ayatollah Khomeini.)

Islam was a conqueror's religion, brought to India by Arab invaders in the eighth century, and even after Partition there were almost as many Muslims in India as in Pakistan. Its message of equality before God was naturally attractive to lower castes within the ridigly hierarchical world of Hinduism. Untouchables became Muslims—a fact that has more than a little to do with Indian attitudes toward Islam. (Many of the Hindus who stayed in Pakistan were Untouchables, and they and their children continued to do the dirtiest work of the society, cleaning streets and toilets. But many of them changed their religion, becoming Christians.)

Pakistani attitudes toward Indians seemed complicated—tortured, really—mixtures of fascination and fear. After losing the three wars over Kashmir and East Pakistan, the Pakistanis appeared to have finally accepted the fact that India rules the subcontinent. There were fewer illusions of political, economic, or military parity. Pakistan must play Canada—an antagonistic Canada—to its more powerful neighbor. Pakistan had many problems, and one of them was maintaining the myth that its people were fundamentally different from Indians, for the similarities between Indians and Pakistanis often overwhelmed the differences—in the eyes of foreigners, at least—and the confusions of that unwanted similarity made the quest for national identity even more difficult and deepened the pervasive inferiority complex of Pakistan.

Pakistanis had not yet defined themselves. That was one of many similarities I thought I found between them and us—between Pakistanis and Americans. There were, after all, more than a few of the untouchables of the Old World among the people who made the United States of America. People didn't come to the New World because they were successful and honored in their own countries. With fewer natural resources—'meagre resources'—and older and more complicated problems and handicaps, and in a more dangerous and difficult time, Pakistanis were trying to do in decades what took Americans more than a century.

When Anwar Kamal, the lawyer in Lahore, talked about the heavens on earth he had seen in Europe and America and how he wanted to be part of building a modern country with his own people, I envied him. Most of that had been done for me; it was something I had read about. I heard Kamal's kind of dedication again and again from Pakistanis. 'Progress' was talked about as a god. But not as God.

Modernization and Islam were often spoken of together, comfortably sometimes, uncomfortably sometimes, but not as mutually exclusive. How could they be, in the Islamic Republic? Islam was the environment. The ideas of Islam were the only way to reach all the people joined together now as Pakistan; they were the shared values, assumptions, and knowledge of the nation. There was nothing else to begin with.

But what is Islam? Who defines the faith? First, the believers did not see it as a 'religion'—as somehow separate from the secular—in the way that most Western Christians and Jews see their religions. 'We can't separate God from Caesar,' Abdullah, the zealous Commissioner of Refugees, had said. 'You do that.'

'Islam is not merely a set of beliefs and a way of worship,' stated a position paper prepared by the government of Zia-ul-Haq to explain its Islamization program to outsiders. 'It is a complete way of life. It provides guidance in all walks of life—individual, social, material, moral, economic, legal, and cultural. It is this-worldly and other-worldly.'

Almost everyone I talked to in Pakistan, even the most Westernized (and personally secularized) of the country's élite, the men and women who went to embassy and consulate parties for the French wine, agreed with that and restated it in their own words. But that was where agreement ended. There were many Islams—sometimes, it seemed, as many as there were Muslims. When the Zia government, with the help of Zia's Saudi Arabian advisers, interpreted the Koran to mean that *zakat*, the alms tax, applied to bank deposits, hundreds of thousands of people took angrily to the streets; they were largely Shia Muslims, the minority in Pakistan, who read the Holy Book differently.

The great division in Islam—though still one division among many—is between Sunnis and Shias. Pakistan is a Sunni nation—eighty-five per cent of the population—and Iran, for instance, is a Shia nation. To a Muslim, that explains almost everything about the differences between the countries, and explains why Pakistan could never become a theocratic state on the model constructed by Ayatollah Khomeini in Iran.

There are no ayatollahs in Pakistan—only local *maulanas*. There is no hierarchy among Sunnis. In that respect, the two sects could be loosely compared with Roman Catholicism (Shia) and Protestantism (Sunni) in the days when Western nations were more inclined to fight religious wars. The Sunnis and the Shias divided over the succession to the Prophet Muhammad after AD 632. The stories that were revealed to Muhammad over twenty years and recorded by scribes as the Koran were of the Flood and Moses and Abraham—fiercer in tone but similar to Bible tales—but Muslims believe that Jesus of Nazareth was the next-to-last in the line of prophets that ended with Muhammad.

After the Prophet's death, Islam (the word is Arabic and means 'submission' or 'surrender') was ruled by a series of caliphs ('successors') selected by the family of Muhammad and the men around him. At the death of the fourth caliph—Ali, the Prophet's son-in-law—there was a dispute among factions, and two lines of succession were established. The Sunni line—to oversimplify—eventually petered out, ending ambivalently in the twentieth century with the end of the Ottoman Empire in Turkey. The Shia line ended, after a fashion, most Shias believed in AD 873, when the Twelfth Imam ('leader') died or disappeared mysteriously. 'The Hidden Imam' became an omnipresent factor in Shiism: 'We are waiting for you, Twelfth Imam' was a revolutionary slogan in Iran, and Ayatollah Khomeini (or Imam Khomeini; the title applies to all Shia leaders) wore, for many, the mantle of the Hidden Imam. That connection gave Khomeini a temporal power over many people that it would be virtually impossible for any Sunni leader to accumulate.

In talking about Pakistan's Shias, the hundreds of thousands of them who demonstrated against Zia's *zakat* proposals, I asked someone what it would take to trigger such a demonstration by the majority Sunni population.

'I don't know,' he answered. 'You couldn't get a hundred Sunnis, much less a hundred thousand, to agree on anything.'

I have obviously simplified all this enough to outrage any thinking Mulsim. But it would be impossible for me to do justice to such disputes. Millions of men have been arguing—and going to war—over these differences for centuries. I have also ignored hundreds of smaller sects that have broken off from the two main sects over those centuries—the Ahmadis, for instance, a sect that followed a nineteenth-century prophet and was declared *kafir* by Prime Minister Bhutto, and the Nizari Ismailis, of the northwest, the followers of the Aga Khan. The closest I can come to describing the passion and the angels-on-the-head-of-a-pin nature of the debates—and, too, the intellectual vitality of Islam—is to compare them with the arguments of American consitutional lawyers working for very high hourly fees.

Apart from sects, the Islam of India and, in time, Pakistan developed in ways unique to the subcontinent. After Arab and then Turkish Muslim armies invaded the territories that would become Pakistan, new invasions, by Genghis Khan and Timur, in the thirteenth and fourteenth centuries, reached Delhi, weakening Hindu rule in all of India. Muslim princes grually took control of more and more of the subcontinent, and in the sixteenth century the great reign of the Moguls was established. In the next two hundred years, those Muslim rulers built the spare and disciplined monuments that came to symbolize India to the world: the Taj Mahal, at Agra; the Red Fort, at Delhi; the Badshahi Mosque, at Lahore. Larger and larger numbers of Hindus were converted to Islam during those years; what drew them from their musical religion of many gods to the faith of the one God was their own ambition—Islam was the religion of opportunity while the Moguls ruled—and the oppression of the Hindu caste system. It was, by and large, Untouchables, beneath the four major castes, who embraced Islam.

In India, higher-caste Hindus—particularly the highest, Brahmans—would not touch food in the presence of Muslims; they were still treated as Untouchables even as they ruled. When the British came, gradually expanding their rule as the Muslim princes divided and were conquered, the Hindus began not only to reassert their numerical superiority—there were two hundred and fifty million Hindus and a hundred million Muslims in India at Partition—but also to seize the opportunities of British education and modernization. The Hindus became the businessmen and bureaucrats of British India; the Muslims, uncertain about confronting new knowledge, remained landlords, soldiers, and peasants. But, whatever the tensions between the religions—village slaughters periodically followed provocations like Hindus' playing music while Muslims prayed, or Muslims' killing a sacred cow—the new religion of one God never totally abandoned the culture and ritual of Hinduism. The Muslims of India and, in time, of Pakistan worshipped at the tombs and shrines of *pirs*—local saints and demigods—in most un-Koranic ways, and sang and danced and threw flowers at weddings in most Hindu ways. One of the enduring traditions of Lahore, which Muslim purists had been trying to stamp out almost forever, was the giving of garlands of rupee notes as wedding gifts—a Hindu custom. Perish the thought in the Islamic Republic, but Pakistani Muslims sometimes seemed more Indian than Muslim.

Then there came a day when the military government ruling the country of those Muslims decided they were not Islamic enough. General Muhammad Zia-ul-Haq decreed Islamization. The official definition of that process was this: 'Islamization in Pakistan is a positive effort to build up a system of human relations—on individual and collective level—on the principles of justice and morality as enunciated by Islam. It is an attempt by the people for whom religion is a living faith to remodel their private and public lives.'

'Who the hell is Zia-ul-Haq to Islamize us?' said a prominent writer. 'I was Islamized a long time ago.'

I heard that question a couple of times a day. The short answer was that he was the man in charge of the Army—and the Army ran the government. He gave a longer answer, of sorts, in a press conference that he held on August 14, 1983—the thirty-sixth anniversary of the country's independence. It was, I thought, one of the most extraordinary performances I had ever seen by a political leader. Humble in personal manner, intelligent, articulate, committed, the self-appointed President of Pakistan suddenly seemed a bit mad to me, drunk on his own power and destiny. I did realize, however, that not all his sense of power was delusionary. 'My only ambition in life is to complete the process of Islamization, so that there will be no turning back,' he said that day. 'The Islamization process is a lifetime job. It is not only the changing of certain laws from the Anglo-Saxon character to Islamic character. Islamization is complete whenever we can have the social environment turned into an Islamic character. You have to bring some of the fundamental elements of the educational system into line with Islamic values. Also, the general society itself. You have to put their aims and objectives straight on the path of righteousness. And that's what I call Islamization.' It might also have been called 'hubris.' The Army Chief of Staff who took over the country—for ninety days, he said at first—thought he could also take over the mission of the gods. Whatever tragedy lay ahead for him and for his nation, Zia-ul-Haq did not seem totally in touch with either the general society or righteousness that day.

'The man in the street—the illiterate masses—knows Islamization is a hoax,' said a young writer who takes his own Islamization seriously. 'It's just a way to keep the military in power. The people know the difference between the way the Prophet lived—the clothes he wore the house he lived in—and the way our leaders are living.'

The word 'hoax,' which was widely used, in safe privacy, by Zia's opponents, was too strong, even if many generals and colonels were obviously feasting on the spoils of power—including the money that the United States was delivering in the name of its own governmental religion, anti-Communism. There were, I was sure, some admirable aspirations behind the quest for a modern Islamic identity. But Islamization fashioned on the austere and repressive monarchical religion of Saudi Arabia was choking Pakistanis, who were coming to despise the Saudis anyway, as stories of life under the Islamic masters of the desert were brought back home by oilfield laborers.

Truly changing the social environment and the behavior of millions of people would require more than arresting young couples for publicly embracing, or putting eighty lashes on the back of some poor soul caught drinking a can of beer or the home brew made in villages. But more substantial attempts at Islamic reform quickly ran into the realities of modern life—the way Pakistanis lived was being changed by modernization more than it could ever be by Islamization—and ran into as much resistance as could be prudently mounted in a police state. Better and presumably more righteous minds in Islamabad had not been able to figure out a way to construct a banking system faithful to their interpretation of the Koranic ban on what Zia often referred to as 'the curse of interest.' The women of the country were in open and (to the Zia regime) dangerous revolt over attempts to institutionalize new laws of evidence, based on the thoughts of some conservative Islamic scholars who were determined to maintain legal male supremacy. So the Islamization of Zia was often reduced to silliness, like his announcement to the nation that he would ask the Shariat Courts—courts created to review all civil and criminal verdicts and sentences to determine whether they were 'Islamic'—to decide whether book piracy was Islamic. Pakistan had never been a signatory to any international copyright agreement. Local publishers just stole any foreign books of local interest—if they were passed by the military censors—and reprinted them without paying royalties or fees to authors or foreign publishers. So a court of *maulanas* was delegated to determine whether the Prophet would approve of that.

But there was more to Islam than things like that, and there could be more to islamization than the hastily conceived and self-serving games being played with the lives of the faithful of Pakistan. It seemed obvious to me that Islam was rich and complex enough intellectually and idealistic enough not only to provide the material for political speeches and clichés but also to create the environment for technological modernization and for modern political systems providing the rule of law, majority rule, social justice, and economic opportunity for most of the people most of the time.

Despite the angry and vengeful message of many Koranic verses, Islam was, after all, the faith of the tonga wallahs—men as good in the eyes of Allah as Zia-ul-Haq. A determined egalitarianism was projected in the pages of the Koran, and the religion had grown on the subcontinent as an alternative to the caste system. Though there were VIP entrances to mosques, the faithful were taught that all men—women were a different matter, as they had been at the beginnings of the United States—were equal if they performed, with belief, the five duties of a Muslim: to say with full acceptance, '*La ilaha illah 'llah, wa Muhammadun rasul Allah*,' the Arabic for 'There is no god but God, and Muhammad is His messenger;' to pray five times daily, facing toward Mecca, and to say Friday-noon prayers in a mosque; to give alms generously; to keep the fast of Ramazan; and once in a lifetime, if it is financially possible, to make the Hajj, the pilgrimage to Mecca.

'Wherein the principles of democracy, freedom, equality, tolerance, and social justice as enunciated by Islam shall be fully observed' is how an initial passage of the Constitution of the Islamic Republic of Pakistan, adopted in 1973, reads. And it says, 'Now, therefore, we the people of Pakistan . . . faithful to the declaration made by the founder of Pakistan, Quaid-i-Azam, Muhammad Ali Jinnah, that Pakistan would be a democratic state based on Islamic principles of social justice . . .' That Constitution was suspended by Zia-ul-Haq, but, as I found out—and, more important, as he did, too—it was still a document of great weight to the people of the country, including the illiterate masses. 'There seems to be a consensus emerging in the Majlis-i-Shura during the debate on the future system of government that the 1973 Constitution was a sacred document that should not be touched under any circumstances,' the *Muslim* reported on page 1 of its 26 July, 1983, edition, during the period leading up to the Chief Martial Law Administrator's promised announcement before Independence Day, 14 August, of a framework for Nizam-i-Mustafa, a 'System of the Prophet.'

The system, Zia had promised, would include elections of some sort—'Islamic democracy.' I asked a Pakistani publisher of an Urdu-language daily newspaper whether there could really be such a thing as Islamic democracy.

'If it's really democracy,' he answered, 'who cares what they call it?'

'Can you preserve the old ways as modernization comes?' I asked a Pakistani intellectual, who had just been telling me how important it was for his people to find their own way instead of simply imitating the West.

'Preserve the way people live here?' he said, with a look I took to be perplexed. 'Why would anyone want to do that?'

Islam tried to resist modernization once—for centuries. The price was enormous, and Pakistan is one of the Muslim countries still paying it. In the Middle Ages—the Dark Ages of Western Civilization—science, mathematics, and medicine all flourished in the Arab world and Persia. It was our ancestors, not Muslims, who were painting themselves blue and dancing around rock piles to combat drought and plague. But over time the efforts of xenophobic Muslim leaders who were determined to resist the sinful advances of Western philosophy and science—earlier and greater versions of the Gujrnawala *maulana* who cast out anyone who believed that men had walked on the moon—drove entire nations back to their origins, back in time to the sullen bliss of the ignorant. But what they didn't know was hurting them. In India, the descendants of the Muslim rulers of the seventeenth century gradually lost their feudal domination of the subcontinent's Hindu population. As the nineteenth century was ending, with the British in control of the subcontinent, earlier roles were reversed as the Hindus grabbed at the opportunities offered by education and the English language while the *maulanas* cursed white men and the darkness. Between 1858 and 1878, of thirty-one hundred graduates of Calcutta University only fifty-seven were Muslims. During the eighteen-eighties, fewer than one in twenty-five of the Indian students in British colleges were Muslims. Some of that was a product of British discrimination against Muslims because of their role in the Mutiny of 1857—an Indian Army uprising against British rule—but much of it was by choice. Muslims buried their heads in the sands of time.

A hundred years later, in 1983, Pakistan, the home of the ninety million descendants of the men who built the Taj Mahal and discovered much of early modern medicine, had twenty universities and thirteen physics professors. There were, according to one study, forty-five thousand one hundred and thirty-six scientists and engineers working on research and development in all the Islamic countries combined, compared with thirty-four thousand eight hundred in Israel alone—or four hundred thousand in Japan, or a million and a half in the Soviet Union.

But there was no debate, not anymore, about whether the Islamic Republic should accept and learn the technological ways of the West. 'We must be like the Mormons I have seen in your country,' said Fazl-ur-Rehman, the *maulana* from Lahore. 'They are a religious people, like us, who have known persecution, as we have. They push their people into technology and the advanced fields. Television and universities are part of their church. They are not only up-to-date. They are ahead.'

The debate now was only over how to become part of that world of 'advanced fields;' and Islam, the vessel of the old ways, was also being used, finally, as the agent of change. The science-and-technology section of the government's Sixth Plan began by quoting the Koran: 'In the change of the winds . . . are signs for a people that are wise.' It then got down to the business at hand: 'Quantum jump in Science and Technology allocations—from Rs. 1,838 million in the Fifth Plan to Rs. 5,855 million—to accelerate progress towards early attainment of self-reliance in Science and Technology.' 'Islam and Science' was practically a standing headline in newspapers.

The Islam I found in Pakistan was a more positive force, or field of force, than I had expected; but it was also less important than I had expected. It was not Islam that oppressed Pakistanis and enslaved the illiterate masses of the country. They were victims not of their faith but of things that have always oppressed men and women—force and greed. The worst thing I could say about Islam was that it made the oppression more bearable. Dreams of the next world, a paradise of gardens for the pure, made men—and women—more tolerant of the injustices of this one.

Islam was used for many things. As Zia-ul-Haq tried to restructure Pakistan to fit his own images by using the phrase 'Islamization,' Zulfikar Ali Bhutto made the same effort before him with the phrase 'Islamic socialism.' That is the way of the words and the worlds spiritual and political. But materialism and self-interest—wanting first what is necessary to survive and then wanting what other people have—are ways of the world, too. Pakistanis did not vote for Bhutto because he was a Muslim. Everyone was a Muslim in the Land of the Pure. In the villages and the slums of the cities, they voted for '*Roti, Kapra, aur Makan.*'

Abdul Hafiz Kardar, a Lahore businessman who was once captain of the national cricket team, told me about the first day he campaigned, in 1971, as a candidate for the Punjab State Assembly on the Pakistan People's Party ticket, headed by Bhutto.

'I went outside the city, where the farms began then,' he said. 'I saw a lady sitting—her husband was farming—and I asked her whether I could talk to her. She just stared at me coldly, and finally said, "Why?"

"Who owns the land where your husband is farming?" I said. She told me a name and pointed to a mosque far away and said this man owned everything up to the mosque. "I'm running with Mr. Bhutto," I said, "and If Mr. Bhutto wins, *you're* going to own the land where you're sitting."

"Sit down, brother," she said. "Tell me about that." '

'My sole aim is to organize free and fair elections . . . Soon after, power will be transferred to the elected representatives of the people,' General Muhammad Zia-ul-Haq announced on 5 July, 1977. The Chief of Staff of the Army was the spokesman for the group of generals that had planned the coup d'état that ended the public life of Prime Minister Zulfikar Ali Bhutto. General Zia pledged that the elections would be held within ninety days. Very little was known about Zia-ul-Haq when he took power. He had been a Bhutto appointee and loyalist, and it was widely assumed, in the country and outside, that he was not much more than a front man acting, perhaps reluctantly, for other military leaders. Even after seven years in power, not much is known about him—at least, not much by the standards of Western democracies with free, inquiring presses and with leaders driven to be liked and so fascinated with themselves that they assume that their people are just as interested in daily details of their lives and thoughts.

The best public information on the man who ran the ninth-largest country in the world was his four-page official biography. I also had some access to classified reports prepared by the United States Department of State and American intelligence agencies. 'God, these things are short on information,' said an American official reading the classified documents for me in Washington, and in terms of usable facts the official Pakistani version was little better. 'Fortified by deep religious conviction, animated by the spirit of Islam, and sustained by an ideological 'élan vital', General Muhammad Zia-ul-Haq, President and Chief Martial Law Administrator of Pakistan, is an enlightened and progressive soldier-statesman. . . .' That was the beginning of the Pakistani biography, and it did not lose its enthusiasm for the subject as it went on. He was born in Jullundur, now part of India's East Punjab, on August 12, 1924, the son of an Army chaplain—a lower-middle-class *maulana* in uniform. He graduated from St. Stephen's College, in Delhi, one of the better English colleges in India, and was commissioned as a cavalry officer in 1945, serving in Burma, Malaya, and Java at the end of the Second World War.

After Partition, according to his biography, Lieutenant Zia, who was already married, attended the Pakistan Army Staff College, at Quetta, and later served as an instructor at the college. In 1963, he attended the United States Command and General Staff College, at Fort Leavenworth, Kansas. In the 1965 war between India and Pakistan, he was a lieutenant colonel, but it was unclear from official biographies whether or not he served in combat. The question of whether or not he led troops in combat five years later, in 1970, when he was in Jordan, had long been debated—in whispers—in Pakistan. Whatever he was doing, he was in Jordan as an adviser to the Royal Army of King Hussein from 1969 to 1971—the period that included the Black September of 1970, when Jordanian troops attacked the Palestine Liberation Organization, driving Yasir Arafat and his troops into Lebanon. Zia, who was by then a brigadier general, returned to Pakistan—after the 1971 war with India over East Pakistan—and worked his way up the command ladder until 1976, when he was plucked from its second rung and elevated to Chief of

Staff by Bhutto. It was generally believed that Bhutto selected Zia because he found him dull, dedicated, loyal and controllable.

Bhutto was wrong, and so was the promise of 'free and fair' elections. The deposed Prime Minister was executed—after a trial on charges that he was an accessory to the murder of a political opponent—and General Zia gradually destroyed the rule of law in Pakistan. By 1983, Pakistanis had no enforceable rights. Each and every person was subject to the judgments of military courts—courts of junior officers; courts without laws or lawyers, judgments without judges or appeals. That done, the dilemma of the commander of the junior officers, General Zia, was to find the right time and the right way to legitimize his rule. He managed through his years of power to maintain the acrimonious divisions between the political parties—keeping the minority parties more against the P.P.P. than for elections—while attempting to create new political leaders and political structures through nonpartisan local elections and the appointed Majlis-i-Shura. He won the backing, or, at least, the tolerance, of most of the Western world—most important, of the United States—by welcoming the millions of Afghan refugees. And he even tried his luck with the general masses; in April of 1983, for instance, he spoke at an announced rally at Gujranwala, which has a population of four hundred thousand, and drew a crowd of about a hundred thousand. That was not considered good enough, however; in that part of the world the carnival spectacle of political rallies is often enough to attract many hundreds of thousands of people.

But, as skillful as Zia was, his time seemed to be running out. Because there is usually little behind the front line of guns, dictators like Zia have to be extremely careful about any domestic confrontations in which the line might be breached or confronted for very long—once it is, soldiers tend to change sides or throw away their uniforms. Zia had been quick to back down at the first marches of any mass movement; when Shia Muslims began demonstrating aginst the *zakat*, their demands were met within days. Further, because unelected governments can rarely trade on either the demonstrated support or the constituent pressures of their nations, they are notoriously weak in negotiations with outsiders. Dictators generally have no voting numbers and few cheers to demonstrate that great numbers of people back their decisions. All they have is the power to impose their will on great numbers, but in that power there is inherent weakness.

'The military regimes look strong, but they are weak, because of the constant uncertainty about the future,' said an executive in Lahore. 'We have an interim, imposed stability, and that may have been necessary. But after a while there came to be uncertainty about the future. No one knew what would happen next. That has great impact on commerce and industry. Pakistan's capital went overseas when Bhutto began nationalizing everything, and it's still there—the money Pakistan needs to build a modern state. The time has come for a change, for a government with prospects for the future. The changeover should have happened about two years ago. But you, the United States, won't allow that. The Americans are what's sustaining Zia now.'

And the Americans had been quietly pressuring Zia for years to reestablish at least the forms of Pakistani democracy. As part of that process, the General began arresting politicians (not for the first time) on 3 August, 1983. Newspapers, in small headlines and stories over the next eight days, reported: '20 Political Workers Detained,' 12 Political Leaders Held in Quetta,' '6 MRD Workers Held in NWFP,' 'MRD Student Body Chief's Father Arrested.' The idea was to make sure that no one would make trouble on 12 August. President Muhammad Zia-ul-Haq was about to speak to the nation on democracy.

'It will be our endeavor, *Insha'allah,* to present a positive framework for a Muslim state and a truly Islamic system before the nation by next Independence Day,' the President and Chief Martial Law Administrator had said as he raised the flag of Pakistan at the country's Independence Day celebration on 14 August, 1982. On 12 August, 1983, he kept that promise in an address to the Majlis-i-Shura. The flags and bunting went up around the old National Assembly Hall in the center of Islamabad the day before. Attendance at the speech was by engraved invitation only, and the small crowd of diplomats, journalists, and VIPs—about a hundred of us—was settled in place in the balcony ten minutes before the President was scheduled to appear.

The President was dressed in a long gray tunic. The two hundred and fifty Majlis members, in some of the many costumes of the country or in Western-style business suits, sat in eleven rows in front of him—ten rows of men and a row of women. ('Majlis,' meaning 'assembly,' was the name used officially for the psuedo-legislature, but people generally called it the Shura, because that word has a double meaning in Punjabi—'adviser' and 'pimp.') After an opening prayer, Zia said that he had been following the debates of the Majlis and the discussions of democracy in the newspapers. He said that he had also studied and consulted with scholars but that he had been most impressed by the opinions and ideas of the public.

'The men who matter perhaps do not give them any importance because they are illiterate or semiliterate,' he said. But he intended to—and he had determined that they wanted one thing above all others: Islamic government. He had determined that, he said, by reading letters to the editor in the newspapers. 'After contemplation and exchanges of views with my colleagues on this subject, I have come to the conclusion that at this time there are three options open to us: First, that the 1973 Constitution be restored . . .' Applause stopped Zia, but it was premature. When he was able to continue, he said, '. . . be restored as it is. Second, that after the abrogation of this Constitution, a new Constitution be framed and approval of the people be sought on it. And, third, that the 1973 Constitution be enforced after necessary amendments.'

Zia picked the third option. Then he sketchily outlined the 'necessary amendments'—destroying the parliamentary form of the Constitution in favor of an indirectly elected President with almost dictatorial powers and a National Security Council of military chiefs with the power to declare a state of 'emergency.' The President would be chosen by elected members of the National Assembly and would then have the power to select and dismiss prime ministers and to accept or reject legislation voted by the Assembly.

'Zia,' the man next to me said, 'He wants to be the civilian President.'

The speech had been going on for an hour and fifteen minutes. Zia was listing what he called the new 'rules and regulations' of the 'elections.' Some members of the Assembly would be appointed rather than elected, to insure that religious leaders and certain professional groups would be represented. 'You should know that personal canvassing is not permissible according to Islam,' he said. And he said,'One person, one vote'—but a quota of women members would be maintained, apparently one in ten.

When? When would elections be held?

Finally: 'Election for local bodies . . . will be completed in the current year' (these elections had, in fact, already been scheduled). 'The elections for provincial and national assemblies and the senate will be held and this phase will, *Insha'allah*, be completed by 23 March, 1985.'

Elections within nineteen months. A Pakistani reporter took out a pocket calculator. When Zia-ul-Haq took power, he had promised elections in ninety days. That was six years one month and seven days ago. So on that basis Zia intended to stay in power for thirty-six years eight months and twelve days longer.

'Martial law will be lifted when the democratic process is restored after this phased election program,' Zia said. 'Oh, the believers, obey God, His Prophets, and those who are in power amongst you,' Zia quoted from the Koran. Then he quoted the words of the Prophet: 'He who obeyed me, verily obeyed the Lord, and he who disobeyed me verily disobeyed the Lord. And he who obeys his Amir [ruler] verily obeys me and he who disobeys his Amir verily disobeys me.'

Zia's listeners were getting a bit weary as he passed the hour-and-a-half mark. But they seemed pleased. The diplomats across the aisle seemed content. The Americans were smiling and nodding to one another. This was 'democratization'—a plan for return to civilian rule. Better than many people expected. Diplomatic service in a far place made one a gradualist; the diplomats took what they thought they could get. So American diplomats were applauding, with a certain enthusiasm.

I was making a list as Zia spoke. What did he represent to the United States? Order. Order was most important to us. Stability—same thing. Efficiency—relative efficiency. Sovereignty. Economic growth—some of that. Another list. What was he against? Change. The rule of law. Political freedoms. Majority rule. Freedom of choice. Democracy. Hope. Add bread, and a couple of other material things, and the second list could be the agenda of the illiterate masses—the ones who didn't write letters to the editor.

At the top of that second list I put 'Them.' At the top of the first list I put 'Us.' Zia was our man. The Chief Martial Law Administrator was pursuing the American agenda as well as he could in that part of the world. And the Americans there I found to be intelligent, practical people representing as well as they could what they understood to be the interests and official policies of the government of the United States of America. They admired and talked of capability and efficiency and technique, not of principles, ideas, and commitments. Diplomacy in practice, after all, was not a business of abstractions. There was a job to be done and you worked with the people you had to work with, and you got along. You began to understand their problems—perhaps a little too well.

'I tried to make it clear every day that our support was not for a man or a system but for a country and a people,' the former American Ambassador, Ronald Spiers, told me in the summer of 1983, after he left Pakistan.

'We made every effort to maintain contact with the opposition to Zia, although I must say I found him to be a more estimable man than most of the politicians. What could we do? I asked politicians and intellectuals the same question each time; I asked it a hundred times: "Should we refuse to give economic aid to the military government—particularly the aid that goes to rural areas? Should we stop that aid? Should we stop the military aid to your country?" Only one man of the hundred answered yes. Then they would ask me why the Americans did not support elections. Why didn't we force Zia to hold elections? Leaving aside the question of whether we actually had the power to do that, my answer was: "That would be gross interference in the internal affairs of your country. Elections are your problem." '

Spiers was a very good Ambassador. I was not the only person who thought that, because in August of 1983 he was appointed Under-Secretary of State for Management. He had, I was told, been quietly effective in persuading President Zia to slow down his country's nuclear-weapons research and to speed up efforts toward conciliation with India. He had also organized, without public embarrassment, functioning support and weapons-supply systems for the Mujahideen fighting the Russians inside Afghanistan. Zia, he thought, was honest and sincere and the best that America could do out there. 'Consultative dictator' was a phrase that I was told the Ambassador used privately to describe the ruler of Pakistan.

That ruler closed his 'democratization' speech with these words: 'Now let us attend to the rights of man, and save humanity, as in it lie the blessings of God and if we are able to gain the blessings of God then we will succeed in this world and hereafter. *Pakistan Paindabad.*' Or 'Long Live Pakistan.'

'Our great ideal, the United States of America and its human rights,' an important Pakistani reporter said the next morning with a mixture of sarcasm and bitterness in his voice. A cynical man. We were whispering, because we were in the President's house, in Rawalpindi, waiting for him to appear for his press conference after the speech to the nation. 'Then, when the Americans come, they talk just like the people who are killing us. You don't have to take us too seriously, do you? We're a frightened people. I'm frightened. Someone talks here, someone gets picked up, and he's beaten up. The better classes here aren't used to that. We get the message, and each of us knows he can't take it. We're too soft. If we get together to do something, they've always got new and better tear gas from the Americans. From you.'

Zia-ul-Haq came in, relieving my discomfort. There were fifty reporters in the room, almost half of them from other countries, and the questions from foreigners, in English, concentrated on two subjects: Was Zia planning to be the new President? Would political parties be allowed to take part in elections?

The questions were repeated again and again, in different forms, but Zia, smiling easily, stuck to his two answers: 'I've never anticipated anything for myself, although I've anticipated many things for Pakistan. So, I'll leave that part out' and 'We'll wait and see about the parties.'

The session went on and on, for more than an hour, with fewer and fewer questions and longer and longer answers.

The President was enjoying himself. 'My only ambition in life is to complete the process of Islamization so that there will be no turning back. . . . The Islamization process is a lifetime job. . . . The general society itself—you have to put their aims and objectives straight on the path of righteousness. And that's what I call Islamization.'

'He used to be sensitive to world opinion, particularly American opinion,' said my friend the Pakistani journalist. 'Bhutto was, too. That was always one of our protections—"The Americans want elections. The Americans don't like torture." But Zia doesn't have to worry about the world anymore. He thinks the Americans will support whatever he does.'

'U.S. Interests and Objectives Regarding Pakistan' was the title of the briefing that the State Department and the Defense Department provided for the House Foreign Affairs Committee on March 9, 1983, and the briefers were direct and clear: 'South and Southwest Asia is a region of critical strategic importance to the United States, presently threatened by Soviet expansionism. We are committed to the search for peace and stability within the region and to the safe-guarding of the supply of oil critical to U.S. and Western security.'

That was the interest: the oil tankers that went through the Arabian Sea from the Persian Gulf to the West. They steamed out there somewhere beyond the ship breakers working at Gadani Beach. Behind the beaches, the deserts of Baluchistan stretched into Iran and Afghanistan and, finally, almost a thousand miles away, to the borders of the Union of Soviet Socialist Republics.

It was in our interest to control that territory—'safeguarding the sealanes' was the term of superpower art—and, therefore, to control the people in it, even the nomads I saw through the mists of dust and time behind Gadani. But that was close to impossible. Pakistan was difficult to define, much less to control; there was too much of it—too many places, too many eras. Perhaps, somehow, it could be conquered, but the United States did not have the national will to undertake conquest. We are materialists—it is our way to buy what we want. Yet, as rich as the United States is, we can't buy nations of almost a hundred million people.

But we could buy the Army and the Air Force and the Navy of Pakistan, and we did that. It was not difficult to make them financially and technologically dependent on us—for everything from F-16 planes and M-48 tanks to the tuition for the children of generals in universities at Palo Alto, California, and Boston, Massachusetts. We bought control of the people who controlled the military. Therefore, it was in the American interest for the military to rule Pakistan.

It was a bargain. The official figure for six years was three billion two hundred million dollars in military and economic aid, and the real figure might be twenty-five per cent higher, but most of that money would be recycled. Some of it was loans. Most of it had to be used to buy American equipment.

Travelling in Pakistan, going back and forth in time, from Gadani Beach to Karachi, from Islamabad to Bumburet, I often found myself thinking that the United States would do better to use its great wealth, which was partly my wealth, just to offer some aid that was not glorious, complicated, or obviously geopolitical, such as figuring out how Pakistanis could teach each other basic sanitation—just the connection between filth and disease—and basic literacy, in any language. The shame of the United States of America was that in countries under American patronage, among them Pakistan, the illiterate masses stayed illiterate, while in countries under Soviet patronage, among them Cuba and Nicaragua, people learned to read and write within one generation.

Why were we the ones afraid of literacy, the great carrier of modernization? I was astounded to realize that my country, the one place and the one people with the most to gain materially and spiritually from the modernization of other people, was out there resisting the most fundamental linkage between the old and the new—literacy. If we believed in the way we lived and in what we said, in our own history and our own spirit, then it was in our interest for people to hear it and understand it—to know more of the ways of the modern world and the ideas that created and moved people like us, living on another level of time. Instead, we picked friends in Pakistan whose stated commitment to modernization emphasized technology over ideas—as if they could somehow use one and reject the other. Zia-ul-Haq, with a perception influenced more by Machievelli than by Muhammad, understood that the more things Pakistanis knew, the worse things were going to be for the military. Mass illiteracy served the purpose of our friends in Pakistan—preservation of the status quo of the masses—and the United States seemed quite comfortable in going along with that. The government of Pakistan at least announced rural literacy programs, even if a proposed study of the accomplishments of three hundred and fifty new schools in the rural Punjab revealed that they existed only on paper. But the government of the United States specifically excluded such programs from its aid package to Pakistan. 'We were just spread too thin to bother with things like literacy,' an official of the Agency of International Development told me after I returned to the United States. 'Why don't you try someone over at the World Bank or the United Nations? That's more their style.'

Usually, the American style was dollars for defense. But those dollars too—at least half of the total of three billion two hundred million dollars—preserved the status quo. And it was not only that the military aid helped keep the military in power. There was also the suspicion among many American officials—angry and dismayed in private—that after Zia and the other generals had painted crescent moons on all their new American planes and tanks their guns would be pointed east—not north toward America's enemy, Russia, but toward Pakistan's old enemy, India. 'The most discouraging thing out here has been trying to nudge the Pakistanis a little closer to the Indians,' one of those Americans said. 'And vice versa for our people in Delhi. It's not only a question of preventing future wars between them and preventing a nuclear-arms race between them—which, God knows, is important enough. It's the realization that real security against Soviet expansionism in this part of the world finally depends on some sort of alliance between Pakistan and India. Pakistan alone could be vulnerable, unless you assume we are going into combat with it—which is ridiculous. Together, though, Pakistan and India would be too much for even a superpowr to confront. But we can't crack the old attitudes.'

Preserving the *status quo* for as long as possible, holding off the future, it seemed, was the most likely historic role and purpose of the rule of Zia-ul-Haq. Talking of elections and of the transfer of power to civilians was generally seen as a trick of the trade of military dictatorship. There was a pervasive and debilitating sense while I was there that General Zia had no intention of giving up power voluntarily. Few people, Pakistani or foreign, believed that the men in uniform intended to hold national elections they did not control, or would allow the installation of a government they did not control. So pressure was bulding as modern power-sharing was forcibly retarded. 'Time bomb' was a cliché, but clichés come into being because they describe people, places, and situations so well—and Pakistan was a time bomb, a nation that might be shattered by explosions if its internal pressures were not vented into the creation of a truly modern state.

From the day it was founded, there has been danger that Pakistan could shatter into modern feudalism. That could happen in much of the Third World as post-colonial Western maps and models prove inadequate to govern the life of the illiterate masses—with changing military or military-based regimes proclaiming central government while violence is the real arbiter of political power in the countryside. If it did happen in Pakistan, then, for a long time, no matter what was written in constitutions and on maps, great areas of its rural regions and urban slums would be little more than fiefdoms—going their own traditional ways under an ignored national flag and faraway superpower patronage. That disintegration, beginning, perhaps, with separatist movements in Baluchistan and Khyber, would be encouraged and helped along as it happened by the Soviet Union—but it would have already been encouraged by America's backing of the historic domination of the nation by the military élite of the Punjab. The United States seemed blindly committed to working on Pakistan from the top down while change in the society was almost certainly coming from the bottom up.

The masses of Pakistan, reacting to a confused identification of military government and semifeudal economics with modern democratic capitalism, might effect change by moving toward socialism. That could begin with some of the excitement of overthrowing the military—celebrations in the name of bread and democracy ending, perhaps, with most of the bindings of authoritarianism, if not totalitarianism. Although it may be heresy for an American to say it, socialism might offer the most stable and most modern and modernizing future for Pakistan—over the next couple of decades, at least. I could not conceive of a lot of short-term benefits in an American-model economic system for most of the people of Pakistan most of the time. American ideas of competition and free enterprise superimposed on an almost feudal economy—on the ship-breaking of Gadani Beach and the agricultural fiefdoms of the Sind and the Punjab—would be an irrational choice for the people of Pakistan at this stage of the country's development, if they actually were ever to have a voice in their own destiny. While Pakistan struggled through the difficulties of modernization, some sort of socialism would probably have much more to offer the country's awakening materialists. They could get some education, maybe some land, if feudal power bases were cracked by a central government that could survive without holding back the power-sharing, materialist forces of the future. But if there were to be a progression to socialism in Pakistan I did not think that it would follow any pattern familiar to Karl Marx, nor would it lead eventually to Communism—neither the pure form he envisioned in Western industrial nations nor the totalitarian perversion practiced and propagated by the Soviet Union.

Men and events in India—and the part of it that became Pakistan—have never managed to accommodate Western analysis and prognosis. The place and the people have never been kind to observers and visitors seeking truth or the power that comes from seeing the future. Another earnest representative of that discouraging heritage, I ended my first visit believing that Pakistan would not become a Communist country—certainly the Muslims would resist Communism mightily—and that Pakistani national history would probably stand Marxist theory on its head. Pakistan, with intelligent help from its friends—which I hoped would include the United States and India—could progress fairly quickly from feudalism, through the jumbled ancient and modern systems that I found, to a few generations of socialism before joining the modern world one day with a mixed economy of centralized planning and free enterprise and a democratic political system compatible with the arguments of Islam.

The next period of Pakistan's history, after almost forty years of attempts, both successful and unsuccessful, to impose Western political and economic systems on the nation, will decide whether or not there will be an Islamic Republic, whether Pakistan can survive as an independent country. Three choices—or projections, since choice might not be much of a factor in what happens next—seemed obvious to me after I was there: one, more military dictatorship, increasingly repressive; two, the violent chaos of the shattering of the country put on maps by British arrogance and Muslim determination; three, a fumbling, frustrating attempt to create a Pakistan that would be more modern and more democratic—economically as well as politically—and more socialist than the countries usually favored by American patronage.

The third option could be the American option. Pakistan has to find its own way to the future. Generations of modernization breaking up the patterns of the past into some sort of centralized socialist (not Communist) state seemed to me to be necessary to create and shape the forces—literacy and rampant materialism among them—that could bring Pakistan into the modern world with a productive economic system that was more free than slave and a democracy that existed off the pages of abrogated constitutions. Pakistanis whose materialist cravings for bread and books were satisfied would be a pretty good bet to begin moving toward abstractions like the rule of law, political freedom, majority rule, social justice, and economic opportunity. Those abstractions are what America is supposed to be about, and if we are wrong in thinking that people anywhere in the world with some security and some education will choose and fight for those things for themselves and their children, then we are wrong about everything. If that is not what being an American means, then we should not worry about trying to make the world think and act like Americans, because we are doomed to fail in our missions in Pakistan and many other places.

I came back thinking that if the United States does fail this time in Pakistan—if we 'lose' Pakistan—it will not be becuase American ideas and ideals were not worthy but because we didn't seem to think that illiterate masses were worthy of sharing them. Without those ideas, what were we out there? Just more people with guns. It seemed possible that we would not be there much longer. On the day after my wife and I went to the Presidency for Independence Day in 1983 and sipped tea with President Zia-ul-Haq, we went to Lahore for, among other things, dinner with a young lawyer and his wife. She came alone. He had been arrested that day. The police had come at two-thirty in the morning, but he had already gone into hiding. In the afternoon, with other attorneys, he had appeared at the Lahori Gate, volunteering to be arrested for violating orders against public assembly. 'Courting arrest' was the local term. He was taken to a jail in a smaller city, a day's drive away. There would be no trial; probably he would be released in quieter times—perhaps in a few months.

'Police started mild caning to disperse the crowd at the gate,' the Karachi daily *Dawn* reported. Still, the dinner was pleasant. The woman spoke of her impressions, generally favorable, of a recent trip to the United States. When we were leaving, she said, 'You realize, don't you, that when Zia goes, you go?'

The young lawyer was one of more than seven thousand Pakistanis arrested during demonstrations and riots in cities across the country after Zia announced there would be no national elections for as much as a year and a half. More than six hundred people were also believed to have been killed in the riots of August and September of 1983. But the lawyer and most of the others arrested were out of jail when I returned almost a year later, in June of 1984.

New restrictions had been placed on the press during the year, and President Zia explained them—from his viewpoint—when we met again in his den at home in Rawalpindi, a manly room of guns and swords and autographed photographs of the leaders of the world. 'The press in Pakistan is as free as it can be under the present circumstances,' he said. 'Except for a little check I've introduced—of not reporting political news. I don't want people to waste their time on politics at the present time. The parties are practically dormant anyway. This is a military regime.'

It was Eid-ul-Fitr again, the holiday of celebration and thanksgiving after the fasting of Ramazan, and the leader of the regime had cast himself in the role of Mogul ruler, receiving all who came to the gate of one of the Victoriangovernment guesthouses in Rawalpindi. For seven hours, Muhammad Zia-ul-Haq stood in a simple white *shalwar kameez*, accepting the good wishes and hearing the complaints of thousands who had waited in line to shake his hand or kiss it, embrace him, receive an envelope with a few hundred rupees.

'What do you think?' a deputy minister asked me as the line moved toward the last man.

'I think it's very impressive,' I said.

'What do you think of the President?'

'I think he's impressive, too,' I said, pausing to choose my words with care. 'Intelligent. Determined. Resourceful. Courageous. Very skillful.'

'It would be very dangerous for people like you to write such things,' he said.

'Dangerous? Why?'

'Because Americans must not believe this is what the people of Pakistan want.'

'What do the people want?' I asked.

'We are speaking unofficially?'

'Yes, of course.'

'People here are the same as people in America. The people want democracy. The people want justice. The people want freedom.'

HOW IS INDIA DOING?

Amartya Sen

'Thou by the Indian Ganges' side / Shouldst rubies find: I by the tide / Of Humber would complain,' wrote Andrew Marvell, outlining to his coy mistress the things they could do if they had 'but world enough, and time.' While not many rubies have been found on the banks of the Ganges, India's reputation as a land of riches is as ancient as the history of its poverty. That mixed reputation has changed in recent centuries, and India is seen these days primarily as a land of poverty, famines, disease, squalor, caste, untouchability, separatism, and chaos. This reputation is not altogether undeserved. But things don't stay stationary, and some changes have occurred in the last few decades. We have to ask: which way is India going? A sixth of humanity is involved.

I start with the economy. What did India look like at the time of independence in 1947? It was poor, obviously, but, more strikingly, almost completely stagnant. In fact, many estimates suggest that a sizable economic decline took place during the last decades of British rule. This is disputed by Alan Heston in his chapter on national income in the recently published *Cambridge Economic History of India* − an impressive two−volume work that is indispensable for anyone seeking enlightenment on India's past.[1] While Heston challenges the thesis of decline, his own estimates indicate a complete absence of growth of per capita income for the three decades preceding independence. Heston also accepts that in these years Indian food output per head was falling, despite the rather low growth of population (around 1 per cent a year).

The average expectation of life at birth in newly independent India was a mere thirty-three years. India also experienced a gigantic famine in 1943, shortly before independence; this killed around three million people. While the Great Bengal Famine was not directly related to the decline in the amount of food available per head (since it took place at a time when there was a comparatively good aggregate food supply), it brought out the disastrous vulnerability of several large occupation groups to the vagaries of economic fluctuations.[2]

Judged against this background, India's economic performance since independence is bound to appear quite remarkable. Its national product has grown steadily faster than population, and there is some evidence even of speeding up in recent years (against the trend of world recession). The long run growth rate of 3 or 4 per cent per year has been comfortably ahead of the population growth of about 2 per cent. Agriculture, no longer stationary, has grown sufficiently for India to be self-sufficient in most years and often more than that. Some regions within the country, e.g., Punjab, have grown at rates high enough to compare with the fast-growing economies in the Far East. The popular world image of India as a model of Malthusian decline survives, but the reality is different.

There have been no major famines since independence. While droughts and floods have threatened famine (for example, in Bihar in 1968, in Maharashtra in 1971–73, in West Bengal in 1978), public action has prevented a traditional catastrophe from taking place. Life expectancy at birth has gone up from thirty-three years to fifty-two years. While the fall in the death rate led initially to a sharp increase in the rate of population growth, that growth has recently been declining because the birthrate has been falling. It still has a long way to fall, and there is little cause for smugness, especially since China and Sri Lanka have achieved so much more in reducing the birthrate than India has. But even the relatively moderate fall in birthrate from 44 to 36 per thousand during the last two decades has now given India the third lowest birthrate among the thirty-three 'low-income economies' covered by *World Development Report 1982*.[3] Some regions in India, especially Kerala, have been more successful in cutting down the birthrate than have others.

The postindependence period has also seen some far-reaching changes in the legality of the caste system, and these have included making the practice of untouchability a criminal offense. India has been many years ahead of the West in introducing its own programs of affirmative action and positive discrimination. The constitution of the republic of India, which came into force in 1950, two and a half years after independence, makes explicit provision for such actions. In the civil service a substantial number of jobs have been reserved for members of the 'scheduled castes' – officialese for traditional 'untouchable' groups. As a temporary measure, a proportion of seats in the House of the People (the lower house of the Indian parliament) were reserved for 'untouchables' (the others being 'general' seats open to all citizens). The same was done in the legislatures of the states. The number of 'untouchables' in positions of power and influence has grown rapidly under these 'positively discriminatory' arrangements.

If all this sounds like a propaganda handout by a pro-India lobby, I should warn that I will presently argue that Indian society is a deeply troubled one, with extreme injustices heaped upon dreadful inequities. But we cannot begin to view India's problems and failures intelligently without acknowledging what has been achieved.

The expansion of science and technology in India – including nuclear power – has received some comment lately. Ved Mehta in his interesting and important book on the grip of the Nehru family in modern India has even argued that 'by some estimates' India 'ranks next to the United States and the Soviet Union in its number of highly trained nuclear scientists.'[4] India's higher education sector is vast. In the number of students enrolled in higher education as a percentage of the population aged twenty to twenty-four, not only is India a considerable distance ahead of any other country of comparable income level, but there is in fact no country with even twice India's per capita income that comes anywhere close to its higher education ratio.[5] In China, for example, the number of students in institutions of higher education is about 1 per cent of the corresponding age group, whereas in India that ratio is 8 per cent. In the number of doctors per unit of population, India is second only to China among all countries having income per head no higher than twice India's.

I ought to discuss two other achievements of some importance before I take up the bad news. Ever since independence, it has been feared that, in view of its regional diversities, India would soon break up. It has also been doubted whether India is, in any sense, one country. The inevitability of disintegration was most plausibly argued. But this has not happened. The so-called most dangerous decades have come and gone. There have been regional tensions, but the social, cultural, and economic bonds have proved to be too strong to snap – or even come close to snapping. I believe the historical basis of Indian unity is often underestimated by those who attribute to the innocent British the creation of a sense of 'Indianness,' which in fact has deeper roots. The first volume of the *Cambridge Economic History of India*, edited by Tapan Raychaudhuri and Irfan Habib, brings out the extent of social and economic integration that obtained in pre-British India.

There are, of course, several peripheral groups, e.g., the numerically small but politically important tribes in extreme northeast India, and retaining their loyalty has often involved the use of force – even brutality. However, for most of the country separatism has proved to be a very weak force much overestimated by 'experts,' foreign and domestic. While various *internal* re-arrangements (such as revision of interstate divisions) have occurred and will no doubt continue to occur, the nation of two – thirds of a billion people, with fourteen major languages, has survived remarkably intact.

The second achievement concerns the effects of the oil crisis and the world recession. India is dependent on oil imports, though attempts have been made recently to find more oil within the country. Despite the hike of oil prices in 1973, which expanded India's import bill remarkably, its foreign exchange earnings also increased rapidly. While India's terms of trade declined sharply with the rise in oil prices, the volume of its exorts increased much faster than the volume of its imports through the seventies. India also earned large remittances from Indians working abroad, especially in the Middle East. India has had more difficulty in coping with the second round of oil price rises, in the late seventies, but all in all it has weathered the storm remarkably well. And in recent years – despite the world recession – the Indian econmy has grown at an unusually rapid rate. Taken together these achievements are certainly impressive. What is the other side of the story?

'Speak of me as I am,' said Othello (shortly before that imperialist agent gave his candid views on 'the base Indian' and 'a malignant and turban'd Turk').

To apply the same principle to India today offers much scope for criticism even without anyone's having to 'set down aught in malice.' One can, for example, point out that while the pace of India's growth has speeded up recently, its long‑term average growth has been much lower than the world average; that Indian agriculture has got by with some help from good monsoons in recent years; that one reason India has weathered the oil crisis so well is that it is relatively near to the Middle East. Even as it has suffered from the rise in oil prices, India has benefited from the consequent shift in world income from the West to the Middle East, which has been much more inclined to buy Indian goods, services and skills.

These facts, however, do not really detract from India's achievements. Judged historically, the speeding up of Indian economic expansion from, at best, just about 1 per cent at the time of independence, to 3 or 4 per cent or higher, cannot be dismissed merely by noting that it is only recently that India's performance has become internationally respectable. Nor can the monsoons – on close analysis – be seen to be the major influence on the change in India's growth performance. And insofar as India has put the Middle Eastern boom to good use, it has been able to do this because of its potential for domestic production, the availability of skilled and semi‑skilled workers, and a willingness to seize economic opportunities as they arise. The real blots on India's performance lie elsewhere.

One of the major blots is the survival of regular malnutrition – as distinct from acute starvation and famines – in most parts of India. At least a third of the rural population seems to suffer from nutritional inadequacies. The deprivation is especially common for landless rural laborers, whose entitlement to food in the market economy of India rests on their ability to sell their labor and buy food. Depending on the varying chances for employment and relative prices, a great many of these families remain hungry a lot of the time. This class of rural wage laborers has been the traditional victim of South Asian famines (e.g., the Great Bengal Famine of 1943, the famine in neighboring Bangladesh in 1974). While this class has not had to face a famine in post-independence India, it has had to live with regular malnutrition and endemic hunger.

Estimates of poverty in India are usually related to nutritional norms such as the amount of calories people need. There have been a great many controversies among Indian economists and nutritionists on the choice of such norms (even on whether thay are meaningful at all) as well as on the use of these norms for statistical analyses of India's performance in relieving poverty. While some estimates show an increase in poverty despite economic growth, others suggest a slight amelioration of the incidence of poverty. But there is no picture whatsoever of a decisive change for the better.

India's 'self‑sufficiency' in food has to be assessed in the light of the limited purchasing power of the Indian masses. Their needs may be large, but their 'entitlements' in the market are small; that the economy produces enough to meet their market demand is not in itself a gigantic achievement. There has been no great 'shortage' in the market – no 'crisis' to deal with – but at least a third of the rural population has regularly – and quietly – gone to bed hungry and malnourished. The government has been able to ignore this endemic hunger because that hunger has neither led to a run on the market, and chaos, nor grown into an acute famine with people dying of starvation. Persistent orderly hunger does not upset the system.

Could India have done otherwise? It could be argued—indeed it is argued—that given the extremely low level of income from which India has started, it could not really do anything else until economic growth put the Indian people at a different level of economic prosperity altogether. Does that argument hold up? The contrast with China is relevant here, but that raises a great many complex issues, some of which I shall take up later. Fewer problems are posed by a comparision with Sri Lanka, which belongs to the same region and has a political system not far different from India's.

For a long time now Sri Lanka has followed the policy of providing extensive social services, including distribution of subsidized rice. The nature of that subsidy has varied over the years – sometimes cheaper rice was made available for all, at other times some rice was given free to anyone qualifying by a means test. While Sri Lanka's per capita income is of the same order of magnitude as that of India and Pakistan, and its total amount of available food (measured in calories) per unit of population is also quite comparable, cases of endemic hunger are much rarer in Sri Lanka than in the subcontinent. And the expectation of life at birth in Sri Lanka – estimated to be about sixty-six years – is far closer to the figures of rich countries than to those of India and Pakistan (fifty-two and fifty years respectively). The rice policy is by no means the only factor responsible for the difference, but it has certainly contributed substantially to the result, and the general program of government-financed social services – of which the rice policy and medical provisions are part – has worked powerfully in that direction.

It is thus not quite the case that India's overall poverty rules out all policies other than the one it has followed. Food subsidies in Sri Lanka have cost no more than a fairly tiny fraction of its GNP, and if they were similarly expensive in India, they would have amounted to less than just one year's growth of GNP at India's recent rates of growth. But India's approach to social services has, in fact, been sadly unimaginative and breathtakingly conservative. The deal that the government of India struck recently with the International Monetary Fund, leading to the approval of the largest loan (exceeding $5 billion) that the IMF has ever given to any country, seems to involve a pattern of development that includes a further move in the direction of the no–nonsense South Korean model and that will have the effect of excluding ambitious programs of social services. There is not much reason to doubt that this type of policy can bring dividends in high economic growth, but its impact on the quality of life will be slow. It is worth noting that South Korea, with five and a half times the per capita income of Sri Lanka, still has a slightly lower expectation of life than Sri Lanka. Nevertheless, the Indian leaders seem to have clearly decided on a strategy focused on growth, with an astonishingly conservative approach to social services.

That conservatism happens to fit quite well with the elitist character of Indian society and politics. The powerful groups have much to gain from high growth. If intensive public efforts were made to eliminate endemic malnutrition immediately, that would benefit groups that are less powerful. It is important to understand the elitist nature of India to make sense of India's policies. The elite groups in India are remarkably powerful, and while they are a small minority of a nation of 700 million people, they are still numerically large. The elite must not be confused with just the industrial leaders or the bourgeoisie. It includes millions of civil servants, business people, commercial farmers, educators, office workers, small landowners. In fact, it includes many people who are themselves poor by international standards.

Nor is it the case that the Indian elite is unenlightened, or indifferent to the rest of the community. The moral and political consciousness of the Indian elite does not permit, for example, a major famine in India, and when a serious famine threatens, public intervention is swift and effective. Even reports on pockets of acute starvation by probing journalists – and there are many excellent ones in India – get prominent attention in newpapers and produce some response. On the other hand, removing the quiet presence of non-acute, endemic hunger does not have high priority in that elitist morality and politics.

The roots of elitism go way back in Indian history. The Hindu view of mankind – stratified and hierarchical – conncects with it. To be born into one of the higher castes does not ensure elite status in the political economy; but in fact most of the elite comes from the upper and middle castes. The firm grip of the elite can be seen in practically every sphere of social activity in India. Recently, the historian Ranajit Guha has argued in *Writings on South Asian History and Society* that it is difficult to disentangle the events of the history of South Asia, since even the writing of history in the Indian subcontinent is so 'dominated by elitism.'[6] As far as politics is concerned, it is remarkable that much of the leadership of all political parties in India – from the extreme right to the extreme left – comes from this elite background. It is not so much that the leaders join the elite when they establish themselves but that they typically come from that stratum already.

Some of the achievements of India that I discussed earlier reflect the success of elitism. The remarkable expansion of higher education is a case in point. This applies to liberal university education, and also to science and technology. The other side of the coin can be seen in the shocking neglect of elementary education. After thirty-five years of independence, only a miserable 36 per cent of adult Indians are literate. In this nation with a nuclear capacity, well-developed scientific know-how, and a higher-education ratio perhaps eight times that of China, nearly two-thirds of the citizens simply cannot read or write.

Speculation on the influence of cultural history is usually rather treacherous, but there might well be some significanc in the fact that in countries molded by the less elitist Buddhist tradition, primary education is much more widespread and higher education much less so than in the land of Hinduism. This applies even to Buddhist countries in the same region, such as Burma and Sri Lanka; their adult literacy rates are 70 per cent and 85 per cent respectively (against India's 36 per cent) and their higher – education enrollment as a proportion of the population aged twenty to twenty – four is 4 per cent and 1 per cent respectively (as opposed to India's 8 per cent).

Underdevelopment of elementary education seems to go hand in hand with limitation of other social services. Kerala, the one state in India that has had a high level of literacy and schooling for a long time, also has a much better developed system of social services, including medical care. The expectation of life at birth in Kerala is, in fact, much closer to that of Sri Lanka than to that of the rest of India. But Kerala occupies an unusual position in Indian history. It has had rather different property laws and tenurial arrangements. Women have had a larger role in property inheritance. It has also been more open to outside influence. Christians came there by the fourth century and Jews shortly after the fall of Jerusalem, and both got on well with the Hindu kings and with the population; there were long-standing and close trading ties with many foreign countries including the Arab world; and Kerala also elected the first communist govrenment in India in the 1957 state elections. The dividing line between the elite and the non-elite has been under pressure for a long time in Kerala.

I mentioned earlier positive discrimination in favor of 'untouchable' groups. Reserving civil service jobs and legislative positions has certainly had the effect of increasing substantially the number of 'untouchables'in positions of power and influence. But there is little evidence that this has contributed substantially to improving the lot of the great majority of 'untouchables' in the country. The high correlation of untouchability with economic disadvantage – in particular landlessness and poverty – makes it difficult to transform the general position of 'untouchables' without very substantial economic change. Moreover, social conventions have been hard to break by puerly legal means, such as the laws against the practice of untouchability.

In fact, in recent years the persecution of 'untouchable' groups by members of some of the rural upper and middle castes seems to have intensified; and in some regions this oppression has even taken a sharply violent form. Members of 'untouchable' communities seeking a better economic or social deal (e.g., less exploitative labor relations) have been subjected to harassment, beating, burning of homes, and even murder. While the offenders have been brought to justice in many cases (often only after newspaper reports and the resulting public outrage), the preventive measures have been quite inadequate, and incidents of such violence continue to occur in different parts of rural India. Because of the rural power structure – even the nature of the police force – it is difficult to wipe out this violence without a much firmer and broader use of central power.

It is also remarkable that those 'untouchables' who are now in a position of influence thanks to positive discrimination have — with a few exceptions—done very little to help others left behind. Recently, the Untouchable Battle Society (Dalit Sangarsh Samiti) has strongly criticized the inaction of 'Dalit legislators, members of Parliament, and ministers in the face of growing atrocities' against other Dalits. Positive discrimination has often done no more than recruit some of the ablest, or most advanced, 'untouchable' members into the charmed circle of the Indian elite. One thinks of Marx's remark: 'The more a ruling class is able to assimilate the foremost minds of a ruled class, the more stable and dangerous becomes its rule.'

The elitist character of Indian society is brought out also by the treatment of women. Many women hold prominent positions in India – as parliamentarians, political leaders, academics, doctors, artists, and others – not to mention the most powerful prime minister the country has had. Although women in elite groups may still suffer from disadvantages, many doors are open to them. But the general position of women in Indian society is nothing short of scandalous. Their mortality rates are typically higher than men's (except for those above forty). The expectation of life at birth is lower for the Indian female than for the Indian male, and this pattern is quite contrary to that of the overwhelming majority of countries. Malnutrition too is more common among females. In studying the effects of the 1978 floods in West Bengal, I found that even among children under five, severe malnutrition was about 60 per cent more frequent for girls than for boys.

All this helps to explain the extraordinary fact that the so-called sex ratio—the percentage of females to males—in India has declined from around 97.2 per cent in 1901 to 93.5 per cent in the last census in 1981. This is, of course, an ominous and startling trend, since with modernization one would have expected a relative reduction of female mortality vis-a-vis male mortality. On the contrary, it appears that with the progress of modern medicine and health services in India, the opportunities have been much more effectively—and unequally—seized by men than by women. The traditional differences have been heightened by new opportunities, and as the absolute positions of both men and women have slowly improved in health and longevity, the *relative* position of women has fallen behind. This does not of course happen among the elite—not much anyway. The peculiarities and inequities of the respective mortality rates of men and women among the nonelite majority in India have not become a major policy issue in elitist India.

Insofar as elitism is seen as one of the main problems with India, a comparison with China is obviously relevant. With the establishment of communist China, anti-elitism immediately became one of the major emphases of its official policy, and during the Cultural Revolution this aspect of Chinese policy became particularly prominent. Certainly, anti-elitist achievements of China are very substantial. The traditional rural power structure was smashed effectively, the hold of the urban elite quite tranformed. Schooling and medical services have expanded rapidly and are much more widely spread than in India. The general level of nurition has vastly improved. Life expectancy—between sixty-four and sixty-nine years according to various recent estimates—is much higher than India's miserable fifty-two years.

But anti-elitism has caused grave casualties too. The chaos and destruction in the old university system that took place during the Cultural Revolution have clearly extracted a heavy price, and while the system is currently being rebuilt, a great deal remains to be done. The tyranny imposed during the Cultural Revolution was also justified by the anti-elitist policy, and even the more moderate accounts suggest a merciless extremism—torture, 'punishments,' killing—in the treatment of a considerable part of the population. India's record in this respect is obviously less disquieting. As Fox Butterfield, who was the *New York Times* correspondent in China, puts it in his disturbing book *China: Alive in the Bitter Sea*, except for the short period of the 'emergency,' which ended in Mrs Gandhi's electoral defeat, India

> has maintained its political freedom; there have been no unchecked Public Security Ministry, no street committees, no network of forced – labor camps, no persecution of whole groups of people because they were intellectuals or had relatives who had once been landlords, no destruction of libraries and universities.[7]

But in view of the price that India has to pay for its political system, it could be asked: are these liberties worth it? Would not better feeding, clothing, and health for the Indian population compensate for the loss of liberty which after all effectively concerns only a minority? I believe this way of posing the choice is both banal and wrong. First, there is little evidence that matters of liberty do not concern most of the people, even in poor countries. Indeed, the response of Indian voters to Mrs Gandhi's 'emergency' rule demonstrated the wider concerns of one of the poorest electorates in the world. It is indeed remarkable that a community of voters who are ready to tolerate so much economic inequity and are so difficult to mobilize against elitist policies could be so quick to move in its rejection of tyranny.

Second, the choice posed is unreal. A regime in which basic liberties are severely suppressed, and in which the government cannot be voted out of office no matter what it does, is deeply unpredictable, and there is no guarantee that even large-scale starvation and famines would not occur under such a regime. Indeed, there is clear evidence now that in China during the three years from 1959 to 1961 a great many people died from lack of food.

The exact size of the extra mortality caused by the food problem remains controversial. One estimate, based on Chinese data sources, indicates that the *extra* mortality during a four-year period including the food crisis years was about 16.5 million. Another, also based on recently available Chinese data, suggests that 'the net loss in 1960-61 would have to be no less than 23 million,' though other evidence suggests that 'the losses during the crisis may not have been as acute.'[8]

No matter which of the various estimates we pick, there cannot be any serious doubt that there was truly appalling extra mortality during the food crisis years. The same statistical approach – focusing on *extra* mortality – used to calculate the size of the Great Bengal Famine of 1943, and the extra mortality during the years from 1943 to 1946 was estimated to be around 3 million (much in excess of the official figure of 1.5 million). On that basis the Bengal famine of 1943 counts as the largest famine in South Asia in this century. The scale of Chinese mortality seems to have been much larger. So the Chinese catastrophe of 1959 to 1961 dwarfs even the pre-independence famines in India, and as I have already noted, there have been no major famines in the post-independence period in India. Although the Chinese have an economic system that makes guaranteeing food to everyone much easier than in the Indian economy, it is China rather than India that has had sudden large-scale deaths from food shortages in recent times.

What is also remarkable is that the news of hunger and death in China could fail to become more widely known. It is only in the last few years—nearly twenty years after the event—that the extent of the calamity has been acknowledged, and this has happened after a major change in the Chinese leadership. In India even a fraction of that death toll would have immediately caused a storm in the newspapers and a turmoil in the Indian parliament, and the ruling government would almost certainly have had to resign. Any government keen on staying in power would have had to avoid such starvation deaths from taking place at any cost. Thus the question of food and starvation is not unrelated to the issue of liberties, of newspapers, and, ultimately, of democracy. The Soviet famines in the thirties point toward the same less. So does the Kampuchean famine of more recent years.

What Wei Jingsheng called 'the fifth modernization'—the establishment of democratic rights – in his famous wall–poster message of December 1978 (after which he was sent to prison for fifteen years) is not only valuable in itself, as he emphasized, but it also has a crucial instrumental function in guaranteeing food and other necessities of life. The Chinese experience brings out the penalites of doing without 'the fifth modernization.' The Indian experience does not contradict the value of democratic rights—it confirms that value—but it also shows how easily terrible inequities can survive *despite* 'the fifth modernization.' The issue of democratic rights is part of a bigger social picture. In itself it does not make the picture, but if it is excluded, the picture has a crucial gap in it.

The strengths and weaknesses of the Indian system are clear enough. It permits endemic malnutrition and hunger that is not acute, so long as these happen quietly; it does not permit a famine both because it would be too acute and because it cannot happen quietly. It permits the injustice of keeping a large majority of the people illiterate while the elite enjoys the benefits of a vast system of higher education. It tolerates the continuing disadvantages of those who formerly suffered from explicit discrimination, even though such discrimination is now made illegal, and even though 'positive discrimination' promotes a small number from the bottom stratum to positions of power and influence as new recruits to the elite. The elections, the newspapers, and the political liberties work powerfully against dramatic deprivations and new sufferings, but easily allow the quiet continuation of an astonishing set of persistent injustices.

This dichotomy seems to me to be the central point in judging how India is doing. It is doing quite well in many specific respects − e.g., in accelerating the growth of income per person, in guaranteeing many traditional liberties, in developing science and technology and higher education, in putting more dynamism into agriculture, in meeting the oil crises and the world recession. But this record has to be assessed in the light of the persistent inequities, and the basic weakness of modern India that sustains them. It is a weakness that is not being conquered.

NOTES

[1] *The Cambridge Economic History of India* (Cambridge University Press, 1982 and 1983). Volume I: c. 1200 to c. 1750, edited by Tapan Raychaudhuri and Irfan Habib; Volume II: c. 1751 to c. 1970, edited by Dharma Kumar with the editorial assistance of Meghnad Desai.

[2] See my *Poverty and Famines: An Essay on Entitlement and Deprivation* (Oxford University Press, 1981).

[3] The World Bank, 1982, Table 18.

[4] Ved Mehta, *A Family Affair: India Under Three Prime Ministers* (Oxford University Press, 1982), p 158.

[5] The real income levels and other comparative data used here and later are taken mostly from *World Development Report 1982*, 'World Development Indicators.' See also *World View 1982: An Economic and Geopolitical Yearbook* (Pluto Press, London, 1982, and Maspero, Paris, 1982).

[6] *Subaltern Studies I: Writings on South Asian History and Society*, edited by Ranajit Guha (Oxford University Press, 1982).

[7] Fox Butterfield, *China: Alive in the Bitter Sea*, Times Books, 1982, p 447.

[8] John S. Aird, 'Population Studies and Population Policy in China,' *Population and Development Review*, Vol. 8 (1982), pp 277−278. The 16.5 million estimate is by Ansley J. Coale, 'Population Trends, Population Policy, and Population Studies in China,' *Population and Development Review*,Vol. 7 (1981), p 89. [Estimates published subsequently indicate an even higher famine mortality level in China during 1958−61. See particularly B. Ashton, K. Hill, A. Piazza and R. Zeitz, 'Famine in China: 1958−61,' *Population and Development Review*, Vol. 10 (1984), which estimates excess mortality of around 29.5 million during 1958−61. A.S.]

CLOSE-UPS

CAPITALIST AGRICULTURE AND RURAL CLASSES IN INDIA

Gail Omvedt

In 1969, two years after Naxalbari, Ashok Rudra and two colleagues published results of a survey on capitalist farming in Punjab. Their rather negative conclusions were responded to first by Daniel Thorner, a longtime observer of India's agriculture, who had concluded from his own rural tours that a new era of capitalist agriculture was beginning: 'Rudra tells us that he is more interested in the 'red revolution' than the 'green revolution.' The colour of the revolution I have seen in one area after another of India in 1960 is steel-grey. I call it an industrial revolution.'[1] Then in 1971 Utsa Patnaik argued, from her own study of 1969, that a new capitalist farmer class was indeed beginning to emerge. Rudra contested this, Patnaik replied, Paresh Chattopadhyay intervened with crucial theoretical points—and the famous Indian debate on the 'mode of production in agriculture' was on. Ranjit Sau, Hamza Alavi, Jairus Banaji, Harry Cleaver and numerous other Indian and foreign scholars became involved, and journals in Europe and elsewhere published summaries and further interpretations.

Clearly the 'mode of production' debate was provoked by real changes occurring in Indian agriculture, expressed politically in the Naxalbari revolt, new organizing of agricultural labourers and the repression of this organizing by the rural elite as symbolized in the 1968 Kilvenmani massacre, first of a long series of 'atrocities on Harijans.' It grew out of a milieu where scholars steeped in the classic Marxist notions of feudalism, capitalism and imperialism confronted a changing empirical reality, and the concern of all participants about the connection of research with revolutionary practice was perhaps best expressed in the catch-phrase, 'Will the Green Revolution turn into a red one?' But reading through the material in retrospect, it is surprising how scanty in fact the data base of the whole debate was. Most of the important economic changes in agriculture can be said to date from the 1960s, when the process of destroying the pre-independence forms of landlordism and laying the foundations of an industrial and infrastructural development that could supply inputs to agriculture was beginning to produce real changes. But though there were a few micro-studies, the only all-India data available was from 1961 (including both the most important data on tenancy and land concentration as well as Census data) and to a small extent from 1964-65 (The Rural Labour Enquiry). And this was rather early to show patterns. In fact, much of the 'mode of production' debate centered more on the colonial

From Bulletin of Concerned Asian Scholars, *July–August 1983. Reprinted with permission.*

Glossary

adivasi: tribal (Scheduled Tribe). Term means 'original inhabitant.'

benami: illegal (literally 'without name') land shown under someone else's name to escape the land ceiling laws.

bhauki: patrilineage.

crore: ten million.

dalit: member of ex-untouchable caste (Scheduled Caste).

gawki kam: 'village work,' literally, but refers to caste-duties of *dalits.*

Harijans: Gandhian term for *dalits.*

jajmani: the social organization of production at the village level according to which each caste performed its specific duties.

jati: caste.

kisan: 'peasant.'

ksatriya: second of four *varnas;* warrior, ruler.

lakh: one hundred thousand.

mahila mandal: 'women's club'—women's organizations usually traditionally run, in villages and cities.

panchayat: village council.

panchayat raj: 'village government.'

patil: village headman.

ryot: usually translated as 'peasant,' but one with rights to cultivate the land. Some *ryots* in British and pre-British times were actually petty landlords.

ryotwari: the land settlement which gave 'ownership' rights to *ryots* rather than landlords or other intermediaries.

sat-shudra: 'clean' *shudra,* term applied to high-status, non-Brahman castes of Tamil-nadu.

shudra: fourth of four *varnas.*

taluka: county; lowest political unit above village.

varna: one of four caste-categories (these were *brahman, ksatriya, vaishya, shudra*) in which actually existing *jatis* were given a place.

veth begar: forced labour somewhat equivalent to feudal corvee but often mediated through the caste system which required caste-specific duties.

zamindar, talukdar, khot, malguzar, jotedar: all terms for various types of non-cultivating landlords or intermediaries who could claim rent from the land. *Zamindars* were lower-level landlords throughout north India and higher level landlords, in Bengal; the term has come to be generally used for 'landlord.' *Talukdars* were higher-level intermediaries in U.P. *Khots* were in the Konkan (western India), *malguzars* in central India. *Jotedars* are now landlords in West Bengal but were before independence sub-holders from Bengali *zamindars.*

zilha parishad: district council.

period, than on analyzing whether a qualitatively different process was at work in the post-colonial phase.

Now, ten years later, many things seem much clearer. To begin with, not only have the patterns that could be seen in outline in 1968-69 developed much further, but there is more data available to confirm them. These include not only many more village and regional studies, but also massive all-India government material—the Census and Agriculture Census of 1971, the National Sample Survey and All-India Debt and Investment Survey whose jointly conducted 1971 survey of 12,452 villages is perhaps the most quoted source of information we have, the Rural Labour Enquiry of 8,512 villages in 1974-75, to mention only the most important. These are heavily infected with bias, as we shall see, and are also ten years old, but biases can to some extent be compensated for, and 1971 was sufficient to reflect the basic pattern of the changes in Indian agriculture. Further, data on production itself—productivity, crop patterns, irrigation, investment and credit, use of tractors, fertilizers and improved seeds, etc.—is available for much more recent years up to 1978. There is, in other words, a basis now that did not exist in 1969-70 to draw more solid empirical conclusions about the agrarian economy and class structure, though there are still important gaps in our knowledge and the state of theory.

Politically also the classes that observers were barely discerning in 1970—a Kulak or capitalist farmer class, and a rural semi-proletariat of agricultural laborers and poor peasants—are now coming forward as clearly powerful rural actors, though not in forms predicted in 1970. Capitalist farmers are the main force behind the 'farmers' agitations' that are dominating the rural political scene: it is no accident that these agitations are centering in the more capitalistically developed regions, that their main demand for higher crop prices itself indicates the commercialization of the rural economy, and that in contrast to pre-independence peasant movements they are not directed against any rural exploiter but rather seek to unite 'all peasants,' with an ideology that claims the 'city' is exploiting the 'countryside.' Thus they show the kulaks on the offensive against the industrial bourgeoisie and seeking to bring other sections of the rural population under their hegemony—with some success in the case of the middle peasants and even among the poor peasants especially where the left parties are there to help them. On the other hand, the increasing incidences of 'atrocities against Harijans' and caste riots, especially those recently in Marathwada and Gujarat which raged in both rural and urban areas, show the capitalist farmers on the offensive against the rural poor (it is again no accident that the most mass explosions and campaigns, including that centering on Kanjhawala, have been in more capitalistic areas) and using a weapon whose potency had also been hardly expected ten years ago—the weapon of caste divisions. It is symptomatic of the current dilemma that the question, 'will the green revolution turn into a red one?' is now being replaced by, 'will the caste war turn into a class war?'

As for the rural poor themselves, agricultural labourers, poor peasants, contract labourers and migrants, whether *dalits, adivasis,* Muslims or caste Hindus, have also been constantly struggling and asserting their rights, sometimes as workers, sometimes for wages or land, sometimes also as oppressed castes, nationalities or women struggling for rights as human beings. Though their movements so far have been comparatively weak and divided—and most weak and divided precisely in the more capitalistic areas—they provide a hint of what might come once they really begin to organize.

This article attempts to use the main all-India empirical data, especially the Agricultural Census, the 1971 National Sample Survey/All India Debt and Investment Survey (NSS/AIDIS) and the 1974-75 Rural Labour Enquiry (RLE), to show something of the structure and characteristics of what we consider to be the main rural classes: capitalist farmers, middle peasants and the semi-proletarianized poor peasants and labourers. Generally it will back up not the hesitant conclusions of most of the participants in the 'mode of production' debate (including myself at the time)[2] who still stressed the dominance in one way or another of semi-feudalism and forces holding back agricultural development or saw the post-colonial period as a mere continuation of colonial patterns in a slightly different form, but rather the bolder, even sweeping, conclusions of Thorner that 'a few pockets of capitalist farmers were to be found in certain regions of India before 1947. But their emergence as a significant group in every state is one of the facets of the industrial revolution that is changing the face of India.'[3] That is, it will stress the growth of capitalism in agriculture and the links between agriculture and industry, city and countryside. But it must not be forgotten that this is a capitalism developing within a post-colonial economy totally bound up with imperialism, affected in specific ways by the disarticulation between small-scale capitalism (including that in agriculture) and large-scale industry characteristic of such economies and by the still-potent effects of backwardness and various types of semi-feudal elements, including caste. It is important to analyze the specific nature and processes of this type of integration with imperialism, rather than simply seeing all kinds of backwardness and distortions of capitalism as signs of 'semi-feudalism.' The article, however, will focus mainly on the growth of capitalism as such.

Transformation of Indian Agriculture

Indian agriculture at the time of independence was predominantly feudal in character, though important elements of capitalism had risen. Various types of *zamindars, talukdars, khots, malguzars* etc., controlled the land in the areas of *zamindari* settlement, even though tenancy acts under the British had already given substantial protection to the top section of the tenantry. Some of these tenants themseleves (for instance those whom Charan Singh represented in UP) were essentially proto-captitalist in character and needed only the final blow of Zamindari Abolition to emerge as Kulaks; others (such as the Bengal *jotedars*) were more feudal in nature in that they sublet the land to share-croppers rather than cultivating it themselves or with hired labour. In *ryot-wari* areas also, the majority of land was informally under control of non-cultivating landlords. These were in some areas merchants or bureaucrats who had purchased it or won rights over it as a result of peasant indebtedness (e.g., western Maharashtra) while in other cases they were village landlords who were recognized by the law as 'ryots' (e.g., Thanjavur). Even where the recognized 'ryots' were those who came from castes with cultivating tradition and took an entrepreneurial interest in the land, they very often relied heavily on the near-slave bonded labor (e.g., the Gujars and Bhils in Dhule district of Maharashtra).

Not only was the majority of the land cultivated under some form of formal or informal tenancy (even formally, area leased-in as a percentage of total land was 35.7 percent in 1950-51) and thus dominated by landlords outside of or at the very top of the village, but inside the village itself specific types of semi-feudal relations continued to prevail.[4] Most of those classed as 'field-labourers' in the colonial period were from untouchable castes who still performed all types of labour service as an obligatory caste duty, though struggles against this had begun and though legal definitions had shifted, by and large their servitude remained in its traditional form. (This is shown in nomenclature: various forms of 'contractual' debt-originated servitude had replaced the pre-British state-enforced caste slavery—and this was an important shift—but locally these almost always continued to be known by the traditional caste-specific nomenclature.) Similarly, most of the means of production for agriculture were provided by artisans working within the traditional *jajmani* system in which their work was a birth-defined caste duty for which they received not exchange but yearly prerequisites in shares of the harvest or occasionally small allotments of land. Together these *dalit* field labourers and the artisans were a significant part of the village population who performed the labour that was crucial for agricultural production but never had any traditional recognition as 'tillers of the soil'; and with the development of the *kisan* movement their labour came to be known as *veth begar*. While a few *dalits* and large numbers of artisan caste people were becoming free wage labourers or small sharecroppers or even landholders, the continued prevalence of caste-defined duties and their importance for the whole process of agricultural production also defined the system as still a feudal one.

Clearly this was a caste-structured form of feudalism. In Indian feudalism prior to British conquest, *jatis* were basic untis of the social division of labour, with the 'twice-born' *varns* and other high castes being landlords, merchants and other exploiters, while the exploited toilers, were divided along caste lines into three main sections—the cultivating *kisan* castes who were traditionally 'tillers of the soil' (Kurmis, Jats, Kunbi-Marathas, etc.), the artisan and service castes who produced the means of production and some consumption goods, and *dalits* (untouchable) labourers who were semi-slaves for the village authorities and some dominant landlord. Where there was a seeming overlap in *jati* between landlords and peasant cultivators, there were always distinctions made between the mainly landlord clan/sub-caste and the others—e.g., between *patils* and 'guest' cultivators, between Shahhanavkuli Marathas and Kunbis, between Reddis and Kapus, etc. Further in the south traditionally landed castes such as the Vellalas or Nayars who did not have *ksatriya* status used other ways to distinguish themselves in *varna* terms from the cultivators as *sat-shudra* versus ordinary *shudras*, or by classifying all others as untouchable. During the colonial period, the state no longer enforced the caste system but rather instituted formal rights to acquire property, education, etc.; with this and with the opening of new factories, mines and schools the old identity of class and caste was broken; some members of low castes and even untouchables found opportunities for education, employment and even landholdings; agricultural differentiation resulted in some traditional landholding peasants becoming poor and going for labour, or in new landlords (especially often from Brahmans or merchant castes) taking control at the expense of old ones. Thus 'caste' and 'class' began to be constituted as separate social phenomena; but there was still a near-absolute correlation between them, with high castes continuing to be the main lords of the land, middle castes remaining as dominantly peasant cultivators and semi-skilled workers in the new factories, and the *dalits* and *adivasis* remaining primarily semi-bound toilers and workers in the most exploitative of the new jobs in plantations and mines.[5]

A hundred years of peasant revolts, *kisan* movements, anti-Brahman movements and organizations of *dalits* and agricultural labourers accompanied India's freedom struggle. Because of the particular caste-form of Indian feudalism, the anti-feudal movement was expressed not only through peasant revolts but also in the radical anti-caste movements of Phule, Ambedkar and Periyar; the anti-caste and social reform movements often contained attacks on moneylenders and landlords, while the most radical peasant revolts and especially the climactic Telengana revolt took up social issues including the fights against *veth begar* and against untouchability. In spite of all this, the independence that was won in 1947 was under the control of the bourgeois-dominated Congress Party; and it was in a bourgeois manner and directed to the needs of capitalist development rather than for the sake of a thoroughgoing agrarian revolution that those in power set out to destroy the semi-feudal system that dominated in agriculture. The government had no intention of giving either 'people's power' or 'land to the tiller,' the main slogan of the Kisan Sabha. But those at the head of the state knew very well that they not only had to yield to the demands of a politicized and mobilized rich peasant section who had emerged at the head of the broader agrarian masses, but also that anti-feudal land reforms and the widening of the rural home market were necessary for any real capitalist development. Thus, the five-year plans not only focused on the building up of a heavy industry, a public sector and infrastructure that included dams, roads and other forms of transportation, but also a series of land reforms and various village developments programs.

The Zamindari Abolition Acts and Tenancy Acts passed in various states in the 1950s did not give land to the landless or land-poor; they were not intended to. They allowed landlords to retain huge amounts of land (usually the best land) and paid generously for what was taken away; and they resulted as often in poor tenants being expelled from the land as in richer tenants getting control of the land. But they did achieve by and large the main *effective* slogan of the Kisan Sabha movement—that of giving land to the tenants.[6] They deprived big landlords to a large degree of their village power, pushed them to turn to farming through hired labour and investing in the land (here compensation money also helped), and laid a basis for the bigger tenants and rich peasant cultivators to come to power in the villages and develop as capitalist farmers. Land concentration as such was little affected by the Acts (it should be remembered there is both feudal land concentration and capitalist land concentration, and these acts struck only at the first type). But a basis was laid for the emergence of a new class in the countryside, bigger and more broad-based than the old landlords, composed in part of some old landlords but numerically more of ex-tenants and rich peasants. This class was 'new' in its relation to the land; its members were no longer living off peasant surpluses but were hirers and exploiters of labour power. It was also new in its different and in some ways wider social base in the villages, its caste composition, its traditions of self-cultivation, and its history of involvement in the anti-landlord and anti-caste struggles. While land concentration remained as high as before, tenancy declined and effective landlessness and proletarianization increased.

The second phase of land reform, the Land Ceiling Acts that began to be passed from 1961 onwards, were very different from these Zamindari Abolition and Tenancy Acts. They were designed to give 'land to the landless' and were not simply anti-feudal reforms but rather challenged land property as such, whether 'capitalist' or 'feudal.' As a result they had little significant effect at all. By 1977, 4.04 million acres had been declared surplus under those Acts, 2.1 million were taken over by the government and 1.29 million were actually distributed—a minute proportion of the nearly 390 million estimated cultivated acreage.

Along with anti-feudal land reforms came programs to increase production, for from the very beginning the Indian ruling class had seen its task of building capitalism as including both the development of heavy industry and of fostering and transforming the small-scale sector which centered on agriculture.[7] Developments often seemed slow and halting, but the government did invest, from the 1950s onwards, in irrigation, dam-building, promoting new seeds and improved breeds, long before the Ford Foundation and international agencies came along with their package programs, selected

IAVP districts, and the 'green revolution.' The spread of education, co-operative credit societies, land development banks, sugar co-operatives, agricultural universities all played a role. One of the most significant steps was the bank nationalization of 1969, which had the effect of channeling an increased share of credit to the countryside. Perhaps more important than any specific program of the whole 'green revolution' package was the increasing ability of the new kulak class to claim an increasing share of government resources for itself, especially after 1965.[8] Government programs and funds played an essential role in helping the new class to increase its productive base.

Finally, on the political side, the new institutions of the *panchayat raj*, credit co-operatives and educational institutions, *mahila mandals* and similar 'village development' institutions, all helped the new class maintain its hegemony in a new way over the increasingly proletarianized and restless rural majority.

All these developments took place very unevenly, for India is a vast and highly varied land, a sub-continent that has become a nation. In areas of *ryot-wari* settlement, where strong peasant or anti-caste movements occurred, it proved easier to move against landlordism and consolidate the gains of the new kulak class. Thus south and western India and the northwest show on the whole a clearer prevalence of capitalist relations of production. (This does not necessarily mean a greater development of the productive forces: the south remains poorer even today, while Punjab and Haryana, where investment in agriculture has been high from British times, maintain their lead in production.) In contrast, the east, the northeast and central regions remain backward, with a significant amount of semi-feudal relations of production. Within these broader regions, within states, and even within districts tremendous differences remain. But on the whole a growth in agricultural production and the transformation of the agrarian relations of production, in short the development of capitalist agriculture—even though it remains a backward capitalist agriculture with tremendous hangovers of feudal relations and remnants—has characterized the Indian countryside since independence.

Development of the Forces of Production

To begin with, let us look at the evidence for the degree of development of the productive forces in agriculture.

On the commercialization of the rural economy, Reserve Bank studies showed that by the early 1960s wages provided either the main or supplementary income for over half of rural families[9]; my estimate now is that this figure is close to 65 percent (see below).

Similarly in the early 1960s the Ministry of Food and Agriculture estimated that 45-47 percent of total crop production was marketed; it seems that about three-fourths of this was marketed by producers while the rest represented crops turned over to landlords or moneylenders who in turn sold them on the market.[10] I know of no recent detailed study of rural marketing that would allow us to estimate the changes in this,[11] but Indradeep Sinha[12] has claimed recently that 'during the last 30 years virtually the entire rural economy has been drawn into the vortex of money-commodity relationships and almost 100 percent of commercial crops and 40 to 60 percent of the food crops are brought to the market and sold as commodities.' This is probably correct, as is his point that village traders and wholesalers are thoroughly integrated into the overall Indian industrial-commercial structure and that this itself is linked to the imperialist chain, so that the life of India's rural population is truly dominated by the crisis-ridden economy of world capitalism.

There is clear evidence for a substantial growth in the use of *capital inputs in agriculture,* such as fertilizers, tractors, oil engines, irrigation pumpsets, etc. As Table 1 shows, there has been an almost qualitative change even in the last few years. Besides these, while the use of wooden ploughs and animal carts remained stagnant, iron ploughs nearly doubled between 1961 and 1971, from 2,298,000 to 5,359,000.[13]

This use of capital inputs has been often provided through the state and co-operative sectors and has been inevitably accompanied by greater dependence on the world market. A particularly stark example is the case of fertilizers. While production rose from 39,000 tons in 1951-52 to 3,490,000 tons in

Table 1
Agricultural Inputs

	1950−51	*1965−66*	*1975−76*	*1978−79*
Net irrigated area as percent of net sown area	17.6	19.3	24.2	NA
Consumption of fertilizer per hectare of cropped area in kgs (all kinds)	0.5	5.1	17.4	29.4
Tractors per *lakh** hectares of gross cropped area	7	34	166	234
Oil engines per *lakh* hectares of gross cropped area	62	295	1,074 (1974)	NA
Irrigation pump-sets with electrically operated tube wells per *lakh* hectares	16	326	1,617	2,308
Consumption of power in kwh per thousand hectares gross cropped area	1.5	12.2	50.0	76.9

Source: Centre for Monitoring the Indian Economy (CMIE), *Basic Statistics Relating to the Indian Economy,* Vol. I., All India, Oct. 1979, Sec. 10.
*lakh = 100,000.

1979-80, imports also rose from 52,000 tons to 2,300,000 tons in the same period. Imports as a percentage of total use declined from 57 percent to 40 percent but the value of these imports rose from Rs 5 *crore* to Rs 600 *crore*[14]; and this does not include the import of crude oil required for the production of fertilizers. India's previous food dependence has now substantially ended, but according to one economist, 'instead of importing food we are importing fertilizers for producing food' (*The Economic Times*, March 4, 1980).

Behind this growth in capital inputs has been a substantial inflow of financial resources to agriculture. This can be measured in various ways. Advances from Scheduled Commercial Banks to agriculture increased from Rs 11 *crore* (2.3 percent of total lending) in 1950 to Rs 67 *crore* (2.2 percent of the total) in 1968 to Rs 1,399 *crore* (10.4 percent of the total) in June 1977; the most dramatic increase was clearly after the nationalization of banks. Co-operative societies of all types numbered 214,000 with 35,600,000 members and a total of Rs 1,637 *crore* of loans outstanding in 1965-66; by 1976-77 the number of societies had decreased to 150,000 but there were 66,400,000 members and Rs 7,102 *crore* outstanding.[15] International funds, especially from the World Bank, going to agriculture substantially increased during the 1970s[16] while the Reserve Bank estimated that institutional finance of all kinds, direct and indirect, to agriculture more than doubled between 1973 and 1978, from Rs 2,621.8 *crore* in 1973 to Rs 5,722.3 *crore* in 1978.[17]

Some effort to quantify the flow of resources going into agriculture, especially between 1961 and 1971, has been made recently by Ashok Mody. He estimates a net inflow of about Rs 829 *crore* into farm households between 1962 and 1971 measured in terms of changes in financial assets and liabilities. He also estimates the average annual net flow of funds on government account into agriculture (public expenditure minus tax burden) as ranging from about Rs 48 *crore* a year to Rs 182 *crore* a year between 1951-52 and 1968-69. This latter figure does not include subsidies to the agricultural sector in the form of low water, electricity and interest rates or in the form of subsidies for food purchases, all of which have become increasingly important in recent years. Finally, terms of trade, which were more or less constant until the mid-sixties, turned steadily in favor of the agricultural sector between the mid-sixties and mid-seventies; though there has again been a reversal in recent years the net result has still been to increase the resource flow into agriculture.[18]

Clearly there have been substantial inflows of resources, largely as a result of state policy, into agriculture though the effects of this on the economy as a whole are still much debated, and just as clearly this has resulted in some growth of capital investment. The results of all this can be measured in three ways: in terms of growth of production, mass welfare, and the changing nature of the rural elite.

First, there has been a genuine, if halting, growth in agricultural production. Since independence the growth in production of all crops has been 2.9 percent a year or 0.7 percent per capita per year (Table 2). The overall rates of

Table 2
Annual Rates of Increase in Agricultural Production

	1951–52 to 1964–75	1964–65 to 1978–79	Whole Period
Foodgrains:			
Area	1.5	0.5	1.0
Productivity	1.5	1.9	1.7
Production	3.1	2.7	2.9
Per capita production	1.0	0.7	0.8
Non-Foodgrains:			
Area	2.5	0.7	1.5
Productivity	1.0	0.9	0.9
Production	3.5	2.5	2.8
Per capita production	1.2	0.1	0.7
All commodities:			
Area	1.7	0.6	1.1
Productivity	1.4	1.4	1.5
Production	3.2	2.0	2.9
Per capita production	1.1	0.5	0.7

Source: Basic Statistics, Tables 11.4–11.6.

food imports have steadily declined. The growth rate in the earlier period, up to 1964-65, was higher than in the later period, but this early growth was primarily due to expansion of cultivated area. Productivity growth rates were more or less constant with some improvement in foodgrains in the later period; there is no marked difference in productivity seen from the time of the 'Green Revolution' because in fact state-sponsored efforts at techonological growth preceded this period. In the early 1970s it seemed the growth rates were slowing and tending towards stagnation per capita; this was part of a world-wide agricultural crisis accompanied by widespread drought, famines and starvation deaths. The later 1970s appear to have reversed this process and led to renewed growth and even 'export surpluses. But it is too soon to define a long-term trend; it has to be noted that even some fairly recent studies (e.g., by the Asian Development Bank) have predicted increased dependence on imports for India in the 1980s. Still, it seems fairly clear after thirty years that in spite of some reversals neither 'semi-feudalism' nor imperialism is successfully holding back the 'growth of the forces of production' in agriculture. Though Indian agriculture is still miserably backward, though progress is slower than it could be under a rational socialist agriculture (it may be noted that China has achieved an estimated 5.3 percent growth rate in almost the same period on an even more crowded land area, cf. *Economic Times*, 26 June 1981), there has been a halting but clear *capitalist agricultural development*.[19]

This development, however, is not leading to any increased overall welfare of the rural (or urban) masses. (Indeed the idea that capitalist development by itself leads to improved welfare, or that immiseration, pauperization, growing landlessness, etc. are themselves signs of 'semi-feudalism' or the lack of capitalist development betrays some strange illusions about the nature of capitalism.) India's agricultural development is development that is accompanied by continuing insecurity in which bad weather leads to famines and by increasing dangers of widespread plant disease and salination, water logging, etc. resulting from major irrigation projects. Most of all, in the context of the imperialist system, it is development accompanied by growing exports of food from undernourished Third World countries to the imperialist centers and to the Arab countries, and by dependence on imperialist countries for imports of food during bad years and of agricultural inputs on a continuing basis; and it is development based on the stagnant and in some respects even declining living standards of the rural poor.

Estimates of per capita availability of foodgrains, pulses and other foods and of the general level of calories and protein consumed show a small rise in the availability of cereals between 1951-55 and 1971-76; but even then there is stagnancy in cereals between 1961-65 and 1971-76, and there is a general decline in almost every other food source over the whole period and in overall estimated calories and protein between 1961-65 and 1971-76 (Table 3). The general rise in agricultural productivity since 1975-76 does not appear to have led to any real change in this trend; in fact the drought year of 1979-80 caused another drastic fall in per capita availabilities.[20] It seems that most of the increasing gains in production are being directed towards export, including not only traditional exports like tea or coffee but also the best of India's rice, fruit, vegetables, onions, meat and fish products. As far as the other major

Table 3
Per Capita Availability of Food Protein and Energy

	(grams per day)		
	1951 – 55	*1961 – 65*	*1971 – 76*
Cereals	354.08	400.42	400.92
Pulses	64.66	60.68	45.40
Milk	131.29	129.90	115.65
Fish	5.67	6.00	8.75
Meat (a)		3.60	3.40
Meat (b)		6.80	6.30
Hen eggs		.50	.30
Reference protein (expressed in egg protein as standard)		29.26	27.57
Energy (kcal per day)		1744.57	1668.80

Meat (a)=from slaughtered animals and poultry.
Meat (b)=from both slaughtered and indigenous animals and poultry.
Source: S. D. Sawant, 'Indian Agriculture: The Protein Crisis', *The Economic Times* 14 Feb. 1981.

items of rural expenditure goes, the most thorough estimate of per capita availability of cloth (including natural and synthetic fibers) shows a rise of 31 percent between 1952 and 1964, from about 11 to 16 meters a year, and then stagnation through 1978.[21]

There is further, every reason to think that the rural poor are getting a decreasing share of this stagnant available product. There are widening inequalities in rural assets, between classes and between regions, which will be discussed partly in Table 7. The NSS estimate of the percentage of households below the poverty line increased in rural areas from 38.11 percent in 1960-61 to 45.12 percent in 1973-74 and close to 48 percent in 1977-78.[22] Agricultural labor remains the main source of income of the rural poor, and almost all studies show that both real wage rates and the days of work available have been declining. While there is a somewhat growing reliance on other sources of income, from low-paid labour in the unorganized sector (organized sector employment continues to show declining rates of growth), from various forms of very petty-commodity production (ranging from lace-making to selling grass in the market), or from ownership of tiny plots of land or a cow or milch buffalo, there is no evidence to show that this is increasing sufficiently to compensate for the decline of income from agricultural labour. The Rural Labour Enquiry itself estimated that the total real earnings of rural workers (defined as those who get the majority of their income ·from rural wage labour and who were 31 per-cent of the population in 1974-75) decreased by 10-18 percent over the period from 1964-65 to 1974-75 (*The Economic Times,*March 9, 1981). In short, we are forced to conclude that in spite of some gains in the years of Independence—increased medical care which has resulted in a lengthening of life expectancy, and some improved access to other amenities such as water, education, electricity and transport—the living standard of India's rural poor outside of a few pockets has actually declined in key respects. This absolute immiseration of a growing proletariat even while capitalist development is preceding on its crisis-ridden path is a sad confirmation of the most dire Marxist views of capitalism.

A third result of the capitalist growth of productive forces in agriculture has been a significant change in the nature of the rural elite. On one hand the inequality of access to the new inputs is stark: while aggregate capital expenditure on farm business rose by 65.7 per cent between 1961-62 and 1971-72, the proportion of rural households making *any* capital expenditure declined from 52.2 per cent to 37.9 per cent. But inequality is not the main point here. What is is the relation of the changing forces of production to class. Rastyannikov[23] points out that in the middle 1960s,

> the distinguishing characteristic of commodity production in India's agriculture prior to the 'green revolution' was the markedly uneven erosion of natural-type relations in both spheres of the reproduction process; the reproduction of labour power was freed from the fetters of the

natural economy to a far greater extent than the reproduction of the means of production . . . The industrial sector, both large-scale industry and small-scale industry, played an insignificant role in the productive consumption of agriculture.

That is to say, the reproduction of labour power had become dependent on the market (on wage labour or selling crops to buy necessities) but the reproduction of the means of production was not: modern inputs were minimal, land was the most decisive factor, and most other means of production were provided by traditional craftsmen and household production. This situation has now substantially altered. The large increments in credit going to agriculture, in fertilizers, improved seeds, pumpsets, tractors, etc., and the importance of irrigation in determining the value of land itself means that now the means of production for the rich farmers who control most of the land are being significantly and increasingly provided through the market and by modern industry and the state. Another indication is that over half of the debt owed by richer farmers comes from modern external sources such as co-operatives and banks in contrast to traditional moneylenders and other agriculturalists.[24] This also reflects the transition of the dominant class in agriculture from being primarily landlords to being primarily capitalist farmers.

In conclusion, there seems to be no basis on which we can argue that India's agricultural is not dominantly capitalist: over half the rural population depend on wages for their survival; all cultivators, including middle and poor peasants, are forced to sell to some extent in the market and their production is governed by the laws of the market; and the means of production in agriculture are now significantly produced industrially, acquired through the market, and monopolized by those who depend on the exploitation of labour power.

Changing Relations of Production:
Decline of Tenancy

In documenting these changes more precisely at the level of relations of production, the most striking, simple but important fact is the decline in tenancy. According to NSS data, area leased-in declined from 35.7 per cent of the total in 1950-51 to 9.25 per cent in 1971-72. The main drop took place before 1961-62, that is during the years of the Zamindari Abolition and Tenancy Acts (Table 4).

Further, there is evidence that tenancy is increasingly a kind of capitalist tenancy, in which land is given not by big landlords to small sharecroppers but by all kinds of land-owners (including even very small owners who cannot work their own land for a variety of reasons) to middle peasants and rich farmers who have the means of production to farm it profitably. From the

112

Table 4
Tenancy Variation over Time

	Percentage of Holdings Reporting Land Leased-in	Area Leased in as Percentage of Total Land
1950-51	NA	35.7
1953-54	39.85	20.34
1961-62	23.52	10.70
1971-72	17.61	9.25

Source: P. C. Joshi, *Land Reforms and Agrarian Change in India and Pakistan,* Reprints from Studies in Asian Development, No. 1 (n.d.); All India Debt and Investment Survey (AIDIS), *Statistical Tables Relating to Disposition of Land Held and Area and Value of Irrigated Land Owned by Rural Households as on June 30, 1971* Bombay: Reserve Bank of India, 1978.

Table 5
Tenancy Variation by States

	Percentage of Land Leased-in	Percentage of Households Leasing in Land	Lowest 50 Per cent Households	Top 15 Per cent Households
Assam	17.0	33.2	60-63	11-12
Manipur	29.5	29.3	55-58	12-14
Orissa	12.8	24.8	45-48	17-18
Himachal Pradesh	11.9	27.8	50	
West Bengal	17.8	29.6	50	
Bihar	12.0	21.8	46	13-14
Uttar Pradesh	5.9	18.7	65-68	9-10
Madhya Pradesh	6.5	16.1	50-55	13-14
Rajasthan	6.8	14.1	48-53	17-18
Jammu and Kashmir	8.6	14.0	60-65	8-9
Haryana	21.7	21.5	45-47	11-12
Punjab	25.7	21.9	30-35	16-18
Karnataka	11.0	16.4		
Tamil Nadu	10.8	17.3	40-41	18-20
Gujarat	3.4	13.0	35-40	20-22
Maharashtra	5.8	10.2	35-40	35-37
Andhra	6.6	10.9	25-30	33-34
Kerala	5.8	10.1	27-28	30-32
INDIA	9.3	17.6	40	24

Appropriate Percentage of Leased-in Land Held by (columns: Lowest 50 Per cent Households, Top 15 Per cent Households)

point of view of capitalist farmers, this 'reverse tenancy' is also a way of increasing land concentration in a period where there are some (even if usually unimplemented) limiations on ownership. Our estimates from AIDIS data show that the 50 percent poorest households held only about 40 percent of tenanted land, while the richest of 15 percent households held about 24 per cent of tenanted land in 1971 (Table 5). There is also significant variation by states.

How accurate is such data? Must we postulate a lot of 'hidden tenancy' resulting from the fact that landlords are actually continuing to sharecrop their land but only shifting tenants around and showing them as wage-labourers instead? The fact is, there is little other evidence to show any significant amount of hidden tenancy; even micro-studies which have gone looking for it have found little of it.[25] And where there is hidden tenancy, as my own study of western Maharashtra villages indicates, it is as likely to be that of land leased-in by rich farmers as by poor peasants, and is part of the general tendency of the rich to hide the extent of their land control. Perhaps most significant of all, though a form of indirect evidence, is the fact that all of those who postulate 'semi-feudalism' in agriculture no longer do so on the basis of tenancy of any kind, but have shifted their arguments to postulating the prevalence of 'bonded labour' and other forms of labour relations that indicate the labourer is 'like a serf' and the landowner is 'like a landlord' or that 'new forms' of landlordism have come into existence. The inescapabe fact is that landlord-tenant relations are now a minor element in the relations of agricultural production, and tenanted land covers only a small proportion of the cultivated area.

Land Concentration and Capitalist Farmers

Assuming that tenancy covers roughly 9-10 percent of the total land, how do we characterize the ownership of (and the relations of production prevailing upon) the remaining 90 percent? There are two issues here. One is that many political activists and theorists argue that big farmers who do not work manually on their own land and rely for labour mostly on indebted, low caste permanent hire labourers are in essence 'landlords'; the labourers are characterized as 'bonded labourers' and the agrarian relations are described as 'semi-feudal.' The varying types of labour relations on big farmers' land will be discussed later. Our opinion is that as long as production is based on hired labour, even where there are elements of compulsion, the land-owner is extracting surplus value. The general conditions in India are such that even the most repressed labourers submit to their 'bondage' for largely economic reasons; generalized commodity production, including the sale of labour power, is the prevalent fact. And, whether or not the landowner himself works manually on the land is irrelevant to determining his status as a capitalist; in fact capitalists in general do not work manually though very small capitalist do so to a considerable extent.

What percentage of land is controlled mainly by peasants working their own land by middle and poor peasants) and what percentage by rich farmers (i.e. predominantly capitalist farmers) who mainly farm this land through hired labour? Answering this question is in part equivalent to answering the question of how much land concentration there is. (Of course the value of land varies immensely depending on its quality and whether it is irrigated, and the amount of land required to make a family a capitalist farmer one—i.e. where hired labour significantly surpasses family labour—varies immensely from region to region; but here we are taking an all-India average and taking amount of land owned as an *index*, not the *essence* of class status.)

The amount of land concentration, however, is not a simple issue because of data bias. There are basically only two types of evidence available at the macro-level. The first is that of the Agricultural Census, which is based on aggregating data from village land records. The other is that of the National Sample Surveys (NSS), the All-India Debt and Investment Surveys (AIDIS), the Rural Labour Enquiries (RLE) and other sample surveys which depend on teams of research assistants asking questions of villagers. A little thinking about these sources by anyone familiar with Indian reality will be enough to cut the ground from under almost any conclusion.[24] In addition, it should be remembered that the most important of such data was gathered in 1971—after the Naxalbari revolt and other outbreaks, after the big left-led 'land grab' movement of 1970, at a time when talk of imposing more rigorous land ceilings was in the air (and land ceilings were lowered in most states in 1971-72)—in short when the rich farmers were well aware of some kind of threat to their property and ready to cover up any record of the extent of their holdings in written form and from anyone who might be thought to be an official observer. Yet data from such sources is cited without exception in all studies and in all journalistic references to rural inequality, and is usually taken at face value.[27] The result of this uncritical use of biased sources, is an underestimation of the power and wealth of the rich, and overestimation of the number and position of middle peasants, and an underestimation of proletarianization—something that has important consequences for political strategy. We shall also use the data, but we try to estimate and compensate for its biases.

First, the Agricultural Census. Table 6 shows the distribution of 'operational holdings'; this shows that the top 15 percent of holdings controlled

Table 6
Size Distribution of Operational Holdings, 1970 – 71

| | Holdings | | Area | |
	Number (Millions)	Per-centage	Hectares (Millions)	Per-centage
Up to 1.0 hectares	35.69	50.6	14.56	9.0
1.0 to 2.0	13.43	19.1	19.28	11.9
2.0 to 4.0	10.69	15.2	30.00	18.5
4.0 to 10.	7.93	11.2	48.23	29.7
10.0 and above	2.77	3.9	50.06	30.9
Total	70.49	100.0	162.12	100.0

Source: CMIE, *Basics Statistics,* Table 10.1.

about 60 percent of the area and the top 4 percent had 31 percent. By itself, this already seems an impressive degree of inequality. But it is clearly an underestimate. Aside from the often notorious inaccuracy of any village statistics, one simple fact indicates this: 'operational holdings' for the Census is defined as land operated as a technical unit whether owned or rented, by one person:

> The concept of holding used in the Census was one of individual as against a family holding. If more than one individual of the same family held land in their individual names (and were shown in the records as such), their holdings were considered to constitute as many separate holdings.[28]

But leaving aside any real *benami* transactions, the true unit of land operation is the family, often a joint family, whose head manages the cultivation of land that is very often put in the names of many members of the family. Rich farmers in particular have almost always already 'distributed' their land under the names of sons, brothers and even distant relatives but continue to operate it as a unit; the Census definition allows them to do so perfectly legally. In addition, the data on 'operational holdings' from the land records does not include landless families, land held in two or more *talukas*, or unrecorded and illegal leasings, land-grabbing, etc.

How can we use such figures? According to the NSS/AIDIS there were 78 million rural families in 1971, of whom 57 million operated land. Thus the top 15 percent of holdings (10.7 million) by themselves would represent about 14 percent of rural families, but there are in addition about 13 million 'extra' operational holdings representing an unknown portion of total land. If we assume that one-half to all of these holdings belonged to the richer farmers (the over4 hectare group) and that they represented about 2 hectares of land each we can estimate that this section, representing abut 14 percent of actual families with land of 10-12 acres or more, controlled about 70-80 percent of the total land in India. This is a very rough estimate, but it is clearly closer to reality than the figure of 60 percent.

Second, the NSS/AIDIS. Table 7 gives data from the NSS 8th round (1953-54) and 27th round (1971-72, the one conducted with the AIDIS) on distribution of operated land. But note that the basis is a sample survey and while researchers might be able to find and interview a valid sample of rural families (hence the reason for taking as roughly accurate the number of families given in this data), there is no reason at all to assume that their respondents tell the truth. In fact, our own experience[29] is that rich farmers lie; so for that matter do many poor peasants, but their amount of cover-up and their incentive and ability to cover up is much less. They 'underestimate' their land holdings even in comparison to existing village records, they underestimate their crop productivity often by laughable amounts, they do

Table 7

Distribution of Land Operated

Size Class (Acres)	Percentage of Households		Percentage of Area Operated	
	1953–54	1971–72	1953–54	1971–72
None	10.96	27.41	—	—
0.01–0.99	31.12	14.93	1.20	1.69
1.00–4.99	29.15	34.38	14.40	22.47
5.00–9.99	14.59	12.94	19.56	22.61
10.0–24.99	9.96	8.10	29.22	30.40
25 and above	4.22	2.24	26.62	22.83
Total number (000s)	61,780	78,370	335,711	310,439

Source: NSS Surveys, cited in Indradeep Sinha, *The Changing Agrarian Scene* Delhi: People's Publishing House, 1980.

not mention land they own in other villages, and they do not mention government-owned 'waste land' that they might be illegally cultivating or land taken on lease or mortgage (often from the rural poor) which is not recorded.

An estimate of the extent of this bias can be easily made: the NSS derives from its surveyed land holdings a figure of 310 million acres total for operated land in India, but the Agricultural Census for the same year (and this can be said to be roughly accurate about the total amount of cultivated land which the village accountants are somehow bound to account for) shows 390 million. In other words, there are 80 million missing acres, one-fifth of the total land area, to represent the land about which the farmers 'forgot' to tell the surveyors. Very approximately again if we assume that three-fourths to all of this land is in fact operated by the top 10 percent of families, we can conclude that the top 10 percent controls actually 57-62 percent of total land, and that the top 15 percent controls about 75 percent. (The NSS figures show a significant decline in the proportion of land held by the top category, 25 acres and over, between 1953-54 and 1971-72. This is often taken as indicating that as a result of land reforms 'middle' farmers gained something at the expense of very big farmers. However, this decline is also likely to be spurious; we simply cannot tell from the data since it is the biggest farmers who have the most interest in cover-up and the most capacity to do so.)

Concentration of marketed produce is higher since rich farmers market at least twice as much of their total produce as the poorer families; this at least was true in 1961-62.[30] And concentration of total assets, taking into account the value of land, as well as buildings, animals, farm machinery, as well as non-agricultural assets is even higher. From the NSS/AIDIS figures three economists have derived information on distributions of assets by decile

Table 8
Distribution of Rural Assets by Decile Groups

Decile Group	Share in total Assets 1961–62	1971–72
0–10	0.26	0.21
10–20	0.68	0.56
20–30	1.18	1.01
30–40	1.80	1.58
40–50	2.76	2.34
50–60	3.88	3.47
60–70	5.79	5.51
70–80	9.11	8.28
80–90	15.83	15.24
90–100	58.71	61.79

Source: R. G. Pathak, K. R. Ganapathy and Y. U. K. Sarma, 'Shifts in Pattern of Asset-Holding of Rural Households 1961–62 to 1971–72,' *EPW* 19 Mar. 1977, p. 507.

groups (Table 8). This is also an underestimate, it has to be remembered, since non-landed assets can be hidden even more easily in land (the farmers 'forget' to mention their house or sheds in the fields or the businesses or houses they share in nearby towns or cities, their profits from trade, etc.)[31] and possibly 80 percent might be closer than 60 percent in representing the actual control of the top 10 percent of families. This is indeed a quite frightening degree of inequality, and the significance of the qualitative gap between the top 10-15 percent of rural families and the rest should also be noted: for it indicates not only inequality, but membership in an essentially different class, property-holding as compared to near-propertylessness.

The nature of rural assets also suggests another fact about the nature of the rich farmers: their property and power is not simply in agriculture. After the coming of independence, rich peasants,landlords and the emerging capitalist farmers began to invest on a wider scale, rather than simply consuming surpluses. The establishment of tiny transport companies, tea shops, small flour mills,oil mills, brick kilns were all part of this process. Some moved more into trade in direct competition with previous merchant classes/castes. With the establishment of co-operative sugar factories the new kulaks fought the domination of urban industrialists and merchants, and in the process transformed some of their wealth into accumulation in India's second biggest industry. The spread of rural education with the establishmentof nemerous societies running schools and colleges has also been largely their work. A rural capitalist farmer family today normally has a well-educated younger generation, and systematically seeks to diversify economic activities, placing some sons in service (making them doctors or lawyers if possible), setting others up with small shops or tiny businesses, and leaving only one or two to run the land and the tractor. By 1971-72, according to the AIDIS (which may be underestimating this as much as anything), about 6 percent of all capital expenditure and 12 percent of gross capital formation of rural households was in non-farm business. This is Thorner's 'steel-grey revolution,' the connection of industry (small-scale) and agriculture.

In class terms, the situation is somewhat complex, for the rural elite (the top 10-15 percent of families) contains an intermixture of small business, merchant, landlord and white collar employee interests along with those of capitalist farmers. Some are becoming small-scale businessmen and engaging in trade, while in a converse fashion many families from traditional merchant castes are now hiring labourers rather than renting out land and engaging in entrepreneurial farming along with their trading activity. Some big farmers continue to give out a portion of their lands on share, while there are also (we can estimate from the AIDIS data) another 1-2 percent of rural families who are not among the top in terms of operated land, but who own enough in terms of assets and leased-out land to classify them with the rural elite. These are the rural families who are primarily merchants or landlords (it should be remembered the majority of merchants and many of the landlords still live in towns). But while there is an overlap of personnel and thus of concrete individual material interests, this is not necessarily true of class interests as such. Small businessmen and capitalist farmers may not have any interests in conflict, but there is clearly a conflict between the industrial bourgeoisie and the farmers over the issue of food and manufactured goods prices and over claims over bank credit and government concessions. Similarly merchant capital has a complex and conflicting relation with the farmers. In the case of landlords, in some areas where semi-feudal relations are still very important, the conflict between landlords and rich tenants/kulaks may have some of its old sharpness; but in the more capitalist areas this conflict is no longer important, the remaining landlords have made a tactical adjustment with the rising kulaks and very frequently the relation is simply that of sharing the surplus extracted from agricultural labourers. The concrete form of these class conflicts is also heavily affected by their historical emergence, including the caste character of their members.

As far as the majority of the rich farmer class itself is concerned, it is no longer appropriate to describe the rurual elite as 'landlords' who appropriate surpluses from the toiling peasantry. Some of the income of the top families comes from urban employment, rent, trade, or money-lending; and the ultimate sources of such income in turn are partly outside the agrarian sector, partly other sections of the rich farmer class (and this involves in turn sharing surpluses extracted from labourers), partly middle peasants, and partly the rural poor. Again this varies by families, and more systematic studies are necessary. Still it seems clear tht the primary aspect of their relationship with the rural poor is as exploiters of labour power, the labour of the agricultural labourers who work on the 70-80 percent of land they control, and the labour of the various other types of rural workers employed in small businesses, mills, road contracting, construction. It is for this reason that we call them basically a class of capitalist farmers.

In analyzing this class it should also be remembered that there is considerable inequality within it—as there is within every capitalist class. The Agricultural Census shows the top 4 percent of holdings opeating 31 percent of the area; the NSS/AIDIS shows the top 2.2 percent of househlds operating 23 percent, while assets concentration figures show that in 1971-72 the top 5 percent of all households had 47.21 percent of total assets and the top 1 percent had 22.96 percent.[32] If we try to compensate for the underestimations in all these studies it might be accurate to say that the top 5 percent of households hold close to 50 percent of total area and more of total assets—though such estimates are very difficult to make. But the degree of inequality, even up to the very top fractions of a percentage, is clear, with the very top households probably merging into the urban and industrial bourgeoisie.

As noted, a small percentage of the top landholders can be characterized as primarily merchants or landlords; the latter in turn might be classed as either 'feudal' or 'capitalist' landlords depending on how much they invest and how much exploitation of hired labour is involved on the leased land. But this class distinction cannot be assumed to coincide with the distinction between size of landholdings and other assets; there are everywhere both small and big landlords as well as small and big agrarian capitalists. In other words, it can no longer be assumed that a 'big' landowner is a 'landlord' while a slightly small landowner is a 'rich peasant.'

Finally, given the general conditions of Indian poverty, the smaller capitalist farmers do not have, by world standards, a very high level of living—which is one reason it is possible for upper-middle class urban and foreign observers to see them as 'peasants.' Some family members do normally work on the land, and though this is mostly supervisory work, such supervisory work itself is strenuous. Finally, given the often violently fluctuating price and market conditions of any capitalist agriculture and the vagaries of weather on top of the normally insecure life of all small capitalists anywhere in the world, their own life is likely to be insecure and unstable. This, along with their social traditions that may include a history of past participation in peasant and nationalist agitations as well as a combination of caste pride and a sense of being 'working cultivators' arising out of specific caste statuses, may well lead to a readiness to participate in such militant agitations as the recent 'farmers' movements' for higher prices. They also have their contradictions with merchants and industrialists, and an ability to appeal to and identify with a wider range of poorer and middle peasants. But all these factors do not change their relationship to the means of production which makes them part of one of the most important exploiting classes in India. This 'rich peasant' section is an important sector to be taken into account in an analysis of India's rural capitalists but there is no reason to conclude there is an essential class difference between small and big capitalist farmers.

Middle Peasants

Perhaps 20-30 percent of the land, then, is under cultivation of the remaining 85 percent of rural families. But these families are also stratified into asset-holding and land-holding families. More important, just as there is a qualitative gap, a class difference, between the capitalist farmers (and other exploiters) and the rest of the rural families, so there is also a qualitative gap among the 'rest,' a class difference between those who are essentially middle peasants and those who are essentially a landless or land-poor rural semi-proletariat. For some among these 85 percent of rural families possess enough land or other assets so that they can survive as petty-commodity producers, working mainly with family labour on their own land (or working as artisans or as petty traders) and some do not, so that they are forced to sell their labour-power on a regular basis.

This is an important distinction, for even though there may be a gradual transition in the sense that some families may seem to be midway between the two classes, or may be in the process of mobility (the same thing is true of the distinction between middle peasants and rich farmers), it still indicates an important class difference and corresponding differences in consciousness. Middle peasants are very small property holders who aspire to increase their property (the AIDIS survey showd 37.9 percent of all rural families making some kind of capital investment on the land, that is, including approximately both capitalist farmers and middle peasants); if they are exploited it is *via* the terms of trade, sometimes by rents when they are tenants, and most often by middlemen (who are often themselves rich farmers) and moneylenders. This is not true of the rest of the rural poor, who make no investment in their property, market very little of their product, cannot realistically aspire to any prosperity and are exploited primarily or partly through the sale of their labour power.

We can estimate the size of the middle peasants if we assume that, on an all-India basis and on average, two and a half acres indicate a cut-off point. Above this families can manage to survive on their own land; below this families cannot and have to rely on their sale of labor power, either in rural area or by migrating to urban areas. This is a highly complex matter, because first the variation from state to state and between regions within states is high (in states like Kerala the cut-off point would be closer to one acre, in others nearer to five or more acres) and second because the survival of a rural family on 'household' income also depends on such things as ownership of milch cattle and buffalo and other forms of petty commodity production. Similarly some forms of putting out of household production which can be said to be essentially forms of exploitation of labour-power also play a role in the income of these rural families.

Nevertheless, 2.5 acres seems to be a reasonable cut-off point. According to the Agricultural Census (Table 6), there were 35,690,000 operational holdings under one hectare in 1971 representing 9 percent of the total cultivated area. The question is, how many rural families (including those with no land) do these holdings represent? We have to assume that in at least a few cases they represent holdings actually operated by relatives or richer farmers. If we assume that two or three million holdings should be thus 'subtracted' we are left with about 33 million families with operated land of under one hectare, or about 40 percent of all rural families. This plus the 25 percent of rural poor families who operate no land (see below for this estimate) gives us 65 percent of rural families who have no land or land below one hectare. These are the rural semi-proletariat who depend on some form of wage labor for their survival. And the remaining 20-25 per cent of rural families, operating between 10-20 percent of the total land area, can be said to be primarily a middle peasant petty-bourgeoisie, including a few families deriving a fairly stable income from artisanship or petty trade.

Nature of Rural Proletarianization

The 65 per cent of rural families who together operate 9 percent or less of the total land in India and own even a lower percentage of total assets are essentially a proletarianized, or proletarianizing, section which requires some other form of income to survive through the year. It is they who provide the labour on the land controlled by the rich farmers, and on the roads and construction projects and in the brick kilns, mills, small factories and other businesses controlled by the rural and urban capitalists and the state.

This rural semi-proletariat itself is a fairly stratified section, as indeed the assets Table 8 suggests. To really analyze its class character, we need to get away from the simple and misleading classification of the rural poor into 'poor peasants' and 'landless labourers.' First, we need to distinguish landless rural families from those who are agricultural labourers (since not all agricultural labourer families are landless, and not all of the landless work on the fields). Second, we need to distinguish the number or percentage of agricultural labourers from agricultural labourer families, since members of primarily poor peasant or even artisan families may also do labour on a regular basis. (The Census of India gives its data by number of labourers; but we shall mainly use figures which show number of families or households on the assumption that, given the ongoing subordination of women in the family and the continuing significance of the patriarchal Hindu joint family, class structure is mainly organized in terms of families.) Third, we need to distinguish agricultural labourer from other (rural or urban) labourer families, since some rural families, both landless and landed, depend primarily for their survival on non-agricultural rural labour or on urban labour income. Finally, we can distinguish labourer families, defined as those who get the majority of their income from agricultural or other wage labour, from poor peasant families, who get most of their income from land but also require some income from wage labour.

This will give some sense of the class fractions of the rural poor, but to analyze their position fully we also have to briefly look at the conditions of labour, the variations in labour relations (e.g., the extent of 'bondedness'), the role of tiny landholdings, and the increasing significance of migration. Finally, of course, the role of caste and the position of women will have to be considered.

In terms of landlessness, the NSS/AIDIS data are fairly clear—and somewhat unexpected. For landlessness in the sense of *owned* land has declined from 22.0 percent of all families in 1953-54 to 9.6 percent in 1971-72, which in part reflects tenancy acts and land ceiling laws and various other government measures giving cultivable waste land, forest land, village grazing land to the 'landless.' But one cannot conclude from this that proletarianization is not increasing. For at the same time the percentage of rural families *not cultivating* land has risen equally decisively from 11.0 to 27.4 percent. In other words, at least 18 percent of poor families who own some land are unable to cultivate it, either because it is too barren or because they cannot afford the inputs. (The figure would in fact be higher because some families who do not own land acquire some for cultivation through sharecropping.) They turn it over to relatives or to rich farmers or middle peasants who can cultivate it, and either migrate for labour or sometimes even continue to work in the same village. (One example of the latter category is a small percentage of widowed or abandoned women, often old, who cannot cultivate their tiny bits of land and so lease it to others, but themselves continue to work as agricultural labourers.)

This 27 percent really gives us a more accurate figure for 'landlessness.' According to the same AIDIS survey, in 1971-72 14.6 percent were landless agricultural labourers, 2.4 percent were landless artisans, and 10.6 percent were 'others.' These 'other non-cultivators' are described as 'a heterogeneous group consisting of absentee landlords, traders, moneylenders, shopkeepers, skilled workers like tractor drivers, mechanics, truck-drivers, electricians workers employed in processing factories and marketing yards, government servants, etc.,'[33] but only a small proportion of them (1.28 percent of total rural households) had enough assets including land to fall above the line demarcating middle peasants from the rural poor. (That is, they had over Rs 10,000 worth of assets and land of an average of 5.32 acres each.) These 1.28 percent were the absentee landlords, merchants, skilled workers, electricians, etc., and the remaining 9.3 percent of rural households were, according to AIDIS data, landless non-agricultural labourer households working at very petty and underpaid manual labour. Thus, assuming that the statistics are roughly accurate and the more substantial 'landless' non-cultivators are no more than 1.5 to 2.0 percent, we can estimate about 25 percent of rural households as the landless rural poor. Aside from the landless artisans, that is very poor petty commodity producers, these are the most fully proletarianized section in the countryside. Most of them work as agricultural labourers, but a significantly large percentage (37 percent of the landless) work on other kinds of low-paid rural or urban labour.

But these are not all of the agricultural labourer or other labourer households in the countryside. There are also landed artisans, landed agricultural labourers, and landed other labourers. They are labourers in the sense that the majority of the income of the household is from wage labour (this is the definition of the RLE), but they have tiny plots of land, sufficient to meet a bit of consumption needs for part of the year or to provide a bit of extra income through sale of some crops. (And we would, to repeat, distinguish these households from the poor peasant households who have significantly more land but still must do some wage labour on a permanent basis.)

How many are these? According to the Rural Labour Enquiry,[34] there were 25.5 percent agricultural labour families and 5.0 percent other rural labour families in 1974-75. (Unlike AIDIS, the RLE data do not include among 'rural labourers' those families who are artisans or who work in urban areas. This is problematic because the distinction between rural and urban non-agricultural labour is often quite tenuous, and somewhat meaningless in economic terms since many small, unorganized and highly exploitative factories are likely to be located in towns drawing their workers from the countryside.) Of these agricultural and other rural labour families, about half were 'landless' (not operating land) according to the RLE while the rest had small holdings, three-fourths of them less than 1.5 acres. The RLE figures for landless agricultural labourers (12.8 percent of rural households) are roughly comparable to the AIDIS figures (14.6 percent) and this comparability generally holds also when looked at state by state (see Table 9). It is significant that the RLE estimates the total number of labourer households to be about twice the number of landless labourer households. If we extend this kind of estimate to artisans and 'other' labourers, we can derive a figure of about 45 percent of rural households being semi-proletarian households in the sense of getting the majority of their income from wage labour, while another 5 percent are poor artisans, and about 15 percent are poor peasants. This estimate, again, is a very approximate one, and the line between poor peasant and landed labourer households is very hard to draw even in principle; but it seems to be a fairly accurate picture of the Indian countryside today.

Regional Variations

Before taking up further issues about the nature of labour relations, it is important to look at regional variations. Given the very uneven nature of capitalist development in India, superimposed upon the uneven impact of colonialism on an already highly varied and immense subcontinent, it is not surprising that there should be tremendous variation in agrarian relations and the development of production. (In a sense it may be equally surprising that there is not more variation, given all these factors.) Some idea of the variation can be had from Table 4 on tenancy and Table 9, which gives data on agricultural labourer and other rural labourer households from both the 1974-75 RLE and 1971-72 AIDIS surveys. (It can be noted that both surveys define 'landlessness' in terms of not cultivating land, and that the RLE definition of 'rural labourer' is not equivalent to the AIDIS definition of the 'other non-cultivator').

On the basis of these Tables the states can be approximately divided into five groups. The clearest contrast is between the first group, the northeastern and mountainous region, which is characterized by relatively high tenancy, more of tenanted land held by poorer households, and relatively fewer landless and labourer households, and the last group of southern and western states which have low tenancy, less of tenanted land held by poor households, and more labourer and landless households. (Kerala is only an apparent exception in terms of landlessness, because the tiny plots of homestead land given to agricultural labourers are counted as 'operated land' on the assumption that labourers maintain garden plots; this assumption is contested by some scholars like Mencher, 1980.)

The three middle groups, however, represent a mixture. West Bengal and Bihar appear to have both high tenancy and a high degree of proletarianization as measured in landlessness and labourer households, while Haryana and Punjab have very high tenancy and a relatively low proportion of agricultural labourers (in spite of being in the forefront of capitalist agriculture in other respects) though they have a very high proportion of landlessness. Similarly, UP and Jammu and Kashmir have low tenancy (but most of it going to poorer households) along with relatively fewer labourer and landless households.

It is tempting to say that the northeast shows a greater prevalence of semi-feudal relations of production while the southern-western group is more thoroughly capitalist. But then we would have to characterize West Bengal and Bihar as a mixture of two forms of exploitation, while Punjab and Haryana also seemingly contain some mixed forms though most of their tenancy is clearly capitalist tenancy with land going to middle peasants and rich farmers. The middle group of states would appear to have a greater prevalence of small or middle peasants within frequently backward forms of production and a likely prevalence of a good deal of trading-moneylending exploitation. In any case there are clearly many factors at work, and a limited amount of overall data. While there may not be much hidden tenancy, the actual degree of mobility and freedom of agricultural labourers is not indicated in these figures, and there is almost no study at all referring to the more important specific element of Indian feudal relations, the degree to which caste-defined duties remain in force (*gawki kam, veth begar, jajmani*, etc.). Thus all

Table 9

Agricultural Labourers and Landlessness

Part 1: RLE Figures (1974 – 75)

	Agricultural Labourer Households			(Percentages)
	With Land	Without Land	Total	Rural Labour Households
Assam	7.3	5.9	13.1	22.1
Manipur	.7	.7	1.3	2.0
Orisa	13.3	7.9	21.2	25.7
Himachal Pradesh	1.4	.4	1.8	
West Bengal*	20.1	23.8	44.0	55.1
Bihar	19.3	13.9	33.3	36.1
Uttar Pradesh	9.0	6.8	15.8	19.1
Madhya Pradesh	11.5	10.3	21.8	24.0
Rajasthan	1.8	2.1	4.0	6.4
Jammu-Kashmir	1.1	.6	1.7	4.8
Haryana	1.5	7.6	9.1	16.2
Punjab	1.8	19.1	20.9	25.6
Karnataka	14.4	16.4	30.8	35.8
Tamil Nadu	13.8	24.3	38.1	44.3
Gujarat	7.7	14.6	22.3	29.6
Maharashtra	15.0	16.9	32.0	36.7
Andhra	14.0	21.8	35.8	39.4
Kerala	23.8	3.6	27.4	42.1
INDIA	12.4	12.8	25.3	30.3

Part II: AIDIS Figures (1971 – 72)—Landless Households

	Agricultural Labourers	Artisans	Others	Total
Assam	6.2	0.8	11.2	18.4
Orissa	12.1	1.7	9.0	22.8
West Bengal	17.4	1.0	14.9	34.2
Bihar	13.4	1.0	5.2	19.6
Uttar Pradesh	8.1	3.6	14.1	25.8
Madhya Pradesh	10.3	1.4	6.3	18.0
Rajasthan	3.3	1.5	8.4	13.2
Jammu-Kashmir	0.7	0.5	4.9	6.1
Haryana	14.7	4.0	20.7	40.0
Punjab	25.8	5.1	26.2	57.1
Karnataka	19.3	2.9	9.1	31.3
Tamil Nadu	26.6	3.8	14.2	44.6
Gujarat	18.3	3.6	14.1	36.0
Maharashtra	19.8	2.9	8.7	31.4
Andhra	23.1	3.3	12.0	38.4
Kerala	3.8	0.6	5.1	10.3
INDIA	14.6	2.4	10.6	27.6

*The West Bengal figures from the RLE for agricultural labourer and rural labour households appear to contain an error, being based on an improbably low number to total rural households (p.22).

Source: Rural Labour Enquiry (RLE), (1974–75), Table 2.1; AIDIS, Assets of Rural Households, Table 1.2.

categorizations must remain tentative, and in any case they indicate only the variation of local relations of production and forms of extraction of surplus under the dominance of a generally capitalist mode of production.

The figures for Punjab, agriculturally the most productive and wealthy state, are however very interesting. Its high tenancy, as noted, is mainly capitalist tenancy. Further, Punjab has the highest proportion of rural landlessness in India: only 43 percent of all rural families actually cultivate land. From the AIDIS (n.d. Section 15) we can see that of the 57 percent non-cultivating households, over 90 percent owned land which they leased out, but the majority of these were poor families with only tiny plots. Only about 15 percent of the non-cultivators (or about 8.6 percent of all households) had assets equivalent to middle peasant status on an all-India scale or above: about 70 percent of these had assets mainly in land. Thus we can estimate that about 6 percent of all Punjab rural households were non-cultivating landlord households, though not necessarily big landlords. The other non-cultivating households—51 percent of all rural households—were mainly proletarian landless households, living on agricultural labour, other labour, or artisan work. The unique feature of Punjab in comparison to other states with more capitalist labour relations is that there is only a tiny percentage of agricultural labour households who also operate small plots of land. Another unique feature is that Punjab's agricultural labourers are almost all *dalits* (see Table 10) and, more recently, migrants; local caste Hindu landless apparently prefer to work at almost any kind of job, rather than as field labourers. Punjab thus has the highest percentage of rural households in the category of 'other non-cultivators' and is (along with Haryana) practically the only area where the category 'scheduled caste landless agricultural labourer' really makes sense.

Specificity of Labour Relations

In analyzing the type of proletarianization that is occurring in India one of the most important features to take into account is the wide extent of tiny landholdings of labourer families. It is not accidental, nor simply due to the fact that proletarianization is 'incomplete' or that these are still mainly 'peasants.' Rather, the fact that half or more of rural wage workers have small plots of land is a fairly permanent feature of the rural scene that must be analyzed in terms of the nature of the imperialist economy today and the fact that the Indian economy is indissolubly linked to it and conditioned by its laws. The fact is that the compulsions of imperialism to compete at a high level of organic composition of capital in the world market force Indian industry (whether multinational or national) to grow in such a way that the organized sector can employ only a small proportion of the total labour force. It is now a general feature throughout the Third World that while a fairly sophisticated and competitive manufacturing sector can grow, employment in it does not keep pace with a growing labour force; the result is a systematic creation of a dual labour market. In India the rest of the manufacturing sector (the so-called 'informal' or 'unorganized' sector) pays such miserably low wages that it is impossible to maintain a family with only one or two working members. The result is that while in some cases the total family need is met at very minimal levels by all (women, children) doing petty labour, in many cases the family survives only because in addition to the wage income there is a bit of help from a piece of land, a milch cow or buffalo, the sale of grass or firewood gathered from forests, or other services. The fact that a large section of proletarians are 'landed proletarians' or 'semi-proletarians' means simply that there is a cushion which helps to dampen their desperation and—just as important—cheapen their labour power. The ability of the unorganized sector to continue operating at such low wage levels depends to a large degree on the existence of this section of rural households with tiny plots of land.

Another major issue is the element of compulsion in the relations of production. As noted above, the continuing existence of 'bonded labour' is a major reason for claiming that these relations in fact continue to be 'semi-feudal.' In this context the most-often cited figure is that of the Gandhi Peace Foundation which has claimed five million 'bonded labourers' in India; but generally permanent agricultural labourers (those serving on a monthly or yearly basis for one landowner) and contract labourers are often simply described as 'bonded.'

What is the real situation? First, it is crucial to understand that there are important regional variations in the actual position of agricultural labourers. In some areas there is a larger percentage of permanent labourers, in others most labourers work on a casual, daily basis. In some areas a large percentage of the daily or permanent wage is paid in kind, in others it is almost all in cash; this also varies from crop to crop. The position of the 'permanent' labourers themselves varied tremendously, from being almost hereditary family servants, or bound by debt from generation to generation or for a number of years to that of being relatively free 'contractual,' labourers who are even in a more privileged position compared to daily labourers because they have security of employment. A 'permanent' labourer who changes employers every few months, even if he is obliged to make some arrangements to repay the debt he has incurred with an earlier employer, cannot realistically be called bonded. But the fact is that this situation varies; and there is no harm in saying that where there are larger numbers of permanent, indebted labourers working for longer periods of time for a single landowner, where compulsion clearly exists and where elements of traditional caste power also enter (that is where the labourer is a *dalit* or *adivasi*), that the relationship is a 'more feudal' one. Similarly the element of compulsion is very high in many forms of contract labour, especially where the contractor has clear and extra-legal links with the police, government officials, local landowners. This again has crucial regional patterning, and it is not hard to identify the large central-India belt

Table 10

Agricultural Labourers, Caste and Landlessness:
Percentage of Households

(Figures in brackets show percentage of landless households)

	Scheduled Caste	Scheduled Tribe	Other	Total
Assam	4.65	1.25	7.17	13.06
	(1.76)	(0.66)	(4.36)	(5.79)
Manipur	—	—	—	1.32
				(.66)
Orissa	5.86	5.55	9.77	21.18
	(2.86)	(1.72)	(3.44)	(7.92)
Himachal Pradesh	1.42	—	.36	1.78
	(0.35)		(.10)	(.36)
West Bengal	17.98	5.32	20.66	43.96
	(10.42)	(2.81)	(10.63)	(23.86)
Bihar	14.01	1.74	16.54	32.29
	(6.84)	(.32)	(6.76)	(13.92)
Uttar Pradesh	9.72	.24	5.85	15.81
	(5.28)	(.17)	(1.38)	(6.83)
Madhya Pradesh	5.99	7.39	8.39	21.77
	(3.11)	(3.41)	(3.76)	(10.28)
Rajasthan	2.37	.66	.99	3.96
	(1.31)	(.27)	(.54)	(2.12)
Jammu and Kashmir	.46	—	.22	1.68
	(.15)			
Haryana	7.22	—	1.89	9.11
	(5.98)		(1.60)	(7.58)
Punjab	18.14	—	2.74	20.88
	(16.87)		(2.25)	(19.12)
Karnataka	8.67	.46	21.24	30.78
	(4.79)	(.13)	(11.48)	(16.40)
Tamil Nadu	16.17	.47	21.11	38.05
	(11.35)	(.33)	(13.59)	(24.27)
Gujarat	4.91	6.79	10.60	22.30
	(3.41)	(4.54)	(6.65)	(14.60)
Maharashtra	7.38*	5.56	19.13	31.97
	(3.89)	(3.67)	(9.67)	(16.93)
Andhra	12.73	1.58	21.47	35.78
	(8.26)	(1.12)	(12.40)	(21.78)
Kerala	7.45	.89	19.06	27.40
	(1.26)	(.26)	(2.13)	(3.65)
INDIA	9.84	2.51	12.93	25.28
	(5.41)	(1.25)	(6.18)	(12.84)

*The Maharashtra figure for Scheduled Castes is an underestimate by nearly half since Mahar converts to Buddhism are not counted.
Source: Calculated from RLE, Table 2.3(b).

with its agricultural backwardness and relatively high *adivasi* population (especially the Jharkhand region: south Bihar, western Orissa, eastern Madhya Pradesh) as the 'bonded labour belt' in India.

But (aside from the theoretical importance of the fact that economic compulsions lie behind almost all these forms of bondedness) several important facts need to be noted here. The first is that the number of 'semi-feudal bonded labourers' in the above sense is a relatively small one in the all-India context. Not all of permanent agricultural labourers or contract labourers can be called 'bonded' in any sense. The highest figure given for the number of such labourers in India (the five million of the Gandhi Peace Foundation) is still a small proportion of rural labourer families. According to the Rural Labour Enquiry (1974-75: Table 6.1) 60 percent of all agricultural labourer families were indebted, and of these only 10 percent were indebted to their employers. Since debt-bondage is defined in terms of the worker who takes a loan and then has to slave for the landowner for years on end to pay it off, this means that at the very most 6 percent of agricultural labourer families are 'bonded' (and again we would not agree that all who take loans from their employer are really bonded); even if the survey can be said to underestimate because labourers are afraid to admit their position, this is a minor proportion.

Second, it is crucial to take account of the trend, of the element of change. From the Gandhi Peace Foundation figures themselves and from all other evidence it seems clear that the old form of hereditary, generation-to-generation bondedness has become an extremely minor element, that even permanent indebted labourers are now working only for some years, that a high turnover is going on. The fact is that the permanent labourers, 'bonded' or not, can organize themselves like other agricultural labourers; they do in fact organize in many areas and where they do so they enter a process of constituting themselves as a more free (proletarianized) wage labour force. Reports from many areas indicate that to the extent we can identify a variation from permanent/indebted/caste-bound labourers to free daily wage workers, the trend is towards the latter. For instance in Sangli district of western Maharashtra where some years ago daily labourers took loans during the rainy season on the basis of agreeing to work at cheaper rates during the harvest season for those rich farmers (still a common practice in many areas) they now refuse to do so: they take loans, but pay interest and refuse to sell their labour cheaply. Similarly, in Khammam district of Andhra it is now reported that labourers almost all work on a daily basis and simply refuse to work as permanent labourers. There are similar reports of *dalits* and other low castes refusing to do their traditional caste duties (*veth begar*) where these still go on. In all these cases it is often said that 'the labourers are becoming aggressive'; the fact is that the process of proletarianization is going on, not only 'from above' as rich farmers or landlords become agricultural entrepreneurs but also 'from below' as the rural poor and downtrodden assert their rights as human beings and workers.

Finally, it can be argued that while compulsion in labour relations is a problem, the focus on 'bonded labour' as such has come as much from the government (that is, the bourgeoisie) as from the left, and it can play a crucial role in distracting the attention of progressive forces from more general problems of all the rural proletariat such as wage levels, price rise, unemployment and landlessness (lack of control over the means of production.) At a minimum, rather than seeking to 'free bonded labour' from their employment, the beginnings of a solution can be found only when they begin to organize where they are exploited at the point of production and in their home areas against the poverty and social conditions (caste traditions, etc.) that often force them into bondage.

Migration and mobility must also be considered as increasingly important features of the rural scene, not simply rural-to-urban, but also rural-to-rural. Here again there are important regional variations. Rudra[35] has argued that in Bengal most labourers in fact are immobile, work only in their own villages and often only for the same few landowners year after year—and gives this as a major reason for saying the relations are not capitalistic. But in contrast, in such areas as western Maharashtra, one can find cases of whole villages whose labourers daily go to nearby villages to work.[36] More significantly, the phenomenon of migration on a seasonal basis from backward rural areas to more developed ones seems to be on the increase. Again in Maharashtra, there are some 1,500,000 migrants from poor peasant and labourer families in dry districts who work from six to eight months a year cutting and hauling sugar cane in the irrigated belts. Besides these there are more regular migrants working as agricultural labourers, for instance those from Sholapur district and northern Karnataka, who have now become regular workers in the fields of western Maharashtra. The most stark example of such migratory connections may be Punjab-Bihar, or more generally northwest India-central-east India: it is now estimated by some that one million workers come every year to labour on the wheat and rice harvests (they also fill in jobs such as permanent labourers or in small industries such as brick-kilns.) These include some *adivasis* from the Jharkhand region whose bonded condition has become notorious, but the majority are caste Hindu poor peasants from eastern UP and northern Bihar. This migration has served to reverse the gains in wage rates that local labourers were making from the 'green revolution,' labour shortage and their own organizing and has introduced new tensions between the migrants and the locals; on the other side it is now said to be 'universal knowledge' in some eastern UP districts that people can make a thousand rupees in the Punjab.[37] There are many, many examples of such type of migration which is becoming increasingly predominant not only in India but throughout the Third World and indicates the way in which the processes of imperialism are increasingly producing 'integrated' (but uneven and exploitative) capitalist development.

Rural Classes: Some Tentative Conclusions

Given the uncertainty and often unreliable data, identification of rural classes on an all-India scale is necessarily a tentative procedure. Nevertheless, in terms of their relations to the means of production, we can identify two main exploited classes and an intermediary section/class.

A toiling peasant class, including both relatively self-sufficient middle peasant and poor peasants who also have to do some wage labour. Poor peasants can be included in this class because their primary relationship to the means of production is as small producers working their own land, and this conditions their way of life and aspirations.[38] But it must not be forgotten that the fact they do wage labour for a significant period of time gives them important interests in common with the rural semi-proletariat. We can very roughly estimate this calss as 35 percent of the total rural population, including 20 percent middle peasants and 15 percent poor peasants.

Rural petty producers and service workers. This is a hard-to-define category including artisans (about 50 percent), plus a wide variety of other rural toilers who survive primarily through such forms of labour as small household industry, *bidi*-making, selling of forest produce (from grass to fodder and other things), and petty trade. The latter are mostly landless and are classified along with actual wage labourers under the category of 'other landless households' in the AIDIS statistics. They are classified as 'self-employed' or 'own account' workers in the RLE survey. But, though they are not strictly speaking wage labour, their work is sometimes in fact a form of piece-work putting-out labour, and is almost always governed by the laws of capitalist production. Thus in fact they are practically a semi-proletariat. We can estimate abut 10 percent of such labourers, making 15 percent total rural households in this category.

A rural semi-proletariat, including 25-30 percent agricultural labourer households (whose main income is from agricultural labour) and 5-10 percent other rural wage labourers, who get their main income from various forms of other direct wage labour, ranging from work in or for sugar factories, road and construction work to work gained by migration to urban or more developed rural areas, in small or large factories, brick-kilns, and urban construction projects (such as Asiad!). I call these a 'semi-proletariat' since about half of their families do cultivate small plots of land, but the land does not make much difference to their way of life. This class totals about 35% of all rural households.

We can sum up the main characteristics of the exploited rural toilers as follows:

(1) This is a highly stratified group, both between and *within* those classified as primarily 'toiling peasants' and those classified as primarily a 'semi-proletariat.' That is, there is a high inequality in terms of income and

life-standard running from those with some significant parcels of land at the top (or those with access to well-paying working class jobs) down to those who are totally landless and nearly without work. This inequality has a regional/linguistic dimension (e.g Punjab/Bihar/Jharkhand) and social dimension that functions primarily in terms of caste. These regional/linguistic/national/caste divisions have in recent years become a severe barrier to the unity of the rural toilers.

(2) In spite of stratification, poverty is the main overall characteristic, even for the better off. Their overall consumption level is incredibly low. At best, the poor peasants and labourers as a whole, representing 65 percent of the rural population, control only 9 percent of the total land and much less of total assets and represents an insignificant section of the rural market (and it is also important that Indian capitalism is in the process of finding ways to go ahead without developing a market based on the rural majority). Their 40 percent poorest, the semi-proletariat, have *at best* only 1.58 percent of total rural assets (see Table 8).

(3) In spite of some elements of bondage, some areas of immobility, and some remaining aspects of caste-defined feudal servitude, this is by and large and increasingly a mobile, migrant and free rural section. Not only the semi-proletariat and poor peasants, but even members of many middle peasant families are ready to go anywhere in search of work, through education and training if this is available, as casual and unskilled labourers if it is not.

(4) Nearly all members of the family, certainly women and in most cases children also, have to work to maintain even the current miserable standard of living. For women from both labourer and toiling peasant families, this means double work in its most exploitative form, with work as hired labourers in the fields or as low-paid home workers producing some kind of goods for the market[39] added to their drudgery of cooking, cleaning, child-care, and fetching water and fuel. The Hindu patriarchal family continues to be strong. Male authority is everywhere, often in brutal forms, even when women are also earning members, and the fact that women remain at the bottom is starkly shown in the Indian sex ratio, where the proportion of females to males continues to be among the lowest in the world.

(5) Not the rural-urban dichotomy, but a rural-urban and agricultural-industrial continuum must be stressed. Not only is migration increasingly important, but a large section of the rural semi-proletariat is dependent on non-agricultural wage labour, both in towns and the countryside. Rural labourers, petty commodity producers *and* poor peasants buy on the market significantly more than whatever crops they may manage to sell and thus are in general *adversely* affected by rising commodity prices. This is a characteristic they share with the urban working majority and which distinguishes them from the rich farmers who are demanding higher agricultural prices in the name of a 'peasant' majority. Even for middle peasants the gains from higher crop prices are offset when the costs of their inputs and consumption goods continues to rise.

(6) It is a striking fact that now India's rural poor toiling majority is no longer primarily a 'peasant' class but an increasingly proletarian one. Even if we classify poor peasants (who also do wage labour) with the 'toiling peasant' class, it can still be seen that the strictly defined rural wage-earning semi-proletariat is at least as large a class and perhaps larger. And, in spite of poverty, ties to the land and remnants of feudal servitude, this is now a class with increasingly wide labour experiences (including some experience of labour organizing) which has some limited access to modern amenities (from education to the cinema) which help to increase its knowledge of the world and change its consciousness. It is a class whose main immediate concern is not land or the price of crops, but rather the price of labour power and the consumption of goods it has to buy. It differs from the factory proletariat in that it labours under extremely backward conditions of production where workers are subjected to more personalized compulsions and repression, but this is true also of a significant section of urban workers. It is true that large numbers of this rural semi-proletariat hold property, that it is stratified in terms of standard of living, and that it is divided by linguistic, caste, sex and other social differences. But such things are true of the urban working class as well and similar factors can be found in every country in the world. In this sense the differences between urban and rural working classes seem more those of quantity rather than quality.

While in some regions (especially backward areas and forest regions) fights for land continue to be crucial, in the large majority of areas the rural poor are organizing themselves on the same kinds of demands as the urban poor, though much more sporadically—for higher wages, for jobs, against price rise, against caste and sexual oppression.

(7) Finally, the revolutionary process in India will be heavily shaped by this rural class structure—given that even in 1981 a high percentage of the population were still living in villages. The specific features of India's 'new democratic revolution' still have to be fully analyzed, but some things seem clear. One is that the 'main enemy' can no longer be defined as simply a landlord, or landlord-merchant class, but must include capitalist farmers (who are often called 'rich peasants' but the traditional left parties) as a whole. These not only exploit labour power and control the majority of land; they also control rural power structures, ranging from *gram panchayats* and *zilha parishads* (village and district councils) to coopertives, education societies, sugar factories, credit societies and banks. Not only do they (capitalist farmers) exploit the rural proletariat, they also exploit and oppress the toiling peasantry through their control of such institutions and they are often the direct intermediaries in the purchase of crops and provision of inputs.

Because the rural semi-proletariat is now the dominant section among the rural poor does not mean that wage issues must be considered primary, let alone the main 'revolutionary' issue. Wages are simply often the most important immediate organizing issue. For a revolutionary rural movement, some other things are as or more important. One is that overcoming internal divisions among the rural semi-proletariat and among rural toilers as a whole requires taking up the issues of *dalits, adivasis,* women, and oppressed nationality groups, which means the proletariat taking the lead in such broad and often 'noneconomic' social movements. Similarly, the question of what is often referred to as 'class alliances' is still a central one. In many areas the struggle for land is still crucial, and this becomes a mass movement normally in the heavily tribal, forest areas. And everywhere the question of uniting with the 'middle peasant' is a live one. Middle and poor peasants very often tail after the capitalist farmers in such movements as the 'farmers' movement' for higher crop prices—but in fact they are often more troubled by problems of price-rises (of consumption goods and agricultural inputs), by the corruption and gangsterism that are characteristic of the operation of all rural power structures, and by their oppression by the intermediaries (whether merchants or sugar factories) who buy their produce. The rural semi-proletariat can take up such issues to split them off from the rural rich and build a broad movement, and in some parts of India such local movements can be seen—whether it may be a sugar factory workers' union leading peasants of their area aginst the corrupt management of the factory, or an 'anti-price rise movement' fought in the form of direct seizure and distribution of goods to the rural poor.

Finally, while it can still be said that in some sense agrarian revolution and 'land to the tiller (or tillers)' is central, this can definitely no longer be seen simply as 'redistribution of land.' First, while poor peasant and labourer committees may take over land, in many areas the conditions may be appropriate for collective and cooperative forms rather than redistribution. And control of land is no longer sufficient: control of inputs, tractors, irrigation facilities, and all the rural power institutions from 'cooperative' credit societies to banks, and schools is equally crucial. Thus 'collective control of the means of production' becomes almost as important for rural as for urban areas.

Caste and Rural Classes

No analysis of class in rural India can be complete without taking caste into account; for not only did Indian feudalism have the specific feature of being structured and shaped through caste, but caste—though in a somewhat different form—remains equally viable and virulent today.

Under colonial rule, as noted above, though the seeds of capitalist development were laid and the feudal form of caste was given a decisive blow, still by and large a correlation between class and caste continued to exist, with high castes (usually the so-called 'twice-born') continuing to be lords of the land, moneylender-merchants and bureaucrats and professionals and middle and low castes mainly toilers.

'Today the development of capitalist agriculture in India has broken down this old correlation between class and caste and reconstituted a new and more complex relationship between the two.'

In destroying the old type of feudal landlordism, the old form of high-caste domination has also been given a decisive blow, though caste itself is far from vanishing. A survey of the main rural classes will give some idea of the situation.

Rich Farmers (including capitalist farmers and landlords) include both the former high-caste landlords (Brahmans, Rajputs, Bhumihars, Nairs, Vellas, etc.) and a large section of the *shudra*-status *kisan* castes (Marathas including those who were former low-status Kunbis, Jats, Kurmis, Yadavas, Kammas, Reddis, Kapus, etc.) The landlords who rent out their land tend to be drawn from mainly the 'non-cultivating' high castes (Brahmans, Kayasthas-Karans, etc.); conversely, the dominant section among the capitalist farmers are the *kisan* castes who have caste traditions of being cultivating peasants and were often in fact former tenants and peasant cultivators. In the more backward and semi-feudal regions, former landlord castes such as the Rajputs, Bhumihars, Brahmans remain powerful and contend with *kisan*-caste kulaks for control of the countryside. In Bihar this conflict expressed as the 'advanced-backward' caste conflict, is still fiercely raging. But in the most capitalistically developed areas the *kisan*-caste kulaks, who were traditionally of *shudra varna* and were often tenants or subordinate peasant cultivators in the past, are now decisively in control: Marathas in Maharashtra, Patidars in Gujarat, Jats in Punjab, Haryana and western UP, Okkaligas and Lingayats in Karnataka and so forth. That is not to say that there are no capitalist farmers or landlords of other castes in these areas. There are (even in western Maharashtra, for example, there are still a fair number of Brahman big landowners), but they are politically and socially subordinate and outnumbered by the dominant caste farmers.

In this sense, the dominant section among the rural rich as a whole, and especially in the more capitalistic states, are those who are *shudra* or 'middle-caste' in terms of *varna* status, who still represent themselves as *kisan* or *shetkari* ('peasant') or *bahujan samaj* ('majority community') and whose caste-cultural traditions combine both a sense of caste-pride and a history of resistance to high-caste and landlord domination.

Middle peasants are made up predominantly of the *kisan* castes. And where such castes (Marathas, Jats, etc.) are in significant proportion in a state or an area, they generally make up an overwhelming proportion of both capitalist farmers and middle peasants. The difference from the capitalist farmers is that the middle peasant class contains almost none or very few of the high castes (Brahmans, etc.) and a somewhat larger proportion of the artisan-service castes. A tiny proportion of *dalits* and *adivasis,* probably no more than one or two percent, are also in this class. This common caste and kinship background, along with the general propertied nature of the middle peasants and the aspirations this gives rise to, facilitates identification of the middle peasants with the capitalist farmers.

The rural semi-proletariat is most divided in caste terms. Here we have, at least for its lowest section, relatively precise data. The Rural Labour Enquiry (see Table 10) gives the proportion of agricultural labour households, both landed and landless, who are *dalits* (Schedule Castes), *adivasis* (Scheduled Tribes) and 'other.' 'Other' is a broad category that includes Muslims, Christians, Buddhists, and Hindus of artisan and *kisan* caste background (generally micro-level village studies and observation back up the assertion that not only artisans and non-*dalit* low castes but also a large section of the *kisan* castes are agricultural labourers in many areas). As can be seen from Table 10, a little over half of agricultural labourers on an all-India basis are 'other,' and the proportion is greater in the southern and western states where proletarianization and loss of land by ex-peasants has gone the farthest. This is a clear refutation of the assumption sometimes carelessly made that agricultural labourers are only or even primarily *dalits* and *adivasis*. Only in Punjab and Haryana does this seem to be true, and here also the in-migration of large numbers of UP-Bihar caste Hindu labourers is changing the situation. Even considering only landless labourers does not make much difference, for *dalits* are only a bit more likely to be landless than the caste Hindu labourers.

Thus, class and caste are no longer absolutely correlated: economic differentiation has affected almost every caste. But this differentiation is itself differentially felt. That is, the *dalits* and *adivasis*, and to a lesser extent the artisan-service castes and other low castes and probably also minorities such as Muslims and Christians, remain primarily proletarianized. Only a small proportion of their members become middle peasants, almost none are capitalist farmers, while somewhat more become socially mobile through urban occupations and service. In contrast, the middle-level *kisan* castes are the most differentiated in class terms, and include all classes from capitalist farmers (and members in high government service, business and politics) to middle peasants to landless agricultural labourers. Further, my own study of Maharashtra suggests that not only are major castes like the Marathas differentiated, but this differentiation extends to practically every *bhauki* or clan among them, so that even the most dominant *'patil'* lineage of a village may contain members who are agricultural labourers.[40] (In other areas, however, where such castes have a status-contempt for doing field labour, poorer members may refuse to work as field labourers in their own village and choose instead to move away or struggle along on reduced levels of consumption.)

Looking at the situation from another angle, while the capitalist farmers are the most nearly homogeneous in caste terms—and this is most true of the more capitalistically developed states—the rural proletariat, in contrast, is most divided. Its members include, and at all levels, from landless to poor peasants, *dalits, adivasis,* minorities and caste Hindus of 'middle-high' status, all present in sizeable sections and with regional/national differentiations often overlapping the caste divisions.

It should be stressed that this caste differentiation among the rural proletariat is not simply a matter of 'social' or 'superstructural' factors. There are still material and economic divisions. Where there is bonded labour, it is mainly among *dalits* and *adivasis,* while these sections and very low-caste artisans are the ones still affected by survivals of *jajmani*-type *veth begar* in some areas. It is still true that the more skilled and privileged labourers are caste Hindus; these are favoured by their caste and kin among the rich farmers and more likely to be hired as permanent labourers where this position provides some security; more likely to get such jobs as tractor drivers, in mills, and dairies. There are still some jobs that for pollution reasons *dalit* labourers are not hired to do in some areas, such as sowing. *Dalits* still live 'outside the village,' in separate settlements with separate water supply and worse roads and other amenities, while caste Hindu labourers live in the village, next door to and to some extent sharing the social life and some material benefits of their richer caste and kin-mates. Finally, there is an important historical difference: *dalit* agricultural labourers, in most cases, have won their current relatively free status along with some access and rights to land and education as a result of their own struggles and movements and so experience their position, however difficult and impoverished it may be, as an advance over their previous feudal bondage. In contrast, the caste Hindu agricultural labourers have often experienced historically a downward mobility, a loss of their former position as subsistence peasants or artisans, a decline of their social status. All of these differences provide a historical and material basis for crucial differences in consciousness and social organization.

The impact of caste on the nature of class conflict in India appears to be a dual one. On the one hand, a Japanese agricultural expert has given his belief that caste is reinforcing class in the countryside:

> It is my impression that the relation between farmer employers and agricultural labourers now prevailing in India is more like an urban market type rather than a patron-client type; this somewhat impersonal market-like relation in Indian village is reinforced by caste prejudice. Class conflict is that much more sharp and explosive ... [It] appeared to me much more tense and sharply felt than in Southeast Asia.[41]

It is true that added to fearsome poverty and exploitation, the bitterness of ongoing caste oppression gives a potentially explosive character to the Indian countryside. It is also true that the specific historical-cultural traditions of *dalits, adivasis* and low-caste non-Brahman labourers are a potentially powerful weapon against oppression that can also help to unite all the toiling masses if the fight against caste oppression and its culture of repression is made an integral part of class struggle. Similarly it must be noted that the massive work participation of women is also a crucial strength that can be drawn on most effectively by developing a genuine toiling women's libertion movement. But this requires a conscious and sustained effort by advanced sections to make the fight for liberation from caste and women's liberation a central part of the organizing of the rural toiling people.

And there is the other side of the situation: the existing class/caste complex also provides a fertile ground for the capitalist farmers to use casteism to appeal to their kin among the middle peasants and labourers, to divide the rural semi-proletariat, and to attack its *dalit* and *adivasi* sections (and their women) who are often the most militant. While 'atrocities against Harijans' are occurring throughout India, it is precisely in the more capitalistically developed areas, where the general class-caste structure described above is most fully present, that they are taking the most widespread forms with even poor and middle peasant caste Hindus sometimes participating in attacks on *dalits* on a mass basis: in northwestern India (in the campaigns centering around Kanjhawala), Marathwada, and Gujarat.

At present (mid-1981) it seems that it is mainly the capitalist farmers who are on the offensive, whether in leading agitations for higher prices for their products or in organizing repression of the rural poor, while the revolutionary potential of the rural proletariat is still to be organized. It is a situation that leads many left and progressive individuals to feel that agricultural labourers and poor peasants cannot really constitute a revolutionary force, that they are inherently weak, that they are incapable of forming a center around which middle peasants and other oppressed sections can be united, that in order not to be 'isolated' it is necessary to ally with the 'rich peasants' (always meaning in effect the village rulers, and capitalist farmers) on issues like higher prices. (This tendency is helped by the fact that the major parliamentary left parties not only possess a political line that in theory says it is necessary to maintain an 'all-peasant' alliance, but have their leading activists drawn not simply from middle peasants but from the kulaks themselves—many of whom were in fact previously tenants of middle peasants fighting landlords.)

But the seemingly repressed and divided state of the rural semi-proletariat today is after all only a phase in a long period of intense and complex class struggle. Though this class has its roots in the *dalits* and agricultural labourers who battled for freedom from feudal bondage, wages and land in the colonial period, it has after all only begun to emerge as an independent revolutionary force. Its weakness is in part only apparent, for there are vast numbers of diverse and unreported or underreported clashes going on among both agricultural labourers and other rural labourers as well as poor and middle peasants. The organization of sugar-cane cutters in Maharashtra in 1980-81 as well as an upsurge of spontaneous rural labourers' strikes in Ahmednagar and other districts (as well as locally organized ones especially in Dhule) are part of this upsurge, as is the decades-long struggle of *dalit* and low-caste labourers in Bhojpur under Naxalite leadership. Confusing the ability to understand this upsurge of the rural toiling masses is the fact that because class exploitation is compounded with caste and national oppression, struggles frequently take place under forms difficult to identify as simple 'class struggle'—for instance under the Jharkhand Mukti Morcha in Bihar or the Dalit Panthers in Maharashtra. It is noteworthy that there was a bigger mobilization for the *dalits'* 'long march' in December 1979 with hundreds of thousands of people taking part in various actions under various types of leadership all over Maharashtra) than there was for the 'farmers' long march' a year later, even though the left parties threw all their energy into helping the latter and only a bit into the former. It is clear that the rural toiling masses have not yet found their own revolutionary party and that in the political vacuum, especially where the opposition (including much of the left) tends to line up with the capitalist farmers, they are giving their support to the authoritarian Indira Congress. But the present lack of leadership, and the consequent prevalence of divisions and fragmentation is due to factors external to the agrarian class situation. It may also be a phase that will pass with the undoubtedly tumultuous political developments that appear to be ahead.

NOTES

1 Daniel Thorner, 'Capitalist Farming in India,' *Economic and Political Weekly (EPW) Dec. 1969, p.A-212.*

2 *Gail Omvedt, The Political Economy of Starvation: Imperialism and the World Food Crisis* Pune: Scientific Socialist Education Trust, 1976.

3 Thorner, p.A-212.

4 It is true that tenancy as such cannot simply be identified with feudalism, that different types of tenancy are associated with varying modes of production and that cash-rent itself can be viewed as a final transitional form to capitalist relations. Nevertheless, where landlord-tenant relations are the most prevalent form in agriculture, and where the surplus is *mainly* extracted in the form of rent (by cash, kind or labour-rent) by big landlords from small peasants who have some kind of claim on subsistence plots, it can be said that feudalism prevails.

5 For a fuller analysis see Gail Omvedt, 'Caste, Class and Politics,' in *Land, Caste and Politics,* New Delhi: 1981.

6 Nearly all Kisan Sabha documents show that the slogan of 'land to the tiller' and the whole analysis of landlordism was mechanically transferred to the Indian context and made equivalent to abolition of Zamindari, which in effect meant 'land to the tenant.' It was assumed that a substantial class of agricultural labourers would go on existing and that low caste artisans or *dalits* toiling as field servants did not really have rights as 'tillers.' Only the Telengana revolt *in practice* brought forward through the application of land ceilings, the notion of transferring land to these sections as well.

7 G.K. Shirokov, *Industrialisation of India*, Moscow: Progress Publications, 1973, pp.62-64.

8 Ashok Mody, 'Resource Flows between Agriculture and Non-Agriculture in India, 1950-1970,' *EPW,* Annual No., Mar. 1981.

140

9 V.G. Rastyannikov, 'The Agrarian Evolution of Indian Society in the 50s and 60s of the 20th Century,' in V. Pavlov, et al., *India: Social and Economic Development*, Moscow: Progress Publishers, 1975, p.140. My estimate now is that this figure is close to 65 percent.

10 Ibid., pp.116-20.

11 One 1976 study does argue that the percentage of gross product marketed remained relatively stagnant between 1961-62 and 1974-75. S.S. Madalgi, 'Trends in Monetisation in the Indian Economy,' *Reserve Bank Staff Papers*I, 1 June 1976. However, this is based on *assuming* that the rural class structure remained essentially the same throughout the period as it was in 1951.

12 Indradeep Sinha, *The Changing Agrarian* (Delhi: Peoples' Publishing House, 1979), p.22.

13 Center for Monitoring the Indian Economy (CMIE), *Basic Statstics Relating to the Indian Economy*, Vol.I: All India, Oct.1979, Sec. 10.

14 Ibid., Table 10.4.

15 Ibid., Sec. 16.

16 Veronica Bennholdt-Thomsen, 'World Bank Investment on the Poor', *Social Scientist* 91-92 Feb.-Mar. 1980.

17 CMIE, *Basic Statistics*, Table 10:11.

18 Mody, 'Resource Flows.'

19 Indian agriculture is still miserably backward. Nevertheless, an over-all 2.9 percent growth rate is significant, though not sufficient. Hayami and Rutton argue that growth rates of 1 percent a year were the best achieved in pre-industrial societies and that only following industrialization were growth rates of 1.5 to 2.5 percent possible. Yujiro Hayami and Vernon Rutton, *Agricultural Development: An International Perspective* Baltimore: Johns Hopkins, 1971, p.27. In this perspective the annual growth rates achieved since the 1950s by some countries (including some Third World countries) on the basis of world-wide technological developments appear as a real gain, and India's 2.9 percent is also not bad. Hayami's own recent visit (1981) sees India's agricultural development as respectable. The point is that leftists should not simply dismiss this as capitalist propaganda, but rather give an analysis of the *type* of exploitative system coming into dominance.

20 CMIE, *Basic Statistics*, Table 1.3.

21 CMIE, *Standard of Living of the Indian People*, Bombay: May 1979, Table 2.1.

22 A.N. Agrawal, *Indian Agriculture: Problems, Progress and Prospects*, Ghaziabad: Vikas, 1980, Table 5.2; *The Economic Times*, 19 April 1981.

23 Rastyannikov, pp.115-16.

24 See Mody, 'Resource Flows,' and note 31. This is likely an underestimate.

25 Joan Mencher, *Agriculture and Social Structure in Tamilnadu*, New Delhi: Allied, 1978 and N.S. Jodha, 'Complex of Concealed Tenancy,' *EPW*, 31 Jan. 1981.

26 In fact it may also be necessary to argue why it *is* possible to use such statistical data. In fact, there is good reason to think the Indian data are as relatively valid as data anywhere (compared to the U.S. census, for instance). Biases to some extent can be compensated for, and there is some independent confirmation provided by the general comparability between, for instance, the NSS/AIDIS (All India Debt and Investment Survey) and the RLE (Rural Labour Enquiry) data on landless labourers. It is likely that the data on the lower class majority is more valid than that on the rich farmers, simply because they have less to hide and less capability of doing so.

[27] For a recent example see Dilip Swamy, 'Land and Credit Reforms in India, *Social Scientist* 95-96, June-July 1980, p.4.

[28] Maharashtra State, *Report on Agricultural Census, 1970-71*, Bombay: Government of Maharashtra, 1976, p.16.

[29] Gail Omvedt, 'Effects of Agricultural Development on the Status of Women, Paper presented for ILO Tripartite Regional Seminar on Women and Development, Mahabaleshwar, April 1981.

[30] Rastyannikov, p.120.

[31] Another estimate of the underestimating in the AIDIS figures is given by Ashoka Mody, ibid., pp.434-36, who compares reported shares and deposits in primary credit societies from the AIDIS with actual holdings. While there was only a minor underestimation in 1961-62, by 1971 AIDIS showed RS 13.3 *crore* in deposits and Rs 121.5 *crore* in shares while the actual deposits were Rs 69.5 *crore* and the actual shares Rs 188.81 *crore*. Similarly in 1971 the AIDIS estimated Rs 724 *crore* in cooperative direct finance to agriculture while the actual figure was Rs 1,419 *crore*. See Mody, Tables 9 and 12.

[32] See tables 5 and 6, and R.G. Pathak, K.R. Ganapathy and Y.U.K. Sarma, 'Shifts in Pattern of Asset-Holding of Rural Households 1961-62 to 1971-72,' *EPW*, 19 Mar. 1977.

[33] All India Debt and Investment survey (AIDIS), *Assets of Rural Households as on June 30, 1971*, Bombay: Reserve Bank of India, 1971, p.8.

[34] Rural Labour Enquiry (RLE) 1974-75, Table 2.1.

[35] Ashok Rudra, 'The Self-Contained Village Society', *Frontier*, 3, 10 & 17 Jan. 1978.

[36] Omvedt, 'Caste, Class and Politics.'

[37] The original version of this paper had included 'poor peasants' with the rural semi-proletariat. On reconsideration it seems more accurate to classify them as part of the 'toiling peasant' class, if we are to define class in terms of relationship to means of production and define the proletariat as mainly sellers of labour-power. For a full discussion of the issues of defining rural classes, see Gail Omvedt, 'Agrarian Economy and Rural Classes,' *Frontier*, 18 Oct., & 8,15,22 & 27 Nov. 1980.

[38] Ibid.

[39] Maria Mies, 'Dynamics of Sexual Division of Labour and Capital Accumulation: Women Lace Workers of Narsapur,' *EPW*, Special No., Oct. 1981.

[40] Omvedt, 'Effects of Agricultural Development.'

[41] Yujiro Hayami, 'Agrarian Problems of India: An East and Southeast Asian Perspective,' *EPW*, 18 April 1981, p.710.

Additional References

Hamza Alavi, 'India and the Colonial Mode of Production,' *EPW* Special No., Aug. 1975.

– – – – –‥, 'India: Transition from Feudalism to Colonial Capitalism,' *Journal of Contemporary Asia*, Vol.10,no.4.

All India Debt and Investment Survey (AIDIS), *Capital Expenditure and Capital Formation of Rural Households*, Bombay: Reserve Bank of India, 1978.

AIDIS, *Assets and Liabilities of Rural Households as on June 30, 1971: Statistical Tables, Vol.I: All India and States, Vol.II: Regions within the States*, Bombay: Reserve Bank of India, n.d.

142

Jairus Banaji, 'India and the Colonial Mode of Production: Comment,' *EPW*, 6 Dec. 1975.

Pranab Bardhan, 'Variations in Extent and Forms of Agricultural Tenancy,' *EPW*, 11 & 18 Sept. 1976.

A. Bhaduri, 'An Analysis of Semi-Feudalism in East Indian Agriculture, *Frontir* 29 Sept. 1973.

N.K. Chandra, 'Proletarianisation in Rural India,' *Frontier*, 3 & 10 Nov. 1979.

Paresh Chattopadhyay, 'On the Question of the Mode of Production in India Agriculture: A Preliminary Note,' *EPW*, Mar. 1972.

– – – – – – . 'Mode of Production in Indian Agriculture: An Anti-Kritik,' *EPW* Dec. 1972.

Harry Cleaver, 'Internationalisation of Capital and Mode of Production in Agriculture,' *EPW*, Mar. 1976.

S.N. Mane, 'Poverty in India,' *The Economic Times*, 10 & 11 April 1981.

Joan Mencher, 'The Lessons and Non-lessons of Kerala: Agricultural Labourers and Poverty,' *EPW* Special No., Oct. 1980.

P.V. Paranjape, 'Kulaks and Adivasis: The Formation of Classes in Maharashtra', *Bulletin of Concerned Asian Scholars*, Vol 13, No. 1 Jan.-Mar. 1981.

Utsa Patnaik, 'Capitalist Development in Agriculture: Further Comment,' *EPW*, Dec. 1971.

– – – – – – –, 'On the Mode of Production in Indian Agriculture: A Reply,' *EPW*, Sept. 1972.

– – – – – – –, 'Class Differentiation with the Peasantry: An Approach to Analysis of Indian Agriculture, *EPW*, Sept. 1976.

Pradhan Prasad, 'Semi-Feudalism: The Basic Constraint of Indian Agriculture,' in Arvind Das and V. Nilakant (eds.), *Agrarian Relations in India*, Delhi: Manohar, 1979.

Ashok Rudra, 'Big Farmers of Punjab: Second Installment of Results,' *EPW*, Dec. 1969.

– – – – – – –, 'In Search of the Capitalist Farmer,' *EPW*, June 1970.

– – – – – – –, 'Reply to Patnaik', *EPW*, 6 Nov. 1971.

– – – – – – –, 'Class Relations in Indian Agriculture,' *EPW*, 3, 10 & 17 June 1978.

Ashok Rudra, A. Majid and B.D. Talib, 'Big Farmers of Punjab: Some Preliminary Findings of Sample Survey,' *EPW*, Sept. 1969.

Ranjit Rau, 'On the Essence and Manifestation of Capitalism in Indian Agriculture', *EPW*, Mar. 1973.

------, 'On the Agrarian Question in India,' *Frontier*, 7, 14, 21, 28 July & 4 Aug. 1979.

Hari Sharma, 'Green Revolution in India: Prelude to a Red One?' in Hari Sharma and Kathleen Gough (eds.), *Imperialism and Revolution in South East Asia*, New York: Monthly Review Press, 1974.

Ranjit Singh and Gopal Iyer, 'Migrant Labourers in Rural Punjab,' Paper given at Workshop on the Trade Unions and Labouring Poor in the Third World,' Delhi, March-Apr. 1981.

H.S. Surjeet, 'General Secretary's Report,' in All-India Kisan Sabha, Varnasi, Mar. 30-April 1, 1979.

DIALECTICS OF CAPITALIST TRANSFORMATIONS AND NATIONAL CRYSTALLISATION

The Past and the Present of National Question in India

Javed Alam

Introduction

There is a growing concern, of late, with questions of national and political unity of India even after more than three decades of independence. This suggests that the forces that tend to weaken or impede the unity of the people within the modern Indian State are still at work. A wide range of problems associated with the different nationality groups in India have come to the fore. These range from: first, conflicts involving the tribal formations, religions, communities, caste groups, sons-of-the-soil movements, etc., obstructing the unification of the people within the major national or cultural-linguistic groups; questions of mutual relations between the different nationalities themselves; and, finally, issues concerning the relations between some of these national groups—the constituent states of India—on the one hand and the Central-state authority on the other. The totality of these issues, problems, conflicts, etc., together constitute the national problem or question that confronts us in India today. In a different terminology this also represents, in scope, what has come to be known as the problem of nation-building although the emphases, problematics and approach of Marxian social analysis remains distinct.

The manifest form of the problem now is obviously different from the one in the 1950s and the early sixties at the time of the struggle for linguistic states; and the latter struggle was very different from the problem before independence when the growth and the political and cultural assertion of different nationalities and of the 'national movement' itself got entwined with the communal problem. It is therefore important to ask: what makes for this heterogeneity of forms and their concrete manifestations in the different phases of the evolution of the national question in India? And what keeps alive, in its varied forms, the problem even today? In seeking to answer these questions it is also necessary to ask: Is it possible to provide explanations to these questions in terms of a unified set of factors or factor that have shaped the growth of modern India? The argument developed in this paper assumes that it is substantively possible as well as methodologically necessary to treat the national question as an integral part of the large-scale socio-economic transformations through the development of capitalism in India.

From Economic and Political Weekly, *January 29, 1983. Reprinted with permission.*

The development of capitalism and of the many sided changes and forms of unevenness brought about by it have been key factors in the emergence of national awareness and national movements. The subsequent differences in the levels of national crystallisation of people with different expressions of ethnic identity have also been conditioned by the nature and varying consequences of the capitalist transformation. While in this respect India and the third world share the historical experience of Europe to a great extent, the patterns and stages of the crystallisation of national entity in the former need not follow European patterns. For these patterns are rooted in different social and political consequences of capitalism today compared to what they were in Europe.[1]

Hence capitalism as a generic form with the radically different and varied and social and political consequences of its development under different historical conditions becomes the basis of investigation in the determination of specific national problems which confront the various multi-national states in the third world today. In more concrete terms, a capitalism in retreat as in the West today or in a situation of structural dependence on the pre-capitalist social forces and economic relationships for its political survival, as in the third world, now becomes, in its essence, a divisive force. The growing capitalism in the period of the genesis and consolidation of European nation-states could relentlessly break down all barriers to its expansion and amalgamate people into new social unities within the emerging nation-states, which provided the market for its consolidation. Today in the situation of post-colonial imperialist domination, as in the colonial phase earlier, capitalism in the third world is no longer capable of totally destroying the pre-capitalist forms and is therefore incapable of creating new social unity on its own terms. Instead, while it undermines the pre-capitalist forms and relationships it is forced to compromise with the forces represented by them. Consequently, its historical significance as a revolutionising force is lost for the third world.

Consider Central or Eastern Europe. The bourgeoisie in the Central European states achieved social hegemony via fascism and the East European states came under the socialist system; and thus, in both the national question got sorted out either through the re-drawing of boundaries or by the success of the struggle against oppression and exploitation. A number of possibilities latent in the situation got frozen. Patterns, tendencies, and possibilities cannot be the same in India where capitalism, however crisis-ridden, moribund and reactionary in its character, continues to expand and grow. But this expansion and growth has however been characterised by a specific retardation: failure to establish its sway over productive economy; and society has forced it to accommodate landlordism with all its pre-capitalist ideologies and pre-modern outlook. In spite of its crisis-ridden nature capitalism in India today has displayed, with the backing of landlords and a united imperialist camp, greater surviving capacity than in Eastern Europe and has been able to push back revolutionary forces from becoming strong enough to capture state power. It is this more than anything else that keeps the national question alive in multi-national countries like India where the formation and development of people with different national compositions and make-up remains incomplete.

Moreover, capitalist growth in India has throughout shown a strong tendency towards self-perpetuating unevenness both region-wise and community-wise. Although capitalist growth everywhere is always uneven, this creates serious problems in multi-national states when it coincides with nationally demarcated regions or contiguous areas within such regions where population composition is different, as for example, the tribal belts.[2] This pattern of development has been taking place when people inhabiting these regions have been at different levels of linguistic and cultural development; in other words, at different stages of national-identity formation. Such a process of capitalist transformation also gives rise to a tendency towards differentiation of such groups from the larger nationalities of which they form unstable parts. The overall tendency of a divisive capitalism is more towards differentiation and separate crystallisation than towards assimilation, as was the case with growing capitalism within the nation-states in Western Europe.

In such a perspective, the national question is not only relevant but also poses an issue of some theoretical importance. Questions of definitions, and distinctions of terms like 'nations' or 'nationalities' or their inter-relations are no longer relevant for understanding the national movements within the new states. This is so because, unlike the historical model of development as in Western Europe, 'nationality' or a well developed cultural-linguistic community is no longer a necessary ground of transition to the emergence of national awareness and movements and their crystallisation in some form of demarcated boundaries. It was so then because capitalism grew, as Marx remarked, out of the womb of the old society. The future was conceived when the past had realised its potential. In a situation of imposed capitalism and its retarded development under colonial patronage this could not be so. The grounds of transition to national movements later were provided by people at different levels of linguistic-cultural developments and social formation. In the course of the growth of self-awareness and national consolidation in countries like India, even the Bengal-Maharashtra-Tamil Nadu pattern could not be gone through by many other national groups when national movements arose among such people after their incorporation in the forces of capitalism. The basis of future national movements in the case of these people were not well-formed linguistic communities with distinct literary traditions as it was in Western Europe or even in regions like Bengal, Tamil Nadu, etc. Therefore the earlier model of transition to national movement and crystallisation is inadequate as an analytical aid. This inadequacy is also due to the fact that terms like nations, nationalities or even ethno-linguistic communities can no longer refer to distinct stages in the development of national identity of people, in terms of which one could specify that national awakening arises only at this stage and not at that; such might have been the case in Western Europe, though even this is by no means certain. The process today gives an indeterminacy to the transitional forms as well as to certain historical concepts like nations and nationalities in relation to understanding the origin and development of the national movements in a multi-national context like that of India. What, therefore, is more important today is to specify the conditions which make possible the rise of national awakening even before nationality formation has reached maturity and the demands such movements may generate, including the one for statehood.

Having provided a perspective as well as a point of departure, I will, first, examine the terms of debate among the Indian Marxist writers keeping in view the national and class cues in the writings of Lenin on this problem. Secondly, as background for my own analysis, I will highlight certain aspects of the capitalist developments in India that seem to me relevant for the national question. And finally, I will consider a few sets of problems which constitute the more important dimensions of the question in India.

The Indian Debate

The prevalence of movements for recognition as distinct national groups, under conditions as noted above, among different peoples in countries like India calls for a radical theoretical break from some inherited traditions of scholarship. An attempt towards this necessitates a review of the debate among Indian Marxist writers on the subject along with an examination of the basis of their arguments. I will take as a sample E. M. S. Namboodaripad, Irfan Habib and Partha Chatterjee and question only their initial propositions which have a methodological relevance.

Namboodaripad is of the opinion that the nations and the national cultures emerged in the late feudal phase, that is, before the advent of capitalism, with the extensive growth of money-commodity relations and the rapid growth in the social use of regional languages both during and after the Bhakti and other religious reform movements.[3] This has been strongly refuted by certain others like Irfan Habib.[4] Partha Chatterjee disagrees with both these positions.[4a]

The evidence is far from clear. In principle, the evidence in an abstracted form is amenable to alternative explanations? it can *support* both the arguments without being able to *establish* either. It, therefore, seems to me that the conclusions are hasty and are based on a faulty use of concepts. The dispute between them concerns the questions of the emergence of nations and/or nationalities and, further, in the case of Irfan Habib and some others, concerns what constitutes or differentiates a nation from a nationality. This is at the root of the confusion. The problem, from the Marxian point of view, relates to the emergence of movements as a specific historical phenomenon and not the emergence of nations, nationalities, or ethno-linguistic communities.

To begin with, it may be useful to recall that Lenin in his numerous writings on the national question nowhere posits the questions concerning the origin of nations and nationalities or bothers about the differences between these terms. He was basically concerned with grasping the logic of historical forces behind the emergence of national movements and the consequent tasks of the revolutionary forces. The historical salience of the problem with Lenin lies in the fact that the 'principle of nationality is historically inevitable in bourgeois society and, taking this into due account, the Marxist fully recognises the historical legitimacy of national movements'.[5] While trying to grasp this logic Lenin takes recourse to a multiplicity of terms in a more or less synonymous manner. Terms like 'nation', 'nationality', 'national population', 'national group', 'national features', 'national distinctions', 'national composition', 'nationally distinct', 'national make-up', etc., have been used in an interchangeable way in the course of building arguments during the polemics he had with the leading spokesmen of European Social Democracy. What seems clear is that Lenin was not bound down to a predefined term in the description of similar phenomena. One may therefore have to ask: is it an instance of carelessness or is there a logic to the way he employs terms?

What seems clear from his writings is that the ground for national movements to emerge is provided by the contiguous presence of people with a distinct identity that is more or less. 'national'. The degree or extent of development of various characteristics and their crystallisation seems to be of secondary importance; in fact, these are never talked about by Lenin. It is plausible to argue that Lenin does so because of the extremely uneven impact of capitalist development on different societies and the consequent great variance in the types of national movements from Europe, and within Europe, to Asia and Africa. In the colonised part of the world, the capitalist incorporation and penetration and the subsequent transformation of different social formations in different parts of the world took place in the context of extremely uneven levels of development of the antecedent societies. Some had advanced to very high levels of money-commodity relations whereas many others were still at the stage of primitive social segmentation. This was so not just across countries; even within a country there were regions which were highly developed while others had not moved out of tribal formations. Capitalist transformation of all these areas began more or less after their colonial conquest and forced incorporation into the economies of metropolitan capitalism. The extraction of resources from these areas and the destruction of indigenous economies was of prime importance in the primitive accumulation of capital for the development of metropolitan capitalism, but they simultaneously led to a massive distortion of the capitalist transformation of these colonised societies. Lenin could therefore assert categorically that 'we cannot say whether *Asia will have had time to develop into a system of independent national states* like Europe, before the collapse of capitalism, but it remains an un-disputed fact that capitalism, *having awakened Asia*, has called forth national movements everywhere in that continent, too, that the tendency of these movements is towards the creation of national states in Asia.'[6] But, he points out, 'theoretically, you cannot say in advance whether the bourgeois-democratic revolution will end in a given nation seceding from another na-tion, or in its equality with the latter.'[7] It is the indeterminacy introduced by the late beginning of capitalism under colonial patronage and its continuation in the era of imperialism that makes Lenin say that 'the working class should be the last to make a fetish of the national question, since the development of capitalism *does not necessarily awaken all nations to independent life.* But to *brush aside the mass national movements once they have started,* and to refuse to support what is progressive in them means, in effect, pandering to *na-tionalistic* prejudices, that is, recognising *one's own nation as a model nation.*'[8] Yet, 'in the leap which all nations have made in the period of bourgeois revolutions clashes and struggles over the right to a national state are possible and probable.'[9]

If one situates what has been quoted above in the totality of Lenin's writing on this problem, one would find that his formulations and assertions closely follow his understanding of the nature and implications of capitalist developments in different parts of the world. He looks at the problem in Western Europe as basically sorted out and therefore of no consequence to the revolutionary movements at that time. The problem in Eastern and Central Europe and Tsarist Russia was not only alive but dangerously so. It had ac-quired an ideological immediacy for the revolutionary movements and strug-gle. It was of this that he was acutely aware. His pronouncements therefore display a categorical assertiveness and a kind of certainty. The very nature of the polemics in the context of the immediacy of the ideological struggle on certain manifest issues led him to underplay others that were not of im-mediate relevance at that time.[10]

In contrast to these, whenever in the few places he talks of what is now call-ed the third world, his formulations and assertions show a great degree of cau-tion and uncertainty. The historical point of time from which he was viewing these societies, the future and the consequences of the capitalist development were difficult to determine with any degree of certainty. Apart from the anti-colonial struggle, it was difficult to be clear about the development of internal forces in these societies. This led Lenin to leave the question open.

In spite of this, the debate is still being conducted in terms of the definite formulations and assertions by Lenin in terms of the East European polemics. As a result, the extremely insightful nuances in Lenin about the future development of capitalist forces and their implications for the third world societies has suffered a costly neglect. For the debate to get a proper theoretical grounding, it is necessary to get back to those themes in Lenin's writings.

There are a few implicit suggestions in what Lenin discerns in the situation which need highlighting. They have a particular relevance for any scientific analysis of national movements in countries like ours. What is obvious, first, is that the model of national crystallisation that emerged in the phase of early progressive capitalism does not generally get repeated later. In other words, tendencies that are inherent may not fructify. It is therefore necessary to be cautious in equating tendencies with necessary features. Secondly, the future basis of transition of a people to a national movement can no longer be the same empirical configurations as were witnessed in Western Europe; alternatively, levels of development from where people take off towards national awareness have changed with the change in the pattern of capitalist development. Thirdly, and this may be of importance, there can no longer be a model of a nation / nationality in the evaluation of a national movement. If 'one's own nation' cannot be a 'model' then it logically follows that no one nation can be taken as a model. It further follows from this that one cannot define it once and for all; for definitions imply a model. This however does not imply that historical categories cannot have core meanings. Around these core meanings many characteristics get attached or detached depending upon how possibilities in a situation get materialised.

Lack of careful attention to some of these changed features is at the root of controversy among certain scholars of eminence on the national question in India. Let us briefly examine a few aspects of this controversy — aspects that have become central, as much of the debate takes off from these premises. The intention here is not so much to criticise but to make an effort, however tentative at this stage, to rediscover the lost theoretical ground.

Take Irfan Habib for instance.[11] He predicates his discussion of the question on a sharp distinction between a nation and a nationality. By treating what to Lenin is only a tendency as a necessary feature for all times, Habib argues to the effect that a nation has to have a sovereign state or else it needs to be classified as a nationality. A nationality to him is one where the 'urge for a separate sovereign state is either (a) not fulfilled, or (b) moderated'.[12] Accordingly *'such people are usually termed "nationalities", not nations, in Marxist usage'.*[13] Moreover, the nationality itself to him is a bourgeois phenomenon: 'there was no basis for the emergence of nationalities before the British conquests, because there was no trace of any emerging bourgeoisie'.[14] It is unclear how these distinctions are, as Irfan Habib asserts, 'Marxist'. The basis for such assertions is the implicit assumption that the consequences of capitalism for the national question are unidirectional under all historical conditions. This seems to be a variant of the Luxemburgian error which Lenin so systematically undermined. The assertions seem to be arbitrary both if one bases oneself on the writings of Lenin or follow the Marxist methodology rigorously. Irfan Habib, however, uses these distinctions for a correct criticism of Namboodripad.

Namboodripad without getting drawn into such distinctions takes a position that is equally untenable. In his examination of the national question in Kerala, he assumes the prior emergence of a 'nation' as a condition for the emergence of national awareness and national movements. Basing himself on Stalin's oft-quoted definition of nation he meticulously searches out and finds all the characteristics of what Stalin says constitutes a nation. Incidentally, he finds what he discovers for Kerala to be widespread in India at that time: '. . . . folk culture was flowering into national culture in Maharashtra, Bengal and other parts of India.'[15] A clear instance of this phenomenon was: 'The great Shivaji and other *national heroes* were coming out as champions of a new form of social and state organisation—an organisation based on *national language and national culture*—although many of them were also *national* oppressor in relation to *nationalities* other than their own.'[16] And therefore: 'The process is thus similar to what took place in Europe.'[17] It is intriguing that a nation and national movement is sought out as existing prior to capitalism. Moreover the assumption is that the pattern of Europe has to repeat itself. Such a searched out pattern is, in plain and simple language, an analytical superimposition on a reality that is so different. It is difficult to accept this contention of Namboodripad in the face of world-wide evidence so meticulously used by Lenin in his arguments. There is also no methodological basis in terms of which such a contention becomes tenable nor the kind of evidence that can clearly establish a case. In the absence of the development of capitalism, a community displaying characteristics that are more or less 'national' and providing the future basis of a movement could have existed. But it is doubtful if one could talk of national question as a problem before capitalism if, as Lenin says in the quote above, the 'leap' is made at the time of bourgeois revolutions.

When the crux of the matter is capitalist transformation then, as an aside, it is useful to note that even if the potentiality of capitalist development existed before the incorporation of India into the British colonial empire no one has so far shown that capitalism had started growing in India. The controversy is only about its possibility and not about its actual development.[18] One can, therefore, legitimately talk of the national question in India only with respect to the period after the colonial conquest.

Now when we are caught up in the problem it is futile and misleading to get lost around the definitions of concepts and terms and a search for their equivalents in the social phenomenon. Engels's warning that we will never find any 'fixed, cut-to-measure, once-and-for-all applicable definitions in Marx's works'[19] is relevant in this context. 'It is self-evident that where things and their *inter-relations are conceived, not as fixed, but as changing,* their mental images, the ideas are likewise subject to change and transformation, and *they are not encapsulated in rigid definitions,* but are developed in their historical or logical process of formation.[20] Lenin similarly uses terms, in the correct Marxist way, to locate the unity of concepts and phenomena that are everchanging and therefore we cannot find in his use of concepts and terms any cut-and-dried meanings. In the way he employs them, terms and concepts change their meanings to mirror the changing phenomena and their ever-changing inter-relations. For our context this is revealed in a significant sentence where Lenin says: 'It is autonomy that enables *a nation* forcibly retained within the boundaries of a given state *to crystallise into a* nation.'[21] The nation as a social form here is, significantly, both prior to as well as the result of the process of crystallisation. Lenin moreover does not, following Marx, begin his account of historical phenomena from concepts but rather does so with historical and contemporary facts and makes use of concepts in relation to conditions in particular societies. Attention to this, and such other, extremely useful nuances in Lenin following the novel use of terms in Marx would not have led to an escalation of this unnecessary controversy.[22]

Partha Chatterjee, in an otherwise insightful piece of analysis on Bengal,[23] proceeds to build up his argument, like Irfan Habib, in terms of Eurocentric presuppositions. Nation he takes to be a phenomenon of the capitalist era. It is an outcome, according to him, of homogenisation, in terms of economic imperatives, of a pre-existing 'cultural community' in a state formation by the bourgeoisie. But he finds a good many of the characteristics assigned generally to a nation existing within these cultural communities. He, therefore, calls such a community 'already possessing a distinct and common cultural identity in the pre-capitalist era, a nationality'.[24] The complete divergence, in his position and the one Irfan Habib takes, is clear and is indicative of the confusion in the way terms have been employed. But this is not the most important aspect for analysis; from this he is forced into an anomalous position when he asserts that characteristics assigned to 'nation' should actually belong to 'nationality'. Accordingly, he argues that Stalin assigns to 'nation' the characteristics which should properly apply only to 'nationality', and this lands Stalin 'in all sorts of conceptual difficulties when discussing the national question in eastern Europe'.[25] It is true that it was Stalin who went in for a detailed elaboration of the characteristics of a nation, and gave a 'once and for all' definition as well as distinguished it from nationality. But what is not clear is how the conceptual difficulties could be avoided if the characteristics found to inhere in one are transferred to the other concept in a sort of musical chair of concepts.

Such a conceptual muddle hinders the process of understanding. Behind these formulations, there are no methodological criteria to decide one way or another. In the absence of any criteria, amorphous evidence from history can be used to support many such positions but does not establish any.

To come back to our problem, the initial awakenings and the subsequent heightening of these and the emergence of movements took place in states and societies which were not only, in many cases, of diverse social-national compositions but also at different levels of identity formation from a 'national' angle. It was in this situation that ill-defined groups having distinct but unstable national features were thrown into a historical flux of which national awareness and national movements manifesting a variety of hitherto unknown forms were a part. In a great many cases in the third world such national movements themselves became instrumental in welding these people into crystallised national groups. In this process nation / nationality distinctions or the precise prior categories of transition are only of peripheral importance, as they have become merely academic.

It was this awareness that probably restrained Lenin from defining the terms and concepts 'once and for all' and helped him to take into his analytical grasp all sorts of situations manifesting diverse national forms in the different periods of emergence of national movements. It was Stalin's error, I would contend, to have closed the concepts and rigidified the terms of debate once and for all, resulting in a fetish of definitions of terms in so much of the otherwise fruitful analysis undertaken by later Marxists.

Stalin's theoretical position that 'it is sufficient for a single one of these characteristics to be lacking and the nation ceases to be a nation',[26] or its reverse—'It is only when all these characteristics are present together that we have a nation'[27]—has led to unnecessarily rigid schematisation which makes the dialectical handling of complex situations extremely difficult. Moreover, it is this that leads to conceptual difficulties and not, I feel, the attribution of characteristics that belong to 'nationality' or to 'nation' as suggested by Partha Chatterjee. It does so because Stalin's approach here is more logical and less dialectical. Moreover, the logical rigour demanded by Stalin for the specification of nations-nationalities as social forms leads him and others to ignore or conflate important distinctions of our era. Consequently, these historical forms look like curiously stationary phenomena in his writings.

To sum up the point, I would suggest that this confusion is largely due to an exclusive reliance on the writings of Stalin. Stalin asserts, on repeated occasions, that the nation emerges at a definite period: 'The process of elimination of feudalism and development of capitalism is at the same time a process of the constitution of peoples into nations.'[28] Or, 'Modern *nations* are the product of a definite epoch — the epoch of rising capitalism.'[29] In clear contrast Lenin equates the same period with the rise of, as distinct from nation, national movements: 'Throughout the world, the period of the first victory of capitalism over feudalism has been linked up with *national movements*.'[30] Or, 'Developing capitalism knows two historical tendencies in the *national question*. The first is the *awakening of national life* and *national movements*, the struggle against all national oppression, and the creation of national states.'[31] The difference, as revealed in the choice of terms used like emergence of 'nations' in the case of Stalin and the awakening of 'national life' and 'national movements' as Lenin stressed, is subtle but extremely significant, with many implications both for theory and practice.

Needless to say, national movements can arise without there being fully developed nationals so long as some distinct national features, however dormant or unstable otherwise, exist among people in a contiguous region at the time of its incorporation into the networks of a capitalist system. Given the weakness of contemporary third world capitalism, it is immaterial whether such a community of people constituted an ethno-linguistic community, a nationality or a nation. In the dialectics of the movement and struggle then, such a community in itself can be a sufficient basis for a future nation—a nation in the sense in which Stalin employs the term. But the reverse is not necessarily true: that there can be a nation without a national movement being its necessary concomitant. It is logical to assert here that one can talk of the national question only when a national movement has emerged. Here the historical evidence is conclusive: there cannot be national movements and consequently the national question before the advent of capitalism. This brings us to the impact of British rule and the development of capitalism in India.[32]

Impact of British Rule and Development of Capitalism

At the level of the economy, the nature of capitalist development during the colonial period has had its inevitable implications for the national question in India. The entire period of about 200 years of the colonial regime has been clearly demarcated into several stages largely determined by the laws of development of British capitalism itself.[33]

The more visible indicators of a 'national' awareness appeared only in the early second half of the last century when the import of British industrial capital was yet to be accomplished in a big way. The next half century saw a full scale stabilisation of British capital in India in a few industries along with a faster development of 'social overhead capital'—transport and communication being the core sectors here.

When India entered the 20th century, industries and trade centres had grown largely around the port cities with industrial investment concentrated around Calcutta (jute) and Bombay (cotton textiles). As A. K. Bagchi points out, both these centres accounted for a major part of aggregate industrial investments; yet their share in the national income was insignificant, and hence modern industry was in the nature of an enclave economy.[34] In addition to this, most of the other enterprises were in the nature of extractive industries largely concentrated in eastern India. What was equally significant was the development of railways and modern transport which effectively linked up the interior to the port cities,[35] facilitating the development of commodity production and exchange as well as giving a spurt to the growth of agricultural raw materials, geared to these industries. The consequent commercialisation of agriculture laid the basis, as Irfan Habib suggests, for the development of landlord and rich peasant agriculture along with the pauperisation of small proprietors contributing to an increase of landless labourers all over India.[36] Railways thus integrated the heterogeneity of different types of production units and economic regions into an economic interacting system. Linked to this, there was an increase in the parasitical pressure on expropriation of argicultural surplus through trade, finance and money-lending capital, and this facilitated the accumulation of money in the hands of traders and moneylenders. Agriculture got encapsulated by capitalism without any profound transformation taking place in the forces of production. Pavlov is right when he observes that a symbiotic relationship 'between capitalist structures and pre-capitalist ones runs through the sphere of accumulation'.[37] Even this limited and highly distorted development of modern industry largely followed and hastened the process of 'de-industrialisation' in most regions of India. It was more complete in certain regions than in others with different consequences for the subsequent growth of industrialisation and class formation. The more successful development of indigenous capitalism in western India, as shown by Bagchi,[38] was partly due to this factor and partly to the survival of the Indian merchants involved in large-scale trade. Moreover, as limited industrialisation followed the earlier massive de-industrialisation it resulted in a great increase of pressure on agriculture with widespread repercussions for rents, shares and wages. The impoverishment of agriculture also had implications for the origin of the industrial working class, and, as recounted in detail by Sukomal Sen,[38a] for their particular work conditions, social-national composition, wages, etc.

Even after the First World War, under the twin impacts of the weakening of British imperialism (and the fears of a loss of Indian markets to other imperialist powers) and the growth of a powerful mass movement for freedom when industrial capitalism under the Indian bourgeoisie expanded much more rapidly, the basic relations already established between agriculture and industry did not change. Bagchi points out that the growth of large-scale industry in eastern and western India did not stimulate the agricultural productivity in these regions. On the other hand, the growth of agricultural productivity and output in certain regions, like Punjab, did not lead to any substantial growth of large-scale industry before independence. Bagchi argues that the colonial economy imposed a 'dual disjunction' between the growth of agriculture and the growth of industry, inhibiting the possibilities of growth of sub-economies in which the two could stimulate each other.[39] Till independence, modern industry kept growing both commodity-wise (steel, cement, refined sugar, paper, vegetable oils, chemicals, etc.) and area-wise (Delhi, Kanpur, Madras, Madurai, Coimbatore, Ahmedabad, and later Gwalior, Bhopal and Indore, etc.). In this pattern of development, certain areas, which remained completely untouched by modern industry, were Punjab, Baluchistan, North-West Frontier Province, Sind, in the north-western border region and East Bengal, as well as certain other interior regions, in spite of the fact that investment in agriculture in some of these areas was higher than in other places and therefore the domestic market was better for industrial goods.[40] Among these regions, in all the areas which were either overwhelmingly Muslim or Muslim majority areas, modern industry did not grow. Moreover, apart from uneven development in regional terms, the development was very uneven in terms of commodities and ethnic groups in the developed areas also: the Muslims and tribals and lower castes were much less affected by these developments. All this had a deep impact in complicating the movements of people in different nationalities as well as in splitting it up both before and after independence.

From the perspective of the development of the national question in India it is also important to note the origin of the Indian capitalist class. The indigenous entrepreneurs in modern industry both before and after World War I came from erstwhile commercial groups who had accumulated capital through trade, finance and money-lending. Shirokov correctly observes that this largely determined the social mentality of the Indian bourgeoisie and forced it to be on the side of 'caution and easy profit'.[41] As such, it also determined the 'sequence of priorities' of this class as and when new opportunities opened. Bagchi further points out that the easy mobility of trading capital between different fields of profitable investment also got translated into a mobility between different regions of India.[42] As an aside, it is also interesting to note that the controllers of large businesses and industrial houses in Pakistan later as well came from amongst the Memons, Bohras, etc.—the traditional Muslim trading communities who migrated to West Pakistan after partition. These mobile groups of capitalists did not as a class belong to any one national group or, more appropriately, did not treat any demarcated national region for favoured treatment. They moved all over the country wherever opportunities for maximising the return on investment were easily available. They thus became, in a real sense, a pan-Indian bourgeoisie but without the revolutionising potentialities of the bourgeoisie as in Western Europe, at the early phase of the bourgeois-democratic revolution. These new industrial capitalists also kept up their links with agriculture through rent, trade, money-lending—in short, through efforts to control the fiscal apparatus of agriculture.

Towards the end of the colonial era in India, we find that the industrial revolution and the capitalist transformation were far from complete. In the phase after independence, building upon this base, acute regional unevenness in both industrial and agricultural development has come to be a permanent feature of Indian economic growth. The states that developed large-scale modern industry have continued to occupy the leading positions in the statewise share of aggregate industrial investment although some states like West Bengal are slipping, while some others like Karnataka and Andhra Pradesh are gaining in relation to others. On the other hand, the states that have achieved substantial progress in agricultural production and productivity have not had industrialisation on any significant scale. Even the extent of monetisation and commercialisation of agriculture remains fairly uneven. This is an important determinant of the extent of erosion of pre-capitalist structures of economy and social power in rural society. All these developments go a long way in conditioning the response of the working class and peasantry in several key areas of political mobilisation.

The comparative roles of the working class and the peasantry in their response to several important issues and problems have varied widely on many occasions. The 'sons-of-the-soil' argument, for example, has taken on one meaning in Maharashtra under Shiv Sena, a completely different one in Assam, and yet another in Telengana region of Andhra Pradesh in the recent past. The land question or the agrarian question in general has not been relevant to Shiv Sena but quite relevant to the recent Assam agitation. The fact that the Akali Dal at times emerged as a major force in Punjab by championing the causes of the Punjabi capitalist landlords and rich peasants along with Sikh religion is yet another example of a highly extraordinary situation, where demand for cheaper electric power for irrigation pumps, or low input and high output prices have gone hand in hand with obscurantist slogans. In West Bengal, on the other hand, Amra Bangali has failed to make any impact. Each situation has been determined by a wide range of factors, including the history of the democratic movement in these regions. But in this history itself, as also in the present day situation as such, the differential nature of the development of the economy of a region has contributed towards the emergence of a relatively distinct sociology of political response, with its necessary connotation for the national question.

One of the unintended consequences of British rule was that capitalism developed first in and around the port cities and therefore affected those areas more where the population that later crystallised into distinct nationalities constituted only a small proportion of the total population of India; it was everywhere in each case less than ten percent of the total population of the country. It was also a fact that the industrial bourgeoisie in these areas did not belong to or could not become the representative of any of these national groups. When industry grew and spread, even after independence, this pattern did not change significantly. They moved to wherever the rate of return was the highest. The bourgeoisie could never, therefore, get identified with any specific nationality or province as its own.

To sum up, even though the development of modern industry remained confined to certain regions, the bourgeoisie has throughout been of a transregional or pan-Indian character in the way it equally exploited the different nationalities for its growth. Equally important, the market was also throughout of a multi-national character; the bourgeois development was not bound up with nationality boundaries as it was in successive stages in Europe. In other words, the two conditions—first, the equation of market and bourgeoisie with nationally demarcated regions leading to progress; and, second, the oppression of other nationalities within the multi-national states of that time giving rise to the slogan of national self-determination—which are a necessary part of the struggle for equality among nations and for the democratisation of the national question were always absent in the pattern of capitalist development in India both during and after colonial rule. Given this, a 'dominant nation' never emerged in the classical Central or East European pattern nor was there a historical need for struggle against 'national oppression' within the multi-national context of India. What instead became crucial was the communal and other primordial divisions cutting across the nationally demarcated regions because of the strength and virulence of precapitalist forces and ideologies, given the peculiarities of the capitalist transformation in India.

The one region—the Hindi belt—with the largest linguistic group comprising more than one-third of the total population of the country, suffered from two disabilities. First, the standardisation of language and associated culture among the masses was far from complete as has been the case with many other regional languages. Secondly, in terms of modern economic developments, it had remained, as it still is, relatively backward. Even the bourgeois groups, who belonged to some areas of the Hindi belt had, and still have, most of their economic investments concentrated in different nationally demarcated regions of India. This foreclosed all possibilities of a 'dominant nation' emerging in India. Corresponding to this, there is also the preponderance of other smaller nationalities in the military and other services. So the multi-nationality that emerged and later crystallised into national groups with the formation of linguistic states was of a different type than the one Lenin was confronted with; it was free of the relations of oppressor and oppressed nationalities. The only context of oppression prior to independence was colonial oppression, which was an externally imposed factor and not one of relationships between national groups themselves. The national question in India is on a footing that is entirely of a new kind. It cannot be conceived of as belonging to any of the categories talked of by Lenin.

Indian Bourgeoisie:
A Supra-National Class

Here was a situation with profound implications for theory. But, then, theory lagged behind actual developments. It was only much later that Marxist scholarship caught up with the situation. Ajit Roy, in the late sixties for the first time clearly formulated the issue.[43] Later, the major communist party, CPI(M), broke off from the tradition and, while recognising this fact, dropped the right of self-determination from its programme.[44]

In actuality, the concrete situation had long shown that the demand for self-determination could never be an issue, given the way the national question in India emerged. The bourgeoisie, from the beginning being of an all-India nature and there being no oppressor nation, when the anti-colonial movement became powerful no national group did or could feel the historical urge or necessity to secede, notwithstanding Pakistan. In fact, one can look at the Indian independence movement or Indian nationalism representing the interests of the multi-national society as a supra-nationality phenomenon. It was so in the sense that it articulated the organically related common needs of a large majority of people belonging to all the national groups in India. We can speak of it in this way in the sense that the unification of India in a vital economic sense, quite apart from the politico-administrative unification, had been an evolving feature that deepened with time. The restricted political platform for constitutional agitation erected in the shape of Indian National Congress, reflected, in part, the underlying fact of this growing unity as well as became instrumental in its furtherance. Much later, when, under Gandhiji's leadership it acquired a mass character, it did so by aggregating the interests of all the classes and by keeping together the main spokesmen of the different national groups. More than anything else, the long drawn out mass movements forged and strengthened Indian unity at the grass-roots by providing common, concrete aspirations to the Indian people. What took shape was a common reference world for ordinary people representing both their contemporary concerns and the traditionally inherited notions about India and its culture. Anti-imperialism and the struggle for political independence provided the basis for the common struggles and active co-operation of the masses and the ruling classes that did cut across the nationality barriers; a short-term congruence of interests in which the initiative always remained with the ruling classes as is evident in the low salience given to the demands of working classes and peasantry.

In the growth of this multi-national unity, if the structural pre-requisite was the all-India market and the pan-Indian bourgeoisie, the active lead was provided by the new strata that emerged out of the English system of education-itself geared to the over-arching interests of the colonial system. It was this 'class' comprising salaried strata and professional groups that became the spokesman of the all-India national movement as well as of the various regional forms of national consciousness. Apart from the bourgeoisie, this was the only group which in its outlook and perspective transcended the bounds of nationalities; yet was firmly rooted through a variety of ties to the indigenous society. It was not fully oriented to the future but also always appealed to the traditional sentiment of people and played upon the vague inherited sentiments of being Indian. This in no small measure contributed to the popular sentiments around inter-class unity. There was no necessary coincidence of interests between the two—the bourgeoisie and the middle classes—all along the spectrum of interests at successive stages of development; in fact, the divergences were pronounced on many important issues at different points of time. But the articulation of historical tendencies and popular urges showed a growing similarity at critical points as the independence movement progressed. There was no fundamental change in this relationship even when the peasantry was actively involved. It is in this specific sense of complementarities that one can characterise the national movement as bourgeois and not in the sense of its leaders being agents of the bourgeoisie. Yet, this in itself does not make Indian nationalism or, for that matter, third world nationalisms unique, as has been made out in some writings. For example, Barun De argues that Indian nationalism had much less to do with the intentions or role of capitalist classes but was rather a product of anti-colonialism, in which the shattered ambitions of middle classes were the motive forces.[45] To talk of it as determined by capitalism or bougeoisie is a case of, according to him, 'over-determination'. With a different emphasis and perspective, Niharranjan Ray also takes the position that although European nationalisms were a product of the bourgeoisie, nationalism in India was due to the penetration of British political authority and colonial economy and not a product of the bourgeoisie as in western Europe.[46] Common to both, from different intellectual perspectives, is the view that it was more an independent response of the 'middle classes' or 'professional elite' which gave birth to the ideology of nationalism. Barun De, in a significant passage, says that the 'egalitarian agitations' of the middle classes 'turned into national movements or freedom struggles, or socialist liberation movements against the colonial order of international capitalist inequality. While imperialism could only create subordinate elites, colonialism dialectically spawned a subaltern middle class intelligentsia, whose *ideology was forced by rude shocks to its innocence into anti-colonial nationalism.*[47]

Looking at or emphasising the role of the middle classes in any historical process by counterposing it to bourgeoisie or to the other main classes in the social process of production is theoretically untenable and empirically inadequate. The term 'middle class' signifies a stratum, in India as elsewhere, that emerged with the capitalist transformation of societies. It was in the structure of occupations and opportunities created by this transformation that the middle class moved – in terms of their hopes, aspirations and inhibitions as well as dissatisfactions and oppositions. The character of a movement—nationalist or of any other type—is not dependent upon which group becomes instrumental in the articulation and percolation of the ideology of the movement. Even in classical bourgeois nationalist movements it was mainly the middle class that was instrumental in the refraction of bourgeois class ideologies among the masses, more so the peasant masses. Their political strength has been a function of their ability to win over or detach the main social classes from the given configurations of power. Within specific circumstances, they could, later on, become either the spokesmen of bourgeois or proletarian ideologies through different kinds of mediations with society at large. By succesfully mobilising the existing resources of people they could become instruments of bourgeois or 'liberal' populism; or, alternatively, by mobilising the people agianst ruling class alignments of power the harbingers of new revolutionary forces—the socialist revolution. In either case, their relationship with and ability to lead the main social classes—the working class, peasantry or the bourgeoisie, established or emerging—played a central role. In Barun De's formulation the middle classes become an independent class force without having much to do wtih either the bourgeoisie or the working classes and peasantry. Moreover, in the context of the third world, given the persistence and strength of the feudal or pre-capitalist relations and forces, the peasant question compeltely evaporates. The empirical inadequcy lies in its over-riding nature; it destroys all criteria of distinction. It cannot explain why all 'socialist liberation movements' after victory moved in the direction of aboli-tion of private property in the means of production, and why most other 'freedom struggles' tried to establish or encourage capitalist development even if it meant naked repression of people in the interests of the ruling classes.

In the specific context of India, their role has also been of a dual nature. They have been the champions of their respective national cultures whether in Tamil Nadu, Bengal, Kerala, Gujarat, etc. and yet could see and articulate the all-India connections and needs of the people. Yet all this does not qualify them to be treated as an independent class force, as tends to become in the above formulations.

The ideology and the actual pattern of development of nationalism in India goes to prove the historical validity of the Leninist formulation on the na-tional question.

> For the complete *victory of commodity production,* the *bourgeoisie must capture the home market, and* there must be politically united territories whose population speak a single language ... . Therein is the *economic foundation of national movements.*[46]

In this formulation, the choice of words point to the implicit chain of historical causation. Whereas the determination between commodity produc-tion and home market and politically united territories is indicated by *must,* the relation of the single language to political unity is merely referred to as a historical coincidence by the use of verb *speak.* And therefore what provided the economic foundation to national movements gets mentioned by the use of *is* as a historical event and no more. Language thus can be a contingent factor and cannot be treated as a necessary condition for all times to come.

When the home market is not a national market, as in the case of India, but a multi-national market the pan-Indian boureoisie does not need any one regional lnguage in the orthodox sense; language here acquires an altogether different connotation. The laws of the motion of capital in their impact on various nationally distinct regions and groups have incredibly complex im-pacts and reactions. Their political manifestations vary widely at different points of time. Before independence, they manifested different relationships between the supra-nationality Indian nationalism and the various regional movements of cultural awakening and communal assertion. After independence, these have assumed distinct modes of articulation around the demands for regional autonomy or struggle for separation from larger groups or demands for special protection of regions and groups, etc.

In the entire range of manifestations, the multi-national market as an expression of the continuing nature of capitalist development remains the determining factor and the control of the growing all-India market does not require the development of any Indian language in the way it was necessary in. Western Europe. The pan-Indian bourgeoisie did not and does not need to champion the cause of any Indian language. Its specific colonial origins and the nature of its operations precluded the need for it to identify with any Indian language. Today, in a world-wide context, the role of language to bourgeois development has undergone a drastic change. The growth and expansion of agency houses and the institution of sales and company representatives who are recrutied from different regions coupled with the fact of simultaneous advertising in many languages acts as a sufficient basis for the process of buying and selling and for commercial intercourse. The free flow of commerce in the classical age of competitive capitalism based on small enterprises was dependent upon direct interpersonal communications and hence the importance of respective national languages for market consolidation. Monopoly capitalism or imperialism, no longer bound to national boundaries, evolves its own sophisticated mediums of impersoanl communication; the scale of production necessitates this. In the changed physical potentialities of exchange, State and other infrastructure for market have become more important than specific national languages. This is not very different when we look at the pan-Indian monopoly bourgeoisie in relation to the multi-national Indian market.

The need for the unification of communication exists largely at the apex and, as far as the pan-Indian bourgeoisie is concerned, this minimal requirement can be easily met by the English language. The domocratic demand for regional languages is either opposed by the big bourgeoisie or at best is reluctantly conceded as was evident during the language agitations in the 1950s. Sections of the big bourgeoisie may have a preference for some of the Indian languages; but to infer from this that it champions the cause of Hindi will be fallacious. The stand of the Indian State for an all-India 'link' or 'official' language is more due to the pressure of the largest language group in the country and not because of the needs of the big bourgeoisie. As such, on the language question the needs of the Indian State and the big bourgoisie do not exactly coincide. It is reasonable to assert that the fight for regional languages and for the complete equality of these languages is a people's cause in no way directly related to the requirements of the big bougeoisie. In fact, the efforts to have a privileged position for specific languages in different regions and discriminations against national minorities seem to be backed up by the locally dominant ruling class groups. This also makes the struggle for equality of languages a part of the democratic struggle against exclusiveness and regional or linguistic chauvinism.

All this shows that the causal links between market and language and capitalist transformation and national question are different from what they were in Western Europe in the era of progressive capitalism. In countries like India, the development of national languages is much more bound up with the democratic movement for state rights and the protection of the languages and cultures of minorities.

Autonomy vs. Self-Determination

It would be worthwhile here to take a closer look at the demands for state autonomy in the multi-national context of India. It is reasonable to assume that the struggle for and the eventual solution of the national question in India will partly centre around these. When the right for self-determination had no historical basis, autonomy in the multi-national states becomes, to quote Lenin (without reviving the ghost of Rosa Luxemburg), a principle of democracy:

> ... It is not difficult to see why, from a Socialist Democratic point of view, the right to 'self-determination' means *neither* federation *nor* autonomy (although, speaking in the abstract, both come under the category of 'self-determination')... . As far as autonomy is concerned, Marxists defend, not the right to autonomy, but autonomy *itself*, as a general universal principle of a democratic state with a mixed national composition, and a great variety of geographical and other conditions.[49]

It, therefore, assumes an importance in restructuring the institutional basis of politics in India towards greater and more meaningful democracy; of course, within the limits imposed by a bourgeois landlord state.

Barring a few, most of the demands for state autonomy, in simple class terms, seem to be an outcome of contradictions between different sections of the ruling classes. The interests of the all-India big bourgeoisie and non-big bourgeoisie or landlords may not always coincide. The development of capitalism necessitates, as one of its conditions, the formation and consolidation of large markets for commodity production. This necessity plus the other requirements of big capital demand growing centralisation. The centralisation of State power is in part a reflection of this law of centralisation inherent in the capitalist path of development. This centralisation however generally proceeds faster than its economic counterpart in underdeveloped, crisis-ridden capitalist economies as is revealed in the experience of most third world countries. India, in spite of its democracy, is no exception to this trend although here it has generally taken place under a constitutional garb. Such a centralised state looks after the interests of the entire ruling classes—a class coalition in which one or the other class plays a leading role by the very logic of the alliance situation. Evidence since the time of the colonial phase of transformation shows that it is the all-India big-bourgeoisie that has historically assumed such a role.

It may so happen at times that the non-big bourgeoisie may be objectively hampered by the operation of the laws of market which favour big bourgeoisie and thus impede the growth of locally placed non-big bourgeois groups. Or, it may also happen, particularly in situation of economic crises, that the state is unable to dole out concessions to the dominant landed interests or it may not be able to do so uniformly in all the states. This is likely to lead to conflicts of interests within the same ruling classes across the regions. In another way, certain in-built tendencies of capitalist development in India have, since independence, increased regional disparities rather than helped overcome them.

Under circumstances like these, the locally placed ruling class groups seek greater powers for themselves through the regional parties in power or in opposition so that these can be used to further their own interests when their interests are perceived as not being best served by the all India ruling class parties. This is one objective ground on which regional movements thrive and seek greater autonomy for the states.

Alternatively, the deepening economic crisis and the mounting mass discontent may so strengthen the left opposition parties in some states that they are in a position to give an electoral rebuff to the manipulations of the ruling classes. When such parties come to power or bid for power in certain states then the necessity of fighting for state autonomy arises out of very different class compulsions. The efforts of the left parties to struggle for democratic economy and democratic polity are obstructed by a centralised state. For the class preferences of the working class and the peasantry to meet with lasting success effective autonomy is a minimum necessary condition. Moreover, for the left this demand is an integral part of the struggle for democracy. This is the other objective ground on which movements for state autonomy have grown.

It follows from the above that the big bourgoisie, being the leading partner in the class alliance which rules India and being in a position to exercise its control and operate through the centre and its decision-making organs, will be extremely reluctant to concede greater powers to the states in any meaningful ways. The centralised state remains a prime necessity for its unhindered growth. It may be better able to meet the demands of the regionally placed ruling class parties by granting greater concessions like more funds, better distribution of budgetary allocations under plan heads, etc. The situation is complicated by the strength of the left parties in certain states where they happen to be in power. The very logic of the class preferences of the working classes and peasantry involve the use of state autonomy for undermining the material basis of power of the ruling classes. The left-democratic concept of state autonomy therefore poses a challenge to the very structure of state power itself where the division of powers between the Centre and the states is directly linked to the question of hegemony of different classes. Here lies another reason for the resistance to the demands for state autonomy.

But in a crisis-ridden situation, monopoly capital may not be in a position to even meet the limited demands of the regionally placed ruling class groups. Moreover, in a situation of stagnation when all sections of capital cannot grow or expand with equal ease the non-big capital is under increasing attack from monopoly capital. The organised pressure for more state protection and privileges for non-big capital may come from parties that are oppositional but function generally within unified-all-India-class-preferences. This demand and the tensions generated by such shifts in the relationship between the Central government and the state movements led by Akali Dal or AIAD-MK/DMK or National Conference can form a complementary objective condition for left-democratic parties.

One can here see how the question of state autonomy is linked to the national question in India. The conditions that facilitate the struggle for democratic economy and democratic polity are also the conditions that help the struggle for the equality of languages and provide the best opportunities for the development of the cultural level of the people. It is this tie which shows that any satisfactory solution of the national question is integrally tied up with the struggle against the dominance of monopoly capital and its allies. The faster the pace of democratisation of the economy and the polity the more rapid would be the development and consolidation of nationalities. The more the struggle for democracy weakens and the pace of democratisation slows down the greater will be the suspicions and bickering between and among different national groups, and more the opportunities for the bourgeoisie to whip up chauvinism and exploit the genuine demands of people for its own reactionary ends.

In the Indian conditions where there are no historic grounds for secession, the demand for the right of self-determination makes no political sense. It can only be a source for the reactionary and imperialist manipulations and of confusion for the people. On the contrary, in such a situation, complete autonomy for all national groups within the Indian Union becomes a prime necessity for democracy—as is centralisation for big bourgeoisie—and to strengthen the grass-root basis of unity. The unsolved communal and tribal problems along with the caste divisions remain major obstacles in cementing the political unity and for democratisation in Indian society. But to grasp these in the context of the national question in India we need to briefly recapitulate the agrarian situation.

The agrarian question, given the particular nature of the capitalist development noted earlier, became and remains the crux of the democratic revolution in India.[50] The persistence of semi-feudal relations of production in agriculture provides the social basis for the continuing hold of pre-capitalist ideologies among the rural population. The dependence of the emergent bougeoisie in India landlordism of a feudal type was the ground for the caste-based development of new classes in rural India. New classes emerged from among the old traditional castes and the class dynamics took the form of inter-caste struggles in rural India. Prakash Karat[51] has surveyed the emergence of this phenomenon with its implications for the national question in different regions of India. Successive efforts at land reforms since the 1950s have done little to wipe out pre-capitalist features from agriculture.[52] This has left open the possibilities of communal and caste-based vertical mobilisation in Indian society. Coupled with the importance of the religious factor in Indian society, conservative social mobilisation has become a constant fact of political life in large parts of India.

These are used as screens to hide the shortcomings or failures of the ruling classes where such slogans provide easily visible targets or scapegoats to divert the anger and exasperation of the people. So long as semi-feudal relations prevail in agriculture they provide, on the one hand, a social basis for such ideologies to thrive on, and on the other, subject the peasant masses to the forces of economic dependence, political compulsions and pressures towards social conformity—ready-made tools for the ruling classes to keep people in bondage. Short of their revolutionary destruction, the only force that can act as a brake upon these modes of political articulation is the ability of left forces to decisively intervene in the situation; but these factors in themselves represent the major obstacle on the growth of popular movement.

On the basis of the above link one can rightly emphasise the dependence of the capitalist classes on semi-feudal agriculture as of decisive political importance. For the bougeoisie there is, first, the undoubted significance of landlords as allies for political hegemony through competitive policies: but even if competitive politics is given up there is no reason to believe that the bourgeoisie can push through with its bourgeois revolution in an authoritarian setting. Evidence from a large number of third world countries also shows that the capitalist classes have found themselves in a position of extremely cautious dealings with the dominant rural groups. Nothing in the situation suggests that India can provide the world with an exception. The capitalist classes have to be so cautious, as Bagchi neatly sums up, 'since by the very nature of their development and their *fear of the peasantry* and the proletariat of their own countries *in the epoch of the socialist revolution,* the capitalist classes of the third world are on the adjust to the demands of the property owning strata in control of sectors characterised by pre-capitalist relations; the resistance of the latter against a rapid rate of transfer of resources to capitalist accumulation aggravates the difficulties of the capitalist classes of the third world'.[53] The importance of this link cannot be underestimated. Growing contradictions between and the eventual split in the alliance of the ruling classes will narrow down the social basis of support of the leading element—bourgeoisie—and thus will weaken its rule. Moreover, since the heightening of contradictions has the potentiality of throwing a section of the erstwhile allies on the side of popular movement the bourgeoisie is forced to accommodate for fear of revolution. Therefore, concretely, the only development that can put a brake on chauvinistic twists that masses are prone to is the growth of left influence which can unleash their strength for democratic struggles and for social emancipation. Such a process having not yet materialised on a national scale a number of other sets of problems connected with the movements of people belonging to religious communities or tribal groups require specific attention. To reiterate the point; it becomes necessary to attend to these groups in the context of the socially and politically divisive consequences of the capitlist development in India and not just because these are distinct religious or tribal groups. Let us take the most important of the communal problem— the Muslim minority—first.

Hindu-Muslim Conflicts

The communal problem in the shape of Hindu-Muslim conflicts has remained as serious today as it was at the time of independence. The presence of large Muslim minorities within different national groups in India, especially the Hindi belt, has further complicated the national problem in India. The Muslim community, unlike other religious groups, has inherited a peculiar store of historical memories and after the Partition is a victim of an equally peculiar amalgam of fears and inhibitions and bravado; over and above these there is a strong sense of community solidarity, historically determined and reinforced both by theology and politics.

It has historically worked as an impediment, as it does now, in the crystallisation of national groups into distinct unities with a clear-cut identity of their own. The most obvious manifestation of this was in the pre-independence period when the Muslim presence in large numbers in different nationalities made it difficult to unify the peasant movements with different national movements and to keep the supra-nationality Indian nationalism united all over northern India including Punjab and Bengal. The landlord dominated communal mobilisations in most of this region grew into parallel movements of the Hindus and Muslims. Among the Muslims they developed separatist aspirations over time as well. What is interesting to note is that in spite of the general backwardness of regions where Muslims constituted an overwhelming majority like in Sind, Baluchistan and North West Frontier Province (NWFP) there was no popular involvement with the demand for Pakistan; in fact, in some parts of these areas the popular leadership of Muslim masses never reconciled to the idea of Pakistan even in 1947. In Bengal and Punjab, even though Muslims constituted a majority with concentrations in somewhat demarcated regions, the communal politics was, for a greater period of time, more in the nature of community oriented demands. It did not become communal separatism as in the United Provinces or Bihar till quite late in the day when it got fused with Muslim League politics and the demand for Pakistan.[54]

It is a well-known historical fact to which reference has been made earlier that modern industry did not grow in Muslim majority areas and that they remained economically backward in spite of favourable factor endowment like in Punjab or Eastern Bengal. Yet, it was precisely in these areas that the movement for self-determination or secession either did not emerge or had weak popular sanction. What took shape as Muslim communalism was, in spite of different specific roots in different regions like Bengal or Punjab, landlord-led Muslim mobilisations (the plural needs emphasis) and only a regionally specific part of it became 'separatist' and that too largely in areas where Muslims constituted minorities, however large. Landlord-led mobilisations were, however, not something unique to Muslims.[55] They were a common feature of Indian politics then and have not become uncommon even now in most regions. What was certainly crucially different with this mobilisation of Muslims in the pre-independence phase was the fact that Muslim landlordism could not be united with the all-India bourgeoisie as the rest of the landlord classes could. It is this that was instrumental, more than anything else, in keeping the Muslim masses away from the all-India movement for independence. This assertion does not invalidate the presence of other contributory factors which reinforced this separate mobilisaton; for example, one can mention their sense of under-representation in the tertiary sector, the ruin of handicraftsmen, the sense of loss of power of the community in northern India, etc. It was only in 1945 or later that the community oriented political formations like Krishak Praja party or Unionist Party moved into the Muslim League. Even so, the demand for Pakistan did not become anything of a national movement; the demand had a weak popular basis in areas like North-West-Frontier-Province, Baluchistan and Sind even as late as the time of independence. So the damand for Pakistan had no basis to be treated as part of even a partial democratic solution of the national question in India.

But in the creation of Pakistan, as distinct from the politics that demanded Pakistan, aspects of nationality in NWFP, Baluchistan and Sind got combined with the communal aspect in Bengal and Punjab and uncompromising separatism of United Provinces, Bihar, etc. This dimension and its intricate expressions in the contemporary politics was unfortunately not clearly analysed by the Marxists and the Communist Party of India.[56] What baffles one is why the Communist Party of India failed to take a more national democratic stand than the Congress, which accepted Pakistan. That this happened in spite of a rich corpus of theory and class and national cues in the seminal writings of Lenin remains intriguing. The then prevailing confusions and misunderstandings and the historical evasion that it involved apart, it raises an important question: why did the demand for Pakistan meet with acceptance, however reluctantly, by the Congress-led movement for Indian independence? The question is important for two reasons. First, the demand was conceded at a time when the Muslim-Hindu divide as expressed in the electoral and constitutional politics of limited franchise and elite manipulations was being contested by the massive displays of unity of Hindu-Muslim masses in popular agitations and at the level of 'barricade' politics. Moreover, there is some evidence to suggest that at the time the Muslim League leadership including Jinnah were losing their grip over the situation.[57] Why then did the 'nationalist' leadership surrender at that time? Secondly, an investigation of this question, however suggestive at this stage, may provide us with interesting clues as to how the ruling classes treat problems of 'national unity' when such unity seems to run counter to their interests. Such clues can help in understanding the limitations of the contemporary role of the ruling classes in India in relation to the long-term secular tendencies among different national groups.

Partial evidence as well as the logic of the situation suggests that it was in the interest of the all-India big bourgeoisie to accept partition of the country. Three sets of circumstances and their possible politcal spin off seem to have been decisive in its acceptance of the demand for Pakistan. Put briefly and a bit schematically, first, researches in history have provided ample evidence by now to show that there was a growing common perception and fear among the Indian bourgeoisie and imperialist-capitalist interests of the growing militancy and potential radicalisation of mass movements in India at that time.[58] There could not have been more clear evidence of this than the naval revolt, the police strike, and the general strike of industrial workers and, more important, the spread of massive peasant movements under the Communist Party's leadership in Telengana, the Tebhaga movement in Bengal, the mass struggles in Travancore-Cóchin, etc, and the mortal fear of the bourgeoisie as well as the imperialists with such developments over which the moderate leadership of the Congress Party had little or no control. Secondly, the generalised atmosphere of violence in urban areas; if this was the forerunner of things to come, then the bourgeoisie, primarily interested in market and profits, was rightly apprehensive and fearful of the loss of market and disruption of trade and commerce. Moreover, it is not unreasonable to assume that a climate of anarchy and violence provides, particularly in colonial situations, a more favourable atmosphere for radical movements to thrive on and expand. These two sets of circumstances were, or could be, the basis of short term fears and were sufficient grounds for the bourgeoisie to panic. Along with these there was also a factor of long-term significance and this is the third set of circumstnces. Here it is difficult to point to any concrete evidence but absence of evidence does not necessarily invalidate an argument; there is also the logic of the situation to go by. In the context of the landlords as the necessary allies of bourgeoisie, for sustained mass support, it seems reasonable to deduce that the Indian bourgeoisie was doubtful of its ability to politiclly unify the Muslim masses under its leadership in the foreseeable future. The above assertion does not seem unreasonable given its failure to win over as allies the Muslim landed gentry and the inescapable fact of landlord-led social and political mobilisation in the Indian politics. If this line of reasoning—that the Indian bourgeoisie was capable of somewhat long term calculations, however vaguely—has any validity, then it is possible to say that it was genuinely apprehensive of exercising its hegemony or domination over state power in independent India; at least, in a stable way.

Here a clarification of sorts is in order: such an interpretation of bourgeois calculations or, rather realisation, can be advanced only on the plausible ground of bourgeoisie's awareness of the powerful hold on the peasant masses whether Muslim or Hindu of the emergent landlord classes within the rural society and hence of their importance for mass support. Moreover, at each stage of qualitative leap in the politics of that time the Muslim constitutional politics was getting more and more estranged from the Congress-led anticolonial strugggle. This had been so all through after the honeymoon of non-co-operation-Khilafat phase, when the premises of unity were communal. Periods of lull were always followed by political developments which widened the gap between the constitutional positions of Muslim leadership and the Indian National Congress. All these sets of circumstances together provided the calculus of immediate fears and long-term prospects to the decision to accept partition as a historic necessity for the class rule — a necessity because other things being equal an undivided India certainly would have provided a larger market and source of raw materials. But, other things being not equal, it was necessary to concede to the demand for Pakistan for the sake of the political hegemony. As an aside, a stable social basis of class rule was necessary if the bourgeoisie's ambitions to become an independent capitalist class were to materialise in independent India. That it did not and could not is an altogether different question into which we need not go here; in any case, the logic of its development has been worked out in impeccable detail by Prabhat Patnaik.[59] To come back to the point, in this limited and qualified sense one can talk of truncated independence as a grand compromise, and not in the sense of sham, as a number of ultra-left groups characterise it. Nevertheless, the compromise is indicative of the inherent limitations of the Indian ruling classes, especially of its leading element, the all-India big bourgeoisie, which force them to compromise with forces that may not be in the long-term national interests. Part of the purpose of going into the story of partition has been precisely to highlight this specific feature of the Indian bourgeoisie which seems to me to be inherent in its character. There is no contrary evidence to suggest that its character has changed since the time of independence. This inherent tendency of the Indian bourgeoisie shows itself repeatedly after independence when it finds an objective complementarity with forces of social reaction to combat people's power. Herein lies a factor of importance that undoubtedly complicates the national question in India even today. As the big bourgeoisie remains the leading class force, thorough democratisation of the national question has to surmount this obstacle.

Therefore, partition and its aftermath did not lead to any lessening of communal tensions and strife. Quite the opposite happened: it left a trail of blood-shed and bitterness with long-term repercussions for Indian politics. Even to-day, more than three decades after independence, the secular tendencies are not strong enough to help overcome the communal virus. Both Muslim and Hindu communalisms and revivalist tendencies in the communities are as strong as ever, with the result that the unification of different national groups on secular lines has not occurred. The nationalities remain divided and fragmented on communal grounds. This is so in all the states of India where there are large Muslim concentrations; the differences across the states in the strength or otherwise of the communal division is dependent upon a variety of factors including the strength of left forces.

The situation while being complex and far from reassuring everywhere may have particularly dangerous possibilities in the Hindi belt, especially in western UP where the concentrations of Muslims are quite large in a con-tiguous area. In a portion of this area the concentration is so large that Muslims constitute more than a 'national minority' in the strict sense of the term. There seem to me to be strong grounds to single out this area. In this region, a clear interlocking of factors, both of a historical nature and contem-porary origin, seem to be taking place. There is first the persistence and heightening of Hindi-Urdu tussle along with growing divergence between the two languages in their vocabulary and literature. All this adds up to a con-siderable difference when scripts are also different. Moreover, the fact of class discrimination against the Urdu language cannot be denied. Urdu has slowly become over time, due to both political and economic reasons, and for all practical purposes, a language only of the Muslims; this notwithstanding pious declarations about its composite character. In practical terms, discrimination against and denial of equal status to Urdu is perceived of as cultural discrimination against Muslims. All this adds up to, subjectively perceived, cultural oppression. Secondly, there is a deep-rooted feeling, bordering on conviction, among Muslims of being discriminated against in jobs and other employment facilities; not groundless in view of the govern-ment circulars that have come to light through disclosures in Parliament in 1977-78 regarding debarring of Muslims from certain jobs. Similar com-plaints have been found to be not untrue about Muslim applicants seeking licences and loans. All this coupled with the fact of historical backwardness of a large part of the community and, perhaps, some downward mobility are perceived as economic oppression. Thirdly, an overwhelming number of han-dicraftsmen in this region are Urdu-speaking Muslims. There is scattered evidence which suggests that over the years there has been a revival of this kind of economic activity due to West Asian trade as well as the interest of foreign tourists in brassware, etc. As a consequence of this increase in trade and commerce, it is conceivable, as preliminary investigations suggest, that a commercial bourgeoisie of sorts has emerged from among the more enterpris-ing elements among Muslims and that this section of the bourgeoisie is getting into greater economic competition with the established traders who happen to be non-Muslims. Given the strength of the communal ties it seems that the Muslim traders have an easier access to the Muslim handicraftsmen and with their links with West Asian trade have grown rather fast in business. If this reading has any basis in fact then it is reasonable to infer that a bourgeois aspiration to grow and prosper has taken root among a section of the well-to-do Muslims. For an emergent bourgeoisie, political unification of the community under its leadership provides a definite means of advancement. All this combines with the fact of the persistence of the hold of Muslim landlords over the Muslim masses. Here is, or can be, a potent combination of an emergent bourgeoisie in alliance with the traditional landed gentry playing up the oppression of Muslim masses to politically unify them under its leadership and using language, culture, economic discrimination and religious susceptibilities to weld the community on a competitive basis for furthering its own material interests. In this region of western UP, given the interlocking of factors—language, community, economy and politics—plus the historical memory of continuous riots since the 1920s, the possibility remains open of Muslims developing nationality type aspirations. To clarify: it is not being suggested that Muslims as such constitute anything that is nationally distinct or a united community which would be a repetition of the unscientific theory of two nations which has been duly buried by the unfolding of history. The argument is only limited to the fact that in certain regions where there is an interlocking of factors, in a given contiguous territory, which have historically been potent in giving a people distinct national awareness of oppression, persecution, and discrimination, such factors have, or can, create incipient tendencies towards nationality formation. Such a tendency obviously cannot operate in all regions, for example, Kerala or West Bengal or Tamil Nadu, where language and cultural distinctions are absent. In these areas it can only lead to communalism or community-oriented politics. But crystallisation towards nationality orientations has a basis in regions like western UP. Further crystallisation towards a separate nationality awareness or its opposite tendency of unification in the larger nationality groups will be dependent upon how persecution-oppression works or is successfully combatted in terms of the openings available for radical emancipation or major changes taking place in the material conditions of the people of this region.

In the larger context of India, the persistence of socio-economic backwardness of Muslim masses, the continuing hold of landed gentry wherever it exists, and the influence of emerging bourgeois elements along with opportunists politically aligned with these forces will keep the communal problem alive. Reinforcement to this is constantly provided by Hindu communalism led by the RSS. What is more dangerous in an immediate way is the inability or half-heartedness of, and deliberate neglect by, the state power to stop and control the riots which represent blatant attacks on the life and livelihood of common people. RSS and other forces of obscurantist militancy do seem to have a hand in riots but what is more ominous is the growing complementarity of interests between the otherwise secular sections of the ruling classes and the obscurantist forces in the persistence of communal (as also caste) riots. The objective complementarity is precisely due to the fact that if riots help the Muslim and Hindu sectarianism to grow they also divide the toiling people on communal lines. Communal divisions hamper the growth of radical possibilities and weaken chances of the people seizing the political initiative. Such divisions do not seem to matter to the so-called secular elements among the ruling classes so long as their political leadership succeeds in aggravating the Muslim and Hindu sectarianism for purposes of political power. In the latest political sociology of riots one can discern an interesting pattern. If one coercive instrumentality of the state power indulges in killings—Moradabad—or if it deliberately neglects it—Bihar Sharif—then another coercive instrumentality of the same state power moves in to check it and bring it under control and reassures the victims of riots. The net result for the ruling classes is the paradox come true: we will have the cake and eat it too. The problem therefore is not just obscurantism and revivalism, but the complicity of the ruling classes as well. The complicity is not merely one of passively allowing the persistence of the socio-economic roots of communalism but also of active compromise, like at the time of partition or now as at the time of riots, with such forces for the sake of its material interests. Over and above everything else, the communal riots in India weaken and put a brake on the long-term secular tendency towards the regional integration of Muslim masses. Instead, they have given rise to, I suspect, a creeping pan-Indian feeling of being Muslim among the masses.[60]

Tribal Movements

Such processes of separate crystallisation, incipient and halting in the case of Muslims, may have a stronger basis in the tribal belts today. In these areas, territorial contiguity of people and their cultural dissimilarity and linguistic differentiations get combined with a distinctive impact of modern capitalist forces. Due to this, the tribal belts today represent a much more direct aspect of the national question.

Some of the tribals in India have had a more definite and historically determined mode of existence than Muslims in general. They have also benefited much less as a consequence of British rule and the subsequent development of capitalism. After early rebellions, British administration took some care to treat them as protected areas and they were allowed to maintain separate institutions and laws nearer to their own traditions and ethos and yet their politics were greatly disrupted. In spite of the protective laws, the tribes could not be kept immune both from the impact of the developments of market forces and money commodity relations and the inroads of British administration and modern communications. The impact was the subjugation of tribal people and the incorporation of the tribal economies into the market forces. This has continued ever since then giving rise to new social forces in tribal society. Three major influences have been noted: first, the breakdown of the communal mode of production; secondly, limited development of commodity production especially through forest products like lac, timber, etc.; and thirdly, the entry of merchants and moneylenders and the consequent intensification of exploitation.[61] Land grabbing by the process of alienation through money-lending went hand in hand throughout the period and continues now. With the 'restricted transfer of land from tribals to non-tribals' and between the tribals themselves like the chiefs and the upper stratum there 'grew up a rich stratum' within the tribal society.[62] Hardly any section of the tribals except some few at the top gained anything out of this development. Even in tribal regions rich in natural resources, like the Jharkhand region, where considerable industrialisation has occurred, tribals have hardly been the beneficiaries; they failed even to gain entry into the working class except as low-paid unskilled workers.[63] In fact, there is evidence of continuous pauperisation without even the marginal effects at lower levels of entry into the working classes etc. as in other non-tribals regions where modern industry grew. It is a fact that in new industries, including the ones in the public sector, the proportion of blue and white collar workers has increased in relation to the unskilled categories. This means that employment prospects are bleaker among the less educated social groups including tribals. The cumulative effect of all these developments has been a complete disruption of tribal life and a deep-rooted suspicion of outsiders and the modern networks. Unlike in other regions, the absence of even a numerous indigenous middle class—the spokesmen and beneficiaries of capitalism—has worked as an impediment for the growth of a sustained democratic movement and for the slow integration of these areas with the rest of the society. It is only in the case of 'tribals' both in the bordering regions as well as in the interior of the country that one discerns all the distinguishing features of an oppressed nationality without there being any oppressor nationality: national oppression exists here irrespective of the fact whether, definitionally, they are ethnic communities or nationalities.

Relative isolation, intense exploitation and a sense of deliberate neglect and discrimination coupled with a different mode of existence has put in motion a tendency towards the crystallisation of feeling, among them, of groups with distinct national compositions. Rise of tribal movements among these people have helped them to come closer and many sub-tribes are in the process of assimilation into distinct overarching tribal identities. Evidence from Jharkhand seems to point to such a process. Attempts are also being made to develop a distinct language or languages. Through a different configuration of circumstances and historical events a similar process has been occurring among tribes of North-Eastern India and the political content of this struggle, as well as its handling by state power in India, has generated, to borrow a term, a 'parallel nationalism' among some of these tribal groups.[64]

Capitalism, in alliance with rural vested interests, is bound to intensity exploitation and along with it the sense of persecution and oppression. Situations of this sort provide an opportunity to the newly arisen groups with bourgeois aspirations or the educated strata manifesting a variety of outlooks from among the indigenous groups of these ethnic communities to unite the people under their leadership to wrest concessions. The bourgeoisie, or bourgeois elements from among the emergent groups with their allies, either capture the culture movements of the people or build them up by involving the people, and divert them into directions which pits them against people of another nationality. By such tactics the sense of oppression among the people is heightened but the source of oppression remains disguised. Nevertheless an objective basis for the consolidation of people as different from others is created. Oppression, and the sense of it, welds people together and separates them from others. A moribund capitalism accentuates differences and is incapable of amalgamating differences in a natural process. Such was the case in the period of progressive capitalism in Europe. This process of amalgamation of pre-existing groups with national features into larger nations led Engels to refer to them as non-historic or non-viable nations. Engels was referring to a tendency of the expansive capitalism that was breaking down national barriers represented by small national groups, some of which were being assimilated through a natural process into the great, and what became the viable, European nations.

Today, because of the retarded and politically divisive nature of capitalism in third world countries, a similar process cannot operate on its own force, unless and until left forces as agents of history can decisively intervene. On the contrary, the tendency would be for these groups referred to by Engels as non-historic to crystallise into separate distinct national groups and to demand separation from the original national groups within which they have lived an unstable existence. The tendency in areas where tribal concentrations exist in contiguous regions will be one of separate crystallisation of these hitherto ethnic groups. So long as left movement is weak in these areas the tendency also may be one of chauvinistic articulations; and as Lenin so clearly foresaw, 'opportunism in the national question will of course find expression among oppressed nations otherwise than among oppressor nations'.[65] But chauvinism in itself cannot be a ground to deny the 'historical legitimacy' of these movements even when one has to politically combat them. It only provides grounds to oppose those movements and the ground may be as sound as the one when the left opposes mass movements with fascist trapping. It is also important here not to get caught in questions of whether the people behind these movements are already crystallised into distinct national groups or not in terms of the rigid criteria of what constitutes nations-nationalities but it will be useful politically to treat them as part of what constitutes the unsolved problem of nationality formation. Such a position may have its pitfalls too. It is never easy to know beforehand all the possible relations between the struggles of toiling masses and the forms that the national urges of such people take, caught as they are in the whirlpools of capitalist upheaval. It is only in the sphere of political activity that one can hope to get clues to overcome such difficulties.

Conclusions

To conclude: this paper has been more in the nature of an exploratory exercise, both methodologically and in terms of substantive issues. A number of questions have not been touched at all; certain other issues have been dealt with very briefly and in a somewhat tentative manner, notably the communal and tribal questions where considerable empirical work as well as problem clarification is badly needed. What I have attempted to do is to see: (1) Why is the national question, at all, relevant today? and (2) How should one approach it?

As far as the first question is concerned, the foregoing analysis has pointed to certain historical forces which lead to two inescapable conclusions. First, a self-perpetuating regional unevenness both before and after independence, identified with state boundaries provides a major cue to the more manifest national problems in India. By an extension of this logic, even within a state, when this unevenness coincides with a series of contiguous districts made up of distinct population compositions or with historically distinct regions it complicates the problem by giving rise to separatist aspirations or nationality claims. Here, in these backward regions, where the Bengal-Maharashtra pattern of development has not been gone through, it can be a people's upsurge for identity — possibly national identity. The diverse manifestations are caused by diverse sets of factors, inter-relations and respective salience varying regionally. Nevertheless, the key question is: how does one unify these with a number of heterogenous democratic movements which are pan-Indian in character? To come to the second point, it is important to look at it through capitalist transformations in third world countries in this era of imperialism. Capitalism has become not only a moribund force all over, but in the third world its growth and expansion have also been marked by retardation and distortions. All this has radically altered the social and political implications of capitalist transformation. It has resulted in a perpetuation and aggravation of pre-existing social divisions along with the creation of new ones. By the fact of these, capitalism does not any longer unify and amalgamate people but divides them and generates separatist tendencies and aspirations. Concrete manifestations of this display a confusing variety and complexity of forms making analysis a really challenging task.

But all this is taking place in a situation relatively free of national domination or identifiable oppressor nations. Moreover, imperialism in crisis, to maintain or strengthen its stranglehold over the third world, tries to weaken and divide modern states and use them for reactionary ends. The divisive tendencies within the multi-national states today are in general not progressive. Without however renouncing self-determination in principle but treating it merely as contingent, the basic task today should be to unify and strengthen the unity of diverse national and ethnic groups *vis-a-vis* imperialism and internal reactionary manipulations. The principle of autonomy for various nationality groups and decentralisation and devolution within autonomous units provides the basis to wage struggle to build and reinforce unity.

As far as the question concerning the approach is concerned the nature of capitalist transformation seems to me to be the most important theoretical dimension for situating any discussion of this problem in historical perspective. Its importance is considerable and its neglect may lead to serious problems of identification and specification. This is what makes it theoretical. The nature of capitalist incorporation and the subsequent content of developments in what has now become the third world has led to a situation where social forms have emerged before the maturity of the elements that constitute a social reality. Immaturity of elements — one or more — that constitute a social reality, for example a nation, can become the cause of controversies about the identification and naming of that reality *qua* reality. Concretely, in our case, on the continuum of national crystallisation, the language or culture or economic development or whatever else may not reach maturation before a people insist upon or force recognition as a nationality; other contingent factors being in favourable combination. To elucidate: the use of the term 'retarded capitalism' points to an organic analogy, but only as an analogy. As in a living body, so here too, retarded growth *ipso facto* implies underdevelopment or absence of maturation of certain organs and/or elements of a system. This should mean, in other words, that in many cases today all that came to characterise a nation may not reach maturity or be present in their fullness. But, by the fact of this, any analytical refusal to recognise them as such will be a case of gross historical error. Theoretically, the question has to be asked: When social conditions corresponding to a determinate level of production have originated but do not seem to be moving towards completion or consummation, what is the nature of social reality which confronts us and how do we conceptualise it? This has led to considerable debate and discussion on the agrarian and peasant questions but the national question has suffered a near total neglect on this theoretical plane.

Within such a situation, variations in the indeterminacy of factors between regions or nations may be wide but variability (range of variations) is determinable. Therefore, even though identification as well as generalisations of empirical patterns may pose problems, broad theoretical formulations may yet be possible. But the theoretical formulations cannot be deduced from or predicated upon previously set meanings of terms or categories, nor upon received, and somewhat ossified, ways of viewing reality. It seems to me imperative to confront afresh the social world of nations, nationalities and national crystallisation in all the variations of their attributes in terms of the dialectical presuppositions of the Marxist method and the class and national cues available in the writings of Lenin. Within the range of my readings, I feel convinced that the writings of Lenin on this problem remain seminal.

NOTES

[1] A detailed study of the patterns of growth and consolidation of national states in Europe is available in Charles Tilly (ed.), *The Formation of National States in Europe*, Princeton, 1975.

[2] The implication and theoretical position of the point being argued here is different from that of Tom Narain, 'The Modern Janus', *New Left Review*, 94, 1975. See also his 'Scotland and Europe', *New Left Review*, 83 and 84, 1973.

[3] E. M. S. Namboodiripad, *The National Question in Kerala*, PPH, Bombay, 1952.

[4] Irfan Habib, 'Emergence of Nationalities', *Social Scientist*, 37, August 1975

[4a] Partha Chatterjee, 'Bengal: Rise and Growth of a Nationality', *Social Scientist*, 37, August 1975.

[5] Lenin, 'Critical Remarks on the National Question', all references to Lenin and Stalin are from *Selections from V. I. Lenin and J. V. Stalin on National Colonial Question*, Calcutta Book House, Calcutta, 1970, p. 9. Henceforth *Selections*.

[6] Ibid., p. 15, emphasis added.

[7] Lenin, 'The Right of Nations to Self-Determinations', *Selections*, p. 19.

[8] Ibid., emphasis added.

[9] Ibid.

[10] For a comprehensive account of the debate at that time see Michael Lowy, 'Marxists and the National Question', *New Left Review*, 96, 1976.

[11] Habib, 'Emergence of Nationalities', op. cit., pp. 14-20.

[12] Ibid., p. 16.

[13] Ibid., emphasis added.

[14] Ibid., p. 18.

[15] Namboodiripad, op. cit., p. 59.

[16] Ibid., p. 59, emphasis added.

[17] Ibid.

[18] The literature on the problem is considerable; both for and against. R. P. Dutt, *India Today*, 1947, presents the view that India was well on the way towards a capitalist revolution. The opposite view is best represented in Irfan Habib, 'Potentialities of Capitalist Development in the Economy of Moghul India', *Enquiry* (New Series), Volume VIII, No. 3.

[19] Preface to *Capital*, Vol. I.

[20] Ibid., emphasis added.

[21] Lenin, 'The Discussion on Self-Determination Summed Up', *Selections*, p. 45, emphasis added.

[22] For an incisive analysis of the ways in which Marx uses his term and concept in the course of building his arguments, see the brilliant work by Bertell Ollman, *Alienation: Marx's Concept of Man in Capitalist Society*, Cambridge, 1971, esp. Part I.

[23] Partha Chatterjee, 'Bengal: Rise and Growth of a Nationality', *Socialist Scientist*, August 1975.

[24] Ibid., p. 68.

[25] Ibid., note 3.

[26] Stalin, 'Marxism and the National Question', *Selections*, p. 69.

[27] Ibid., p. 70.

[28] Ibid., p. 73, emphasis added.

[29] Stalin, 'Theses on the Immediate Tasks of the Party in Connection with the National Problems', *Selections*, p. 124, emphasis added.

[30] Lenin, 'Right of Nations to Self-Determination', *Selections*, p. 14, emphasis added.

[31] Lenin, 'Critical Remarks on the National Question', *Selections*, p. 6 (emphasis added). The second tendency that Lenin talks of has to do with 'the development and growing frequency of international intercourse in every form, the breakdown of national barriers, the creation of the international unity of capital, of economic life in general, of politics, science etc.'

[32] The debate on the possibilities of development of capitalism in India has gone on. Without going into details, my position, tentatively, is to go along with Irfan Habib. See 'Potentialities of Capitalist Development in the Economy of Mughal India', *Enquiry* (New Series), Vol. III, No. 3.

[33] For a discussion on this see Irfan Habib, 'Colonisation of the Indian Economy, 1757-1900', *Social Scientist*, March 1975, pp. 23-53.

[34] Amiya Kumar Bagchi, *Private Investment in India, 1900-1939*, Cambridge, 1972, pp. 3-24; also p. 424.

[35] A. I. Levkovsky, *Capitalism in India: Basic Trends in its Development*, PPH, Bombay, 1966, p. 45.

[36] Irfan Habib, *Colonisation of Indian Economy, 1757-1900*, pp. 42-44.

[37] V. Pavlov, 'India's Socio-Economic Structure from the 18th to Mid-20th Century', in V. Pavlov, V. Rastyannikov and G. Shironov, *India: Social and Economic Development*, Progress Publications, Moscow, 1975.

[38] Amiya Kumar Bagchi, 'Reflections on Patterns of Regional Growth in India During the Period of British Rule', *Occasional Paper No. 5*, Centre for Studies in Social Sciences, Calcutta, 1976, published in *Bengal Past and Present*, Vol. XCV, Part 1, No. 180, January-June 1976, pp. 28-33. See also his 'De-industrialisation in India in the Nineteenth Century: Some Theoretical Implications', *Journal of Development Studies*, Vol. 12, No. 2, 1976.

[38a] Sukomal Sen, *Working Class of India: History of Emergence and Movement 1830-1970*, Bagchi, Calcutta, 1977.

[39] Bagchi, 'Reflections on the Pattern of Regional Growth in India During the Period of British Rule', op. cit., p. 51. For details see section V of this paper.

[40] Bagchi, 'Private Investment in India', op. cit., pp. 433-37.

[41] Shirokov, 'Industrialisation and the Changing Pattern of India's Social and Economic System', in *India: Social and Economic Development*, op. cit.

[42] Bagchi, 'Reflections on the Pattern of Regional Growth in India During the Period of British Rule', op. cit., p. 51.

[43] Ajit Roy, 'Some Aspects of the National Question in India', *Marxist Review*, October 1967.

44 Communist Party of India (Marxist), 'Note on the National Question', Adopted by the 9th Congress, Madurai, 1972. It states: 'There is no compelling reason why it should be obligatory to insert this slogan in our programme, and that, too, when we cannot postulate the division of Indian nationalities into what are called oppressor and oppressed, and when the big bourgeois landlord Government on the one hand and several chauvinist and jingoist groups in different nationalities on the other are endangering working class unity by fostering separatist and disruptive forces, thus pushing into the forefront of the proletarian party the foremost task of fighting against these trends.'

45 Barun De, 'Complexities in the Relationships between Nationalism, Capitalism and Colonialism', in Debiprasad Chattopadhyaya (ed.), *History and Society: Essays in Honour of Professor Niharranjan Ray*, Bagchi, Calcutta, 1976, pp. 479-512; see esp. pp. 496-500.

46 Niharranjan Ray, *Nationalism in India*, Aligarh, 1973, p. 10.

47 Barun De, 'Complexities in the Relationships between Nationalism, Capitalism and Colonialism', op. cit., p. 499, emphasis added.

48 Lenin, 'Right of Nations to Self-Determination', *Selections*, p. 14, emphasis added.

49 Lenin, 'The Social Revolution and the Right of Nation', *Selections*, p. 29.

50 Among others, see Prakash Karat, 'Theoretical Aspects of National Question', *Social Scientist*, April 1977.

51 Prakash Karat, *Language and Nationality Politics in India*, Orient Longman, New Delhi, 1973.

52 See among many others Charles Bettleheim, *India Independent*, London, 1968, Ch. II and VIII; see also E. M. S. Namboodiripad, *The Economics and Politics of the Socialist Pattern in India* for an analysis of the political forces and calculation behind and the economic and social consequence of land reforms in India. P. C. Joshi's *Land Reforms in India* (Allied, Delhi, 1975) contains a detailed survey of literature and has a comprehensive bibliography.

53 A. K. Bagchi, 'Relation of Agriculture to Industry in the Context of South Asia', *Frontier*, Vol. VIII, Nos. 22-24 (October 4 - October 18, 1975), p. 13, emphasis added.

54 In the case of Bengal, Partha Chatterjee shows how the turns and twists at the level of constitutional politics were related to the specific nature of demands of Muslim peasantry. See his 'Bengal Politics and the Muslim Masses, 1920-1947', *Journal of Commonwealth and Comparative Politics*.

55 On this point see, among others, Peter Hardy, *The Muslims of British India*, Cambridge, 1972, esp. Ch. 9.

56 See G. Adhikari, *Pakistan and National Unity*, PPH, Bombay, 1944; or P. Sundarayya, *Vishal Andhra*, PPH, Bombay, 1946, where he bluntly asked the Congressmen as to why refuse to accept the demand of Muslims in Baluchistan, Punjab, Sind and Bengal when they could accept the demand of the Andhra nation. It is interesting that Bengal and Punjab on the one hand and Baluchistan and Sind on the other are clubbed together.

57 See Peter Hardy, *The Muslims of British India*, op. cit., pp. 251-52.

58 See, in this connection, Sumit Sarkar, 'Popular Movements, National Leadership and the Coming of Freedom with Partition 1945-1947' (mimeographed); Paper submitted at a Seminar on Aspects of the Economy, Society and Politics in Modern India, 1900-1950, December 1980. Nehru Memorial Museum and Library, New Delhi.

59 Prabhat Patnaik, 'Imperialism and Growth of Indian Capitalism', in Burt Sutcliff

and Roger Owen (eds.), *Studies in the Theory of Imperialism*, Longman, London, 1972. Also published in Robin Blackburn (ed.), *Explosion in the Sub-Continent*, Pelican, 1975, and in Matthew Kurien (ed.), *India: State and Society: A Marxian Approach*, 1975.

60 The position adopted here is different from that of Irfan Habib, 'Problems of the Muslim Minority in India', *Social Scientist*, June 1976, as well as in Suneet Chopra's rejoinder to him under the same title in *Social Scientist*, September 1976. Habib assumes that, given a variety of factors, historical as well as contemporaneous, and the fact of converse 'psychological make-up', they already constitute a pan-Indian community. In contrast to this Suneet Chopra, while rightly, perhaps, questioning a sense of such a community, feels that given the heterogeneity of factors — cultural, linguistic, etc. — such a sense of community cannot emerge. Such a view ignores the crucial role of politics, particularly the sociology of riots, in generating such tendencies among Muslims which go to negate the long-term secular tendency towards regionalisation.

61 See K. S. Singh, 'Colonial Transformation of Tribal Society in Middle India', *EPW*, July 29, 1978.

62 Ibid., pp. 1227-28.

63 See Nirmal Sengupta, 'Class and Tribe in Jharkhand', *EPW*, April 5, 1980, pp. 664-71.

64 See Shibani Kinkar Chaube, Sunil Munsi and Amalendu Guha, 'Regional Development and the National Question in Northeast India', *Social Scientist*, August 1975, pp. 40-66. See also Udayon Misra, 'The Naga National Question', *EPW*, April 8, 1978, pp. 618-24.

65 Lenin, 'Right of Nations to Self-Determination', *Selections*, p. 20.

ETHNO-NATIONALISM

K. R. Bombwall

Ours is, and has been for over two centuries, a world of nation-States. As a form of territorial-political organisation, the nation-State emerged at a particular stage in history and as a result of a set of socio-economic developments. Nevertheless, there has been a persistent tendency to view the nation-State independently of the historical and socio-economic pre-conditions of its genesis and to treat it not only as the highest but also as the ultimate structure in which large human aggregates, most of them diverse and heterogeneous in their ethnic configurations, live and to which they do or must render willing and terminal, if not undivided, allegiance. The viability and near eternality of the nation State have come to be accepted almost as givens of the human situation.[1]

All the same, recent decades have been a witness as much to the crisis as to the triumph of the nation-State which is currently facing a two-fold challenge. The challenge, both to the conceptual precision and the functional viability of the nation-State has arisen at two levels. On the one hand, the challenge comes from the appearance and relative success and durability of supra nation-State organisations such as the EEC, the COMECON, the NATO and the Warsaw Pact which, in varying degrees, are offering to the citizens of the nation-State alternative foci of loyalty and identification and alternative channels and instrumentalities for the articulation and fulfilment of some of their material and psychological urges and needs.

Internally, and more potently, the challenge to the nation-State comes from numerically significant ethnic groups which have retained, or have developed or are in the process of developing self-awareness and which demand formal recognition of their distinct identities. These demands range all the way from legal and institutional safeguards against discrimination through cultural autonomy for identity preservation, increasing federalisation of the State structure and decentralisation of political power to separate homelands.

Ethno-nationalism is found in two varieties: one, the 'national' self awareness of ethnic groups concentrated in compact geographical areas and, two, territorially scattered ethnic minorities which nevertheless, claim to possess a 'national' identity.[2] The Sikhs in the Punjab, the tribals of Jharkand living in geographically contiguous areas currently divided among four States of the Indian Union and the Assamese, presently engaged in an 'anti-foreigner' campaign, are examples of the first type of ethno-nationalism. It is this form of ethno-nationalism that led to the linguistic reorganisation of Indian States in 1956 and subsequent years. The second variety of ethno-

Courtesy: Punjab Journal of Politics, *July-December 1983,* and *Seminar,* February, 1984.

181

nationalism is exemplified by a religio-linguistic minority like the Indian Muslims which is dispersed throughout the country, and, therefore, cannot claim any compact territory as its 'home'.[3]

It is the challenge posed by the first of these two categories of ethno-nationalism that forms the focus of the present paper which attempts a discussion of the nature of this challenge and the problem of poltical management it poses for scholars and statesmen in multi-ethnic States like India. The discussion is conducted around a brief and necessarily tentative analysis of the emergence, growth and consolidation of identity-consciousness in a major ethnic aggregate in India, viz. the Sikhs, and the demand for a self-determined political status for Sikhs articulated by the Shiromani Akali Dal which has officially adopted the position that Sikhs are a nation.[4]

It is the central argument of this paper that the conceptual ambivalence and programmatic ambiguities that characterise the ongoing nation-building[5] endeavour in India arise largely from the failure, at the scholarly as well as elite levels, to grasp two important realities: one, that some of India's ethnic groups, particularly those concentrated in compact territories, are nations or possess the potential of growing into nations, and two, that nation-building in this country is essentially a problem of the political integration of a multi-ethnic and multi-national State.[6]

It is not without significance that even eminent Indian social scientists have had some difficulty in coming to grips with the full implications of ethno-nationalism in India. The difficulty is reflected in the effort to coin the concept of 'sub-nationalism' for what we have called ethno-nationalism and, then, to be in some doubt as to whether the phenomenon of sub-nationalism is to be accepted as a fact of life with which one must learn to live or whether it is to be treated as a nuisance to be converted. This kind of intellectual dilemma can be seen in two mutuallly incompatible formulations which M.N. Srinivas offers in his booklet, *Nation-Building in Independent India.* In one of these formulations, Srinivas avers, 'those who deplore various forms of sub-nationalism such as ethnicity, communalism, linguistic consciousness and regionalism are unaware that they are all part of the package of nationalism itself when it hits a developing country and the danger that sub-nationalism may overwhelm nationalism is an ever present one.[7]

A little earlier in the same booklet, Srinivas advocates the formation of smaller States and maintains that, among other benefits, this 'would also counter the powerful sub-nationalism of linguistic States and cease to pose a threat to the integrity of the Union'.[8] Now, to recognise sub-nationalism in all its forms as 'part of the package of nationalism itself' and then to project it as 'a threat to the integrity of the Union', a threat which has to be countered and eliminated is a feat of intellectual tight-rope walking if not an exercise in academic double-think, albeit unwitting. In fact, the very use of the term sub-nationalism reflects an effort to accord a lower order of legitimacy to the nationalism of ethnic groups whose members are conscious of and emotionally attached to an identity distinct from and independent of the pan-Indian identity which, to most scholars and, more so, to most politicians, is *the* nationalism and to which all varieties of sub-nationalism must be subordinated if they cannot be made to merge and dissolve themselves in it.

II

The unwillingness or inability, or both, to come to terms with ethnonationalism are rooted in two main causes: one, a tendency to forget or ignore an empirical reality and, two, the influence of the functionalist model presented by theorists of nation-building; Karl W. Deutsch being the best known representative of this school. The empirical reality which is often forgotten or ignored is that very few existing nation-States are ethnically homogeneous and mono-national.

Writing in 1972, Walker Connor noted that[9] 'of a total of 132 contemporary States, only 12 (9.1 percent) can be described as essentially homogeneous from an ethnic viewpoint. An additional 25 States (18.9 percent of the sample) contain an ethnic group accounting for more than 90 percent of the State's total population, and in still another 25 States the largest element accounts for between 75 and 89 percent of the population. But, in 31 States (23.5 percent of the total), the largest ethnic element represents only 50 to 74 percent of the population and in 39 cases (29.5 percent of all States) the largest group fails to account for even half of the State's population. Moreover, this portrait of ethnic diversity becomes more vivid when the number of distinct ethnic groups within States is considered. In some instances, the number of groups within a State runs into the hundreds, and in 53 States (40.2 percent of the total), the population is divided into more than *five* significant groups.'

Connor correctly concludes that 'the problem of ethnic diversity is far too ubiquitous to be ignored by the serious scholar of 'nation-building' unless he subscribes to the view that ethnic diversity is not a matter of serious concern.'[10]

The fact is that, in varying degrees, ethnic diversity and the associated phenomenon of ethno-nationalism characterise most contemporary nation-States irrespective of whether they are western or non-western, developed or developing, liberal democratic or authoritarian, capitalist or communist. Canada and Belgium are developed western States and both are facing serious difficulties in accommodating the conflicting demands of major ethnic groups within their existing political structure. France and Italy have long been regarded as homogeneous but have, in recent years, been obliged to adopt measures of regional decentralisation to meet the urges of alienated or dissident ethnic groups: Bretons and Corsicans in France and Sicilians and South Tyreleans in Italy. Non-western developing countries, both democratic and authoritarian, which are facing problems related to ethno-nationalism include

Ethiopia, Nigeria, Burma, Malaysia, Thailand, Sri Lanka, Pakistan and India.

On the other side of the ideological divide, we have Yugoslavia and the USSR which have frankly accepted the fact of being multi-ethnic and multinational and have made appropriate institutional and policy responses to this fact. The success achieved by the USSR in graduating from a 'prison of nations', as the country was under the Czars, to a 'fraternity of nations' organised in a federal structure founded on the principle of self-determination for the nationality-based constituent union republics, is often held out as a model for many similarly placed developing countries including India.[11]

Perhaps the most telling example is that of Great Britain which is confronted with the problem of Scottish and Welsh national movements despite the fact that Scotland and Wales have been integral parts of a unitary British State for centuries and the Scottish and Welsh people have been subjected to systematic and intensive acculturation and assimilation for many generations. This has compelled several writers to recognise the empirical reality of Great Britain being a multinational State instead of a homogeneous mononational one as it has all along been categorised.[12]

The second reason for academic and elite ambivalence in discussing and dealing with the phenomenon of ethno-nationalism may be traced to the influence of what we have earlier described as the functionalist or diffusionist model of national-building. Karl W. Deutsch, whose influence has been most pervasive in this area, has from time to time changed the direction and emphasis of his theorising. Two points, however, stand out rather clearly in his model. First, he distinguishes nation-building from national growth and treats the former as a species of social engineering. Thus, he writes,

> 'Nation-building, by contrast, suggests an architectural or mechanical model. As a house can be built from timber, bricks and mortar, in different patterns, quickly or slowly, through different sequences of assembly, in partial independence from its settings, and according to the choice, will and power of its builders, so a nation can be built according to different plans, from various materials, rapidly or gradually, by different sequences or steps, in partial independence of its environment.'[13]

Secondly, answering his own question: 'how and when do nations break away from larger political units, and how do they triumph over smaller units, such as tribes, castes or local States, and more or less integrate them into the political body of the nation.'[14] Deutsch hypothesizes that cultural differences between the core and peripheral groups of a nation-State are gradually dissolved under the impact of industrialisation, mass communication, personal mobility and the increasing activities of the national governments.

Plenty of empirical evidence is, however, available in modern as well as modernising countries to show that Deutsch's portrait of 'plasticity and change' is overdrawn. While it would be wrong to advance a pessimistic counter-hypothesis that modernization necessarily accentuates ethnic dissonance in multi-ethnic States and, thus, to posit an 'iron law of disintegration', Walker Connor is correct in pointing out that 'if the processes that comprise modernization led to a lessening of ethnic consciousness in favour of identification with the State, then the number of States troubled by ethnic disharmony would be on the decrease. To the contrary, ethnic consciousness is definitely in the ascendancy as a political force. . . . Multi-ethnic States at all levels of modernization have been afflicted.'[16] It is the persistence and durability of ethnicity and the resurgence of ethnic consciousness in recent years that has caused even the US, popularly projected as the world's most successful 'melting pot', to move towards a formal recognition of the separate identities of racial groups.

Nathan Glazer, who is concerned at this shift in official policy, nevertheless agrees that 'developed and developing countries alike have been struggling with problems of old ethnic groups, demanding conditions in which their cultures would be preserved and assisted and their people would advance economically and their homelands would be granted a degree of autonomy from central governments.'[17] The demand of the Tamils of Sri Lanka for a separate *eelam*, the Basques' demand for autonomy in Spain, the demand raised by the French-speaking Swiss of Berne for political separation from their German-speaking compatriots, the recalcitrance of Kurds and Arabs in Iran and the sharp and escalating discord between Wallens and Flems in Belgium are only a few of the cases that go to prove the virtual indestructibility of ethnic identities.

III

Where do the Sikhs of the Punjab fit into the analytical framework developed in the preceding paragraphs? There has been a great deal of loose and often motivated talk of Sikhs being a nation. But despite the heat and dust raised by the violent activities and a small group of extremists calling for the establishment of a sovereign *'Khalistan'*, the issue has not received adequate academic attention. This is surprising because from Cunningham's famous *History of the Sikhs* written in the early years of the present century to the resolutions passed by the Shiromani Akali Dal and the SGPC in 1981, the idea of Sikh nationhood has been frequently projected from different perspectives. A prominent theme in Cunningham's book is the growth of the Sikhs from 'a sect to a people' under Guru Gobind Singh and 'from a people to a nation' under Maharaja Ranjit Singh.[18] In a more recent work, Khushwant Singh has also viewed the heroic Sikh resistance to the British and in particular, the second Anglo-Sikh War of 1848, as a 'national war of Independence.'[19]

The Akali Dal's Sikhs-are-a-nation thesis is, therefore, new only in the sense that it has become a rallying cry for the achievement of an objective to which the party has been committed for almost four decades, *viz.* the attainment of a self-determined political status for Sikhs. Before we subject the Akali Dal's claim and the implications of a self-determined political status for Sikhs to a brief analysis, it would be appropriate to refer to Paul R. Brass's path-breaking study, *Language, Religion and Politics in North India*[20], in which he has put forth an interesting theory to explain how an ethnic group develops into a nation or nationality.[21]

The process whereby Sikhs achieved self-awareness as a distinct ethnic group and differentiation from Hindus, began in the penultimate decade of the nineteenth century. Until then, Sikhs were, more often than not, treated as one of the many components of the conglomerate Hindu society. Despite the objective marks of differentiation which the Sikhs possessed, the social and psychological distance between them and the Hindus was minimal. Inter-marriages were quite common. Most Hindus showed as much deference to the Sikh Gurus and the *Adi Granth* as the Sikhs themselves and they could be found in substantial numbers in Sikh religious congregations. Reciprocally, many Sikhs made pilgrimages to Hindu shrines. A common personal law and shared social customs and mores limited differentiation largely to external religious symbols. Brass refers to the confusion caused to British census authorities in the nineteenth century when many Hindus declared themselves 'Hindu Sikhs' and several Sikhs wanted to be recorded as 'Sikh Hindus'.[22]

It was the growing fear that Sikhs might be absorbed into the Hindu social system and thus lose their distinct communal identity that prompted the Sikh elite to conduct an institutionalised campaign for the assertion of a separate Sikh identity. The campaign was spear-headed by the Singh Sabha Movement and the Chief Khalsa Diwan to promote social mobilisation of the Sikhs, strengthen internal communication and define clear boundaries between the two communities. Although an acrimonious pamphlet war betwewn Arya Samaj activists and Sikh leaders, on the question whether Sikhs were Hindus, continued right into the second decade of the present century, it is clear, as Kenneth Jones has held, that, 'by 1900, the Sikhs were less and less willing to class themselves automatically with the Hindu community.'[23]

The progress of social differentiation received a boost when the British conceded separate electorates to the community in 1921. It received further sustenance from the Gurdwara Reform Movement and the emergence of the Shiromani Akali Dal and the SGPC as the political and religious custodians respectively, of the Panth. The process was aided also by the opposition of Hindu chauvinists to the Punjabi Suba movement and the deliberate language shift manipulated by Arya Samaj and Jana Sangh propaganda persuading large numbers of Punjabi Hindus to repudiate their mother tongue during the censuses of 1961 and 1971 thereby handing over to the Akali Dal the guardianship not only of the Panth but also the Punjabi language and its Gurmukhi script. That added to the separatist armoury a new symbol, that of language, besides an already powerful set of religious symbols.

That Hindu chauvinism has learnt no lesson from recent history may be seen in the continued insistence of the Rashtriya Swayam Sewak Sangh that 'history bears testimony that the Sikh creed was founded for the protection of Hindu society, its dharma and Sanskrit[24] and the inclusion of Sikhs, along with Jains and Buddhists, in its definiton of Hindu'. This stance of Hindu 'reaction' helps merely to reinforce the fear of Sikh orthodoxy of being sucked back into the Hindu fold. The inevitable result is increased emphasis on a separate Sikh identity.

There is no problem in going along with Brass in his analysis of the development of Sikhs as an ethnic group, from a religous sect to an objectively differentiated and subjectively self-aware community possessing a set of symbols and myths as also heritage to which its members are attached and around which a distinct identity has taken shape. To salvage and preserve this identity is a concern shared by most Sikhs.[25] In fact, the recent demand articulated by some Akali leaders that laws like the Hindu Marriage Act and the Hindu Succession Act should not apply to the Sikhs is to be seen as part of a continuing process of the consolidation of a separate Sikh identity.[26] It is when Brass proceeds to say that 'during the past century, the Sikhs of the Punjab have developed from a distinctive religious sect to a subjectively conscious nationality'[27] that some difficulties arise. And, these difficulties are not merely semantic but substantive.

For one thing, the application of the concept of nation to the Sikhs raises problems of internal consistency. In view of the success of several multinational States, Brass is justified in departing from the common position and maintaining that 'the term nation or nationality [which he equates] can be applied to an ethnic group' whose political goals do not *necessarily* include separate sovereignty.[28] It is surprising, however, that although the American edition of his book was published in 1974, i.e. after the Akali Dal had adopted the Anandpur Sahib resolution, he appears to think that the establishment of the Pubjabi Suba in November 1966 represented the fulfilment of the political objective of the Sikh nation. The exponents of Sikhs-are-a-nation doctrine themselves appear to be less certain on this point.

True, apart from a miniscule group of Sukhjinder Singh, none of the Akali Dal factions has defined Sikh nationalism in terms of a sovereign Sikh State as its objective. However, it was after the establishment of the present Punjab in which the Sikhs constitute a majority that the well-known Sikh scholar-politician, Kapur Singh, declared the Sikhs to be '*sui generis*' a free and sovereign people'[29] and that it is the birth-right of the Sikh people to claim and establish a sovereign political status for themselves,[30] by creating a 'Sikh homeland'.[31] He, however, made it clear that 'sovereign political status' and the 'homeland' were possible within 'the sovereign and territorial integrity of India.'[32]

In 1978, SGPC President, Gurcharan Singh Tohra, redefined Kapur Singh's concept of Sikhs as 'a free and sovereign people' by contending that 'Sikhs are a nation *sui generis* as well as a national minority',[33] but he too did not press the logic of his formulation to a demand for a sovereign 'homeland'. His complaint was that the present Constitution of India contained provisions, 'which militate against not only the autonomy but also the very self-identity of the minority nations and nationalities'.[34] The suggestions he made for the 'federalisation' of the Indian polity indicated that, in his view, the aspirations of the Sikh nation could be satisfied in a somewhat reconstituted but more autonomous Punjab.[35] This is clear from Tohra's reiteration of the Akali Dal's commitment to the 'historic' Anandpur Sahib resolution[36].

Some more water has flowed down the Sutlej since Tohra's address to the Ludhiana Akali Conference and the two main factions of Akali Dal ('L' as well as 'T' now formally united) have formally declared that Sikhs are a nation. No mention is now made of their being a national minority. However, neither faction has pushed the concpet so far as to include a demand for a sovereign Sikh State. It would, therefore, seem that while Sikh nationalism possesses strong 'social bases' it does not belong to the category of what A.H. Birch has called 'aspiring nationalism' i.e. a nation whose focus is a 'national State' but the focus is located in the future.[36] The Akali formulation of self-determined political status,[37] comes very close to but does not catch up with the well known principle of national self-determination which, in its Leninist version, includes the right of secession.

Another difficulty about Sikh nationalism is that while its social bases—religion, language and script, historial traditions—are in no doubt, it lacks a clear economic foundation. What is being suggested here is not the Marxist view that the development of capitalist relations of production is a necessary precondition for the emergence of nationalism. What is, in fact, being suggested is that the Sikhs, as a group, do not suffer from economic deprivation, absolute or relative even though one does hear of 'simple minded' Sikhs being short-changed by cunning Hindus. Since they are not being subjected to economic exploitation and social repression by a dominant nation, they do not fit into the concpet of 'internal colonialism'.[38] Doubtless, the Akali leadership has sedulously cultivated among the Sikh masses a paranoic discrimination complex, charges of discrimination and injustice against Sikhs figure prominently in party resolutions and public speeches of party leaders.[39]

While a subjective perception of discrimination does exist among members of the Sikh intelligentsia and the Sikh elites generally, there is not enough objective evidence to generate or sustain xenophoic hostility agains the Hindus or a sense of alienation against the Centre. The point is important but need not be pressed too far. The separatist movement of the Basques in Spain and the insistence of their distinct identities among Slovenes and Croatians in Yugoslavia go to prove that national consciousness can emerge even among ethnic groups which are economically as advanced as, or even more advanced than, the politically dominant groups in multi-ethnic States. What is crucial for the existence of a nation is its self-view or its psycho-cultural essence, not real or imagined economic deprivation. The economic factor is important but is no match for the emotionalism of ethno-nationalism.

A further difficulty with Sikh 'nationalism' relates to the question whether it is, as yet, an elite phenomenon or whether 'national' consciousness has become so widespread as to have attained the proportions of mass consciousness. Brass raises the question but does not quite get to grips with it. He has stated correctly that 'elite consciousness is a precondition for and, therefore, must precede the development of mass consciousness.'[40] Two problems arise here, however. In the first place the Sikh elite are themselves divided on the issue of Sikh nationalism. Those affiliated with political parties other than the Akali Dal have publicly dissociated themselves from the claim that Sikhs are a nation. Secondly, the Skihs are by no means a monolithic social group. The community has achieved a definitive external differentiation, (i.e. differentiation *vis a-vis* the adjacent social group, the Hindus) and its members have developed a subjective awareness of a distinctive ethnic identity and of common religio-cultural interests.

However, like all other communities in India, the Sikhs are internally segmented. They are divided by caste, class and urban-rural cleavages. How far the consciousness of a 'national' as distinguished from ethnic identitiy has spread beyond the Akali Dal and a section of the urban intelligentsia and, further, how far the Sikh peasantry, as a whole, comprehends and shares the political demands of the Akali Dal are questions to which no categorical answers are available.

This is an area in which the need for intensive empirical research offers a challenge to social scientists. Meanwhile, some impressionistic propositions may be in order. To all appearances, it seems doubtful whether the broad Sikh masses have made the quantum jump involved in crossing the threshold from ethnic consciousness to national consciousness. The two are qualitatively different and national consciousness cannot be regarded as an extended form of ethnic consciousness.[41]

Take, for instance, the case of scheduled caste or Mazhbi Sikhs who constitute a substantial proportion of the community. There is little doubt that they share ethnic consciousness with higher caste Sikhs. It is known, however, that on crucial political issues they have taken a stance different from that of the Akalis. Their attitude towards the Akali movement for Punjab Suba ranged from indifference to opposition because of the feeling that the creation of a unilingual Punjab would intensify the domination of Jat Sikh landholders over them. Similarly, they have shown little enthusiasm for the Akali demand for greater autonomy for the States in terms of the Anandpur Sahib resolution. A Punjab State Scheduled Caste Convention held at Jullundur in February 1979 was reported to have 'expressed concern of the minorities and weaker sections caused by the autonomy demand,' which was seen as a veiled demand for ultimately establishing an independent State.[42]

Finally, the fact that the Akali Dal is the principal champion of a nation-status for Sikhs has important effects. It rubs off on Sikh ethno-nationalism some of the ambiguity resulting from the Akali Dal's claim to be simultaneously the defender of the Sikh faith and a party committed to promoting the interests of the Punjabi language and region. The political strategy of riding two horses, one theo-political and the other linguistic-regional, and the consequent mixing of religious and secular symbols may give the Akalis some political mileage and some advantage in the competitive game of electoral politics. It has, however, a limiting effect on Sikh nationalism by preventing it from emerging with contours as clearly defined as, for instance, is the case with Tamil, Bengali or Andhra ethno-nationalism. In the latter case, religion—undoubtedly powerful electoral ammunition in itself—does not weaken the regional-linguistic foundations of ethno-nationalism.

In articulating the specific demands of the *Panth*, such as the demand for an All India Gurdwara Act, a holy city status for Amritsar and the installation of a radio transmitter in the Golden Temple on the one hand, and on the other, regional demands such as those for greater autonomy for States, inclusion of left-out Punjabi-speaking areas in the present Punjab, ampler financial resources for the State and a more favourable allocation of inter-State river waters, the Akali Dal appeals to two different and non-coinciding constituencies. In fact, the Akali Dal's split personality and dual orientation make even the latter class of demands suspect in the eyes of those non-Sikhs who would otherwise lend their support tot them since they concern the interests of Punjab as a region and not Sikhs as a religious community. As the present writer has said elsewhere, the Akali doctrine of Sikh nationhood (and the related demand for a self determined political status for Sikhs) is seen as a repudiation and disruption of the Punjabi nationality based on territory, language and culture.[43]

The questions raised here do not necessarily imply a dogmatic rejection of the theory that Sikhs are a nation. What we have called ethno-nationalism may well evolve into a full scale nationalism with all the political implications of the concept. The questions posed here are, in fact, a plea for a constructive academic debate on the issue involved.

IV

We may now summarise the major conclusions which memerge clearly or by implication from the analysis presented here:

1. There is need, at all levels, for a general internationalisation of the empirical reality that India is a multi-ethnic and multi-national State. The formulation is no longer a Marxist preserve. Even the well-known liberal scholar, Suniti Kumar Chatterjee, had no hesitation in describing the country as 'a united nations' of India.[44] Most contemporary States are, in fact, multi-ethnic and multi-national.

2. The package process described as modernisation does not necessarily erode or destroy the particularism of ethnic groups. On the contrary, increasing mobilisation of these groups and the growth and intensity of inter-group and intra-group communication tend to sharpen and consolidate identity-consciousness and primordial loyalties. It is, however, not necessary to proceed from this and posit an 'iron law of disintegration'.

3. Concepts such as 'Indianisation' and *Hindu Rashtra* are counter-productive in so far as they generate fears of Hindu hegemony among non-Hindu and non-Hindi speaking ethnic groups. In a multi-ethnic and multi-national State, enduring loyalty on the part of ethnic groups to the State is not impossible to achieve. However, it is unrealistic to look for the acceptance of a monolithic pan-Indian identity by all the ethnic-national identities that make up the composite Indian identity. Nor can identities by arranged on an hierarchical scale. The possibility of a two-track identification, i.e. identification with an ethnic group and the multi-ethnic State has to be accepted.

4. For a multi-ethnic and multi-national State to achieve the enduring allegiance of different ethnic groups living within its territory and, thus, achieve stable political integration, it must be responsive to the aspirations of ethnic groups including their aspiration for a real rather than a symbolic share in political power at all levels of the polity. This alone can give them a sense of belonging and a stake in the maintenance of the State. Patriotism cannot be made to order at any rate in a liberal democracy. With a slight alteration in phrasing, we can say with Renan that the allegiance of ethnic groups to the State is the result of 'a daily referendum'.[45] It is the present writer's belief that the secular-federal Indian polity possesses the requisite institutional and processual flexibility and resilience to accommodate ethnic and regional discord while, at the same time, defining the parameters within which such discord will be tolerated.

NOTES

[1] A common tendency to equate 'State' with 'nation' is evident in a number of texts on international relations. Thus, in his *World of Nations*, Washington, 1967, Dunkwart Rustow speaks of 'more than 130 nations', while he is, in reality, referring to the then existing 130 odd States. And this despite the fact that, in the same text, he makes a distinction between the two. The same tendency to ignore the difference between the two concepts is seen in *World Politics*, New York, 1968, p. 12, wherein A.F.K. Organsky claims that 'the story we are about to tell is a tale of nations'. Surprisingly, even Karl W. Deutsch falls a victim to the same semantic confusion in his *Nationalism and Its Alternatives*, New York, 1969. At one place in his book, Deutsch defines 'nation' as a people i.e. 'an ethnic group in charge of a State' (p. 15) and at another speaks of the different ethnic groups living in Spain and Belgium as 'Nations' (pp 13 and 70).

[2] 'Nation-states', writes Roy C. Macridis, 'are beginning to get an unpleasant taste of the heady medicine of nationalism which first brought them into being. It is what has

been referred to as *ethno-nationalism*, the search for and expression within the nation-State of particular ethnic, cultural, regional or linguistic autonomy. These separatist movements range from outright independence and the assumption of state-hood to requests for 'self-government'. *Contemporary Political Ideologies*, Cambridge, Mass., 1980, p. 278.

3 The case of Indian Muslims is roughly parallel to that of the blacks in the US whereas that of the Sikhs corresponds broadly to that of the French Canadians of Quebec. To say this is certainly not to imply that, in India, Muslims as a group are subjected to the same kind of racial discrimination and material deprivation as the blacks are in the US.

4 It was at an educational conference, convened in March 1981, by the Chief Khalsa Diwan that an American Sikh, Ganga Singh Dhillon, put foward the claim that Sikhs are a nation and spelled out some of the implications of this claim e.g. the demand that Sikhs be allowed 'associate' membership of the United Nations. Later, the Working Committees of the Shiromani Akali Dal and the Shiromani Gurdwara Parbandhak Committee passed resolutions declaring Sikhs to be a nation.

5 Both concepts, nation-building and political integration suffer from definitional infirmity and have been used by different writers to convey different meaning. Nation-building as used by Karl W. Deutsch carries monolithic implications in so far as it presumes the possibility, if not inevitability, of the assimilation of ethnic particularisms under the homogenising impact of modernisation. See his *Nationalism and Social Communication: An Enquiry into the Foundations of Nationality*, Cambridge, Mass, 1966, his paper entitled 'Nation-building and National Development: Some Issues for Political Research' in Karl W. Deutsch and William J. Foltz, eds., *Nation-building*, New York, 1963 and his *Nationalism and its Alternatives*, New York 1969. As pointed out by A.H. Birch, the meaning given to nation-building by Deutsch seems 'to exclude the possibility of a stable multinational state'. *Political Integration and Disintegratoin in the British Isles, London, 1977, pp 32.*

'Political integration', in its most common usage, has a rather limited conceptual reach. Stricty defined, it excludes social, cultural and economic factors all of which are involved in the process of nation-building. So defined, it has primarilty a territorial and political connection and refers to the creation of political institutions, a structure of administrative authority and communication networks which develop multi-channelled linkages between the centre and the periphery. In this narrower sense, political integration is a process India may be said to have successfully completed. In this paper, the author follows A.H. Birch in using 'political integration' in a broader sense 'so as to include social and other factors which contribute to (or hinder) the development of integration'. Ibid, p 33. Used in this broader sense political integration and nation-building (shorn of its monolithic implications) become more or less interchangeable.

The present paper avoids the term national integration, which is very popular in India but which is also very loosely employed. It is not merely 'tautological' as Claude Ake has pointed out. (*A Theory of Political Integration*, Illinois, 1967, p. 14). It is far too totalistic to capture the diversities of India. It tends to imply a complete submergence of the various distinct elements of a plural society in a monolithic, pan-India identity. It is evidently for this reason, that in a press interview, Sikandar Bakht, General Secretary of Bhartiya Janata Party, objected to the use of this term which, in his view, denoted 'incoherent homogeneity' and loss of socio-religious identity of religious minorities. *The Tribune*, 11 October, 1980.

6 In India, Marxists are about the only group who, since the forties, have consistently described the country as multi-national although in recent years, they have stressed the territorial integrity of the Indian State and the inappropriateness of the right of secession for its constituent units on the ground that there is no single nationality exploiting or repressing other nationalities in the country. For a recent example, see K. Mathew Kurian and P.N. Verghese eds., *Centre-State Relations*, New Delhi, 1981. Akali leader Gurcharan Singh Tohra has also stressed the multi-national character of India in his pamphlet, *Federal Polity*, Amritsar, 1978, p. 6. 'The diversity' writes Tohra, 'is reflected in the variety of nations, nationalities and minorities living in India, making it a multi-national society as the empirical level.' Ibid. Paul R. Brass has also described India as a 'developing multi-national State'. *Language, Religions and Politics in North India*, Delhi, 1975, p. 5.

7 M.N. Srinivas, *Nation-Building in Independent India*, Delhi, 1976, p 30.

8 *Ibid.*, p 24.

9 Walker Connor, 'Nation-Building or Nation-Destroying?', *World Politics*, Vol 24, No. 3, April 1972, p 321. (Italics in the original).

10 Ibid, p 322.

11 'The historical experience of other countries shows that federal polity ensures unity, integrity and progress on an enduring basis' Gurcharan Singh Tohra, op. cit. He specifically cites the case of USSR noting that each Union Republic is 'not only autonomous but sovereign' possessing 'the right freely to secede form the USSR'. Tohra however, does not advocate the right of secession for the States of the Indian Union.

12 In *Politics in England*, Boston, 1964, Richard Rose wrote of the 'absence of major cleavages along the lines of ethnic group, language or religion' (p 10) and described 'the solidarity of United Kingdom' as 'real and important'. Six years later, however, he came out with another book which he entitled *The United Kingdom as a Multi-National State*, Glasgow, 1970, and in which he took issue with a number of writers, including himself oddly enough, who had failed to grasp the potential signfinance of ethnic cleavages in the country. In his *Political Integration and Disintegration in the British Isles*, London, 1977, A.H. Birch includes two chapters dealing respectively with 'Scottish Nationalism', (pp 98-115) and 'Welsh Nationalism' (pp 116-133).

13 Karl W. Deutsch in Deutsch and William J. Foltz, eds., *Nation-Building*, op. cit.

14 Ibid., p 4.

15 Elsewhere Deutsch is less optimistic about casual relationship between assimilation and mobilisation and is inclined to think that the relationship between the two processes is chronological; the crucial question being which precedes and out-paces the other. 'The decisive factor,' he writes, 'is the balance between the two processes. . . . If assimilation stays ahead of mobilisation or keeps abreast of it, the government is likely to remain stable, eventually everyone will be integrated in one people. . . . On the other hand, where mobilisation is fast and assimilation is slow the opposite happens.' Karl W. Deutsch, op. cit.

16 Walker Connor, op. cit., p 327. According to Connor 'the substantial body of data which is available supports the proposition that material increases in what Deutsch termed social communicaton and mobilisation *tend* to increase cultural awareness and to exacerbate ethnic conflict.' Ibid., p 328, (Italics in the original).

17 Nathan Glazer, 'Ethnic Revival, America and the World', *Span*, Vol. 21, No. 5, May 1980, p 21.

194

18 Joseph Davey Cunningham, *A History of the Sikhs from Origin of the Nation to the Battles of the Sutlej*, Delhi, 1966, p 92.

19 Khushwant Singh, *The Fall of the Kingdom of the Punjab*, Bombay, 1962. See also his *A History of the Sikhs*, 2 Vols, Bombay, 1977, *Passim*.

20 Paul R. Brass, op. cit.

21 Brass does not make a clear distinction between 'nationality' and 'nation' and uses the two concepts as if they were interchangeable. In fact his preference is for 'nation-State', for a nation which achieves political independence and 'nationality' or 'nation' for ethnic groups whose political goals do not necessarily include separate sovereignty, Ibid., p 9, f.n. 1.

22 'Since the British saw the two religions as distinct, they expected the believers to see things the same way and they ultimately enforced their conceptions in the census by refusing to record such ambiguities'. Ibid., p 27.

23 Kenneth W. Jones, 'Communalism in the Punjab, the Arya Samaj contribution', *Journal of Asian Studies*, Vol. 28, No. 1, November 1968, p. 50.

24 *Indian Express*, 25 February, 1969, cited in Boris I.K. Luyev, *India: National and Language Problem*, New Delhi, 1981, p 308.

25 The fear of 'deliberate and persistent attempts to devalue and liquidate the Sikh people in free India', (Jaswant Singh Mann, ed, *Some Documents on the Demand for the Sikh Homeland*, Chandigarh, 1969, p. 35) and determination to resist such attempts to disintegrate and dissolve the Khalsa (ibid., p. 72) have formed the refrain of numerous resolutions passed by the Akali Dal and public pronouncements of Akali leaders.

26 Such a demand was made, for instance, by Jiwan Singh Umranangal in a meeting of Akali Dal (L) workers at Gurdwara Bir Sahib near Amritsar held on 4 July, 1981. Umranangal was, at the time, acting President of the Party, *Times of India*, 5 July, 1981.

27 Paul R. Brass, op. cit., p. 9.

28 Ibid., p. 334 (Italics added).

29 Jaswant Singh Mann, op. cit., p 78.

30 Ibid., p 90.

31 Ibid., p 91.

32 Ibid., p 78. Referring to a resolution passed by the Akali Dal (Master Tara Singh) working committee on 20 July 1966, Kapur Singh stated that 'a new Punjab sould be given an autonomous constitutional status on the analogy of Jammu and Kashmir'. Ibid., p. 36. The position was reiterated at an Akali Conference held on 11 December 1966, i.e. after the formation of the Punjabi Suba. Ibid., p. 39.

33 Gurcharan Singh Tohra, op. cit., p. 6.

34 Ibid., pp 13-16.

35 Ibid., p. 4.

36 A.H. Birch, op. cit., p 30.

37 As early as in May 1965, the Akali Dal (Master), which spoke for a minority of the Akalis, asserted that 'there was no alternative left for the Sikhs, in the interest of self-preservation than to frame their demand for a self-determined political status within the republic of the Union of India.' Cited from Ajit Singh Sarhadi, *Punjabi Suba*, Delhi, 1970, p. 402. The constitution of the united Akali Dal, approved on 2 September, 1974 included among the party's objectives 'the preservation among the Sikhs of a consciousness of an independent Panthic identity and carving out a territory and era (*desh* and *Kal*) wherein the national sentiment and nationhood of the Sikhs Panth may find the fullest embodiment and expression.'

195

38 For an exposition of the concept see Micael Hechter, *Internal Colonialism: The Celtic Fringe in British National Development, 1536-1966*, London, 1975.

39 While the point does not need much documentation, a highly melodramatised articulation of the charge may be seen in the following observation of Kapur Singh: 'Under the disguise of democracy, secularism and theory of one-nation subtle schemes and policies are being adopted with the aim of first disintegrating the *Khalsa* into individual Sikhs and then debasing the individual Sikhs into secular citizens so that they may make good cannon fodder, good *Chowkidars* and good chauffeurs for expensive limousines of industrial magnates of a united Indian nation and thus they are deprived of their history-making potency and dynamism. To reduce the Royal Khalsa of Guru Gobind Singh into the secular proletariat of hewers of wood and drawers of waters for the traditional higher classes of Hindus and the new privilegentia of free India, is the greatest betrayal of the trust created by the sacrifices of those, who have through the ages, toiled and suffered for the freedom of *Dharma*, that is India, that is Bharat.' Jaswant Singh Mann, op. cit., p 72.

An SGPC pamphlet, *Sikh Ate Bharti Rajniti*, (Sikhs and Indian Politics), published in 1974, included five pages listing complaints of 'economic attacks on the Sikhs by the Centre', 'injustice to the Sikh religion', 'political excesses against the Sikhs' and 'discrimination and excesses on all sides.' The theme of *Sikh Kaum Nal Dhaka* (injustice to the Sikh Nation) also figured prominently in Jagdev Singh Talwandi's Presidential address at the Ludhiana Akali Conference, October 1978. The theme also runs through the 45-point charter of the Akali Dal (Sant) recently submitted to the Prime Minister which is the basis of the current negotiations between the central government and the Dal.

40 Paul R. Brass, op. cit., p 37.

41 Boris I.K. Luyev, op. cit., p 234.

42 *The Tribune*, 5 February 1979.

43 On the point see also Avtar Singh Malhotra, 'Centre-State Relations-4', *Nawan Zamana*, 6 February, 1979.

44 Cited from A.R. Kamat, 'Ethno-linguistic issues in the Indian Federal Context', *Economic and Political Weekly*, Vol. 15, Nos 24-25, June 1980. p 1062.

45 Ernest Renan, 'What is Nationalism' in Hans Kohn, ed., *Nationalism: Its Meaning and History*, New York, 1965, p 140.

THE POLITICIANS

Rajni Kothari

With the decline of institutions and the rise of both the cult of personality and the politics of survival and insecurity on the part of dominant individuals, there has taken place a dramatic transformation in the composition of India's political elite. We are witness to new faces everywhere. Over the long run, this may make room for truly new forces taking us towards a post-crisis, post-transition scenario. For the moment, however, the newness seems to herald nothing except a deep vacuum in the structure of power at various levels. The vacuum is filled by people who were never trained in the art of politics, ill-at-ease with the complex procedures and niceties of a democratic polity, unwilling to abide by any institutionalized discipline, indulging in and encouraging in others a zero-sum approach to power, to this end providing scope for and often conniving with professional fixers and their mercenaries, all this together moving the political process towards a free for all.

The new faces do not represent a generational change in any basic sense, even though some of them are no doubt younger, more flashy, more ruthless, less bound by older conventions and values, than the ones they have displaced. Nor are they representative of more native, underprivileged, 'vernacular' strata as had been predicted by both alarmists and enthusiasts as the prospect of Indian democracy touching base, going interior and bringing forth less urbanized and cosmopolitan leaders to the fore.[1] On the contrary, it was precisely the fear of such elements both within the Congress and through Opposition formations that led to a near dismantling of the party system by the English-speaking elite who found in Mrs Gandhi a leader who could successfully throw back the rising tide of regional leaders representing the middle and lower middle tiers of rural India and its extension in small and medium sized towns. I have dealt with this overall phenomenon of urban backlash in Indian politics in earlier issues of *Seminar*.[2] Here I am more concerned with the even more recent phenomenon, spurred first by Sanjay Gandhi and subsequently consolidated by Chief Ministers and others to whom State and district party organizations were entrusted by him in 1980.

The new politicians do come from new strata but in a very different sense than was happening in the sixties. They represent not the traditional hinterland of rural India dominated by caste and tribe, but the hinterland of the modern class structure, namely, the educated and semi-educated hordes of lumpens. Finding ready employment in the occupying spaces at lower and middle reaches of both the polity and the economy, largely in the 'informal sector' of each but gradually also making their way to the formal apparatus of

From Seminar, *July 1984. Reprinted with permission.*

government and economic organisations, they have systematically moved into the vacuum created by the ouster of party politicians.

The twin engines of this transformation from party and region based leaders slowly graduating to power to a rapid rise of non-party, almost non-political, individuals to all echelons of power have been corruption and criminality. Everyone seems to agree on the decline of the party system and party organization. What is not readily perceived to observers and editors, and if perceived not said, is the displacement of party by a new infrastructure of politics made up of musclemen and local mafias.

These are either directly paid for or thrive on dens of illicit liquor, gambling and all manner of entertainments (now aided by the video revolution that is sweeping across the country like a torrent). Many of these happen to be relatives of ministers and other important politicians. And many of them have had strong international ties through smuggling, international drug traffic and foreign exchange rackets and through close contacts with the Persian Gulf and its Sheikhs. Massive transactions in money and kind have taken place in the process, some of which was sent right up!

I discussed this whole phenomenon of criminalization of politics at greater length in an article in 1981.[3] Then it had shocked many. It may not any more, though there still seems to be little realization of the dramatic change which has taken place in the role of crime in the political process. As I had said then, the role of gangs and bullies in Indian politics has undergone both a quantitative and a qualitative change. Even in the old days when party bosses in the much maligned 'syndicate' structure of the Congress Party held sway (the S.K. Patils and Atulya Ghoses), use was made of local bullies holding sway over specific *mohallas* or *chawls*. But, the process was largely limited to congested urban areas, it was sparingly used and was much less intense and ruthless, and was almost wholly limited to election periods. And, above all, there was never any question as to who was the master—it was always the party politicians at whose behest the musclemen went into action.

The relationship entered its second phase in 1969 when the party organisation as the main lever of political mobilization got undermined. After this and until the Emergency the balance between the politicians and lumpens began to get more and more even. With the 1980 election and the meteoric rise of Sanjay Gandhi to the top of the effective political pyramid, the lumpens, which included a large number of persons with a record of either criminal or civil offences, emerged from the backstage and entered the political stream as MLAs, MPs, ministers and still higher.

Since then, during the more than three years of operating at various levels of the system, these 'goonda' politicians have given rise to a truly new infrastructure of politics. They lend support to feuding factions within the ruling party, stormtroop the Opposition meetings (earlier Sanjay and his cohorts had stormtrooped into courts and newspaper offices), settle scores between the landed and propertied interests and the defiant members of the poor and peripheral communities in the rural areas and, either in collusion with the police or with the latter standing by as onlookers, terrorize the rural areas. Often the police itself (and the local bureaucrats) are terror stricken by the 'goonda' politicians, largely because of the support they wield in State governments or at still higher levels.

Nor is this new politics limited only to the ruling party. In point of fact, the technique of using musclemen and 'mastaans' was first tried out in a systematic manner in West Bengal, starting with the confrontation between the communist parties and the Naxalites, later with the Youth Congress using the same technique and defeating the communists at their own game. In Maharashtra and Tamilnadu too, the same technique has been employed over a long period between various Marxist-Leninist groups and betweeen them and the CPI(M). In north India the politics of rigging by booth-capturing as well as of settling personal, factional and inter-party feuds between different opposition parties have led to the rise of 'goonda' politicians. Chiman Patel of Gujarat, now in the Janata Party, had as Chief Minister employed a crude mixture of corruption and vandalism against his own party MLAs in 1974, spurring the massive Navnirman movement and his ouster from office.

No such movement has taken place against more recent perpetrators of corruption and criminality like Antulay and Gundu Rao (the former was removed by a court verdict; the latter by electoral defeat). This itself is a symptom of how far the politics of bullying and fear has overtaken us. No doubt, the mass of people do react when given a chance as happened in the masive defeat of the Congress (I) in Andhra Pradesh and, to a lesser extent, in Karnataka.

But what happens when the masses react against a corrupt and non-performing regime and want a clean change? Are they able to draw upon alternative structures and images from within the democratic political spectrum or, finding no such clear alternatives, are they found to turn to forces outside the political sphere? Here we come across yet another ingredient in the changing composition of the political elite. This is the rise of the playboy on the political stage—the hold of MGR on Tamilnadu politics for over a decade, the meteoric rise of NTR in Andhra Pradesh, and the growing rumblings of Raj Kumar and his fans, of Shivaji Ganesan, Jayalalitha (both of whom are now in Parliament) and the considerable political clout being worked out for gymnast Amitabh Bacchan as the playboy of the Congress (I) and its *Inquilab*.

A peculiar combination of cultural reaction to centralised politics and a substitution of elite culture by mass culture lies behind this phenomenon. In Tamilnadu, then the State of Madras, where the first systematic and successful regional response against the Congress monolith emerged, the Dravida Kazhagam (DK) which was a cultural movement against Brahmin domination was followed by the Dravida Munnetra Kazhagam (DMK) in the form of a political party aimed at a demand for substantial autonomy for the State, at times invoking seccessionist symbols. The latter was soon contained and, under the leadership of Annadurai and later Karunanidhi, participation in the federal polity was combined with regional, linguistic and cultural assertion and firm political consolidation and monopoly at the State level (since 1967). It is the widespread corruption and machine politics that subsequently ensued that led to populist reaction, epitomized by the pious and virtuous mythological image of G. Ramachandran whose coming on the scene shifted the whole emphasis from pragmatic politics to mass idolatry, the latter filling the vacuum created in the public mind.

In the cultural domain, too, a dramatic change had come about which contributed to this transformation. This consisted in the undermining of the powerful upsurge in consciousness and the deep intellectual stirrings and public debate on basic cultural themes which accompanied Tamil renaissance by a kind of pop culture of film and soap opera which swept across Tamilnadu. Both authentic politics and authentic culture, as well as regard for basic values and liberties of dissenting elements, became casualties in this transmutation of a genuine urge towards regional autonomy and cultural identity into a celluloid culture and inane hero-worship. It is hero-worship, moreover, which has no political basis but in fact adopts a stance and imagery which are in essence anti-political.

In Andhra Pradesh, too, more than fifteen years later, a similar phenomenon took place, not in the sense of any great upsurge of a distinctive culture—authentic culture having everywhere been undermined in the intervening period—but in the sense of a gross reaction to a highly centralized political process. This had resulted in its growing alienation and insensitivity to grassroots reality, imposition of leaders from an alien Centre and a humiliating situation in whch a highly politicized region was reduced to a non-entity. Once again the regional response came not from an organised political force but from yet another mysterious rise of a mythical presence in the form of N.T. Rama Rao, who, in turn, did not hide his contempt for normal politics and went on to combine in his being a patron saint of the people and a real saint above that—the mythical NTR in real life.

This rejection of normal politics is spreading in many regions. So is the impact of celluloid and of mass culture, further galvanized by the advent of the mass media. These tendencies are likely to become more powerful with the explosive impact of electronic networks, satellite communication, capsuled entertainment and the use of public television and video channels for partisan ends. There is going to be an intense battle for the control of and access to these channels and, with that, further accentuation of regional-national confrontations. As this confrontation will be waged less through parliamentary and more through theatrical politcs, the role of playboys in politics—there are other (non filmic) kinds of playboys coming up too—will become endemic.

Both the growth of lumpen politicians and the spread of playboys in politics, replacing or undermining or at best 'servicing' the normal vocation of professional politicians, are symptomatic of a deeper shift in the constitutional fabric of Indian society, namely, a growing decline in legitimacy of normal politics combined with a sense of exhaustion and drift on the part of both party leaders and the Indian State as a whole. The resulting vacuum is being filled by the 'goondas' and the playboys.

It is also filled by a whole new set of actors and phenomena—the vulgar *nouveau riche* occcupying new avenues brought forth by a rapid growth of metropolitan towns and blind and uninhibited westernization thereof, the fantastic sweep of advertisement agencies catering to these new tastes, the growing use of sex symbols that is undermining the whole balance of the Indian psyche, the invasion of social mores and ethics by the video and the tantalising esoterica that accompanies it, the whole Amitabh Bacchan phenomenon, the prompting of rabid consumerism by new professionals making you buy what you do not want with money you do not have. All this is leading to a basic lumpenization of the economy, in turn relying on the political patronage of the lumpen politicians and the new playboys with high political connections.

Into this world of drift and decay are entering two 'dynamic' strata of India's industrial culture. Leading lights of the corporate sector are moving into influential positions in the process of government, either through direct entry into the political arena as found in the support mobilised by the top brass of the ruling Congress Party for K.K. Birla or indirectly in the form of providing an overarching economic philosophy as in the case of J.R.D. Tata. The growing influence of FICCI in the economic policy-making is not any longer even papered over by public sector slogans and socialist invectives; it is a case of deliberate and openly admitted collaboration.

Alongside this local phenomenon of the permeation of the Indian State by the rich is an even more open-ended collaboration with rich Indians abroad. Finding in the changed Indian scene great prospects for both investment and markets, bringing in a whole new generation of bright young people from abroad to displace the natives, destabilizing established concerns with the active help of ministers and the Prime Minister, coopting even the public sector in this new economic dispensation, and spreading the idea of the need to restrain the democratic process and especially mass aspirations if the country is to 'move forward' and become a great power, the foreign-based tycoons are about to have a field day in the 'poor India' they are out to transform. Swraj Paul fully epitomizes this new thrust of the economic wizard into the national political process. It is not an accident that the author of the latest biography of Indira Gandhi is none other than Mr Paul.

Do these various constituents of the new elite—the lumpens, the playboys, the blackmarketeers, the advertisement and media wizards, the business tycoons gunning for power, the tycoons abroad—cohere into a common interest? Unfortunately, yes. What seems to hold them all together is a belief in their capacity to rip a whole civilisation apart and put it together in a new and malleable form, ever to be pressed into fulfilling new and innovative ideas—exactly in the image of the new hardware and the new software they are all peddling. A full apotheosis of modernity writ large across the length and breadth of India!

Capping all these changes in the composition of the ruling elite and the vision that holds it together is, of course, the cadre of managers and technocrats surrounding Rajiv Gandhi and the strategic-military experts advising the Prime Minister through the good offices of a plain-clothes diplomat like G. Parthasarathi. The age we are moving in has already been proclaimed by Asiad, Chogm, the space odyssey and the 'prediction' of a war with Pakistan. Whether we move towards a Presidential system with its accent on a centralised technocratic State which will consummate this age or not, the transformation in the composition of the new elite in India as highlighted in these pages already heralds a basic change in the politcal system.

Unless it is arrested by a determined leadership which can 'restore the political process'. . .

NOTES

[1] The alarmist view was best portrayed in Selig S. Harrison, *India: the Most Dangerous Decades* (Princeton, 1960). A much more positive interpretation was provided in my *Politics in India,* (New Delhi and Boston) 1970.

[2] See for instance 'Democracy: Retrospect and Prospect', *Seminar,* 122, April 1977.

[3] 'Where Are We Heading?', *Indian Express, Sunday Magazine,* November 29, 1981.

PLANLESS IN PAKISTAN

Kaiser Bengali and Khalid Nadvi

The Plan is dead. Long live the Plan. Launched only a year and a half ago amidst glittering media fanfare, th Sixth Five Year Development Plan was even then dubbed by many as being still-born, given its unrealistic targets and faulty premises. Now it hs been effectively buried and replaced by a Three Year Rolling Plan.

However, Dr Mahbubul Haq, the Plan's author, puts it differently. According to him, it is 'the government's intention to *rationalise* the Sixth Plan by evolving a Three Year Rolling Plan envisaging a 10-15 percent downward revision in the size of the overall Sixth Plan . . . and to design a concrete programme, project-by-project and sector-by-sector which must be implemented *at all costs* . . . irrespective of any shorfall in the resources.' Verbal and statistical jugglery is by now a perfected art in Islamabad. The fact that the Third, Fourth, Fifth and Sixth Plans all met with premature deaths and had to be replaced with Annual, Interim and Rolling Plans indicates that ad hocism has become a national way of life.

Details of the composition of the Rolling Plan are yet to be announced. One clear casualty is likely to be the Kalabagh Dam which is now being considered for inclusion in the Seventh Plan! That may be a blessing in disguise for Sind and NWFP, as the economy of both these provinces is likely to suffer from ecological damage as a consequence of the construction of the dam at Kalabagh. And given the absence of representative government, the smaller provinces are not in a position to represent their interests. Another constituency whose case may go by default is the man in the street; the improvement in his quality of life was the main selling point of the Sixth Plan. However, if adjustments in previous five year plans are any guide, the axe will inevitably fall on education, health and other social sectors.

The apparent reasons for the failure of the Sixth Plan to take off and achieve its targets even in its first year, the massive planning exercise notwithstanding, are attributed to the reduced inflow of remittances and foreign aid and the reverses in agriculture. But the malaise lies much deeper.

The two years before 1984 were particularly good for the economy. The gross national product (GNP) in 1982-83 increased by 6.5 percent with real per capita income recording a rise of 3.5 percent. Agriculture grew by 4.8 percent and manufacturing by 8.3 percent. The balance of payments gap showed a tendency to narrow, mainly due to enhanced exports and a freak 29 percent rise in remittances, and international reserves almost touched the 3 billion dollars mark.

From Herald, *January 1985. Original title: 'So What Else Is New?' Reprinted with permission.*

The good fortune, influenced by favourable weather, generous aid and the spurt in remittances was mistaken by Islamabad economic pundits as good performance in economic management. And a political climate fed by obscurantist abstractionism and spurious rhetoric tended to blot out saner voices which have continued to maintain, *ad nauseum* that the economy was basically weak due to structural imbalances and, far from taking off into sustained growth, it was heading towards a severe crisis.

As early as 1981, independent economists had sounded the alarm of a return migration of the Gulf labour force bringing in its wake not only the problem of their absorption in productive employment, but also a potential reduction in remittances. One study estimated that some 600,000 of the 2 million-odd Pakistanis working in the Middle East would have to return home due to lack of jobs. Another study warned that the wheat surpluses of the early eighties were a transient phenomenon and predicted that wheat imports would have to continue well into the late eighties. Both the forecasts are now appearing to be correct.

The net result is that the bubble has burst and the economy is headed for the rocks. The Gross Domestic Product in 1983-84 grew by 4.5 percent as against a planned target of 6.3 percent. Agricultural growth was a negative 4.6 percent; cotton, wheat and rice output declined by 40 percent, 11.9 percent and 3 percent, respectively; the manufacturing sector recorded a growth of 7.7 percent as against a target of 9.3 percent; while public administration and defence grew by 15.5 percent as opposed to a projected 3.5 percent.

The deficit on the current account increased from 558 million dollars in 1982-83 to 700 million dollars in 1983-84, and the ratio of aid disbursement to commitment fell from 98.4 percent to 63.7 percent during the same period. With remittances also down by 3 percent, the balance of payments situation registered a deteriorating trend, with a deficit of 267 million dollars over the year. Consequently, gold and foreign exchange reserves are down to just 900 million dollars. A potent indicator of the sinking economy is the unabated decline of the rupee, which has depreciated by almost 50 percent since it was delinked from the US dollar in 1982.

The social aspects of the economy are not too encouraging either. Inflation has reached double digit figures, according to official estimates, while independent sources place it at above 15 percent. Unemployment, which has been officially placed at the absurd level of 3.5 percent, continues to be a serious problem, particularly in the interior of Sind and Baluchistan. Even a casual visitor to Dadu, Larkana, Khairpur, Gwadur or Sibi would find scores of unemployed youth whiling away their time in the towns' cafeterias. The employment problem is likely to be further aggravated by returning migrants from the Middle East.

The return migration trend is fraught with grave socio-economic consequences. Firstly, a long-term reduction in remittances will have a catastrophic effect on the balance of payments. With the severe trade deficit, which in the first four months of the fiscal year 1984-85 alone was Rs 17 billion (an increase of around 30 percent over the figure for the same period in the previous year) any sustained reduction in levels of remittances will lead to a major financial crisis compounded by high US interest rates and the rising value of the dollar.

Secondly, the issue of absorption of the returning migrants within the domestic economy is likely to reach crisis proportions. One study suggests that the manufacturing sector would have to expand by an additional 7 to 9 percent over and above that projected for in the Sixth Plan, in order to absorb the returning labour. Not only is that well nigh impossible, but the tendency of the industrial sector to adopt capital intensive techniques of production and the growing mechanisation of agriculture has meant that the labour absorption capacity of the economy is being steadily reduced. The implications, therefore, of large-scale unemployment and the ensuing political and economic conflict are very real.

The prospects for the new year are, therefore, grim. Domestically, the economy does not have much to offer to effect a recovery. The cotton crop is likely to be good, but world production is also estimated to be a record 76 million bales, thereby depressisng world cotton prices and adversely affecting Pakistan's export earnings. Private sector industrial investment has also failed to respond to the government's overtures, as is perhaps indicated by the fact that as against Rs 4953 million worth of sanctions given during July-October 1983-84, only Rs 551 million sanctions have been given during the corresponding period in 1984-85. The Export Processing Zone at Karachi has also not been the hoped-for success. Out of 45 projects sanctioned, only about 10 are complete or near completion. As a result, the authorities are considering a proposal to allow Pakistani capitalists to invest in the EPZ as well, thereby diluting the very purpose of establishing a tax-free zone.

Externally, Pakistan has to commence repayment of the External Fund Facility, availed from the IMF during 1980-83 in order to avert the then serious possibility of a default in debt repayment. It appears that Pakistan is now back to square one. Of the total aid commitment of 2.2 billion dollars for 1984-85, 1.5 billion dollars alone will have to go to cover debt servicing charges on the 13 billion dollars debt already accumulated. Actual disbursement, however, is only expected to be around 1.2 billion dollars.

It will, therefore, be necessary to mobilise 1 billion dollars in order to meet the shortfall of 300 million dollars for debt servicing and 700 million dollars for financing domestic development efforts. The prospects for any debt rescheduling, however, appear slim, given the poor performance in agriculture and the sharp reduction in the level of overseas remittances. Both these factors have been serving as Pakistan's international collateral and any reduction in their value clearly makes further loan facilities increasingly difficult.

On the other hand, little effort has been made to significantly expand internal resource mobilisation. The call by leading economists to introduce a progressive agricultural income tax continue to fall on deaf ears, an indication of the might and influence still exerted by the large farmers' lobby within the corridors of power. This group continues to be subsidised, both directly and indirectly, by the state.

As to the arguments on 'growth with a social conscience' expounded within the Sixth Plan, the reality is that equity and redistribution remain low in the list of national priorities, as perceived by the planners. The instruments of Islamic social welfare in the form of Ushr and Zakat have had a negligible effect on poverty and income inequality. The mechanisms of raising and distributing Ushr and Zakat have both been prone to extensive corruption.

Corruption and graft also continues to widen the spread of the parallel black economy. Sustained by wide-scale smuggling, the drug trade and tax evasion, it has permeated all aspects of economic life. Corruption has become institutionalised. The various incentive schemes introduced by the government to legalise such 'earnings' have been totally ineffective. Prize bonds, land and more recently the stock market have become the regular avenues to launder black money into white. According to one report Rs 10 billion of black money is annually injected into the economy, not to mention the fact that Rs 5 to 7 billion is illegally transferred abroad every year.

The much talked-about Islamic system is yet to be realised. The banking sector remains confused as to the meaning and working of Islamic financing and consensus has not been reached by decision makers on the modalities of the Islamic economic system. Meanwhile, the modaraba schemes have achieved a rare notoriety and the private sector has not welcomed projects that do not leave it free to produce two sets of accounts.

The inherent weakness of the economy and the overwhelming dependence on external assistance has effectively mortgaged the country to the international banking system. The IMF and the World Bank dictate not only matters of economic policy, but even such mundane issues as the price of wheat, gas and railway fares. Important donor countries exert pressure for acceptance of projects which have little relevance to Pakistan's priorities and needs, but generate significant job opportunities in the donor countries. The abject subservience of the country to foreign interests is amply illustrated by the fact that the World Bank refused permission to the Planning Commisssion to instal a computer required for processing the enormous amount of data!

LAND REFORMS IN PAKISTAN:
A RECONSIDERATION

Akmal Hussain

Introduction

Before the introduction of the high yielding varieties of food grain in the late 1960s the argument for land reform was a simple one. It was observed that small farms had a higher yield per acre than large farms,[1] so it was argued that a re-redistribution of owned land in favor of the smaller farmers would improve average yields in agriculture. Hence land reforms were considered advisable both on grounds that they would reduce the degree of inequality of rural incomes, as well as on grounds of efficiency. The efficiency argument for land reforms in Pakistan gathered momentum in the 1950s when agricultural stagnation began to fetter the growth of industry.[2] Agriculture provided not only food grains for the rising urban population but also provided most of the foreign exchange with which industrial machinery and raw materials were imported.[3] Accordingly, slow agricultural growth generated both a crisis in the balance of payments as well as food shortages in the urban sector.[4] In such a situation even the technocrats who were merely interested in the growth of GNP joined the cry of the social reformers for a land reform. It began to be seen as a necessary instrument for accelerating agricultural growth and thereby releasing the constraint on industrial growth.

When the Green Revolution technology became available in the late 1960s, the ruling classes could breathe a sigh of relief. The new technology made it possible to accelerate agricultural growth substanitally through an 'elite-farmer strategy' which concentrated the new inputs on large farms. Now the crucial determinant in yield differences became not the labour input per acre in which small farms had been at an advantage, but the application of the seed-water-fertilizer package over which the large farmers with their greater financial power had superior access. Thus the technocrats felt that the Green Revolution had made it possible to accelerate agricultural growth without having to bring about any real change in the rural power structure.

Today after more than a decade and a half of the 'elite-farmer strategy,' the imperative of land reform is re-emerging, albeit in a more complex form than in the pre-Green Revolution period. As the large farms approach the ceiling on yield per acre with the available technology, further growth in agricultural output will increasingly depend on raising the yield per acre of smaller farms.

The small farm sector whose yield potential remains to be fully utilized, constitutes a substantial part of the agrarian economy. According to the Pakistan Census of Agriculture 1972, farms below 25 acres constitute 88 percent of the total number of farms, and 57 percent of total farm area. From the

From Bulletin of Concerned Asian Scholars, *June–March 1985. Reprinted with permission.*

viewpoint of raising the yield per acre of small farms, the critical consideration is that 54 percent of the farm area in the small farm sector (below 25
acres) is tenant operated. Since tenants lose half of any increase in output to
the landlord, they lack the incentive to invest in raising yields. Tenants also
lack the ability to raise yields in a situation where, because of their financial
and social position, they are unable to ensure optimum quantity and timing in
inputs. The ability of the tenant to invest in increasing yields is further erod-
ed by a whole nexus of social and economic dependence on the landlord which
deprives the tenant of much of his investable surplus.

The objective of raising yields in the small farm sector is clearly inseparable
from removing the institutional constraints to growth arising out of the fact of
tenancy. A land reform program that gives land to the tiller is therefore an
essential first step in providing both the incentive and the ability to the small
farmer to raise yields. The imperative for land reform today arises not only
from the need to accelerate agricultural growth, but also from the need to prevent the developing social crisis associated with the impact of the Green
Revolution on Pakistan's rural society. I shall argue in this paper that in a
situation where the distribution of landownership was highly unequal the
adoption of the Green Revolution technology set in motion powerful
economic forces which rapidly enriched the large farmers and brought a sharp
increase in rural poverty, unemployment and the pressure on big urban
centers. I shall discuss the following four contradictions generated by the
growth process in Pakistan's agriculture during the Green Revolution period:

(1)   The rapid mechanization of large farms in an economy characterized by
        a 'labor surplus.'

(2)   The polarization in the size distribution of farms accompanied by a
        growing landlessness of the poor peasantry. The polarization consisted
        of an increase in the percentage shares of large and small farms at the ex-
        pense of medium-sized farms (8 to 25 acres).

(3)   The growth of capitalist farming together with a growing social and
        economic dependence of the poor peasantry on large landowners.

(4)   An absolute deterioration in the economic condition of the poor
        peasants alongside the growing affluence of the large farmers.

The Attempts at Land Reform and their Failure

Before embarking on an analysis of the four contradictions specified above
and their link with an unequal distribution of landownership, the land
reforms of 1959 and 1972 will be briefly examined.

The Land Reforms of 1959

The 1959 land reforms fixed the ceiling on the private ownership of land at 500 acres irrigated and 1,000 acres unirrigated. The fundamental feature which rendered this reform incapable of reducing the power of the big landlords was that the ceiling on ownership was fixed in terms of *individual* rather than family holdings. This enabled most of the big landlords to circumvent the ceiling by transferring their excess land to various real and fictitious family members. Moreover, a number of additional provisions in the 1959 land reform allowed landlords to retain land far in excess of the ceiling even on an individual basis. For example, and individual could keep land in excess of the ceiling so long as his holding was an equivalent of 36,000 Produce Index Units (PIUs). A PIU was estimated as a measure of the gross value of output per acre of land by type of soil and was therefore seen as a measure of land productivity. The flaw in this provision was that he PIUs were based on pre-partition revenue settlements. Since the gross value of output was dependent on the quality of land and prices, values of PIUs fixed before 1947 would grossly underestimate land productivity in 1959. M.H. Khan estimates that even if the PIU values published in 1959 were taken as a correct representative of land productivity, the allowance of 36,000 PIUs for an individual holding would leave a substantially larger area than that specified in the ceiling.[5] Another provision which enabled landlords to retain land above the ceiling was the additional area allowed for orchards.

Given the fact that in the 1959 land reforms the ceiling was fixed in terms of individual rather than family holdings, and given the existence of additional lacunae in the provision, most big landlords were able to circumvent the ceiling and retain their land without declaring any land in excess of the ceiling. Those who actually declared excess land were super-large landlords who even after making use of exemptions still could not conceal their entire holding. Thus the average owned area per declarant landlord in Pakistan was as much as 7,028 acres and was 11,810 acres in the Punjab province. It is interesting that even out of the land declared in excess of the ceiling only 35 percent (1.9 million acres) could be resumed by the government. After the government had resumed whatever excess land it could, the average owned holding retained by the declarant landlords was as much as 4,033 acres in Pakistan and 7,489 acres in Punjab province.[6] Thus the land reforms of 1959 failed to have the significant effect on the economic power of the landed elite in Pakistan. The final gesture of benevolence by the government towards the landlords was to be seen in the fact that of the land actually resumed under the 1959 land reforms, as much as 57 percent was uncultivated. Most of this area needed considerable land improvement before it could be cultivated. Yet the government paid Rs. 89.2 million to the former owners as 'compensation' for surrendering land which was producing nothing.[7]

The Land Reforms of 1972

The 1972 land reforms shared with the 1959 land reforms the essential feature of specifying the ceiling in terms of individual rather than family holdings. However the ceiling in the 1972 land reforms was lower, being 150 acres for irrigated and 300 acres for unirrigated. The 1972 land reforms allowed an area equivalent to 12,000 PIUs (with a bonus of 2000 PIUs to owners of tractors or tubewells) which enabled a de facto ceiling on an individual ownership far above the ceiling. The reason for this discrepancy between the de jure and de facto ceiling was that the basis of estimating the PIUs was still the revenue settlements of the 1940s. The considerable improvement in yields, cropping patterns, and cropping intensities since the 1940s meant that the use of obsolete PIUs in 1972 considerably understated land productivity. M. H. Khan has estimated that due to the understatement of land productivity throughout the PIUs provision, the actual ceiling in the 1972 land reforms was 466 acres in the Punjab and 560 acres in Sind for a tractor/tubewell owner. If an owner also took advantage of the provision for intra-family transfers the ceiling came to 932 acres irrigated in the Punjab and 1,120 acres in Sind.[8]

Of the land that was declared above the ceiling by landlords after making use of the provisions for circumventing the ceiling, only 42 percent was resumed in the Punjab and 59 percent in Sind. The area actually resumed by the government under the 1972 land reforms was only about 0.6 million acres, which was even less than the area resumed under the 1959 land reforms (which was 1.9 million acres). The resumed area in 1972 constituted only 0.01 percent of total farm area in the country. Moreover in the case of the Punjab 59 percent of the area resumed by the government, was uncultivated. Consequently the land reforms of 1972, like the land reforms of 1959 failed to affect the power of the big landlords.

Agrarian Structure and the Impact of the New Technology

The land reforms of 1959 and 1972 failed to alter significantly the highly unequal distribution of landownership in Pakistan. As much as 30 percent of total farm area in Pakistan is owned by large landowners (owning 150 acres and above), yet these landowners constitute only 0.5 percent of the total number of landowners in the country.[9] The overall picture of Pakistan's agrarian structure has been that these large landowners have rented out most of their land to tenants with small-and medium-sized holdings.[10] In such a situation when the HYV technology became available in the late 1960s the large landowners found it profitable to resume some of their rented-out land for self-cultivation on large farms, using hired labor and capital investment.[11] It is this process of the development of capitalist farming which has generated new and potentially explosive contradictions in Pakistan's rural society.

Farm Mechanization and the Problem of Employment

During the period when the HYV technology was being adopted in Pakistan there was also a rapid introduction of tractors. The number of tractors increased from only 2,000 in 1959 to 18,909 in 1968. The rapid increase in tractors continued and by 1975 there were 35,714 tractors in Pakistan. Between 1976 and 1981 an additional 75,859 tractors were imported into the country.[12]

It is significant that most of the tractors were large. According to the report of the Farm Mechanization Committee, 84 percent of the tractors were above 35 horsepower, while only 1 percent were in the small-size range of less than 26 horsepower.[13] Two questions arise: why were predominantly large-sized tractors introduced in a rural sector where 88 percent of the farms are below 25 acres in size[14] and why did tractorization occur at all in what is commonly regarded as a 'labor surplus' economy? Both these questions can be understood in terms of the fundamental features of Pakistan's agrarian economy arising out of the highly unequal distribution of landownership.

First, the distribution of farm area in Pakistan by size of *owned* holding is much more unequal than the distribution of farm area by size of *operated* holding. My estimates based on the 1972 Census of Agriculture show that as much as 30 percent of total farm area in Pakistan was owned by landowners in the size class of 150 acres and above; by contrast the percentage of farm area operated by farmers in this size class was only 9.2 percent. The difference in the degree of concentration of farm area between owned and operated holdings suggests that many of the larger landowners must be renting out some or all of their owned area to smaller farmers. This proposition is supported by the data which shows that the large landowners (150 acres and above) were even in 1972 the biggest renters out of land, compared to any other size class in Pakistan and Punjab respectively.[15]

Second, the larger landowners attracted by the high profitability of owner cultivation following the availability of HYV technology, tended to resume their formerly rented-out land for self-cultivation on large farms with tractors. Evidence for the resumption of land during 1960 and 1978 for owner cultivation on large tractor farms is provided by field survey data, which shows that farms in the size classes 50 to 150 acres and 150 acres and above have experienced a substantial increase in their area over the period.

In the case of farms in the size class 150 acres and above, the increase in farm area over the period 1960 to 1978 constituted half their total farm area in 1978. In terms of the source of increases, 65 percent of the increase in farm area of large farms came through resumption of formerly rented-out land. Thus resumption of formerly rented-out land was by far the biggest source of increase in farm area of large farms (see Table 1).

There is evidence that the resumption of rented-out land for self-cultivation on large farms was associated with the purchase of tractors by those farmers.

Table 1

Increase in Farm Area since 1960 by Source of Increase and Size Class in 1978 (in Acres)

			Increase in Farm Area by Source between 1960 and 1978				
Size Class	*Size of Farm*	*Increase in Farm Area 1960 to 1978*	*Total Farm Area in 1978*	*Resumption of Rented-out Land*	*Increase in Rented-in Land*	*Net Purchase (Purchase-Sale)*	*Net Other Sources**
Small	Less than 8	−20	52	4	−5	0	−19
Lower Medium	8 to 25	−81	209	0	−50	2	−33
Medium	25 to 50	+48	407	45	+8	4	−9
Upper Medium	50 to 150	+448	711	340	+24	40	+42
Large	150 and over	+3338	6464	2172	+38	1493	−365

*Other sources of increase or decrease in farm area are: (1) land brought by wife as dowry; (2) land appropriated by government, following land reforms; (3) farm area reduced through fragmentation following decision by family members to cultivate individually in independently operated plots.
Source: Field Survey, 1978.

My field survey data shows that whereas in 1960 almost 60 percent of the farmers in the large size class (150 acres and above) were without tractors, by 1978 all of them had at least one, and 41 percent had three or more tractors.[16]

Evidence at the all-Pakistan level is provided by the Report of the Farm Mechanization Committee. It shows that within the farm area operated by tractor owners, the percentage area operated by large farmers was as high as 87 percent.

An important reason why large-sized tractors began to get introduced during the 1960s was that large landowners responding to the new profit opportunities began to resume rented-out land for self-cultivation on large farms. Given the difficulty of mobilizing a large number of laborers during the peak seasons in an imperfect labor market and the problem of supervising the laborers to ensure satisfactory performance, the large farmers found it convenient to mechanize even though there may have been no labor shortage in an absolute sense.

Polarization in Rural Class Structure and the Increase in Landlessness

An examination of Census data for the period 1960 to 1972 shows that in the Punjab province (where the New Technology had its greatest impact) a polarization occurred in the size distribution of farms. The percentage shares of both large- and small-sized farms increased while that of medium-sized farms (7.5 to less than 25 acres) decreased (see Table 2). This polarization was essentially the result of large landowners resuming for self-cultivation some of the land which they had formerly rented out to tenants.[17]

The process underlying the polarization in rural class structure was as follows:

(1) Large landowners resumed for self-cultivation land which they had rented out to both small and lower-medium-sized (7.5 to less than 25 acres) tenant farmers. However, the resumption hit lower-medium farms to a much greater extent than small farms due to the considerably greater degree of tenancy in the former size class.

(2) As tenants operating lower-medium-sized farms lost some but not all of their land following resumption, many of them shifted into the category of small farms over the inter-censal period.

The evidence shows that polarization in the size of farms was accompanied by a growing landlessness of the poor peasantry. My estimates based on population census data show that from 1961 to 1973, 794,042 peasants entered the category of wage laborers, that is, 43 percent of the total agricultural laborers in Pakistan in 1973 had entered this category as the result of the proletarianization of the poor peasantry.

Given the unequal distribution of landownership in Pakistan, when the New Technology became available, it induced a process of land resumption by big landlords. This resulted in a polarization in the size distribution of farms on the one hand and an increased landlessness of the poor peasantry on the other.

Table 2

Percentage of Farms and Farm Area by Size of Farm 1960 and 1972 in Punjab (Adjusted* and Unadjusted Agriculture Census Data)

Size of Farm (Acres)	Number of Farms 1960		1972	Farm Area 1960		1972
	Unadjusted	Adjusted		Unadjusted	Adjusted	
Less than 7.5	63.35	35.53	41.28	19.07	9.93	11.80
7.5 to 25	29.81	52.82	46.88	45.27	51.15	46.42
25 to 50	5.42	8.88	8.81	20.21	20.23	21.30
50 to 150	1.27	2.49	2.72	10.57	12.94	14.72
150 and above	0.14	0.27	0.30	4.88	5.76	5.77
Total	100	100	100	100	100	100

Summary Table

Size of Farm (Acres)	Number of Farms		Farm Area	
	Col.(a) 1960 (Adjusted)	Col.(b) 1972	Col.(c) 1960 (Adjusted)	Col.(d) 1972
Less than 7.5	35.5	41.3	9.9	11.8
7.5 to 25	52.8	46.9	51.2	46.4
25 and above	11.6	11.8	38.9	41.8
Total	100	100	100	100

*The columns may not add up to exactly 100 in every case due to rounding errors.

Sources: 1960 Pakistan Census of Agriculture and 1972 Pakistan Census of Agriculture.

The Growth of Capitalist Farming and the Economic Dependence
of the Poor Peasantry

The growth of capitalist farming was accelerated considerably in the late 1960s as large landowners began to resume their rented-out land to operate their own farms with hired labor and capital investment. The particular form of the development of capitalism in Pakistan's agriculture was such that instead of being accompanied by a growing independence of the poor peasantry (as in Europe), in Pakistan's case capitalism in agriculture was accompanied by an increased social and economic dependence of the poor peasantry on the landowners. The reason for this was that capitalist farming in Pakistan developed in a situation where the power of the landlords was still intact. Consequently the emerging market was mediated by the social and political power of the landlords. The local institutions for the distribution of agricultural inputs and credit and of sale of output are heavily influenced by the big landlords. In order to acquire the inputs, credit and facilities for transport of output to the market the poor peasant has to depend on help from the landlord. In many cases the poor peasant in the absence of collateral cannot get credit from the official agencies at all, and has to depend on the landlord for loans. In addition to this he or she often has to purchase the tubewell water from the landlord and use landlord transport for taking output for sale to the market. Thus as the inputs for agricultural production become monetized and insofar as the access to the market is via the landlord, the poor peasant's dependence has intensified with the development of capitalism in agriculture.

With the development of capitalist farming, the poor peasant is subject to a triple squeeze on real income.

Increased Money Costs

Inputs which were formerly non-monetized (seed, animal manure and the like) or inputs which were formerly not used at all (such as tractor ploughings, tubewell water, pesticides) now have to be purchased with money. It might be asked why the poor peasant now has to buy fertilizer and hire tractors. The answer lies in the inability of the poor peasant (whether owner or tenant) to maintain as many farm animals as before. The reasons for this are:

(1) Pastures devoted to fodder have been reduced on poor peasant farms as farm size declined following loss of some rented land due to resumption.
(2) The poor peasant's access to the fodder and pasture lands of the landlords was reduced as the latter mechanized and began to grow cash crops over much of the area formerly devoted to pastures or fodder.

Thus mechanization and the development of capitalist farming on large farms has adversely affected the poor peasants' ability to keep animals thereby making them more vulnerable to market pressures.

The second factor in the rise in money costs is the shift from sharecropping to money rents which are rising sharply. The money rent is often fixed by the landlord not on the basis of the actual yield of the tenant-operated farm, but its *potential* yield if it were being cultivated at peak efficiency.

Slow Growth in Yield Per Acre

While there has been an increase in cash rents payable by the poor peasant and thus in rental burden, yields per acre have not increased proportionately. The latter is due to the fact that the poor peasant has neither the financial and political power to acquire all the required inputs (seed, fertilizer, supplementary tubewell water, pesticides) nor to control their timing.

Selling Grain Cheap and Buying Dear

The third pressure on the real income of the poor peasant is that in a situation of rising cash requirements and indebtedness, they are forced to sell a part of their subsistence output at harvest time at low prices. Then at the end of the year they have to buy grain in the market at high prices. Thus selling grain cheap, and buying dear, is another squeeze on the poor peasant's income.

The squeeze on the real income of the poor peasants is reflected in the changes in the quality and quantity of their diet since 1965, in Table 3. Table 3 shows that the class of poor peasants (with farm size below 25 acres), con-

Table 3

Percentage Change in the Quantity and Quality of the Diet of Farmers between 1975 to 1978 by Size Class of Farm

Size of Farm (Acres)	Quantity of Diet[1]				Quality of Diet[2]			
	Diet has improved.	Diet has deteriorated.	Diet has remained unchanged.	Total	Diet has improved.	Diet has deteriorated.	Diet has remained unchanged.	Total
Less than 8	11	33	56	100	0	67	33	100
8 to 25	0	25	75	100	0	69	31	100
25 to 50	0	0	100	100	0	25	75	100
50 to 150	0	0	100	100	0	0	100	100
150 and above	0	0	100	100	0	0	100	100

1. Quantity of Diet. A reduction in the quantity of diet refers to a reduction in the quantity of one or more of the following items, without an increase in any: (i) number of chappattis consumed during the day; (ii) quantity of milk consumed during the day; (iii) quantity of lassi consumed during the day; (iv) number of times during the day that lentils or vegetables are eaten along with chappattis.

2. Quality of Diet. A reduction in the quality of diet refers to a change of one or more of the following; (i) a reduction in the quantity of milk with an increase in the quantity of lassi; (ii) a reduction in the frequency of meat consumption per month by the peasant households; (iii) a replacement of homemade butter and ghee with canned vegetable cooking oil purchased in the market. The latter has a much lower fat content than homemade ghee and is also often adulterated according to the respondents.

Soucre: Field Survey, 1978.

tains a substantial number of farmers who have suffered an absolute decline in the quantity of food and contains an even larger number of farmers who have suffered a decline in the quality of their diet.

Conclusion

In Pakistan, with its highly unequal distribution of landownership, the introduction of the New Technology in agriculture has unleashed powerful contradictions which are not only likely to become constraints on continued agricultural growth, but are also generating acute social tensions. The nature of the economic progress, in the absence of an effective land reform, is such that it is enriching the rural elite and the expense of the rapid deterioration in the economic and social conditions of the majority of the rural population. Four major contradictions can be seen in the process of agricultural growth since the adoption of the New Technology:

First, there has been the rapid adoption of large tractors in a labor surplus economy where 88 percent of the farms are below 25 acres. This has happened as the result of large landowners resumng their formerly rented-out land for self-cultivation on large mechanized farms. Labor displacing technology is being used by large farmers not because there is an absolute labor shortage, but in order to overcome the problem of supervision of labor and the difficulty of mobilizing labor within a short time period.

Second, a polarization in the size distribution of farms has taken place, with the percentage shares of large and small farms increasing at the expense of medium-sized farms (8 to 25 acres). This has also resulted from large landowners resuming their formerly rented-out land. Land resumption has hit medium-sized farms to a much greater extent than small-sized farms, pushing many of them into the category of small farms following resumption.

Third, the development of capitalist farming has occurred in a situation where the prevalence of feudal power by the big farmers has deprived the poor peasant equal access to the market. Consequently the poor peasant has become more dependent on the big farmer for conducting his production process.

Fourth, rising money costs for the poor peasants—in a situation where they are locked in a structure of dependence—have placed the poor peasant into a triple squeeze which is resulting in a rapid deterioration of their economic condition. Each of the contradictions specified above stems from the fact that the New Technology became available in a situation where economic and social power was concentrated in the hands of the big landlords.

Agricultural growth during the 1960s and 1970s was predicated on the rapid increase in yields of the larger farms, but continued growth in the next two decades will have to be derived from increasing yields per acre of the small farmers. An essential pre-condition for this is institutional and economic changes which will give the small farmer better access over the new inputs and greater control over the production process and investable surplus. In this sense, an effective land reform is now not only an imperative of a more equitable economic growth but also of growth itself.

NOTES

[1] There was a lively debate on the factors underlying the inverse relationship between farm size and productivity. One of the more elegant explanations for this phenomenon was offered by A.K. Sen who suggested that with traditional technology small family farms could produce a higher yield per acre than large farms through a higher labor input per acre. This could happen because small farms using family labor applied labor input beyond the point where the marginal product equalled the wage rate, while large farms using hired labor could not afford to do so.

[2] Annual growth rate of large-scale manufacturing during 1950-55 was 23.6 percent, while that of agriculture during the same period was only 1.3 percent. During the period 1955-60, annual growth rate in large-scale manufacturing declined to 9.3 percent, while that of agriculture was only 1.4 percent. See S.R. Lewis, Jr., *Economic Policy and Industrial Growth in Pakistan,* London: George Allen and Unwin Ltd., 1959, p.3, table 1.

[3] Cotton and jute constituted 85 percent of total commodity exports up to the mid-1950s. See S.R. Lewis, op.cit., p.7, table 5.

[4] Import of foodgrains and flour as a percentage of total commodity imports increased from 0.5 percent in 1951-52 to 14.6 percent in 1959-60. See: A Hussain, 'The Impact of Agricultural Growth on Changes in the Agrarian Structure of Pakistan.' D.Phil. Thesis, Sussux Univerity, 1980, table 3, p.16.

[5] M.H. Khan, *Underdevelopment and Agrarian Structure in Pakistan.* Vanguard Publications Ltd., 1981, chap.5.

[6] *Land Reform in West Pakistan.* Vol.III, appendix 18, Government of Pakistan, 1967.

[7] See M.H. Khan, op.cit., chap.5.

[8] Ibid.

[9] These figures are estimated on the basis of combining Land Reforms Commission data and the Agriculture Census data. The 1972 Agriculture Census data alone gives an incorrect figure for land owned by the large landowners because its sampling procedure is such that absentee land is systematically excluded. For details of my estimating procedure see: A. Hussain, op.cit., appendix 2, pp.219-21.

[10] As late as 1972, 46 percent of the total farm area in Pakistan was tenant-operated, and of this tenant area, 50 per cent had been rented out by large landowners (owning 150 acres and above). My estimates show that as much as 75 percent of area owned by large landowners in 1972 was rented out to smaller tenants. See: A. Hussain, op.cit., chap.3.

[11]For detailed evidence and analysis of this tendency of land resumption by big landlords, see: A. Hussain, 'Technical Change and Social Polarization in Rural Punjab' in Karamat Ali (edited), *The Political Economy of Rural Development*. Vanguard Publications, 1982.

[12]Finance Division, Economic Adviser's Wing, *Pakistan Economic Survey 1980-81*. Government of Pakistan, Islamabad.

[13]Ministry of Agriculture and Works, *Report of the Farm Mechanization Committee*. Government of Pakistan, March 1970.

[14]Ministry of Food and Agriculture, Agriculture Census Organization, *Pakistan Census of Agriculture: All Pakistan Report*. Government of Pakistan, table 1.

[15]See: A. Hussain, op.cit., table 5(a), p.194 and 6(a), p.198.

[16]A Hussain, op.cit., chap.5 and Appendix.

[17]This picture emerges when the 1960 Census data is adjusted for biases inherent in its methodology in order to make it comparable with the 1972 Census methodology. A. Hussain, op.cit., chap.3.

NOTES ON
NATIONAL UNITY AND
REGIONAL IMBALANCES

Shahid Kardar

The concept of national integration encompasses political, social, cultural and economic integration. In Pakistan the centre-province relations have always been tenuous behind the facade of public order and public quiescence. The disgruntlement simmering in the provinces manifested itself as an explosion in the late sixties resulting in the dismemberment of the country. The presence of a representative government and the availability of channels for expressing these sentiments during the following six years did not guarantee management of dissent within tolerable limits. The reappearance of the army in 1977, and the introduction of legislation which has taken away from the people political rights procured after a lot of sacrifices, has re-instated in a paramount position in the political arena the question of provincial autonomy and the decentralization of the power structure. The centre-province relations have become politically explosive and the events in the smaller provinces, especially in Sind, over the past few years have a significance more fundamental than suggested by their apparently short-lived repercussions.

This article attempts to examine the social, political and economic backgrounds of the demands being made on the Pakistani State of the eighties by the increasing clamour for provincial autonomy.

Political Dimension

The British, because of their own peculiar circumstances as colonisers, had installed a well-greased administratively efficient centralised system. These centralized decision making structures and institutions were retained after political independence in complete contrast to one of the fundamental desires of the Movement—to create a Federal State. It was agreed that there were four (considering only the present territory) distinct ethnic/national groups. For such a structure to sustain itself it is necessary that the desires of the participating units, regarding effective participation in decision making and equitable distribution of national wealth, be met. I.A. Rahman argues in the *Viewpoint* of March 22, 1984 that historically the Indian subcontinent comprised 'kingdoms and principalities'. Even when they were conquered by a superior military power, the internal structures were left intact, although assimilated into a bigger entity. The British gave the subcontinent some sort of political unity whereas before them these geographical units had developed

From Viewpoint, *December 27, 1984 and January 3, 1985. Reprinted with permission.*

into separate social and cultural units. So, centre-province conflicts are not new, demands for greater provincial autonomy have historical moorings.

Economic growth, urbanisation, increased education and political consciousness instilled during the seventies have encouraged the inhabitants of the smaller provinces to demand their due political, social and economic rights with a greater degree of vociferousness.

The political parties and intellectuals of all shades of opinion in the smaller provinces are now demanding a wider distribution of power. They feel that within the prevailing institutional framework effective restraints cannot be placed on those who use this power from Islamabad. It is widely felt that even the 1973 Constitution falls short of the requirements generated by a radically changed political climate. It does not have a list of subjects which could be treated as prerogatives of the provinces.

The disgruntlement of the smaller provinces is over the enormous leverage that the centre holds over any dispensation in the provinces. The centre is all powerful. Its legislative, executive, administrative and judicial powers appear to have no legal boundaries. It can, and does, practically control the administrative, legislative and judicial decisions and actions of the provinces. Not only does the centre allocate resources for development and non-development expenditure to the provinces, it also appoints the administrative bureaucratic teams which are supposed to implement these projects and policy measures. Furthermore, the centre, and now under RCO 1985 just one man, decides the governors, judges, chief ministers and key officials of the province. A large proportion of the important bureaucratic positions in the provinces (in the revenue departments, in the judiciary and amongst those responsible for implementing and executing important provincial policies) are occupied by those appointed by the Federal Government. The Centre can bring the provinces under its direct control in a 'law and order situation' without even seeking the consent of the provincial government, although law and order is constitutionally a provincial subject. The intervention in Baluchistan during the PPP regime is a case in point.

The provinces are seeking greater provincial autonomy as against the regime's interest in a strong centre which can freely allocate the domestically generated surplus. To them political, executive and economic authority rests either with the Punjabis or the Urdu-speaking refugeees with their control over the military and civil services which consume over 60% of the government's revenue. Of the foreign loans, whose debt servicing costs consume over 25% of the revenues, the vast majority are utilised in the Punjab or areas dominated by the Urdu speaking refugee population. The industrial structure is such that 70% of the industry is concentrated in 8 districts and of which almost 43% is located in Karachi.

The Case of Punjab

The Punjab operates from a position of strength because of its historic dominance of the military and bureaucratic institutions. Even in a democratic set up it would retain this dominance because of the sheer size of its population—56% of the national population; it can outvote all other provinces. Moreover, because of the disproportionate representation of the Punjabi and the refugee elements in the powerful central elites (as I would prefer to call them) in the civil and military services, the public sector—industrial and trading—and capitalist classes, it also means that in absolute numbers quite a few Punjabi households have a stake in the status-quo. Their interconnections are further cemented by inter-marriages, ethnic relationships and the social and cultural values linked with a joint family system. This entrenched position of the Punjab, which it would maintain in any form of political structure, only serves to reinforce the sense of alienation felt by the other provinces thereby rendering more daunting the task of national integration and unity. They feel that they would be subjugated to the whims and wishes of the Punjab on an eternal basis.

The Case of Sind

Sindhi politicians even before independence were primarily engaged in propagating provincial causes. In 1947 the Sind Muslim League had demanded complete autonomy for the provinces and sought equal participation in the legislature and executive functions. Therefore, it was not surprising that Sind was in the forefront of the opposition to the creation of One Unit. The formation of One Unit also worked against Sindhi representation in the military and civil services (in which their representation was historically nominal) aggravating the already deep seated resentment because of reasons enumerated below.

Sindhi became the official language of Sind in the late 19th century. Amongst the regional languages Sindhi was the most developed. It was the medium of instruction in schools at the time of independence and boasted of newspapers with a fairly wide circulation. One of the first translations of the Quran in the subcontinent was in Sindhi. So, to a Sindhi, his mother tongue, apart from its historical importance, is a symbol of nationalistic pride, especially because the non-Sindhi residents of the province speak Urdu. Moreover, even India had accepted Sindhi as one of its regional languages as against the position after independence.

The vast majority of the refugees from India settled in Sind—with almost 70% settling in the urban areas. Being better educated than the locals they replaced the fleeing Hindus. They also took over the property of the Hindus, giving rise to a sense of deprivation amongst the Sindhis. Evacuee property was allocated to the refugees which involved large scale eviction of tenants—involving, according to one estimate, almost 40% of agricultural land. The demand by the Sind Assembly to return this land to the original Sindhi owners was rejected. Then came the allotments of barrage lands (Sukkur, Guddu and Ghulam Mohd) to non-Sindhi officers from the civil and military services. Even today this policy of allotments to non-Sindhis is taking place in spite of the extremely sensitive situation in the province. According to a report in the *Muslim* of May 3, 1984 the most productive land on the National highway in Thatta District comprising 38,000 acres was being leased out for 30 years at a laughable rate of Rs. 7 per acre to high government officials (in the police and revenue departments, PWD and WAPDA) or to those with access to corridors of power—mostly Punjabis and refugee settlers from India—at the expense of the rightful claimants, the poor Haris. Some of these individuals even got themselves registered as Haris.

The state sponsored financial institutions for providing financial assistance to farmers are also suspected of granting most of their loans to the non-Sindhi, absentee landlords. A similar step-brotherly treatment is accorded to Sindhi farmers when it comes to electricity and water connections, distribution of irrigation water and inputs like seeds, fertilizers and pesticides.

According to one estimate, 60% of the population in rural Sind lives below the poverty line with monthly per capita income of Rs. 124 and savings of 1% of Gross Provincial Product. Overall, 20.3% of households in Sind earn Rs. 200 and below, accounting for 3.4% of total income.

Sind unlike the other three and especially the Punjab, did not share in the Middle East bonanza—very few Sindhis went to the Gulf. The two major cities Karachi and Hyderabad and a large proportion of the medium-sized towns are dominated by non-Sindhis, mainly Urdu speaking refugees from India. The civil bureaucracy in the province is also largely non-Sindhi.

The termination of civilian rule by the armed forces largely belonging to the biggest province and the death of the most popular Sindhi ever has minimised the participation of Sindhis in the decision making process and only served to estrange them. These factors and the use of force, under the pretext of a law and order situation, has left the Sindhis with a feeling of a nation whose self-respect, dignity and honour has been violated.

These three factors and the land awards in Sind to Punjabi army officers (as in the Pat Feeder area in Baluchistan) has exacerbated the frustration and disillusionment of the youth in the province. The deprived youth have become bitter and are protesting against 'injustices', and the Sindhi Waderas,* afraid to lose their political influence, have been forced to lead this protest, as they found that the common ground between them and the militant cadres of the PPP and the Sind Awami Tehrik (SAT) was fast disappearing; a situation whose persistence they could ill-afford if they wanted to preserve their political existence. Furthermore, the regime was attacking and

* Waderas: Landowners

attempting to destroy the social power of these Waderas in their areas who were therefore forced into expressing their discontent and resentment through the only avenue available to them: they supported the popular rebellion which erupted in Sind in 1984.

The Case of NWFP

Although at the time of independence Ghaffar Khan and his Khudai Khidmatgars represented an organised group actively engaged in the opposition of the Muslim League, the situation of the NWFP has changed radically. In the Frontier, Punjabi is well understood in some areas while Urdu is spoken by a sizeable proportion of the population. The reason is not only that half the population is non-Pushto but that there is Pathan representation in the civil and military services, business circles and in the labour force in Karachi in industry and the informal service sectors like transport, construction etc. Some Pathans like General Habibullah, Gohar Ayub, the Hotis rank amongst the big Pakistani capitalists. Hence, the Pathans have a stake in the status quo.

Moreover, there are around 0.3 million Pathans in the Middle East who are sending in almost $0.5 billion, adding to the prosperity in the province. A lot of Pathans have also prospered from smuggling of foreign goods (found in the 'Bara' markets) and heroin.

The above factors, the present rather personalised influence of Fazl-e-Haq in the politics of the province and the presence of 2 million Afghan refugees have contributed significantly to the absence of any political agitation in the region.

The Case of Baluchistan

In Baluchistan trade and commerce and the civil services are controlled by Pathans, who even provide labour for the ship breaking industry in Gadani. So, the Baluch also lack representation in the civil and military services and in industry—their stake and interest in the status quo is limited, if any.

Of the 85 established industrial units in Baluchistan (practically all owned by non-Baluchis) 50 are located in Quetta and the rest in Hub—both being essentially non-Baluch areas. The province suffers from acute shortages of adequate infrastructure; even safe drinking water and rudimentary health facilities are difficult to come by.

Sui gas field in Bugti area meets almost 80% of the gas needs of the nation. Foreign exchange savings from Sui and other gas fields in Baluchistan are almost Rs. 8 billion a year as against royalties paid to Baluchistan of under Rs. 0.6 billion. The Baluchis also claim that the mining conditions and operations are not being improved and the surplus generated in the province is consumed (or accumulated) outside the province generating it.

The youth have become politicised to the extent that they are now a militant force. They and the dissident factions dislike the apparently conciliatory policies of even the most polished and articulate Baluch politician, Bizenjo. They have now, like their Sindhi counterparts, become the most important pressure group in the politics of the province.

The feeling is that there is no option left—the national question cannot be resolved within the present political structure. It is argued that even under the democratically elected Bhutto government the democratic spirit of the 1973 Constitution was trampled upon and the provincial government disbanded—even the armed forces were used to suppress them. Thus it is understandable that the Baluch no longer appear to be willing to enter into a dialogue on the political future.

The provinces seek greater autonomy as against the interest of the military regime to centralize and have control over the domestically generated surplus. As defence and administration consume over 60% of domestic revenues it is understandable why the regime cannot afford to give the purse to a 'third party', a truly representative legislature, and also vest it with the discretionary power to distribute the coffers as it best pleased. This brings us to the importance of the representativeness of the civil and military services.

In a highly centralised system, and especially one in which the military-bureaucratic oligarchy (to borrow a phrase from Hamza Alavi) has ruled for almost 20 years of the life of the nation, an effective participatory role, in advancing regional interests, decision making and policy execution, can only be performed through representation in the civil and military services. In this sense obstacles to minority representation in the military bureaucratic set up can be alternatively construed as a lack of political representation and hence a negation of the goal to promote national cohesion and unity. The present regime has compounded the complexity surrounding this sensitive issue by creating a 10% quota in the civlian bureaucracies and the governmental sector for those from the armed forces, which in turn have a heavy Punjabi and Pathan representation.

In the Federal Government secretariat and related departments, Punjab has around 56% of the posts, approximately equal to its percentage of national population. Rural Sind has around 3%, NWFP around 11% and Baluchistan around 2.5%, while urban Sind (especially Karachi and Hyderabad), comprising mainly Urdu-speaking Mohajirs and Punjabis, i.e. non-Sindhis, an almost 25% representation. In the Government sector Corporations, Punjab has about 41% of the middle and senior level posts, Urban Sind 47%, Rural Sind 3.5%, NWFP 6% and Baluchistan 1%. These figures were compiled on the basis of domicile certificates. But these domiciles do not indicate an individual's real ethnic background. These statistics therefore understate Punjabi and Mohajir representation in such institutions.

The primary issue is not merely the creation of an efficiently run economy but how the various nationalities perceive themselves to be the participants in the development proces and in the management of the affairs of the nation. The pattern of growth witnessed in Pakistan has resulted in the fruits of development bypassing large sections of the community and in such a manner that the haves and have nots (in the loose sense of the terms) could also to some extent be split on the basis of nationalities. If the reason underlying the pursuance of this path to economic development was an efficient and optimum utilisation of all resources, including human resources, then the whole approach was extremely myopic. We had surely not sought independence from the British merely to administer our affairs more efficiently: our overriding concern was with social justice.

The Economic Dimension

The major objective of a Federal State should be to ensure that the constituent parts consider themselves to be active, even if not equal, participants of the development process and regard themselves to be some sort of beneficiaries of the gains accruing from economic growth. This approach envisages comprehensive and well laid out policy measures to minimise interprovincial disparaties in incomes and quantum and quality of social services (sponsored and financed by the State).

Since independence Pakistan has unquestionably recorded impressive growth figures e.g.

(i) food production has managed to stay ahead of the startling increase in population;

(ii) the mortality rate has been reduced by 50%

(iii) the growth in domestic industrial production has outstripped, by many a mile, the situation in 1947.

But the above figures obviously do not indicate the distribution of growth not only amongst the various classes but also amongst the different provinces and nationalities. The problem is not of economic stagnation but that of increasing differentials between the rich and the poor.

At independence it was acknowledged that there were wide inter-provincial differentials. Subsequent governments made various attempts to redress the grievances of the lesser developed provinces by adopting policy measures aimed at reducing the disparities in the levels of development. Let us now examine the outcomes of such exercises and whether the outcome of 'planned development' was in consonance with the national objective of balanced regional development.

In 1947 there were large disparities between the Punjab, Karachi and the other poor areas. These differentials were compounded by the differences in cultural traditions, historical characteristics and administrative systems. With the exception of a few enclaves there was general backwardness i.e. most 'remained in the backwater of economic development'. The modernized industrial sector was small and could be found almost entirely in Karachi, Lahore and Faisalabad. Therefore, any industrial expansion, at least in the short-term, had to be concentrated in these areas. It was only in the second half of the sixties that there was some emphasis on the location of industrial units in backward areas, especially public sector projects. This, however, was not to lead to any concrete steps and visible outcomes. Whatever little was established was because of the ready availability of raw materials like tobacco, paper, cement, natural gas etc. in these areas.

The discussion on the issue of regional imbalances was severely circumscribed because there were only few resources available to fund the development effort. The ruling elite were thus under pressure to categorise as traitors any group or section of the community protesting against this inequitable state of affairs. The regional dimension was therefore only paid lip service, if that. The multinational aspect of the country was ignored because, apart from interests of the dominant elites, it was also perceived that economic activity could be better monitored in a unified economy. It was considered that allocations from the centre could look after the development needs of the provinces thereby serving the requirements of national integration, cohesion and solidarity.

The growth in the industrial sector between the fifties and the early sixties was financed by the agriculture sector through the over valued rupee and the unfavourable terms of trade of agriculture products *vis-a-vis* industrial goods. Prices of agricultural inputs of the industrial sector were kept below world prices while that of industrial products higher than world prices. Because of this policy, the poorer regions, being mainly agricultural areas, suffered the most. In Baluchistan, for example, agriculture accounts for 56% of the provincial gross domestic product and accommodates 65% of the labour force. Bureaucrats argue, however, that the main reasons for varied agricultural growth are to be found in differences in the natural resource endowment – availability of land, quality of soil availability of water etc., but then this fails to explain why, if Baluchistan is acknowledged to have about 15 million acres of rich cultivale land, only 3 million acres are under cultivation. Why was so little attention paid to the exploitation of undergound water and improving infrastructural facilities in respect of a transportation network, electricity, training schools for imparting technical skills etc.?

The fiscal powers of the provinces are extremely limited and the revenue they can mobilise from their own resources are woefully inadequate to meet the task of development. Because of the historically high incidence of poverty and general backwardness in Baluchistan and to some extent NWFP, these provinces have difficulty in generating adequate resources from their narrow and limited resource base to finance their development and essential social service programmes. Provinces in general finance under 20% of their expenditure (both development and non-development) from their own revenue sources. So, they have to rely on allocations from the centre either under some fiscal arrangement or on the recommendations of the Planning Commission and Ministry of Finance, as the principal source of funds for regional investments.

Under the 1973 Constitution, the centre allocates funds on sector-wise basis rather than on provincial basis. The centre surveys the situation only in the national context and allocates resources to sectors based on their assessment of a sector's potential to contribute to development—everything else is accorded secondary importance.

There have been demands from certain quarters that provincial allocations by the centre should be made in proportion to the tax and revenue contributions of the provinces. But such a proposition is untenable in view of Karachi's unique position as a port and the government's taxation structure largely dependent on custom duties, which by their very nature are applied at the port of entry or discharge. Again, although sales and property taxes (including land revenue) are collected by the provinces, incomes of manufacturing and service sectors are taxed where they accrue i.e. based on location of head offices rather than where they arise i.e. the location of production. Furthermore, excise duties on production and custom duties on imports are collected elsewhere as against the wide dispersal of consumers. Therefore it can be argued that transfers from the centre have to some extent ensured some allocations for the backward regions as redistribution of income tax collections is done largely according to population.

The more backward regions showed poor growth rates because of poor credit absorptive capacity on account of inadequate infrastructure and a weak credit delivery system. So, unless something is done urgently the regional imbalances will get accentuated. A much higher level of public sector investment could have ameliorated the dire circumstances of the poor regions by providing necessary infrasturctural facilities. This could help attract private investment and minimise the substantial outflow of resources, capital and labour to the more prosperous areas of Karachi, Lahore, Faisalabad, Multan etc. Although the need for creating conditions for balanced regional development is widely touted, regional integration has been disregarded as a key policy instrument. Policies designed merely to accelerate industrial and agricultural growth have been cloaked in populist rhetoric. The outcome of the economic measures was not in consonance with the stated objective of narrowing differentials. Regional disparities worsened and sharpened the polarized nature of development and growth.

A comparison between provinces based on certain development indices (including social indicators) is certain to show Punjab as the best placed, Sind as number two, followed by NWFP and Baluchistan. These positions will emerge if an examination were to be made on an all provincial basis although for some indices Sind would show a higher level of development than the Punjab; but there would be a need for a more detailed analysis of such a composite result. The results would be highly skewed because of the special positions of Karachi, Peshawar and Quetta. As already explained above Karachi, Hyderabad and most of the large, more prosperous cities and towns have a non-Sindhi predominance while Peshawar is largely a non-Pushto city and Quetta a non-Baluch city whose administrative, trade and commercial control is in non-Baluch hands.

The situation is more acute than depicted by the province-wise data on education, health, housing, transportation and communication etc. because, while most of the national population in the smaller provinces lives in rural areas, the facilities are concentrated in the smaller, non-native urban sector. Therefore, a clearer picture of the extent of inequalities betwen provinces would emerge from an examination of the rural areas—where the majority are national and ethnic communities. The results of this exercise are given in the tables which follow:

Average Monthly Incomes

	Punjab	Sind (Rupees)	NWFP	Baluchistan
Urban areas	1,213	1,476	1,607	1,357
Rural areas	828	794	936	762

Rural areas – Percentage of households Monthly income groups

Below Rs. 1000	77.5%	80.3%	72.8%	82.3%
Above Rs. 3500	0.9%	0.3%	1.5%	0.5%

Percentage of Total Farms (in brackets percentage of total areas) – 1981 Census

Farms below 5 acres	31% (7%)	26% (6%)	61%(16%)	28% (3%)
5 – 25 acres	58%(54%)	68%(60%)	34%(41%)	54%(34%)
25 – 150 acres	9%(33%)	7%(27%)	5%(29%)	16%(41%)
Above 150 acres	–(6%)	–(7%)	–(14%)	1(22%)

Percentage of Total Farms (in brackets percentage of total areas) – 1972 Census

Farms below 5 acres	26% (5%)	18% (5%)	56%(13%)	24% (2%)
5 – 25 acres	62%(54%)	73%(63%)	37%(30%)	53%(26%)
25 – 150 acres	12%(36%)	7%(24%)	6%(33%)	21%(40%)
Above 150 acres	–(6%)	–(8%)	–(14%)	2%(32%)

ADP Allocations for Agriculture (Utilization in brackets)

1980–81 Rupees in	454 (281)	109 (100)	93(76)	65(76)
1981–82 Millions	482 (282)	133 (101)	107(90)	114 (87)

Punjab's share in ADBP loans increased from 57% in 1973–74 to 76% in 1979–80.

Loans – Rupees per cropped Hectare

1973–74	21	47	9	32
1979–80	43	36	15	11

Loans outstanding –

| Rupees in Million | 3,537 | 829 | 579 | 451 |

Irrigation Intensity (Irrigated Area as a percentage of Cultivated Area)

	Punjab	Sind	NWFP	Baluchistan
1946–62	71%	62%	42%	15%
1970–80	86%	58%	36%	38%

Punjab has 88.3% of tubewells, Sind 5.6%, NWFP 2.6% and Baluchistan 3.5%.

Use of inputs – Percentages of total farm

Fertilizers only	60%	42%	16%	5%
Manures only	8%	1%	19%	13%
Insecticides	6%	4%	3%	9%
Tractors	17%	8%	Information not available	

Punjab has 80.5% of total tractors in the country.

Fertilizer consumption Kgs per cultivated hectare

1971–72	23	18	20	1
1979–80	62.5	12.5	7	21.5

Villages Electrified – Number

Up to 1959	100	–	519	–
From 1960–1971-72	907	204	790	–
1972–1980–81	4,214	2,180	1,388	255

Percentage of Total Villages Electrified

1959–60	58%	4%	38%	–
1971–72	49%	8%	43%	–
1979–80	52%	22%	24%	2%

Percentage of national production

Wheat	72%	15%	8%	5%
Rice	56%	41%	3%	–
Cotton	71%	29%	–	–
Sugarcane	72%	17%	11%	–

Of the total value added in the manufacturing sector, as per the 1981–82 Census, 48% was added in Sind of which 67% in Karachi and 8% in Hyderabad.

8.5% was added in NWFP of which 56.6% in Peshawar, 23% in Mardan and 16% in Abbotabad – largely non-Pushto speaking cities.

From the above analysis the following conclusions can be drawn:

(a) Within the NWFP rural and urban incomes tend to be less concentrated compared to other provinces.

(b) Although in Sind urban incomes are higher compared to the Punjab and Baluchistan, this position has emerged purely because of Karachi. Urban incomes in Sind also appear to be grossly under reported for higher levels of income.

(c) The problem of fragmentation of holdings is fairly widespread. However, it should be noted that the inforamtion available is in respect of 'operated holdings'. The information above gives no indication of the distribution of land ownership.

(d) Mechanisation in agriculture has proceeded at a much faster pace in the Punjab compared to other provinces.

(e) Fertilizer use is concentrated in the provinces of Punjab and Sind indicating exposure to and adoption of modern agricultural techniques.

(f) Despite ADP allocations for agriculture of almost twice as much as the other provinces put together, the utilization record of the Punjab is abysmal compared to the other three. Punjab's share of agricultural credit has continued to rise at the expense of the other provinces.

(g) Attempts to bring Sind and Baluchistan and some backward regions of the Punjab into the 20th century, through electrification of villages, only took place over the last 10 years.

Other development indicators

Literacy Ratios	Punjab	Sind	NWFP	Baluchistan
Urban	46.7%	50.8%	35.8%	33.2%
Rural	20%	15.6%	17.3%	6.2%

Institutions per Million Population (Numbers)

	Punjab	Sind	NWFP	Baluchistan
Primary Schools				
1960–61	460	794	223	524
1977–78	735	719	609	677
Middle Schools				
1960–61	49	25	34	58
1977–78	74	49	59	76
Colleges				
1960–61	3	4	2	3
1977–78	5	8	7	8
Post Offices				
1977–78	152	73	123	163
Telephones				
1977–78	2763	6342	5042	1582

But these figures do not portray the plight of the Sindhi and Baluch areas. This becomes conspicuous after the figures for Karachi and Hyderabad in Sind and Quetta in Baluchistan are segregated.

Enrolment in Primary Schools in Sind – Karachi and Hyderabad figures in brackets

1974–75	987,000
of which in Karachi and Hyderabad	(538,000)
1976–77	1,094,000
	(582,000)
1979–80	1,292,000
	(653,000)

Of the total enrolment in degree colleges over 85% takes place in Karachi and Hyderabad.

Schools in Baluchistan

Primary Schools		*High Schools*		*Enrolment in Colleges*	
1976–77	132	1977–78	8	1977–78-1979–80	444
of which in Quetta	(35)	of which in Quetta	(4)	of which in Quetta	(295)
1979–80	154	1979–80	9		
	(38)		(4)		

Health

Sind

	1976–79	1979–80
Hospitals		57
of which in Karachi and Hyderabad		(13)
Beds	Not available	9,800
	for 1976–79	(5,600)
Dispensaries		85
		(58)

Baluchistan

	1976–79	1979–80
Hospitals	29	35
of which in Quetta	(6)	(9)
Beds	1850	1964
	(1173)	(1239)
Dispensaries	398	335
	(22)	(22)

Health Facilities in Rural Areas – Percentage of households

	Punjab	Sind	NWFP	Baluchistan
Maternity and Health Care Units	6.8%	–	2.6%	–
Rural Health Care Centres	14.6%	4.3%	11.7%	58.3%
Hospital Clinics	19.4%	21.7%	35.1%	–
Private Clinics	27.7%	35.9%	2.6%	–
None	31.3%	38%	48%	41.7%

Housing Census – Rural Areas

	Punjab	Sind
Rooms per housing unit		
– average	2	1.5
Concrete outer walls	5%	3%
Source of drinking water inside		
– pipe	2%	1%
– handpump	54%	19%
Electricity as a source of lighting	14%	11%
Cooking Fuel used		
– gas and electricity	14%	3%
– wood and coal	76%	87%
– kerosine oil	1%	–

Comparisons of development indicators at the district level in our federal structure would give just about the best portrayal of the extent of deprivation faced by the most vulnerable sections of the different nationalities. According to a study carried out by the Applied Economic Research Centre, Karachi University, post-independence development tended to be more widespread in the Punjab compared to the other three provinces where the fruits of development became disproportionately concentrated in Karachi, Hyderabad, Peshawar and Quetta. The second and third quartiles of population in terms of level of development have a very large Punjabi representation. The most underdeveloped areas in Sind are Dadu, Khairpur, Larkana and Jacobabad—areas which, incidentally, have amply demonstrated, over the past two years, their extreme sense of dissatisfaction. Excepting Quetta all districts in Baluchistan were found to be in the bottom 25%. The rural areas of Punjab were found to be best placed when evaluated according to generally accepted socio-economic indicators.

Conclusions

Seven years of fierce authoritarianism has decisively altered the political structure of this country. The demands on the Pakistani state of the eighties have become quite complex. Not only is the society polarized, it is also split along ethnic and regional lines. The national question is now the central issue. The failure of the military and the dominant elites to create political and social institutions, like a free legislature, free judiciary and free media which could be used for voicing such and other demands, has resulted in social crisis. The institutional structures which could facilitate decentralisation and help in resolving the regional differences are conspicuously absent. By failing to provide channels (mainly those promoting active participation in national affairs) for expressing dissent the central elites have alienated major sections of the population in Sind and Baluchistan. It would be naive to expect the military (considering the internal pressures to centralise and expropriate large chunks of the surplus—after all, defence consumes almost half of revenue collections) to come up with a solution to the national question. The traditional political leadership itself is also unprepared for the explosion of these regional demands and the manner in which they should be settled. There is no charismatic leader whose appeal and political constituency extends beyond ethnic boundaries.

When the central elites, those reaping the major benefits—the land-owning classes, the industrialists and the merchants—and those involved in decision making—the military-bureaucratic oligarchy—have disproportionate representation of nationalities— regional factors will tend to get highlighted. Admittedly there are historical reasons as well, e.g. infrastructural facilities (education, commerce, etc), recruitment by the British for their military from certain areas, etc. But, by taking refuge behind the timeless phrase 'historical reasons', there is a suspicion that a lot is being swept under the carpet. These reasons cannot become an excuse for not making concerted and visible efforts to narrow the differentials.

The recent explosion in Sind has highlighted the heightened sense of frustration and economic deprivation being felt by an increasingly politicised youth. The ferocity of the protest has compelled the regime to respond.

It is felt, however, that the measures being considered are neither adequate nor sufficiently broad based to elicit support and allegiance except from a handful who are likely to benefit from the patronage being extended by Islamabad. The fundamental problem of the extent of provincial autonomy, decentralisation of the decision making process or diffusion of the power structure can no longer be wished or prayed away. The outwardly blissful state is not a guarantee of its continuance *per se*. Contradictions have reached alarming levels. There is discontent and despair in the air although still highly diffuse, fragmented and disorganised—awaiting a mechanism for mobilisation.

There is also the economic dimension of the political factor which has to be attended to on an urgent basis, that relating to the sharing of the national cake. The structural distortions of the development process have worsened the regional imbalances as the Punjab and non-Sindhi Sind grew either at the expense or to the exclusion of the other areas; the structural mechanisms at work enabled the developed regions to siphon off the surplus generated in the poorer regions. The insistence of the regime on the preservation of a market economy will only aggravate the regional disparities.

The right balance has to be found, and soon, over the extent of political and financial autonomy. With time running out, the failure to resolve the crisis will mean that there will be no escape from the logic and dynamic of the movement towards the country's disintegration; everything else will then be rendered meaningless.

CHANGING PERSPECTIVES

CULTURE AND CULTURAL PLANNING IN INDIA

P.C. Joshi

Let us approach the question of culture in India today with a sense of history. Two important points emerge from D.P. Mukerji's analysis of India's cultural problem offered in his *Modern Indian Culture* (1947) which are worth recalling today. Firstly, in Mukerji's view what is called modern Indian culture was shaped by historical circumstances, by economic, political and cultural impact of British colonialism. He believed that all major problems of India including the cultural problem had their source in the colonial impact and in India's response to this impact within the limitations of a colonial India. Thus the cultural renaissance and the anti-colonial national struggle had the same historical genesis and both were expressions of people's search for a national identity. The cultural workers of the pre-independence period did not live and work in a social vacuum or in ivory towers. They were deeply involved in the social problems and challenges of their times. They did not believe in the philosophy of art for art's sake. The anti-colonial struggle at its best assumed the form of a cultural movement and the cultural movement grew as an anti-colonial mobilisation in the realm of consciousness.

In India as in other colonial and semi-feudal societies culture and politics were closely related and a whole galaxy of men and women distinguished themselves in both the spheres of culture and politics. Take Rabindra Nath Tagore, the most towering figure in the realm of culture and consider the contradictions of his own personality. As an artist, Tagore had deep reservations about politics and he was highly critical of the parochial and anti-intellectual tendencies within Indian nationalism which sought to create a cultural wedge between India and the West. Tagore regarded the Indian national awakening as a fruit of India's cultural contact with the West which he welcomed wholeheartedly. And yet Tagore could not remain insensitive to India's great tragedy and indignity as a colonised nation nor could he remain indifferent to the heroic crusade of his countrymen against colonial oppression and tyranny. Time and again he was pulled out of his ivory tower. Shocked and aggrieved by the national tragedy enacted at Jallianwala Bagh, Tagore renounced his knighthood. All his life he carried on a continuous dialogue with the political leaders of the Indian National Congress on all major issues facing the nation.

To Tagore goes the historic honour of giving to the resurgent Indian nationalism its National Anthem. To Tagore goes the honour of raising creativity in an Indian language to such heights of excellence that Indian literature even under the constraints of colonial rule was put on the world map. If the

From Economic and Political Weekly, *December 10-17, 1983. Reprinted with permission.*

country had lost its identity by first losing its pride in its own language and literature, the recovery of the national pride also began first in the sphere of language and literature. And in this sense the indirect contribution of the builders of language and literature to national consciousness was as great as the contribution of the direct promoters and participants in the political struggle for freedom. There were many stalwarts like Gandhi, Nehru, Maulana Azad and Narnedra Dev who contributed as much through creative writing as through participation in the freedom struggle. Indeed, in that historical epoch in all enslaved countries including India, culture became the fountain-head of political awakening; and politics stimulated creative acivity leading to an unprecedented flowering of national art and culture.

Why is it that politics and culture were so intimately related to each other in the pre-independence period? As Mukerji explained in his writings modern Indian culture was a response to India's 'Great Denial' under British rule. The defeat in the First War of Indian Independence of 1857 and the total subjugation of India by colonial masters was a traumatic experience without parallel in Indian history. The British invasion, unlike invasions in past Indian history, shattered the entire socio-economic basis of Indian life. As Marx aptly stated, India under the British suffered from 'a peculiar type of melancholy' resulting from the fact that she was brutally uprooted from all her past traditions and denied all opportunities for growth in modern times. The colonial rulers tried to undermine the faith of the Indian people in their culture—in their age-old concepts, beliefs, values and institutions—which had given meaning and direction to their life all through the ages. Moreover, colonialism was not directed only at economic, political and military occupation of the subject country; it was also aimed at achieving ideological hegemony over the minds of men in the colonies. Promoting mental colonialism was as important a part of British policy in India as promoting economic, political and military domination. The self-questioning by the Indian people, therefore, began with an encounter with colonial ideology or culture which aimed at destroying the very roots of India's identity.

The encounter of nationalists with colonial ideologists and theorists first began with questioning of the doctrines of the 'white man's burden' and of the 'civilising mission' of the West in the colonies. In its subtler forms the colonial theory and ideology propagated the concept of the chronic incapacity of Asiatic Society to outgrow its pre-industrial backwardness and to evolve a technologically developed economy and a modern society. Since imperialism very effectively employed the weapon of culture for the domination of the Indian people, it was a historic necessity that the battle for Indian independence should begin in the realm of culture.

Let us turn to Rabindranath Tagore for an insight into injuries to India's self-respect under British rule. To quote:

> In India the only assistance we get is merely to be jeered at by the (English) Nation for lagging behind. While depriving us of our oppor-

tunities and reducing our education to the minimum required for conducting a foreign government, this nation pacifies its conscience by calling us names, by sedulously giving currency to the arrogant cynicism
that the East is East and the West is West and never the twain shall
meet. If we must believe our schoolmaster in the taunt that, after nearly
two centuries of his tutelage, India not only remains unfit for self-
government but unable to display originality in her intellectual at-
tainments, must we ascribe it to something in the nature of Western
culture and our inherent incapacity to receive it or to the judicious nig-
gardliness of the Nation that has taken upon itself the White Man's
Burden of Civilising the East?

It should be noted that as the internal bulwark of colonial ideology and
culture the British tried to promote the growth of an Anglicised middle class
through modern education in colonial universities. Here was a class accepting
the superiority of the culture of the colonial masters and denigrating its own
people and their traditions. Such a middle class easily accepted the colonial
myths and beliefs and the fundamental cultural premises of colonial rule. Indian national consciousness first grew in the process of self-questioning
within the sensitive sections of the Anglicised middle class itself. It grew as a
result of rejection of colonial assumptions and premises and in the struggle for
restoring the self-respect of the Indian people.
Such was the predominant ethos of this period that every sensitive Indian
tried to relate even his personal problem including the choice of his profession
to the service of his country. The concept of the 'Servant of India' or of a
patriotic *karm yogi* became a talisman for every honest Indian in that formative age of Indian nationalism. Radha Kamal Mukerjee has aptly described
the dilemmas of a sensitive Indian intellectual in the pre-independence period
and his agonising search for identity. To the question what profession he as a
self-respecting intellectual should choose for himself, Mukerjee said, he found
three choices open to him under colonial rule. He could become a poet or a
writer to rouse his people from their passivity and to infuse in them a new
spirit of self-questioning, self-respect and dignity. This was in his opinion
what Tagore and others having the genius for creative writing did in Bengali
and in other Indian languages. He could also opt for the medium of history as
Jadunath Sarkar or his own brother, Radha Kumud Mukerjee, and many
other patriotic historians did; they tried to interpret past history in a manner
that the Indian people became aware of their glorious heritage and of their
contribution to world culture and civilisation. This helped to lift up the
morale of the people who were losing hope and confidence in themselves. One
must note that when the present of the Indian people was ugly and dark and
the future was uncertain, patriotic intellectuals could use the past alone as a
source of strength and inspiration in the struggle for a bright future. The exploration of the past resulted in the blossoming of art and culture; this up-

surge of creativity gave us our historical novels and short stories, dramas and plays, poems and songs, and finally essays and historical writings having the stamp of creative writing.

And, finally, R.K. Mukerjee said, the third choice open to him was that of becoming an economist who portrayed the great contrast between the potential for India's growth and its deplorable economic conditions under British rule. He could thus provide an indictment of colonialism which had converted India into an agricultural hinterland of the British Empire. Mukerji's pursuit of scientific enquiry into Indian economy and society acquired a cultural significance as part of his search for an alternative to the colonial pattern of economy, society and culture in India.

What I wish to emphasise is that the activity of political workers social scientists, historians during the pre-independence period had a deep cultural significance. Further, the cultural activity then was also not just a matter of providing mere entertainment or recreation to the Indian people. It had a political significance. It was a *political* weapon in the fight against colonial domination and oppression. Cultural workers in the pre-independence period thus talked of the cultural front as one of the forums of anti-colonial mobilisation. For instance, Uday Shankar who had built up a cultural centre at Almora, was fully aware that he was fighting the battle of Indian nationalism in the realm of culture. From this standpoint, poets, novelists, musicians, dancers and other types of cultural workers played a vital role in the spiritual and mental awakening of the Indian people and in building their national cultural identity.

We are aware of the sweep and grandeur of India's national struggle which developed as a multi-regional and multi-class movement against British rule. The cultural renaissance was the scene of this broad-based anti-imperialist struggle in the country. In Bengal this renaissance started with Raja Rammohun Roy and was sustained by a whole galaxy of cultural figures including, Rabindranath Tagore and later by the progressive cultural workers constituting the well-known 'Parichaya Group' and the Indian People's Theatre Association.

The cultural renaissance which first began in Bengal later enveloped other regions of the country in its fold. In the pre-independence period and even during early years of independence, one finds the cultural movements nourishing the roots of political consciousness and the political movement nourishing the roots of the critical national consciousness. In that heroic age of Indian nationalism politics was transformed into a cultural force and culture into a political force. In fact, in the case of many national leaders it is very difficult to say whether they should be called political leaders heading a political awakening or cultural leaders heading a cultural awakening.

Nehru who was the leader of a new thrust in national politics was also the author of *The Discovery of India* which is an epoch-making contribution to modern Indian culture. In the earlier period Tilak was a militant national political leader and also the author of a major cultural work, 'Karmayog in Gita'. Moreover, there is a continuous dialogue and interaction between political leaders like Gandhi and Nehru and cultural leaders like Tagore and many others.

Further, many political leaders played a very vital role in promoting cultural organisations and movements. To this category belong political leaders like Jawaharlal Nehru, who created the massive infrastructure in independent India both for India's scientific advance and its cultural development. In *The Discovery of India* Nehru evolved the vision of a New India combining the best of the scientific progress of the West and the spiritual and cultural heritage of the East. Nehru rejected both blind anti-Westernism and blind idolations of India's past. He made a distinction between two Englands—the England of modern science and technology and the new concepts of freedom, equality and democracy on the one hand and the England of colonial tyranny, exploitation and racial superiority and arrogance on the other. Similarly, Nehru also made a distinction between two Indias—the India of saints and sages like Buddha and Kabir with their message of compassion, human brotherhood and equality on the one hand and the India of caste, untouchability, religious superstition and bigotry on the other. In Nehru's view India's freedom struggle and cultural regeneration was directed *against* the alliance of the racist and the colonialist England with the India of casteism, communalism and blind religiosity. It was aimed at forging a new alliance between the anti-colonial movement and forward-looking social forces both in India and in England (or in India and the rest of the world). Nehru's vision of a New India, therefore, was derived from synthesising the humanistic values, ideals and the scientific spirit of the West and the wisdom and the enduring cultural traditions of the East. Nehru thus contributed towards the philosophical basis of India's new culture; he also built the institutional framework and the organisational structure for realising the vision of a New India. For India's cultural reconstruction, Nehru created an impressive infrastructure in the form of the three academies—The Sangeet Natak Academy, the Lalit Kala Academy and the Sahitya Academy supported by a chain of State level academies which were to be vehicles of the new creativity.

There is another figure in the political field to whom also goes the credit of bringing closer the two currents of culture and politics in India. He is the late P.C. Joshi who was an outstanding leader of the Indian socialist movement and the principal promoter of a people's cultural movement. The Indian People's Theatre Association promoted by him brought close to each other stalwarts of the classical arts on the one hand and folk artists on the other. IPTA represented a new philosophy of art. According to this philosophy, a new art and culture must serve anti-imperialist and anti-feudal political movements; and the radical political forces must draw upon art and culture for people's mobilisation. IPTA thus initiated a new type of bridge-building between culture and politics. It sought to elevate people's culture to a sophisticated level and inspired artists from the elite classes to learn from people's art and culture.

In short, within the Indian National Congress and in the Indian socialist movement there were outstanding leaders who did not take up a compartmentalised view of life, considering art and culture in isolation from politics. They treated life in its totality on the basis of an integral vision of India's past, present and future. They were involved in reshaping the life of their people and they discovered through their own experiences that the battle of national regeneration had to be fought on several fronts including the cultural. They gave great importance to the cultural dimension and great respect to the builders of art and culture. In order to appreciate the contribution of Indian cultural renaissance to Indian political awakening, one must ask: would the political awakening have been possible without the cultural awakening? One must also ask: would the cultural renaissance have been sustained without the support of political awakening? As noted earlier, it is through the cultural movement that the Indian people derived a sense of their own identity and their self-respect. Without this recovery of their self-respect one cannot conceive of a sustained political struggle by the Indian people against the mightiest Imperial Power of that period.

No doubt the cultural perspective of Indian nationalism had its own weaknesses insofar as its contribution to national consciousness was sometimes achieved at the cost of its contribution to the *critical social consciousness*. This weakness is dramatically illustrated by the fact that in the major works shaping national consciousness like Bankim's 'Anand Math', Maithili Saran Gupta's 'Bharat Bharati' and Hali's 'Musaddas', nationalism is sustained not by a critique of India's society and culture but by its uncritical idealisation. Such forms of cultural revivalism blunted the critical social consciousness of the Indian people. But under the historical constraints of the colonial period, these cultural contributions were of major significance in the anti-colonial struggle. The correctives to this revivalist trend also appeared both within the political and the cultural movements. We have already explained how Nehru made a distinction between two Englands. In his view there was 'the England of Shakespeare and Milton, of noble speech and writing and brave deed, of political revolution and the struggle for freedom, of science and technical progress' which Nehru asked India to accept wholeheartedly. But there was also the other England 'of the savage penal code and brutal behaviour, of entrenched feudalism and racism' which he asked Indians to resist and oppose with all their might. What is specially important to note is Nehru's stress on the fact that this 'wrong England' had come to India and was encouraging the 'wrong India' through her domination of India. This sharp attack on the alliance between the forces of foreign colonialism and indigenous feudalism and traditionalism was a very great contribution made by Nehru towards the understanding of India's cultural problem.

Earlier Tagore had also made a sharp distinction between two Europes, one which we must acclaim and admire and the other which we must resist and reject. There is 'the Europe who in her literature and art pours out an inexhaustible cascade of beauty and truth, fertilising all countries and all time; the Euorpe who with a mind which is titanic in its untiring power, is sweeping the height and the depth of the universe, winning her homage of knowledge from the infinitely great and the infinitely small, applying all the resources of her great intellect and heart in healing the sick and alleviating those miseries of man which until now we were contented to accept in a spirit of hopeless resignation; the Europe which is making the earth yield more fruit than seemed possible, coaxing and compiling the great forces of nature into man's service'. There was also, however, 'the other Euorpe which was too consciously busy in building up her power, defying her deeper nature and mocking it, heaping up her inequities to the sky, crying for God's vengeance and spreading the infection of ugliness, physical and moral, over the face of the earth with her heartless commerce outraging man's sense of the good and the beautiful'. Tagore further observed that 'Europe is supremely good in her beneficence where her face is turned to all humanity; and Europe is supremely evil in her maleficent aspect where her face is turned only upon her interest, using all her power of greatness for ends which are against the infinite and the eternal in men'.

It must be noted that even under the shadow of total confrotntation between colonial England and enslaved India, the leaders of Indian culture and politics did not allow their long-term vision to be blurred and their objectivity to be coloured by the anti-British and anti-West sentiments which were sweeping the East. They resisted the tendency to attack the West from a revivalist and traditionalist standpoint. This is a permanent legacy of Tagore and Nehru to modern Indian politics and culture which must be remembered and carried forward.

It must also be put on record that both Tagore and Nehru played an outstanding role in making Gandhi aware of certain aspects of his politics which in the context of India could be interpreted as a major support for revivalism. The following observations of Gandhi which have become our national credo on culture were in response to Tagore who prompted Gandhi to spell out clearly the cultural premises of his politics:

> I do not want my house to be walled in on all sides and my windows to be stuffed. I want the culture of all lands to be blown about my house as freely as possible. But I refuse to live in other people's houses as an interloper, a beggar, or a slave.

> I want to write many new things. But they should all be written on the Indian slate.

Tagore's conception of the link between politics and culture is also very relevant and valuable today. Tagore made the following remark on this issue:

We must remember whatever weakness we cherish in our society will become the source of danger in politics. The same intertia which leads us to our idolatry of dead forms in social institutions will create in our politics prison-houses with immovable walls. The narrowness of sympathy which makes it possible for us to impose upon a considerable portion of humanity the galling yoke of inferiority will assert itself in our politics in creating the tyranny of injustice.

Tagore noted the fact that the very people who are upholding the ideal of nationalism are 'conservative in social practice'. In his view a genuine nationalism could never be built on the foundation of social conservatism. Nehru and Tagore emphasise the bond between true nationalism and critical social consciousness or between national emancipation and social and cultural emancipation. This is a cultural legacy of our national movement which we seem to be disowning in practice today.

Why is it that this link between culture, politics, national and social emancipation has been broken in contemporary India? Why is it that all the major political parties in India, the Indian National Congress and the socialist parties, have no clearly defined perspective on culture? Why is that the representatives of the nation-State have not given to culture an overriding priority that it deserves in a country like India?

Certain aspects of the Indian scene lead one to ask whether the cultural task is not going by default. We seem to be functioning without a national perspective on culture; this is specially the case with the Academies, the All India Radio, the Films Division, Doordarshan etc. The State patronage of art and culture seems to be getting interpreted narrowly as organising Award Distribution Ceremonies at regular intervals presided over by luminaries of the State; or into having cultural festivals from time to time in metropolitan centres; or into disbursement of grants to certain institutions and individuals in an *ad hoc* manner from year to year. In the absence of a unified perspective on development and culture, there is no integration between development programmes and cultural programmes.

In taking decisions about economic affairs, we never consider the implications of these decisions for cultural life. For instance, in considering what kind of property structure and motivations will promote economic development, the questions should also be posed whether strengthening private property *vis-a-vis* community property and individualist motivation *vis-a-vis* community motivation will not impoverish the quality of social life or erode the cultural ethos of co-operation and sharing. Enormous possiblities exist, for instance, for using economic growth as a means of cultural development in areas where economic surpluses have been generated through the application of new technology. We have, however, allowed these surpluses to be dissipated in forms of conspicous consumption which are culturally degrading and debasing.

Similarly, we know that in underdeveloped regions cultural backwardness itself is a powerful contributor to poverty and economic backwardness. In such regions the battle against cultural backwardness (illiteracy, ignorance and superstition) is a ncessary condition for any economic break-through in the near future. A perspective on culture is thus lacking in agencies which are drawing plans and programme for economic growth; a perspective on development is lacking in institutions which are entrusted with the responsibility for promoting art and culture. The consequences of such fragmented perspectives are very disastrous.

In this context we may take note of certain features of the present Indian scene. Firstly, our State-sponsored cultural activities are restricted to urban India and even within urban India to metropolitan centres. We have taken no major initiative after independence for preventing the rapid disintegration and even destruction of the folk, peasant and traditional art forms of India. In the second place, in India's open society and polity the processes of foreign cultural penetration are already posing a serious threat to our national cultural identity and are resulting in almost complete alienation of the youth from their national cultural moorings. Thirdly, the forces of ignorance, obscurantism, superstition and intolerance are eroding our commitment to a secular and scientific ethos, to learning and enlightenment, and to an egalitarian and just society. Further, the recent atrocities on women, Harijans and other weaker sections of society are only symptoms of a deep malaise and reflect the erosion of values and the breakdown of moral consciousness. Finally, the concept of unity in diversity, the consciousness of an Indian identity and the vision of a new India which inspired generations of freedom-fighters are being undermined by the growing forces of regionalism, communalism, linguistic and ethnic fanaticism. The problems mentioned above are not chance occurrences. If they have now acquired a menacing form, it is because the major political parties, the devleopmental and cultural leaders and functionaries have allowed the malaise to grow from bad to worse. They have not taken up the challenge of resisting the erosion of values, morals and ethics in all spheres of our life.

Attention needs to be drawn to the paradox of a country or a region within a country growing in material terms but becoming a desert in the cultural sense. This is how many leaders and intellectuals of Punjab and Haryana, the centres of the Green Revolution, have described the cultural scene in these States which present the serious problem of material prosperity not yet contributing to the enrichment of the quality of life. We must not overlook that the debasement following the acquisition of wealth among the new rich or the 'first generation rich' is much worse than the degradation associated with persistent destitution and poverty. The phenomenon of this debasement is aptly captured in Oliver Goldsmith's unforgettable words from 'Deserted Village': 'Where wealth accumulates men decay!'

If you add to all these negative tendencies of the Indian cultural scene the massive disorientation of consciousness in urban India resulting from exposure to commercialised feature films as the predominant form of mass entertainment, one begins to have an idea of the colossal dimensions and ramifications of the cultural problem and also the perils to which India is exposed if it does not recognise them and does not devise an approach for grappling with them. And yet these are not the issues on which cultural workers in India are concentrating their attention. The best and the most creative in the field of art and culture are retreating into their ivory towers regarding the entire cultural scene as entirely hopeless and unredeemable. One must ask whether the fruits of government patronage are really going to the first raters or are being appropriated to a large extent by second raters and third raters. And finally, there has emerged (very much like the parallel black economy) the commercialised, and semi-underground or underground world of culture where cultural goods of cheap, vulgar and obnoxious varieties are manufactured on a mass scale for debasing popular taste and for vulgarising mass consciousness.

In spite of such grave developments, political parties and their workers do not seem to have much time left for cultural debates or cultural controversies. One recalls with some nostalgia the Great Cultural Debate of the pre-independence period. Political parties do require the help of cultural workers, especially of obliging cinema stars mostly at the time of elections to attract crowds for their meetings, to mobilise funds, or to sing a song or present a dance recital. But the hiatus between culture and politics and between cultural and political workers was never as deep and wide as it seems today. What is much worse lowering of the level of political consciousness and activity debases popular taste and attitudes and thus further lowers the general level of culture. The lowering and debasing of cultural levels and activities in turn lowers the level of politics. Considering the overall Indian scene, one notes with alarm a regression into cultural nihilism. The most agonising is the erosion of the major political force in the country, the Indian National Congress, as a cultural force; equally distressing is the disintegration of the parties of Indian socialism as a cultural and moral influence.

It is pertinent to recall in this context D.P. Mukerji's lament during the early years of independence that 'our politics has ruined our culture'. On the basis of our experience since independence we can say that this statement is still valid. One may like to add, however, that our culture has also failed our politics. Further, the key, to the qualitative transformation of our politics seems to lie in the regeneration of our culture. In fact, India's dramatic entry into the age of the modern communication revolution poses fresh challenges in the fields of culture.

Before we explore this vast but unexplored problem-area we must draw attention to the sharp contrast in the cultural scene in the pre-independence and the post-independence period. It may be noted that India's technological backwardness specially in the field of communication did not hamper the creative flowering of her culture and her politics in the colonial era. In fact, India learnt during the period of anti-colonialism to transform her technological backwardness from a liability into an asset. Despite her technological and economic lag, India's genius blossomed in the personality of a Gandhi in the realm of politics and of a Tagore in the realm of culture. Gandhi evolved new techniques of communication and social mobilisation suited to a technologically backward country of peasants and artisans. He mastered the art of converting technological backwardness into a stimulus for creativity in the field of political communication and mobilisation. Tagore's greatness lay in the fact that he identified in art and culture the deeper sources of a country's strength and vitality; that in language and literature he identified the key to a country's spiritual and mental tranformation or to the revitalisation of national character of an enslaved people. Both Gandhi and Tagore who were the products of a society still steeped in technological backwardness were the living affirmation of the idea that man was superior to technology.

Gandhi and Tagore both in different ways conveyed the message that it will be suicidal to equate technological development with cultural development; that technological development created both opportunities and dangers for Indian culture and civilisation. Today when India is poised for a gigantic leap in communication technology with its potential for linking together every part of India with the centre (or centres) of power, it is pertinent to keep in mind this message of Gandhi and Tagore. We must not forget that technology is only a *means* of culture; and it is not the *substance* of culture. Further, modern technology is not culture-neutral; it is closely intertwined with the Western way of life, with an acquisitive and consumerism-oriented culture. In this context the following words of Tagore are as valid today as they were yesterday when they were first spoken:

> We cannot imitate life, we cannot simulate strength for long, nay, what is more, a mere imitation is a source of weakness. For, it hampers our true nature, it is always in our way . . .
> At the imitative stage of our schooling we cannot distinguish between the essential and the non-essential, between what is transferable and what is not. But while our greed delights in wholesale appropriation, it is the function of our vital nature to assimilate, which is the only true appropriation for a living organism. Where there is life, it is sure to assert itself by its choice of acceptance and refusal according to its constitutional necessity. And only thus can a living organism grow strong, and not by mere accumulation or by giving up its personal identity.

In Tagore's view India must not attempt 'a mere reproduction of the West'. India must apply its own mind 'to cut out a new path for this great unwieldily car progress'. He reminded his countrymen that 'what is merely modern—as science and methods of organisation—can be transplanted; but what is vitally human has fibres so delicate and roots so numerous and far-reaching that it dies when moved from the soil'. India, in his view, had to recognise that 'there are grave questions that the Western Civilisation has presented before the world but not completely answered.'

These words of wisdom are highly relevant today when independent India has entered the path of modern economic revolution along with the modern communication revolution. Will these revolutions result in a burst of indigenous creativity in the realm of the spirit and the mind? Or will these put in jeopardy India's national identity and cultural integrity which was so far sheltered by her technological primitiveness and backwardness? These are the vital choices facing India today.

We may recall again Nehru's reference to the alliance between the racist and the colonialist England and the casteist and obscurantist India in the pre-independence period. We may also recall Tagore's reference to the alliance between self-seeking forces of both Europe and India which were responsible for Indians' political enslavement and cultural degradation. A similar but a more sinister and subtle alliance is taking shape today between the acquisitive consumerism of the affluent classes of the post-industrial societies of the West and the parasitic greed and conspicious consumption of the New Rich of Indian society, which is in transition from pre-industrialism to industrialism. The modern communication revolution is turning into a promoter of this evil alliance in many developing countries.

We witness in India today the aggressive emergence of a new elite, a new middle-class, which seeks to emulate not the way of life of the Puritans of England, the Jacobins of France, the Samurai of Japan and the Bolsheviks of Russia who provided the motive force of the Industrial Revolutions in each of these countries. Decisively breaking away from the parasitism of the feudal and mercantile elites, the industrial middle-class in these countries identifed itself with productive values of the working people. In sharp contrast, large sections of today's emerging Indian elite still represent a hybrid culture of decadent feudalism of the East and resurgent consumerism and naked hedonism of the post-industrial West. If these tendencies are not checked, communication technology may not serve as a promoter of India's cultural regeneration; it may accentuate the erosion of India's cultural identity.

We learn from India's history that the roots of its cultural and economic backwardness lay in the wide hiatus between the producing classes which managed material production and the thinking classes which managed spiritual and mental production. The communication technology is so far not being utilised for bridging this chasm by linking the producing classes with mental enlightenment and the thinking classes with material production. This technology seems to be perpetuating and further widening the hiatus between the elites and the masses. If the communication technology is utilised as a means of heightening the consumption appetites of the dominant classes, then it has a dangerous potential of accentuating the envy and the sense of deprivation of the vast masses. The linking of remote but underdeveloped regions of India through modern communication with the developed regions may not also turn out to be an unmixed blessing. People in far flung regions of India were so far sheltered and immunised from the shocks and traumas of a commercial and acquisitive culture. People in these regions had also not experienced the corrosive impact of feudal decadence—of caste, untouchability, religious obscurantism and male dominance. Will modern communication become a means of exposing these societies untouched by feudal decadence and commercial ethos to new culture-shocks, thus profoundly disturbing and destablising their own way of life? Or will modern communication be the means of introducing the commercialism-and-feudalism stricken regions of India to the invigorating winds and currents of a non-commercial and egalitarian culture from the remote regions?

Modern communication technology offers vast opportunities for preserving and promoting unity in diversity in the field of culture. It also poses serious dangers in terms of imposing cultural homogeneity and of destroying cultural diversity. What the great anthropologist Claude Lévi-Strauss said about the impact of Western colonialism on indigenous environments and cultures of non-Western countries is worth pondering upon by us who are experiencing the spread of the evil aspects of Westernism. To quote:

> I understand how it is that people delight in travel books and ask only to be misled by them. Such books preserve the illusion of something that no longer exists but yet must be assumed to exist if we are to escape from the appalling indictment that has been piling up against us . . . There is nothing to be done about it. Civilisation is no longer a fragile flower, to be carefully preserved and reared with great difficulty here and there in sheltered corners of a territory rich in natural resources: too rich almost, for there was an element of menace in their very vitality; yet they allowed us to put fresh life into our cultivations. *All that is over; humanity has taken to monoculture, once and for all, and is preparing to produce civilisation in bulk, as if it wre a sugar beet. The same dish will be served to us every day.*

It is still not too late to raise once again the issue of the relationship between politics and culture on the one hand and technology and culture on the other which D.P. Mukerji raised during the early years of independence. Warning aginst a mechanical view of cultural unity he observed:

> Politicians, language enthusiasts and employers, all want unity; the first as loyal adherents to every important decision of a new born state in dif-

ficulty, the second in the name of a need for cultural homogeneity, and the third for uniform conditions of production. I want you to consider carefully if this type of uniformity is sanctioned by Indian history, even though it be a grave need of the hour. You are also to enquire into the corollary of the above *viz*, the ecology and value of regional cultures, if they have or have not actually contributed to or can still influence the mosaic of culture, or if their descent into the level of subcultures will or will not lower the quality of Indian culture itself. You may also have to relate Indian culture to the world context.

At this point it is necessary to stress that the question of language is fundamental to culture. A creative approach to modern culture is possible only if there is an imaginative approach to the question of language which is the main source of a sense of identity. On the question of language it is as erroneous to under-estimate the depth of sentiments, emotions and loyalties to one's language learnt in childhood as to underrate the importance as well as the potentialities of being multi-lingual in a dynamic world shaped by modern science and technology. Fundamental to cultural policy, therefore, is the question of language policy in a developing country of sub-continental dimensions like India. Unity and diversity of cultures pre-supposes unity and diversity of languages. It will be wrong to deny either the need for unity or the importance of diversity.

We must take note of the fact that so far the concept of cultural unity in diversity was sustained in a large measure by India's technological backwardness specially in the field of communication. India's rapid transition in the age of modern communication, therefore, poses new challenges in the field of culture. Modern technology creates the grave danger of erosion of cultural unity based on cultural diversity. Such a danger, however, arises not from communication technology itself but from the absence of a framework of planning for culture and from the lack of a cultural policy.

It is pertinent to recall that Mukerji had also posed the question: to what extent can culture be planned? Dissociating himself from the view that culture should be left to itself, he took the position that planning of culture was imperative in the scientific and technological age. At the same time his view of planning of culture was not co-terminus with bureaucratic management and dirction of culture. Cultural planning had two basic ingredients. Firstly, planning of culture meant for him creating the conditions for the development of culture. It is in this sense that cultural planning gets linked with economic, educational, scientific and technological planning on the one hand and town and country planning on the other.

Secondly, State and soceity must co-operate in creating conditions for the existence of a 'body of men devoted to the enrichment of popular consciousness through the prestige of their own disinterested, detached and scientific analysis' who would be 'very useful in saving our culture from the degrading pull of partisanship'. Mukerji was very clear in his mind that such a class cannot be 'created by a fiat of the government overnight'. Further, 'even if it can be done, the principle of birth which is very much with us in the shape of nepotism will convert a brain-trust of planners into a caste'. One has, therefore, to guard against 'the degeneration of such an elite group, either by the contamination of the caste system or by the tendency towards unrelated, unreal, sectional and bureaucratic specialisation and similar other evils. And yet the necessity of such a group will always be there.' Perhaps the resilience of such a group is closely related at one end to the moral rigour and intellectual vitality of this elite group expressed in the strict observance of the rules of the game in the professional sphere. At another end, it is related to the cultural enlightenment of the people as a whole who are the ultimate source of continuing renewal and revitalisation of this elite group.

It is obvious that our perspective on culture does not allow for regression into the pre-technological age. Nor does it posit technolgoical primitivism or backwardness as a security against cultural homogeneity and a support for cultural diversity. A dynamic view of culture suited to the technological dynamism of the scientific age must be based on a conscious direction of technological change. It cannot be based on a Luddite-like opposition to modern technology. Planning of culture in the modern context, therefore, requires the planning of technological change. It must be noted that modern, post industrial technology—specially communication technology—is infinitely permissive in its concrete application and utilisation. It allows at once for centralisation or decentralisation, cultural homgeneisation or deversification, cultural elitism or a participatory mass culture, cultural dualism or cultural integration. It can promote one-way communication from the elite to the masses which is the hallmark of a pre-democratic age. Or alternatively, it can promote a two-way communication from the elite to the masses and from the masses to the elite which is the basis of a truly democratic culture. Which of these cultural possiblities will be realised or cultural options exercised is not a technological but a social and political question. Insofar as technology operates through the socio-political framework and the class structure, planning of culture also involves fundamental structural change. Then alone will modern technology not result in the emergence of a dual society and a dual culture. Planning of structural change is, therefore, as fundamental to the planning of a modern, egalitarian culture as the planning of technological change.

It must be remembered that in any society, the pattern of distribution of means of culture (or the access to culture) is closely related to social organisation of material production and the distribution of the fruits of production. The right of the vast masses to the means of culture is, therefore, dependent on their right to the means of production or to the fruits of material production. In this context, what Tawney said long back is still relevant for a society like India:

To one who thinks calmly over the recent experience of mankind, there is something unbearable in the reflection that hitherto, outside a small circle of fortunate families, each generation, as its faculties began to flower, has been shovelled like raw material into an economic mill, to be pounded and ground and kneaded into the malleable human pulp out of which national prosperity and power, all the kingdoms of the world and the glory of them are supposed to be manufactured.

It is clear that planning for access to culture for the masses involves planning for their access to the fruits of material production. There is thus an indissoluble bond between economic planning and cultural planning. Further, the economic structure will also determine the scope and quality of culture. If this structure promotes a balance between competition and co-operation, personal gain and collective good, security and enterprise, surplus accumulation without class exploitation in production process or the work sphere which are fundamental to preservation of life, only then will possibilities emerge for the growth of a cultural superstructure of a new type. Distorton of economic life or alienation in economic life is the basic source of disorientation in the cultural life of a country.

One should also pose at this point the question of the relation between science and culture. Insofar as science demystifies nature and society, it destroys the symbols, the mythology, and the cosmology which constituted the base of the pre-industrial culture. To think that science is only the destroyer of art and culture is to ignore the enormous potentialities of a new cultural *renaissance* in the scientific age. The fears of cultural impoverishment and erosion arising from scientific and technological development have their roots in the historical experience of the industrially developed countries of the West. This has been aptly captured by A.N. Whitehead in the following words:

In regard to the aesthetic needs of the civilised society the reactions of science have so far been unfortunate. Its materialistic basis has directed attention to *things* as opposed to *values*. The antithesis is a false one, if taken in a concrete sense. But it is valid at the abstract level of ordinary thought. This misplaced emphasis coalesced with the abstractions of political economy, which are in fact the abstractions in terms of which commercial affairs ar carried on. Thus all thought in terms of material things and of capital. *Ultimate values were excluded.* They were politely bowed to, and then handed over to the clergy to be kept for Sundays. A creed of competitive business morality was evolved, in some respects curiously high; but entirely devoid of consideration for the human life. The workmen were conceived as mere hands, drawn from the pool of labour. To God's question, men gave the answer of Cain: 'Am I my brother's keeper?' and they incurred Cain's guilt. This was the atmosphere in which the industrial revolution was accomplished in England, and to a large extent elsewhere.

Further:

> The evils of the early industrial system are a common place of
> knowledge. The point which I am insisting is that stone-blind eyes with
> which even the best of men of that time regarded the importance of
> aesthetics in a nation's life. I do not believe that we have as yet achieved
> the right estimate. A contributory cause of substantial efficiency to pro-
> duce this disastrous error was the scientific creed that matter in motion
> is the one concrete reality in nature; so that aesthetic values form an
> adventitious irrelevant addition.

What Whitehead has said should be a matter for profound reflection by
latecomers to the modern scientific and industrial revolution. The pre-
industrial culture and civilisation in India was based on the concept of harmony between the principles of the good, the useful and the beautiful. Should
India's pursuit of material advance or of the useful be such that it causes
alienation from the good and the beautiful as it did in the case of the West?
What grave tension and disorientation can result from such lack of harmony
between 'innate disposition and mode of life' is summed up by Bertrand
Russell from the experience of Japan. To quote:

> One cause of this malaise is the rapidity of change in material condi-
> tions. When I was in Japan in 1921 I seemed to sense in the people with
> whom I talked and in the faces of the people I met in the streets, a great
> nervous strain, of the sort likely to promote hysteria. I thought this
> came from the fact that deep rooted unconscious expectations were
> adapted to old Japan, whereas the whole conscious life of the town-
> dwellers was devoted to an effort to become as like Americans as possi-
> ble. Such a maladjustment between the conscious and the unconscious
> was bound to produce discouragement or fury, according as the person
> concerned was less or more energentic. The same sort of thing happens
> wherever there is rapid industrialisation. It must have happened with
> considerable intensity in Russia.

Further:

> Science, while it has enormously accelerated outward change has not
> yet found any way of hastening psychological change especially where
> the conscious and the sub-conscious are concerned. Few men's un-
> conscious feels at home except in conditions very similar to those
> prevailed when they were children.

If the West paid a heavy penalty of being the first in the race for material
progress, it is possible for the late-comers to exploit the full advantage of being latecomers and to explore using material power for social betterment and

cultural enrichment. In this context the full potentialities of culture can be understood and explored if we recognised another negative feature of western industrialism highlighted by Whitehead. He argues that 'during the last three generations the exclusive direction of attention to the aspect of struggle for existence in a fixed environment has been a disaster of the first magnitude. The watchwords of the nineteenth century have been struggle for existence, competition, class warfare, commercial antagonism between nations, military warfare. The struggle for existence has been construed in the Gospel of hate.' Whitehead suggests that 'the full conclusion to be drawn from a philosophy of evolution is fortunately of a more balanced character. Successful organisms modify their environment. Those organisms are successful which modify their environments so as to assist each other. This law is exemplified in nature on a vast scale. There is something in the ready use of force which defeats its own object. Its main defect is that it bars co-operation. Every organism requires an environment of friends, partly to shield it from violent changes and partly to supply it with its wants. The Gospel of Force is incompatible with a social life. By force, I mean antagonism in its most general sense.'

If avoidance of force and the insistence on co-operation is one major lesson, the avoidance of uniformity is another major lesson to be learnt both from natural and social history. To quote Whitehead again:

The differences between the nations and races of mankind are required to preserve the conditions under which higher development is possible. One main factor in the upward trend of animal life is the power of wandering. When man ceases to wander, he will cease to ascend in the scale of being. Physical wandering is still important, but greater still is the power of man's spiritual adventures—adventures of thought, adventures of passionate feeling, adventures of aesthetic experience. A diversification among human communities is essential for the provision of the incentive and material for the Odyssey of the human spirit.

India's entry into the scientific and technological age can become a true blessing if it is turned into an aid to the people for this 'Odyssey of the human spirit', for 'a true migration into the unchartered seas of intellectual and spiritual adventure'. As Whitehead aptly states, 'the middle class pessimism over the future of the world comes from a confusion between civilisation and security'. This is much more so in the case of India than in the case of many other countries. And yet the coming of science and technology to India marks a watershed in India's cultural history. In the coming decades we shall witness in India the exciting human drama arising from the creative tension between modern science and technology on the one hand and culture on the other. Will science assist a new flowering of culture based on the release of the creative energy of the vast masses? Or will it follow the Western path of exclusion of aesthetic quality from material progress?

If the first possibility has to be realised, culture has not to be treated as a residual and secondary issue in planning for a new India. Culture in fact has to be the determining principle, the basic frame of reference for considering all the issues of scientific policy, economic strategy and social engineering. This is a challenging task without precedents and parallels from past history. But India at her best has not avoided creative challenges and adventures of the mind and the spirit. As Mukerji said 'our heritage does not allow us to bury the talents but to invest them; in risks and uncertainties.' Doesn't the *Upanishad* give the ringing call, *Charebeti, Charebeti* (March forward, march forward)?

I wish to emphasise again that a perspective on culture will not be relevant today if it does not put into the centre of the stage the issue of the relation of science and culture. The issue of the relation of politics and culture was central to India's regeneration as a modern nation in the colonial period. The central issue for India's transformation into a developed and civilised nation today is that of the complementarity and co-operation between science and culture and between scientific and cultural workers. In this respect the legacy of the West with its acute tension, nay antagonism, between science and culture is neither illuminating nor helpful. It is pertinent to recall the negative lessons drawn by eminent scientists from Western history. J.D. Bernal makes the following observation which has great relevance for us today:

> The more honest (of the intellectual classes in the West) could not help using their eyes and their noses to realise that there was something desperately wrong at the very heart of nineteenth century prosperity. Artists, poets and writers were moved to protest against the horrors of the new industrial towns, *against the universal degradation of beauty*, against the vulgar flaunting of wealth. In opposing them these intellectuals found their first support in an attempt to return to an idealised 'Middle Ages'.

Bernal further observes how this reaction to industrialism became the basis for hostility to science itself. It led to a sharp cleavage between scientific workers and cultural workers:

> Rejecting industrialism, the literary and artistic movement also rejected science, which they felt, with some justification, had identified itself with machine production and all that it had brought in its train. It was from this period in mid-century that the split between the humanists and scientists, which is such a feature of our times first became serious. Its first effect was to prevent the co-operation between the two branches of intellectuals without which no constructive criticism of the economic and social system was possible. The humanists never knew enough of how it worked, to have other than ineffective emotions about it; the

scientists were blunted by a quite deliberate turning away from everything—art, beauty, or social justice—that did not come within the purview, of their, by then, highly specialised work.

Such a hiatus between science and culture led to disastrous consequences, limiting the possibilities and distorting the direction, of both scientific and cultural development. To refer to Bernal again:

> In this age the new capacity for handling the material world has been gained well in advance of the appropriate patterns of cultural, political, or economic life. This situation is often described by the pundits of science and religion in terms of man's material powers having outrun his moral stature, with the implication that science must be halted or turned back until man has been spiritually regenerated. This, however, is not in the least likely to occur, science is too useful, if only for destruction. Rather must we look for the opposite solution and seek, through a better ordered society , to raise the moral level of humanity.

The need in other words is for a scientific humanism (or scientific culture) and for a humanistic (or culture-oriented) science. J.B.S. Haldane has also expressed alarm at the situation created by the loss of belief in religion and by the acceptance of science as technique without the acceptance of science as outlook or philosophy. In Haldane's view the basic malaise of Western civilisation arises from the fact that 'there has been a basic failure to integrate into its intellectual structure the scientific ideas which have furnished its material structure'. Again:

> Far more serious is the spiritual decay which is going on now and will go on as long as our attitudes do not alter. Religion is declining for the very simple reason that all religions are full of obsolete science of various kinds; especially obsolete cosmology and obsolete psychology.

In this background of 'general lack of belief in transcendental ideals, such as truth and beauty, that is going on', it is quite possible that 'science will tend to degenerate more and more into medical and engineering technology, just as art may degenerate into illustration, and, religion into ritual when they lose the vital spark'.

Haldane in this context looks for a way out in the 'unification of human effort, the marriage of the mind and the heart, the moralisation of science and the rationalisation of ethics'. If I remember correctly, Haldane during his stay at the Indian Statistical Institute, Calcutta, said time and time again that he expected such an effort to come from India. This continues to be the challenge which India is equipped to take up; India which produced Mahatma Gandhi upholding the principle of primacy of ends over means;Rabindranath Tagore upholding the principle of beauty and joy as the basis of a good life; and Jawaharlal Nehru working all his life for synthesising modern science and the enduring values of India's traditional civilisation. The Indian genius which is synthesis-oriented can achieve the much-desired integration of science and culture; and the construction of a new world-view.

The second major issue requiring reorientation of science and culture is the relation between national identity and class identity, national culture and class culture. In this sphere also the Western legacy has sharply negative features. Bernal's *Science in History* captures adequately the negative features relating to both science and culture being a 'class monopoly' except 'for a short time during the Renaissance and the Enlightenment when class barriers were partially broken down'. In Bernal's view, 'The existence of class-divided societies does not affect only the material consequences of knowledge; it cuts deep into its roots in ideas. The literate and the cultured are the ruling class and the basic ideas that find expression in literature and science are inevitably tinged with ruling class conceptions and self-justificatons. At the same time the fund of practical experience which comes with the daily work that maintains society is cut off from literary expression . . . .'.

Another, perhaps the most important, feature of Western history which is crucial from India's point of view, as pointed out by George Thompson, is that 'hitherto bourgeois culture has always grown and spread at the expense of pre-capitalist culture. In the conditions of capitalism which turns the peasantry into proletarians, this was inevitable'.

Must India repeat this experience of a new national culture growing at the expense of class culture, that is at the expense of the culture of the working peasantry including the tribal people? This is a question which cannot be resolved by intervention in the cultural sphere alone. The determinants of the processes of cultural change lie outside the sphere of culture, in the realm of political economy. They are closely related to the future pattern of agrarian reconstruction, indeed reconstruction of the economic order as a whole. These are challenges of vast dimensions both in the sphere of the economy, polity and culture to which economic planners, political workers and cultrual workers have to jointly address themselves. The modern communication revolution may render powerful aid in the tackling of this problem provided it is used imaginatively.

We are discussing the problem of *values* in the scientific and the technological age in which India has entered in a big way. This is the time, as D.P. Mukerji said, 'to save certain old values and create new ones'. This is the national task of cultural transformation. Again, as Mukerji noted 'Universities and research Institutes have a part to play in this tranformation. Values are too valuable to be trusted entirely to politicans banking on the old techniques'.

REFERENCES

J.D. Bernal: *Science in History*, Watts, London, 1954.

J.D. Bernal, *Social Function of Science*, London, George Routledge, xvi, 482 p, 1939.

J.B.S. Haldane, *The Inequality of Man*, Penguin Books, 1932.

Claude Lévi-Strauss, *A World on the Wane*, Hutchinson of London, 1961.

Karl Mannheim, *Freedom, Power and Democratic Planning*, Routledge and Kegan Paul, 1951.

D.P. Mukerji, *Modern Indian Culture*, Hind Kitab, Bombay, 1942.

D.P. Mukerji, *Diversities*, People Publishing House, Bombay, 1958.

M.G.K. Menon, 'Basic Research as an Integral Base of Science and Technology, Its Relevance, Support, Areas of Thrust', Presidential Address, 69th Session Indian Science Congress Assocation, Mysore, 1982.

Jawaharlal Nehru, *The Discovery of India*, Meridian Books, London (1946).

Jawaharlal Nehru, *Anthology*, edited by S. Gopal, Oxford University Press, 1980.

Bertrand Russell, *Power*, George Allen and Unwin, 1957.

Bertrand Russell, *The Impact of Science on Society*, George Allen and Unwin, London, 1952.

Vikram Sarabhai, *Science Policy and National Development*, Macmillan, 1974.

R.H. Tawney, *The Acquisitive Society*, The Fontana Library, Collins, 1921.

Rabindranath Tagore, *Nationalism* Macmillan, London, 1920.

A.N. Whitehead, *Science and The Modern World*, Pelican Books 1938.

George Thompson, "Marxism and Poetry", Lawrence and Wishart, London 1945.

SOCIAL HISTORY: PREDICAMENTS AND POSSIBILITIES

Sumit Sarkar

Over the past generation, the focus of interest in modern Indian history has shifted decisively from viceregal policies, external relations and administrative developments towards an increasingly sophisticated economic history on the one hand, and studies of the national movement, now being broadened rapidly to include various forms of popular protest, on the other hand. But even a passing glimpse of current historiographical tendencies elsewhere brings a painful awareness of the relative poverty so far of researches on modern Indian social history.

In an influential article published in 1971, E.J. Hobsbawm noted that social history 'as an academic specialisation' was 'quite new', but commented on 'the remarkably flourishing state of the field. It is a good moment to be a social historian. Even those of us who never set out to call ourselves by this name will not want to disclaim it today'.[1] The growing importance, respectability, and even predominance, of the genre would be evident to any reader of the stimulating British historical periodicals of the 1970s and early 80s: *Past and Present, History Workshop* and *Social History* can claim preeminence here. The *Annales* of course had acted as the pioneer, while in the USA 'social history has gradually come to supplant political history as the dominant concern of the academy'.[2] It is symptomatic of changing historiographical moods or fashions that a volume published in 1982 in honour of E.J. Hobsbawm did not have a single article on specialised economic history, even though that had been his original field of expertise.[3]

The social history boom in the West has gone alongside of shifts in the meaning of that convenient but vague label. Already in 1971, Hobsbawm dismissed what he described as the 'residual view of social history'—Trevelyan's 'history with the politics left out'—as something requiring 'no comment'. He distinguished two other earlier connotations-lower class, labour or peasant protest, conventionally often labelled as 'social movements', and the social as (and usually secondary) adjunct of the economic—till the growth of a specialised, quantitative, 'hard', economic history enforced a rupture between cliometricians and lesser folk. The real burden of Hobsbawm's paper, however, had been a call to broaden 'social history' into 'the history of society'. The debt here to Marc Bloch and Lucien Febvre's programme for 'integral', 'global' or 'total' history was obvious and acknowledged. The two leading features of the recent boom in social history have been in fact a tremendous broadening in the scope of historical research

From Economic and Political Weekly, *June 22–29, 1985. Reprinted with permission. First presented as the author's Presidential Address to the Modern India Section of the Forty-Fifth Session of the Indian Congress at Annamaliai on December 27–29, 1984.*

to cover multifarious aspects of the lived experience of the past, bringing within its scope numerous dimensions and themes left only yesterday to antiquarians, folklorists and anthropologists, and an openness towards the concepts and methods of other social sciences. Among these, social anthropology today can claim something like a primacy so far as the current debts of historians are concerned.[4] The shifts have been extensive and rapid, so that even an article like Keith Thomas's 'History and Anthropology' published in 1963, conveys a curiously dated flavour today: anthropology then was still being identified by this British historian with structural functionalism with no reference at all to Lévi-Strauss or stuctural linguistics, and education, family and the history of mentalities were described as subjects hardly explored so far in Britain.

The expansion, as one would expect, has been not without tensions, debates, and sharp antinomies, some of which I intend to touch upon and try to relate to our own historiographical problems a little later. For the moment it might be convenient to remind ourselves that 'total' history has been used in a number of different senses, not all of them of equal potential value, relevance or practicality in the context of existing source material and resources in India. It can imply efforts to define entire epochs and/or their succession over time: civilisations, 'traditional' as distinct from 'modernising' societies (a sociological-cum-political scientist vogue now happily somewhat in decline), modes of production and social formations. The latter, Marxian tradition, despite repeated vulgarisations to an almost equivalent extent by believers and traducers alike, has retained a coherence and heuristic power unequalled by its rivals. Fruitful when related imaginatively and effectively to specific empirical contexts, such a conception of totality can degenerate into scholastic labelling exercises in lesser hands. The most effective Marxist interventions in academic history writing have usually been at a somewhat lower level of abstraction and ambition. We may admire (with qualification) Perry Anderson, but would have been really impoverished without Thompson, Hill, Hilton or Hobsbawm.

With the partial exeption of Marc Bloch's 'Feudal Society',[6] the bulk of the classic work of the *Annales* school operated with a somewhat different concept of *l'histoire integrale*: the study of a region over the *longue duree*, hopefully 'total' in scope, proceeding systematically through the various 'times', 'geographical', 'social', and 'individual' relevant for the historian.[7] Braudel on the Mediterranean, and LeRoy Ladurie on Languedoc have been the two outstanding exemplars of this mode of history-writing, which became associated for a time in the 1950s and 60s with a denigration of political, narrative or episodic *(evenementielle)* history. Event, agency, and process tended to be marginalised in the quest for long-term structures, ecological and demographic, and Ladurie even talked of a 'history that stands still' till the 18th-19th century break, coming surprisingly and perilously close to modernisation theorists.[8] It may be doubted whether such works have really been as 'total' as they had set out to be[9] and in any case we sadly lack in India the necessary infrastructure of 'a prodigious body of articles, papers, books, publications, surveys, some purely historical, others no less interesting, written by specialists in neighbouring disciplines' which Braudel used to write about 'the Mediterranean and the lands illumined by its glow'.[10]

It is 'total' history in a third sense, however, which I feel might prove the most fruitful and realisable in the Indian context: focused on a fairly well-defined theme, problem, or even the once-abused 'event' or 'episode', but trying to study it in depth, and looking at its various dimensions. Many of the more recent works in the *Annales* tradition have themselves moved in this direction, including Ladurie's two best-sellers, 'Montillou' and 'Carnival at Romans'. The currently very fashionable history of *mentalite* still often seeks the *longue duree*, but chooses for intensive study one aspect of human sensibility in its bid to explore the 'ideas concerning childhood, sexuality, family and death ... the attitudes of ordinary people towards everyday life . . .'.[11] It thus seeks to implement a programme outlined by Lucien Febvre more than a generation back.[12] Independent of each other, contemporary feminism and new techniques of demographic research have led to a vast and extremely fruitful expansion of the field of family history and women's studies in Western Europe and America: once again anthropology has become a major influence here.[3] The partial rehabilitation of *l'histoire evenementielle*—what Lawrence Stone recently described as the 'revival of narrative'[14] has had as one of its significant consequences a new mode of writing political history, no longer an outcast from total history but transformed into a 'history in depth by becoming the history of power', with a new focus on the 'semiology of power', investigating signs, symbols, and a variety of non-written documentation.[15] A study of ruling groups, of changing patterns and symbols of domination, or even of diplomacy, it needs to be emphasised, can be as genuine and valuable a work of social history as research on popular movements or popular culture. The identification of lower-class protest as 'social', as distinguished from the history of elites to which the term 'political' has to be confined, is an unfortunately deep-seated historical habit which is unhelpful and indeed illogical.[16] 'Social history' cannot really have a separate domain, marked off from 'economic' or 'political'; the differentia must consist in approach and methods, not necessarily subject matter.

In the hands of the best practitioners of social history today, practically any event or aspect of past experience can be made to yield far-reaching insights. The testimony before the Inquisition of a totally obscure 16th century Italian miller, rituals and festivals of inversion, the French *Charivari* and the English 'rough music', serve as starting points for fascinating reconstructions of the world of popular culture.[17] Food riots become indicators of a partially autonomous 'moral economy' of the crowd.[18] The 'black act' of 1723 and studies of crime and law provide pivots for a major reconstruction of 18th century English history which turns Namierism on its head.[19] The diaries of A.J.

Munby and Hannah Cullwick, minor Victorian poet and his servant-cum-mistress, illuminate intricate nuances of gender and class relations.[20] The prints of Hogarth, or New Year festivities in remote Newfoundland villages, lead on to major theoretical discussions of concepts of culture and class.[21]

II

Research on modern Indian social history, here or abroad, cuts a rather sorry figure if set besides such abundance. Recently an applicant for a college job in Delhi, asked to name a single good general work on the social history of modern India, replied that there is no such book. The selection committee, I am told, was dissatisfied with the answer: as sometimes happens, here the experts were wrong and the candidate right. The 'residual' approach, dismissed so cavalierly by Hobsbawm, still flourishes among us. A survey of 18th century social life published in 1976 hailed G.M. Trevelyan's 'Social History' as a 'brilliant example', and went on to give scattered details about religious sects, education, caste, family life, the position of women, and various 'social evils' before embarking on a more congenial summary of economic conditions.[22] For the 19th century, there has often been a more surprising, indeed possibly unique, redefinition: social history is tacitly equated with the history of 'social reform' initiated by and confined overwhelmingly to educated 'middle class' groups, set against the background of British educational and 'social' policies. Thus V.A. Narain's *Social History of Modern India* (1972) deals successively with Company 'social policy', missionaries and 'humanitarianism' and English education, followed by nine chapters on social reform movements.[23] R.C. Majumdar's *History of Modern Bengal* (1978) seems to promise a little more, with its long chapters on Religion and Society based on extracts from contemporary journals collected by Benoy Ghosh. The absence of any theoretical framework, however, leaves us in the end with bits and pieces of scattered information.[24] The most eminent of historians thus seem curiously uncertain in the domain of social history when they venture out of safe confines of sati, widow-remarriage, Brahmoism or 'Hindu revival'. Similar assumptions, confusing a not-unimportant but undeniably limited sector with a potentially vast field, underlie many University syllabi on 'social history' – including that of my own, though fortunately this has been ignored in practice and is now under revision.

Prospects appear somewhat brighter as regards the two other sub-types of traditional social history distinguished by Hobsbawm: the social as an adjunct of the economic, and studies of popular protest. A number of historians have tried to work outwards from analysis of economic structures of particular regions to changing social and political relationships: Ravinder Kumar's study of Western India and some of the articles in his recently-published *Essays on the Social History of Modern India* can serve as good examples of this genre.[25] Numerous and varied attempts have been made to relate nationalism to its social and economic 'basis': educated 'middle class' grievances, bourgeois upthrust, elite competition, material interests of local patron-client networks, the contrasting implications of wet and dry farming and the emergence in certain areas of rich peasant groups.[26] In recent years there has also been a notable effort to develop a distinct sub-discipline of urban history.[27] And 'history from below' flourishes today, with a large number of publications or research in progress on protest movements of tribals, peasants, and (to a lesser extent) industrial workers.[28] Attempts at 'total' histories of whole regions over longish time-spans remain inhibited by inadequate source materials and lack of a necessary infrastructure of micro-studies, but a work like Chris Bayly's *Rules, Townsmen, and Bazars* does represent a heroic and fascinating effort to transcend traditional barriers between the economic, the socio-cultural and the political.[29]

A number of major limitations persist. A considerable gap still remains between our understanding of the basic structures and tendencies of the colonial economy—considerably deepened today by recent research—and the much-explored history of political movements in late colonial India, generally subsumed, a little too readily perhaps, under the rubric of nationalism. More precisely, this area of silence relates to the vast and virtually unexplored terrain of forms of popular consciousness and culture, as distinct from ideological currents within the intelligentsia on which there has been considerable work of a rather old-fashioned, 'intellectual history' type.[30] The gap is obviously related also to the very evident lack of fruitful dialogue between history, sociology and social anthropology. Our sub-continent provided the subject-matter for some of the earliest classics of anthropological field-work—most notably Radcliffe-Brown's study of Andaman islanders—and yet it is only quite recently that professional historians have started getting interested in tribal societies (and even then, mainly in tribal rebellions). Caste for long remained almost a taboo word among many of us. It occurs only three times in the index of R.P. Dutt's *India Today*,[31] and—to indulge for a moment in an auto-critique—I feel now that a serious lacunae in my study of the Swadeshi movement in Bengal consisted in my inability or unwillingness to relate the data on 'caste movements' of Mahishyas, Namasudras, and others to my overall analytical framework.[32]

Such silences have had manifold consequences. Not only do large tracts of human experience remain unexplored: studies of women, for instance, only just beginning to attract serious historical attention, and even so somehow automatically relegated to women colleagues and usually confined to limited themes like education and social reform. The absence of genuine social history also produces low-order explanation even in apparently much-trodden areas. It is not really possible, for example, to bridge the gap between colonial structure and nationalist or other protest by means of an insufficiently analysed, rigid, and over-general concept of 'class', abstracted from any real empirical analysis of the concrete problems of class-formation through conflict between living human beings in groups.[33] Such 'Marxism' is all too-easily 'refutable', for textbook or programmatic formulas regarding the 'national' bourgeoisie or the working class soon reveal their inadequacies when confronted by micro-studies bringing out the reality of enormous variations, the persistence and even refurbishing of 'traditional' ties of caste and religion, or the importance often of vertical patron-client linkages. It may be argued, further, that a historiography limited to conventional tools and sources has an almost built-in tendency to become more elitist as it turns more sophisticated, and that this has been happening in our field: for private papers, accepted now-a-days as the most 'authentic' source of all, are bound to have an overwhelmingly official or upper-class origin in a largely illiterate country.

So far as studies of popular movements are concerned, the failure to grapple seriously with problems of consciousness and culture leads repeatedly to inadequate or even trite explanations, in particular the two related poles, trenchantly and effectively attacked recently by Ranajit Guha, of economic reductionism and mobilisation by great leaders/ideologies or skilful manipulators of patron-client linkages.[34] Rebellion is presented either 'as an instinctive and almost mindless response to physical suffering of one kind or another',[35] or simply a matter of effective organisation from the top: both tend to exclude the insurgent as the subject of history.[36] It is not that economic pressures, outsider leadership interventions, or even on occasion factional linkages are unimportant or not worth exploring, but surely we need to remember Thompson's withering comment about a simple hunger-protest nexus being as self-evident and as limited as the fact 'that the onset of sexual maturity can be correlated with a greater frequency of sexual activity'.[37] As for automaticity of the second type, otherwise inert masses responding to politico-ideological stimuli, or coherts of 'clients' meekly trooping off at the command of their 'patrons', Thompson's analysis of 18th century English 'paternalism' and 'deference' appear again extremely relevant: deference 'could be seen from below as being one part necessary self-preservation, one part the calculated extraction of whatever could be extracted'.[38] Patronage in other words can be a far more complex, nuanced, and varying concept than imagined by the so-called 'Cambridge school'.

The virtual absence of research on popular culture creates problems even for radical-minded historians who would like to avoid any ascription of inertness or passivity to tribals, peasants, or workers. Repeatedly evident here are signs of romanticisation, anachronism, and teleology: an implicit assumption about a kind of innate popular militancy or rebelliousness; a concentration on moments of open rebellion alone; tendencies to view all manifestations of plebian initiative or autonomy as laudable and progressive; the ascription of present-day political and socio-economic concerns to leadrs like Titu Mir, Sidhu and Kanhu, or Birsa Munda;[39] and persistent, at times almost desperate, attempts to relate all popular rebellions to general currents of anti-imperialism or social change. Such romanticisation appears particularly inappropriate in a country which has just witnessed the undoubtedly plebian appeal of Bhindranwale as well as the 'popular' Hindu communalist backlash following the assassination of Indira Gandhi.

To make the discussion more concrete, I would like to take up now two examples from areas which have been central to my own teaching and research work: popular, more specifically peasant, nationalism in the 20th century, and the intellectual history of 19th century Bengal. In both fields one notices a repeated tendency for interesting historiographical departures to get bogged down in old and sterile polemics, and it is such mental blocks that have made me increasingly aware of the need for the development of a genuine social history.

'Subaltern studies', with its critique of all varieties of 'elitism', whether colonialist, nationalist, or even 'Marxist', its focus on lower class initiatives, and its pioneering efforts to tackle problems of popular consciousness with the aid of tools adapted from antrhopology and structural linguistics, does represent a major breakthrough in our history-writing. A not-uncritical reviewer has even compared the possible impact of Ranajit Guha's *Elementary Aspects* with that of D.D. Kosambi a generation back. Yet much of the debate provoked by this departure seems to have already acquired a certain staleness, an incapacity to pinpoint the real problems. Personally I am neither provoked nor particularly enthralled by the term 'subaltern'. 'Plebian' (as used by E.P. Thompson for 18th century England) or 'popular', could have also served much the same purpose, related to the need for some kind of omnibus category in precapitalist situations where class-formation is still relatively inchoate. 'Subaltern' does have a certain advantage, however, insofar as it is used to pinpoint basic relationships of power, of domination and subordination—relationships which may often be cross-cutting, involving distinction of caste and gender as well as of class, and in which the 'subaltern' of one specific context may well be simultaneously the dominant group in another. An obvious example might be an exploited intermediate caste male peasant employing low-caste landless labour and lording it over his wife and children.[40] Such terminological issues apart, it is unfortunate that the subaltern studies enterprise is often being viewed through the very old prism of an organisation/autonomy debate, endemic in Indian Marxist circles since the 1920s, with Guha and some of his associates charged with the heresy of 'populism', of denying the role of vanguard elements. At times we seem to be going back to the well-established Gandhi-as-great-man/Gandhi-the-great-betrayer-syndrome, and the dust raised by such sterile debates only obscures some of the real problems with Guha's approach: the extent of relevance of somewhat simplistic binary models, for example, or the dangers of a certain abstraction from specific contexts of time and region involved in a quest for 'elementary aspects'.[41]

The tendency for new endeavours to get sucked back into old debates has shown itself also in the controversies about the relevance of the 'renaissance' model for understanding 'middle class' intellectual history of 19th century

Bengal. Some of us had argued that the analogy was inappropriate, based as it was on a unilinear concept of historical development which gave inadequate attention to the peculiar twisted logic of colonialism. The search for distant progenitors of present-day values, most notably in Rammohun, represented a kind of 'Whig' interpretation which had to be overcome if we wanted to avoid the pitfalls of anachronism and teleology.[42] Attempts were made to situate Rammohun, David Hare, Young Bengal, and Vidyasagar more firmly within their specific contexts.[43] But many mistook all this as some kind of exercise in debunking or iconoclasm, and soon we were back to a great/little man debate, about the 'role', 'progressive' or otherwise, of particular movements or personalities.

I have come to feel increasingly that such polemical bogs can be avoided only through a major broadening of approach, sources and methods, a leap towards genuine social history. The organisation/autonomy debate in the history of mass nationalism, for instance, can be transformed if re-read in terms of a common 'language', permitting a communication and yet susceptible to a variety of nuance of idiom, style and meaning as different social strata interpreted it in the light of their specific and often conflicting interests and traditions. I have in mind something along the lines of W.H. Sewell's recent fascinating study of the 'language of labour' in late 18th and early 19th century France, in which the 'corporate' idiom is revealed to have been capable of a multitude of subtle shifts over both time and social space.[44] There is considerable scope here for methods of semiological analysis, having as their subject matter both verbal and non-verbal communication: the rich ambience, for instance, acquired by signs like charkha, khadi or salt, the importance of which surely far transcended the immediate material gains they might have brought to their patriotic users.[45] Such approaches may give us new insights into the strength and strange persistence of Gandhi's appeal, despite numerous 'betrayals', by focusing on its deeply religious nature, its dominant idiom of sacrifice and renunciation.[46] The complex intermingling—indeed, often the near-identification—of the language of patriotism with that of religion demands a subtler, analysis than that offered by assumptions about distinct 'secular' and 'revivalist' trends, with 'nationalism' a thing apart from 'communalism', and politicians only 'using' religion.

Starting from a specific area, movement, or even perhaps a single well-documented incident, analysis of this type may go very much deeper: many of the rumours about the Mahatma as miracle-worker collected by Shahid Amin from Gorakhpur, for instance,[47] can make sense only if placed in the context of traditions of popular culture. The problem of interaction between levels of nationalism leads on, therefore, to that of levels within society, culture and religion—a problem which in the context of Hinduism has already provided the staple for a central and recurrent debate in social anthropology.[48] Historians need to participate in that debate, and make their own specific contributions to it, keeping in mind E.P. Thompson's warning that while entering into a necessary and fruitful dialogue with anthropology, history cannot cease to remain 'a discipline of context and process'.[49] Similar problems, about the validity of elite/popular distinctions in culture, as well as the need to recognise both the possibilities of communications across social strata and of autonomous variations or interpretations, have come to occupy a central place in the concerns of social historians in many parts of the world.[50]

The somewhat arid field of the nineteenth century 'renaissance', for long left to middle class self-praise or flagellation, can also be transformed if brought into relationship with this central problematic. I feel that a close reading of the multitude of texts left by our nineteenth century worthies—religious treatises, literary works, autobiographies, the rich collection of vernacular tracts at the Indian Office Library—can still reveal unexpected treasures, particularly if brought into juxtaposition with evidence concerning earlier religious traditions and contemporary popular culture. Recently I have been trying to do some work on one such text, extremely well known in Bengal but untouched so far by professional historians: the *Ramakrishna-Kathamrita*, remarkable, indeed unique, for its verbatim recording of actual conversation, for a period of some six years, 1881-1886, between the saint and his disciples. A conversation, moreover, which represented a leap across social space, for Ramakrishna was a rustic Brahman with a family holding of only one-and-a-half bighas and a little formal learning, his disciples by the early 1880s entirely educated Calcutta *bhadralok*. The *Kathamrita* provides an index to changing *bhadralok* mentalities—for Ramakrishna acquired a middle class clientale only in the later 1870s and early 1880s, more than twenty years after he had settled at Dakshineshwar—and more interestingly, some clues for understanding the mental world of rural Bengal.[51] As such, it can be a valuable supplement to the efforts being made today to reconstruct peasant consciousness from moments of rebellion alone.

As the conversation of a man involved in a process of social ascent, the *Kathamrita* proves to be a valuable text for probing into basic relationships of power. A central image in it is the richly ambiguous figure of the *babu* or *baromanush*: living in idleness, chewing *pan* without care, with well-trimmed moustaches, far away from thoughts of *Iswara*,[52] and yet someone who has to be pleased, whose patronage is essential for survival, whose heart can be won through devotion and love, and who often becomes strangely homologous with divinity itself.[53] Ramakrishna's attitudes towards authority inextricably combine subservience and, not exactly revolt, but certainly resentment: a reminder, perhaps, that a binary model of subordination/revolt is not always helpful. He loved to recall the days of his 'madness' or ecstasy when he 'had no fear of big people', and had even slapped his patron Rani Rashmoni once for being inattentive during a devotional song.[54] In one, isolated, but remarkable, conversation, Ramakrishna identified himself for a brief moment with the apocalyptic *Kalki-avatar*: 'A Brahman's son—he knows nothing—suddenly a horse and sword will come . . .'[55] And yet Ramakrishna also recalled how he had become sure of his stature as a holy man only after the zamindars of his village home paid their respects to him.[56] Struck down by cancer at the height of his prestige among the *bhadralok*, he pleaded with the doctor: 'Babu, please make me well ... Babu! Babu! You must cure me'—like any peasant or poor man begging a favour from a social superior.[57] Subservience and resentment are reconciled in Ramakrishna through *bhakti*, representing a simultaneous internalisation and humanising of *adhikar-bheda*, or hierarchy, social as well as religious. In a series of homologous parables, the social inferior—servant, poor man's son, client—is shown as obtaining the favour of the king, *baromanush* or *babu* through *bhakti* and *seba* (devotion and service), at times brushing aside the *amlas* or intermediaries who try to block his way.[58] *Bhakti*, as perhaps through much of Indian history, seems to provide a kind of 'living-space' for the downtrodden: a living-space which is also a trap, for it has helped hierarchy and oppression to endure by making them appear less unendurable.

The servant can hope to relate himself through *bhakti* to the *babu*, clearly portrayed as a patron of a 'traditional' or 'paternalistic' type—but there is in Ramakrishna a second kind of model of subordination, much less acceptable: *chakri* or office-work, implying *dasatya* (bondage, slavery) under a *manib* (master, employer). What seems to make *chakri* intolerable for Ramakrishna was its connotation of an impersonal cash nexus, embodied above all in new, rigorous, discipline of time. He once told a disciple: 'your face seems to have a dark shadow upon it. That's because you are working in an office. In the office you have to handle money, keep accounts, do so much other work; you have to be alert all the time.'[59] One is irresistably reminded of E.P. Thompson's seminal essay on the transition from peasant-artisan to industrial time, and the plebian hostility to the change-over to the more rigorous routine of capitalist society.[60] In nineteenth century Bengal, it needs to be added where the few factories were owned by foreigners and employed mainly non-Bengalees, and there was no capitalist breakthrough in agriculture, the principle locii for the imported ideas of bourgeois time and discipline became the office and the new type of schools and colleges.[61]

Space forbids any further exploration here of the unexpected riches of the *Kathamrita*[62] but I must add that it—together with *Lilaprasanga*, the standard biography of Ramakrishna—is replete with references to popular religious and cultural traditions which become meaningful only when read in conjunction with data collected by folklorists and anthropologists. Sacrilegious though it must sound, the intertwining submission and resentment in Ramakrishna's discourse remind one of James Freeman's life-history of Muli, a Bauri pimp of a village near Bhubaneswar whose 'ambivalent responses reflect respect for, affection for, resentment of and rebellion against the same person'.[63]

III

So far I have pleaded for a greater openness towards anthropology and more awareness among us all of the work on social history going on in other countries. To avoid any possible misinterpretation, I would like to add now that I do not mean by this any wholesale borrowing, or a surrender of the necessary autonomy of our own discipline. Awareness is required precisely to avoid being swept away by the 'latest' intellectual fashions, which in any case usually reach our country after a considerable time-lag, and then tend to persist long after they have become outmoded elsewhere.[64]

It is necessary to recall, therefore, that the social history boom in the West has been accompanied by considerable, at times extremely trenchant, criticism. A young historian in 1979 went so far as to declare, in a conscious reversal of Hobsbawm, that 'this is a bad time to be a social historian'.[65]

Both the great possibilities and the real problems of a social history impregnated with anthropology can be brought into focus through the basic concept of 'culture'. Anthropologists have been using it to signify 'a whole way of life', the complex of interlocking institutions, customs, values and myths revealed through fieldwork: as Keith Thomas argued twenty years ago, the resultant perspective of totality has often given 'a better impression of what *l'histoire integrale* might be' than much conventional history-writing.[66] Through anthropology, and today social history influenced by it, 'behaviours and beliefs traditionally seen as senseless, irrelevant, or at best marginal curiosities (for instance, magic and superstition) have been analysed at last as valid human experiences'.[67] Yet a dialogue with anthropology, as E.P. Thompson reminded a session of this Congress in 1977, was necessary but bound to be difficult.[68] The Genoveses, themselves major social historians, have bitterly attacked much contemporary social history for its abstraction from political and economic structures and processes, for threatening to develop into a kind of neo-antiquarian description of everyday life.[69] The ghost of Trevelyan's 'history with the politics left out' has proved much more difficult to exorcise then Hobsbawm had expected.[70] Ranajit Guha's insistence on the centrality of the 'political' derives its value from an awareness of such dangers, and can be of help provided the 'political' is construed in terms of a variety of complex attitudes and actions generated by fundamental relationships of domination and subordination, and not identified only with open rebellion.

At a more general level, structural functionalism—still the dominant in Indian anthropology—does raise serious problems so far as most historians, and particularly Marxists, are concerned. The emphasis on 'functional' integration, cohesion and solidarity, derived from a combination of Durkheim with field-experience among (mostly) primitive groups, often appears as irrelevant or even some kind of prettifying neo-traditionalism in studies of more developed societies, shot through as they are by sharp conflicts of rank, caste or class. To many historians, it might make more sense to interpret culture as a 'whole way of conflict' rather than an undifferentiated 'whole way of life' common in the same way to all members of a society.[71] What adds considerably to the problem is that dominant schools of anthropology, structuralist as much as structural-functionalist, have a built-in preference for synchrony over diachrony, for more-or-less unchanging and uniform structures, and not processes or events; *langue* rather than *parole*, in Saussurean terminology. Some of Lévi-Strauss' techniques may be helpful for us, but on the whole an anthropologist like Clifford Geertz has more to offer to historians, with his quest for 'thick description' of a specific situation, akin to an imaginative literary reading of texts rather than a formal 'decoding' operation.[72] And I feel that there is a lot to learn from Carlo Ginzburg's recent methodological essay on the 'conjectural paradigm', proceeding through a ferretting-out of 'clues', as the approach most suited for history, which 're-mains a science of a very particular kind, irremediably based on the concrete'. Unlike the natural sciences, history cannot really afford to abstract from the qualitative and the individual,[73] and perhaps the same warning is applicable to the kind of anthropology most relevant for historians.

The convergence—despite all problems and tensions—between some of the most interesting types of anthropology and history today is illustrated by the similar conclusions arrived at, quite independently of each other and through work in utterly different styles and intellectual traditions, by E.P. Thompson in his *Poverty of Theory* (some polemical excesses apart) and Pierre Bourdieu in his *Outline of a Theory of Practice*. Both the polemic against Althusser and the critique of structuralist and structural-functionalist anthropology focus on the problem of structure and agency, fundamental to the social sciences since at least Vico onwards: history is made by human beings, yet the products of their labour and thought repeatedly acquire an externality, an objectified or alienated chracter which dominates the makers and mystifies the cultural into the natural.[74] A 'scientific' and 'objective' focus on structures alone involves therefore living in and a surrender to a fetishicised world. In anthropology, Bourdieu has argued, 'model' and 'rule' have to be replaced by 'strategy', and he tries to arrive at a dialectical understanding of the tension between structure and agency through his basic concept of 'habitus'.[75]

The writings of Thompson or Bourdieu and the current 'state of play' between history and anthropology[76] convey simultaneously a vivid awareness of the rich possibilities of work in a creative Marxian tradition, and a sense of acute dissatisfaction with much that passes under that label. Thompson's books and essays are replete with instances of his capacity to give 'familiar sociological concepts . . . a new dialectical ambivalence: an "act of giving" must be seen simultaneously as an "act of getting", a social consensus as a class hegemony, social control (very often) as class control . . .';[77] Bourdieu situates himself in a philosophical tradition going back to Marx' 'Theses on Feuerbach' and yet both would no doubt be regarded as heretical by many.

Marxism of a certain type has acquired considerable influence over Indian historiography in recent years, and today even dominates a number of areas. But one sometimes fears whether the success has not been too easy, and due largely to the weakness and lack of sophistication of alternative traditions.[78] Certainly Marxism has often reigned among us in considerably simplified forms: a rigid, virtually *a priori* conception of class-interest, derived automatically from economic conditions; and unquestioned acceptance of formulas of base and superstructure; faith in the primacy of the 'economic', balanced by the usual ritual concessions to interaction and relative autonomy; a consequent playing down of problems of culture and consciousness. Yet serious doubts have been raised elsewhere about the value of the base-superstructure model. It was only an analogy, after all, and by no means the only one which Marx experimented with;[79] and in any case it is important to remember that really original thinkers often have difficulties in conveying the full richness of their ideas through a language necessarily borrowed from others (in the case of the founders of Marxism, Hegelian, followed by positivistic). Again, it is surely impermissible to identify the mode of production with the 'economy', since it is very difficult to conceive of any system of productions relation abstracted from culture, law, and politics i e, elements of the so-called 'superstructure'.[80] One of Marx's most profound insights was precisely that the rigorous separation and 'primacy' of the economic domain ('economic man') was a construct of bourgeois society and ideology.

Thus we need to move towards both 'a materialist and relational concept of culture' and 'a more culturally embedded analysis of the material world'.[81] A social history developing through a fruitful, because critical, dialogue with anthropology can help us 'in locating new problems, in seeing old problems in new ways, in an emphasis upon norms and value systems and upon rituals, in attention to expressive functions of forms of riot and disturbance, and upon symbolic expressions of authority, control and hegemony'.[82] I feel that it is in such ways that the very rich Gramscian concept of hegemony can develop into a significant tool for historical analysis, and be rescued from the danger, which threatens it now that it has become quite fashionable, of becoming yet another cliché or formula. A Marxist historiography which is content only with the narrowly 'economic' or the 'political' is as emasculated as much contemporary Marxist practice, condemned in the absence of effective counter-hegemonic strategies to oscillate between economism and 'sectarian' adventures or 'reformist' opportunism in politics.

Exploring ever-new realms of lived experience, social history today is contributing to a realisation that 'the seemingly most intimate details of private existence are actually structured by larger social relations',[83] bringing history much nearer to its writers or readers in an interaction that can deepen critical awareness of both the past and of ourselves. Focusing on 'cultural and moral mediations . . . the way . . . material experience are handled . . . culturally',[84] it enters a world in which agency, values, or moral choice can never be entirely submerged in a more or less passive contemplation of structures. Such awareness is not, however, always very comfortable, and this may help to explain some of the suspicion and hostility which social history seems to arouse at times. I am reminded of a discussion on syllabus revision that took place some months back in my University, in which a very young teacher, passionately pleading for a greater emphasis on social history, argued that history to be really meaningful could not remain unconnected with his everyday life, his relations with parents, loved ones, or neighbours. A senior academic pulled him up sharply for becoming so 'individualistic'. I do feel, however, that a history detached from such concerns, even when it is radical or Marxist in appearance, can never become more than—at best—a pleasnt academic diversion, or—at worst—a way of entering the rat-race for jobs, promotions, and patronage. To adapt and expand a slogan of the women's liberation movement, 'the personal is the political'—and it must become the historical, too.

NOTES

[1] Specialised journals in social history, Hobsbawm remarked, were rare till *Comparative Studies in Society and History* (1958). E.J. Hobsbawm, 'From Social History to the History of Society', *Daedalus*, V, 100, Winter 1971.

[2] Elizabeth Fox-Genovese and Eugene Genovese, 'The Political Crisis of Social History: A Marxian Perspective', *Journal of Social History*, x, 1976; reprinted in *Ibid, Fruits of Merchant Capital: Slavery and Bourgeois Property in the Rise and Expansion of Capitalism*, OUP, 1983.

[3] Raphael Samuel and Gareth Stedman Jones, ed, *Culture, Ideology and Politics: Essays for Eric Hobsbawm*, History Workshop Series, London, etc, 1982.

[4] Thus Lawrence Stone talks about 'the replacement of sociology and economics by anthropology as the most influential of the social sciences'. 'The Revival of Narrative; Reflections on a New Old History', *Past and Present*, No 85, November 1979.

[5] Keith Thomas, 'History and Anthropology', *Past and Present*, No 24, April 1963.

[6] Possibly influenced to some extent by Marxian conceptions—see Andre Burguierre, 'The Fate of the History of Mentalities in the Annales', *Comparative Studies in Society and History*, Vol 24, 1982.

[7] Fernand Braudel, 'The Mediterranean and the Mediterranean World in the Age of Philip II', Volume I, Fontana, 1976. Preface to the First Edition, p 21.

[8] As well as to a remarkably uncritical appreciation of Fogel and Engerman's 'Time on the Cross'. E.Le Roy Ladurie, 'History that Stands Still' (1973), reprinted in his *The Mind and Method of the Historian*, Harvester, 1981.

[9] 'The Mediterranean' after all, will remain immortal not for any major revaluations of the Renaissance, the Reformation or the battle of Lepanto, but for its superb and poetic evocation of 'man's contact with the inanimate', in which the flowers 'come back every spring, the flocks of sheep migrate every year . . . the ships sail on a real sea that changes with the seasons', Braudel, op cit, p 27.

[10] *Ibid*, p 18.

270

11Patrick H. Hutton, 'The History of Mentalities: The New Map of Cultural History', *History and Theory*, Vol XX, 1981. See also Emmanuel Le Roy Ladurie, 'Recent Historical 'Discoveries'', *Daedalus*, Vol 106, 1977; Stephen Wilson, 'Death and the Social Historian: Some Recent Writings in French and English', *Social History*, V, 3, 1980; Philippe Aries, 'The Hour of Our Death', Peregine, 1981; and, for more critical assessments, Andre Burguierre, op cit; and Stuart Clark, 'French Historians and Early Modern Popular Culture', *Past and Present*, No 100, 1983.

12Lucien Febvre in 1941 called for 'a whole series of studies none of which have yet been done, and as long as they have not been done *there will be no real history possible*. No history of love, just remember that. We have no history of death, or of cruelty. We have no history of joy . . .'. 'Sensibility and History: How to Reconstitute the Emotional Life of the Past' in Peter Burke, ed, *A New Kind of History: From the Writings of Lucien Febvre*, London, 1973, p 24.

13Ellen Ross and Rayna Rapp, 'Sex and Society: A Research Note from Social History and Anthropology', *Comparative Studies in Society and History*, Vol 23, 1981.

14Lawrence Stone, op cit.

15Jacques Le Goff, 'Is Politics Still the Backbone of History,' *Daedalus*, Vol 100, Winter 1971.

16Even a historian of the stature of E.J. Hobsbawm has frequently made a distinction between the 'political' and the 'social', most recently in hist article in E.J. Hobsbawm and T.O. Ranger, ed, *The Invention of Tradition*, Cambridge, 1982.

17Carlo Ginzburg, 'The Cheese and the Worms: The Cosmos of a 16th Century Miller', New York, 1982; Natalie Z Davis, 'Reasons of Misrule and Women on Top' in her *Society and Culture in Early Modern France*, London, 1975; E.P. Thompson, 'Rough Music: le Charivari anglais', *Annales ESC*, Vol 27 ii, 1972.

18E.P. Thompson, 'The Moral Economy of the English Crowd in the 18th Century', *Past and Present*, No 50, February 1971.

19E.P. Thompson, *Whigs and Hunters: The Origins of the Black Act*, Penguin 1977; Hay, Linebaugh, Rule, Thompson and Winslow, ed, *Albion's Fatal Tree: Crime and Society in 18th Century England*, Penguin 1977. Cf. particularly in this collection Douglas Hay, 'Property, Authority and the Common Law'.

20Leonore Davidoff, 'Class and Gender in Victorian England', in Newton, Ryan, Walkowitz, ed. *Sex and Class in Women's History* History Workshop Series, London, etc, 1983.

21Hans Medick, 'Plebian Culture in the Transition to Capitalism', in Samuel and Jones, ed. *Culture, Ideology and Politics*, op cit; Gerald M. Sider, 'Christmas Mumming and the New Year in Outport Newfoundland', *Past and Present*, No 71, May 1976, and 'The Ties that Bind: Culture and Agriculture, Property and Propriety in the Newfoundland Village Fishery', *Social History*, Volume VI, 1980.

22K.K. Datta, *Survey of India's Social Life and Economic Conditions in the 18th Century*, Delhi, 1976, 1978, Chapter 1 contains the reference to Trevelyan; Chapters 2-4 are entitled, respectively, 'Trends of Relgious Thought', 'Education', and 'Social Life'; Chapters 5-8 (148 out of a total of 221 pages) deal with economic conditions.

23V.A. Narain, 'Social History of Modern India', Meerut, 1972.

24Thus Chapter 7, entitled 'Society' has the following sub-headings: urban society; prostitutes; amusements and festivals; cruel practices; expensive practices; opposition to sea voyage; some characteristics of Bengal urban society—drinking, imitation of Englishmen, social reform; advancement of women; abolition of slavery. R.C. Majumdar, 'History of Modern Bengal', Calcutta, 1978.

[25]Ravinder Kumar, *Western India in the 19th Century*, London 1968; 'Nationalism and Social Change', 'Social Theory and the Historical Perception of Modern India', and 'The Changing Structure of Urban Society in Colonial India' in *Essays in the Social History of Modern India*, OUP, India, 1983.

[26]A representative, more or less, of each type: B.M. Cully, *English Education and the Origins of Indian Nationalism*, New York, 1940; R.P. Dutt, *India Today*, Bombay, 1947; Anil Seal, *Emergence of Indian Nationalism*, Cambridge, 1968; Gallagher, Johnson, Seal, ed, *Locality, Province and Nation*, Cambridge, 1973; D.A. Washbrook, *The Emergence of Provincial Politics: Madras Presidency 1870-1920*, Cambridge, 1976, and D.A. Low's editorial introduction to *Congress and the Raj: Facets of the Indian Struggle*, London, 1977.

[27]See, for instance, J.S. Grewal and Inder Banga, ed, *Studies in Urban History*, Amritsar, n d.

[28]A very partial list: the work, published or in progress, or Majid Siddiqi, Gyan Pandey, and Kapil Kumar on Uttar Pradesh; Walter Hauser, K. Suresh Singh, J. Pouchapadass, Stephen Hennirgham, Arvindnarayan Das, Saradindu Mukherji, and Alok Sheel on Bhiar; Benoy Chowdhuri, Kalyan Sengupta, Hitesh Sanyal, Partha Chatterji, Sunil Sen, Rafiuddin Ahmad and Tanika Sarkar on Bengal; Amalendu Guha on Assam; Biswamoy Pati on Orissa; David Arnol on Andhra and Tamil Nadu; D.N. Dhanagare, Stephen Dale and Conrad Wood on Malabar; Ghansyam Shah and David Hardiman on Gujarat; Ravinder Kumar and Gail Omvedt on Maharashtra; Hari Sen on Rajasthan; Ravinder Kumar and Mridula Mukherji on the Punjab. Significant work on labour includes R.K. Newman on Bombay, Ranajit Dasgupta and Dipesh Chakrabarti on Calcutta, Chitra Joshi on Kanpur, and R.P. Behal on Assam plantations.

[29]C. Bayly, *Rulers, Townsmen and Bazars*, Cambridge, 1983.

[30]For the distinction between ideologies and *mentalite*, and the consequent relative decline of intellectual history, see M. Vovelle, 'Ideologies and Mentalities', in Samuel and Jones, ed, *Culture, Ideology and Politics*, op cit; William J. Bouwsma, 'Intellectual History in the 1980s: From History of Ideas to History of Meaning', *Journal of Interdisciplinary History*, XII, 2, Autumn 1981; and Patrick H. Hutton, 'The History of Mentalities: The New Map of Cultural History', *History and Theory*, Vol XX, 1981.

[31]R.P. Dutt, op cit, Index, p 524.

[32]I have tried to rectify the error to a partial extent in my 'The Conditions and Nature of Subaltern Militancy: Bengal from Swadeshi to Non-cooperation, c 1905-1922', in R. Guha, ed, *Subaltern Studies, III*, Delhi, 1984.

[33]Cf particularly the extremely valuable critique in E.P. Thompson, 'Eighteenth Century English Society: Class Struggle without Class?', *Social History*, III, 2, May 1978.

[34]Ranajit Guha, *Elementary Aspects of Peasant Insurgency in Colonial India*, Delhi, 1983, Ch I, and *passim* see also Guha, 'The Prose of Counter-Insurgency', in Guha ed, *Subaltern Studies, II*, Delhi, 1982.

[35]Guha, 'The Prose of Counter-Insurgency', op cit, p 3.

[36]Guha, *Elementary Aspects*, op cit, p 4.

[37]E.P. Thompson, 'The Moral Economy of the English Crowd in the 18th Century', *Past and Present*, No 50, February 1971.

[38]E.P. Thompson, 'Eighteenth Century English Society: Class Struggle without Class?', *Social History*, III, 2, May 1978.

[39]For an effective critique of such anachronism as manifested in the writings of a radical scholar, see Guha, 'The Prose of Counter-Insurgency', op cit pp 35-38.

[40]I do not feel happy, therefore, with Guha's attempt in his introduction to 'Subaltern Studies, I' to arrive at a general enumeration of subaltern groups in colonial India by simply subtracting certain 'elites'.

[41]I owe many of these points to discussions with two Delhi University students, Saurabh Dube and Dilip Menon, and in particular to Saurabh Dube's 'Peasant Insurgency and Peasant Consciousness', published now in *Economic and Political Weekly*, March 16 1985.

[42]See the articles by Ashok Sen, Barun De, Sumit Sarkar and Pradyumna Bhattacharya in V.C. Joshi, ed, '*Rammohun Roy and the Process of Modernisation in India*', Delhi, 1975, and Barun De, 'A Historical Critique of Renaissance Analogues for Nineteenth Century India', in Barun De, ed, *Perspectives in Social Sciences, I*, Calcutta, etc, 1977.

[43]Apart from the articles on Rammohun cited above, there was an unpublished paper by Barun De on David Hare; Sumit Sarkar, 'The Complexities of Young Bengal', *Nineteenth Century Studies*, October 1973, and Asok Sen, 'Iswarchandra Vidyasagar and His Elusive Milestones', Calcutta, 1977.

[44]W.H. Sewell, *Work and Revolution in France: The Language of Labour from the Old Regime to 1848*, Cambridge, 1980.

[45]Satinath Bhaduri's fascinating Bengali novel *Dhorai Charit Manas*, Calcutta, 1949, depicts villagers in north Bihar identifying the charkha with the *Sudarshanchakra* of Krishna. For the nuances of salt, see Tanika Sarkar, 'National Movement and Popular Protest in Bengal, 1928-34', unpublished thesis, Delhi University, 1981.

[46]I attempted a preliminary, and I feel now in many ways quite inadequate, analysis of these problems in my 'Conditions and Nature of Subaltern Militancy: Bengal from Swadeshi to Non-Cooperation, 1905-1922', in R. Guha, ed, *Subaltern Studies, III*, Delhi, 1984.

[47]Shahid Amin, 'Gandhi as Mahatma: Gorakhpur District, Eastern UP, 1921-22' in Guha, ed, *Subaltern Studies, III*, Delhi, 1984.

[48]Cf, for instance, Louis Dumont 'On the Different Aspects or Levels in Hinduism', in Dumont and Pocock, ed, *Contributions of Indian Sociology, III*, 1959. For a very similar debate on levels within Chinese religion, see Arthur Wolf, ed, *Religion and Ritual in Chinese Society*, California, 1974.

[49]E.P. Thompson, *Anthropology and the Discipline of Historical Context*, Midland History, 13, Spring 1972.

[50]See, for example, Stuart Clark, 'French Historians and Early Modern Popular Culture', *Past and Present*, No 100; Carlo Ginzburg's preference for the concept of 'popular culture' as against the non-class implications of 'mentalities', in 'The Cheese and the Worms', op cit, pp xxiii-xxiv, and the anthropologist Michael Gilsenan's comment that 'the different interpretations of and selections from an essentially common body of myth within a society or cult are historically quite critical', 'Myth and the History of African Religion', in T.O. Ranger and J.N. Kimombo, ed, *The Historical Study of African Religion*, London, etc, 1972.

[51]Ramakrishna by virtue of his caste status could never have been a working peasant, but his lack of formal education made him a participant of the folk culture of the peasantry.

[52]Mahendranath Gupta, *Sri Sri Ramakrishna-Kathamrita* (henceforward K) 5V, Calcutta 1902-1932, Volume V, p 44, June 2, 1883, My translations, from the 1980-82 edition.

[53]K IV, pp 11, 68; KV, p 104.

[54]K II, p 2, (October 16, 1882).

[55]K IV, p 101, (June 20, 1884).

[56]K II, p 49, (June 4, 1883).

[57]K IV, pp 254-5, (September 1, 1885).

[58]Instances abound: see for example, K II, p 63 (June 15, 1883); K III, pp 82-3, 190-191, (June 30, 1884, May 9, 1885, June 13, 1885), K IV, pp 11, 67-8 (February 25, 1883, February 2, 1885). Note the contrast between the troublesome *amla* and the distant overlord who can be reached directly through devotion, evocative of peasant dreams in so many countries of the just king or 'little father' of the poor.

[59]K I, p 121, (June 15, 1884).

[60]E.P. Thompson, 'Time, Work-Discipline and industrial Capitalism', *Past and Present*, No 38, December 1967.

[61]It may not be irrelevant to mention here that Mahendranath Gupta, who kept the record later published as the *Kathamrita*, was a school-teacher who encouraged his pupils to cut classes to come to Ramakrishna. He was dismissed later by Vidyasagar for neglecting his school duties.

[62]The text is a valuable source also for explaining gender relations, for instance. For a detailed analysis of the *Kathamrita*, see my 'The Kathamrita as a Text: Towards an Understanding of Ramakrishna Paramhansa', Occasional Paper, Nehru Memorial Museum and Library, New Delhi, 1985.

[63]James M. Freeman, *Untouchable: An Indian Life History*, London, 1979, p 354.

[64]Thus Ranke's sublime faith in the total impartiality of historians was still being echoed by scholars like R.C. Majumdar in the 1960s: the Anglo-Saxon vogue of economic history of the 1930s, reached India about a generation later; French structuralism has just started affecting some of us.

[65]Tony Judt, 'A Clown in Regal Purple: Social History and the Historians', *History Workshop*, 7, Spring, 1979.

[66]Keith Thomas, 'History and Anthropology', op cit.

[67]Carlo Ginzburg, 'Anthropology and History in the 1980s: A Comment', *Journal of Interdisciplinary History*, XII, 2, Autumn 1981. See also, in the same issue, Natalie Z. Davis, 'Anthropology and History in the 1980s: The Possibilities of the Past'.

[68]E.P. Thompson, 'Folklore, Anthropology and Social History', *Indian Historical Review*, III, 2, January 1977.

[69]Elizabeth Fox-Genovese and Eugene Genovese, op cit.

[70]Tony Judt, op cit; see also Geoff Eloy and Keith Nield, 'Why Does Social History Ignore Politics?' *Social History*, V, 2, May 1980.

[71]Hans Medick, 'Plebian Culture . . .', op cit.

[72]Clifford Geertz, 'Thick Description: Towards an Interpretative Theory of Culture; The Cereberal Savage; On the Work of Claude Levi Strauss; Deep Play: Notes on the Balinese Cockfight', in Geertz, *The Interpretation of Cultures*, London, 1975.

[73]Carlo Ginzburg, 'Morelli, Freud and Sherlock Holmes: Clues and Scientific Method', *History Workshop*, 9, Spring 1908.

[74]E.P. Thompson, *The Poverty of Theory*, London, 1978; Pierre Bourdieu, *Outline of a Theory of Practice*, Cambridge, 1977. See also Peter L. Berger, *The Social Reality of Religion*, London, 1967, Chapter I; Philip Abrams, 'History, Sociology, Historical Sociology', *Past and Present*, No 87, May 1980; and, for the mythification involved in the reduction of culture to nature, Roland Barthes, 'Mythologies' London, etc, 1973.

[75]Defined as 'Systems of durable *dispositions*—an endless capacity to engender pro-

274

ducts, thoughts, perceptions, expressions, actions—whose limits are set by the historically and socially situated conditions of its production—the freedom it secures is as remote from a creation of unpredictable novelty as it is from a simple mechanical reproduction of the initial conditionings', Bourdieu, op cit, pp 72, 95.

[76]Bernard S. Cohn, 'History and Anthropology: The State of Play', *Comparative Studies in Society and History*, V, 22, 1980. See also his 'Anthropology and History in the 1980s—Towards a Rapproachment', *Journal of Interdisciplinary History*, Autumn 1981.

[77]E.P. Thompson, *Folklore, Anthropology and Social History*, op cit.

[78]The undoubted strength of the British Marxist historical tradition, in contrast, has been attributed by Hobsbawm in part to the formidable level of its academic adversaries: 'The advantage was that we could not get away with bullshit', Interview with E.J. Hobsbawm, MARHO, 'Visions of History', Manchester, 1983, p 30.

[79]Cf, for instance, the 'Grundrisse' formulation: 'a general illumination which bathes all the colours and modifies their particularity . . . a particular either which deterines the specific gravity of every being which has materialised within it'—Karl Marx, 'Grundrisse', Penguin, 1973, p 107, E P Thompson cites this passage in his *Folklore, Anthropology and Social History*, op cit. Cf also his 'The Peculiarities of the English', *Socialist Register*, 1963, and Raymond Williams, 'Base and Superstructure in Marxist Cultural Theory', *New Left Review*, November-December 1974.

[80]E.P. Thompson, *Whigs and Hunters*, Penguin, 1977, p 261.

[81]Gerald M. Sider, *The Ties that Bind . . .*, op cit.

[82]E.P. Thompson, *Folklore, Anthropology and Social History*, op cit.

[83]Ellen Ross and Rayna Rapp, *Sex and Society . . .*, op cit.

[84]Interview with E.P. Thompson, MARHO, 'Visions of History', op cit, p 20.

Seeing the Straws; Riding the Whirlwind: Reflections on Unions and Popular Movements in India

Peter Waterman

Eight Propositions

Two short trips in two successive years (1980, 1981) provide a narrow base on which to generalise about labour and popular movements in what amounts to a half continent. If I nonetheless set out certain ideas and impressions here, it is to provide some kind of base line for myself and to provoke a response from readers. Another purpose is to remind socialists of the existence of the world's major unstudied working class—and draw attention to the New Indian labour studies that are discovering it (NILS 1980, and the Bibliography below).

I prepared myself for my trips—which covered but a half-dozen Indian cities and peri-urban areas—by seeking out the best thought of socialist works on India. Hiro (1979) gives an excellent introduction to the social and political tension within Indian society, but his labour movement chapter is entirely devoted to the traditional national trade union centres. Selbourne (1977) provides a horrifying account of the disasters and terrors unleashed on India—and Indian workers— by Mrs Gandhi's Emergency. Written at a time when the European labour movement was either silent about or *supporting* Mrs Gandhi, this was an important task, but one which left little space for dealing with popular resistance. When I turned to a Marxist activist's history of the Indian working class (Sen 1977), I found that despite its claim to continue to 1970, it allowed but 50 pages to the whole period since Independence and none to changes in wage employment or working class structure itself. It was only after almost completing this paper that I read Gail Omvedt's latest book (Omvedt 1980a). Is it despite or because of the fact that it deals with a *brief* upsurge of *just* women's struggles in only *one* Indian state, that it actually conveyed to me more of the general problems of labour and popular movements in India than any other I have read (Waterman 1981a)?

Turning to a new and competent work on labour relations (Ramaswamy and Ramaswamy 1981) proved of little assistance, since the authors define 'industry' so as to cut off the vast majoirty of Indian wage-earners and focus on the problems of management and state—and sociologists—rather than those of labouring people (Waterman 1982).

The major source of perceptive and detailed studies on the new movements is the press—particularly *Economic and Political Weekly, Frontier, How,* and *Business Standard.* These have provided the outlets for such outstanding

From Journal of Contemporary Asia, *Vol 12, No.4, 1982. Reprinted with permission.*

labour journalists as Timir Basu, Sandeep Pendse, Radha Iyer and—again—Gail Omvedt (see Bibliography below). The fact that the latter are themselves activists, Marxists, but mostly outside the traditional labour organisations, probably explains their sensitivity to new developments.

Finally, there is a welcome resurgence of university-based—but far from academic—socialist labour studies. Most of this is in the form of unpublished dissertations (e.g. Chhachhi 1978) or conference papers (e.g. Ram 1981; Sengupta 1981; Upadhyaya 1981; Banaji 1980). Little of this more-theoretical, generalising or synthetical work seems to have got into newspapers, magazines and journals in India or abroad (but see Ghosh 1980 and Gerhardt 1980).

A reading of such material did suggest to me that major changes were occurring within labour and social movements in India. I will set these out as three negative, one ambigious and four positive propositions:

1. There is a *policy* crisis of the traditional national union leaderships, which are decreasingly able to obtain improvements, or to prevent worsening conditions even within the modern private or state sector.

2. There is an *organisational* crisis of the same unions, which continue to be marked by factional splits, stagnant or falling affiliations, and an inability to win over the autonomous unions which are in a majoirty in India (crucially in the modern industrial sector).

3. There is a *strategy* crisis, due to the same organisations' common formal acceptance of highly legalistic industrial relations machinery as the framework for industrial protest, and of parliamentary parties and elections as the framework for political protest. Paired with this is the use of ritualised forms of protest that do not raise consciousness for independent class action.

4. There appears to be an increasing unwillingness of what in India are officially called 'the weaker sections of society' to accept either their traditional lot, or the paternalism, tokenism and electoral manipulations to which they have been subjected: but demands for their legal rights by womem, *harijans* ('schedules castes'), *adivasis* ('scheduled tribes') and oppressed national/language groups are—in the absence of adequate self-organisation or support from the labour movement—so far provoking violent represssion rather than winning significant victories.

5. Repeated industry-wide, city-wide—even state-wide—strike waves are being organised, often under joint action committees, often rejecting traditional leaderships.

6. Traditional leaderships are increasingly being challenged by populist/syndicalist/Marxist leaderships (the distinctions are not always clear between these), organising mass actions that break through legal niceties and traditional forms.

7. There may be a tendency toward worker-led unions, distinguishing them from both the traditional and the populist leaderships (both drawn overwhelmingly from the middle strata).

8. There are increasing cases in which unions (at industry, city or state level) are taking common action with other labouring and oppressed sectors.

To these impressions drawn from written work, I wish to add those drawn from observation on my two visits. I will supplement these impressions with liberal references to books, papers and articles. This is to draw attention to apparently related cases or arguments, and to draw attention to the wealth of material now awaiting synthesis into textbooks and policy proposals for the Indian and international labour movement.

The Crisis of Traditional Unionism

Recognition of the crisis of traditional unionism was best expressed to me by B.T. Ranadive, a leader of the CITU, in 1980. This is especially significant given the fact that the CITU is considered to have been the most successful of the trade union centres recently (Jeuken 1978; Gerhardt 1980).

Ranadive recognised the extent to which 'rural poverty limits the urban wage', and the manner in which the existence of unorganised labour in small enterprises can be used to threaten the power of the organised workers. He then accused the trade union movement of never having done anything to organise outside large-scale enterprise, of being 'dominated by reformist economism', or being 'a silent spectator' to repression and exploitation elsewhere, of failing to come to terms with the fact that 'maybe 50 percent of the workers have land'.

When asked how CITU had avoided the error of 'economism' (a traditional communist pejorative for a narrow wages-and-conditions unionism), he declared that it, too, was guilty of this error. He cited an illustrative case. There had been a CITU-led sugar mill workers strike some four or five years back in Tamil Nadu. This had been aimed against the mill owners, who also controlled the local plantations. It had, however, failed to take up the demands of small sugar-producing farmers also being exploited by the factory owners, and the factory owners had been able to use the farmers against the workers (for a more recent parallel case, see G.O. 1979, 1980; Abraham 1979).

Ranadive was sober to the point of pessimism. Even when he contrasted the above case with a recent major jute mill workers strike during which the union had pressed for a higher government purchase price for the jute growers, he declared the demand to have been no more than 'symbolic' (an opinion confirmed by Basu 1980). He pointed out that there had been no mass working class reaction to the imposition of the Emergency (CITU adopted a policy of tactical retreat during this period), and that when a protest movement had developed it had been for economic demands rather than for democratic ones. There had been a failure of the unions to present themselves as part of the democratic movement, to take up civil rights issues, the rights of peasants, the 'residential dimension' of working class life, the rights of working women and of tribals. In 1981 I heard similar sounds from the lips of ex-Cabinet Minister, Social Democratic politician and railway union federation leader, George Fernandes. But this time it was in public and at length.

The failure of the Congress-aligned INTUC to recognise these problems (but see its perceptions in Nair 1980) may be due to its preoccupation with numerous ambitious 'rural development projects', financed from above (through state agencies and banks) and outside (ILO; the Dutch Union centre, FNV; the Danish state development agency, Danida; etc.). Whilst I was in the INTUC headquarters in Delhi in early 1980 there were present a couple of Norwegians from a Labour movement development agency. These were supposed to be examining a large number of projects in a matter of days, and were said to have been negotiating $200,000 worth of aid for projects in Bhojpur, Bihar. I was also told that Danida had donated or was negotiating a $500,000 project for Bombay. And during the few hours I was in the INTUC offices, I also met the Singapore-based Projects Officer of the Asian Regional Organisation of the ICFTU, Gerhard Schulz.

On returning to Holland I discovered that the Dutch unions were channelling almost *one million* guilders (around US$350-400,000) to the ICFTU for projects in Asia in 1979-80. 143,989 guilders went to one rural development project alone. This was for the INTUC's Organisation of the Rural Poor, Ghazipur, Uttar Pradesh—a project the dubious nature of which has eventually led to public criticism of the FNV in Holland (Leiten 1981; Goedhart 1981).

The impression of INTUC incorporation into an extensive network of international union and state development agencies was reinforced by visits to two international union offices, and to the Ambekar Institute for Labour Studies, Bombay. The ICFTU-ARO has its headquarters and a trade union school in a Delhi suburb, where there can also be found a regional office of the International Metalworkers Federaton (IMF). The AILS (supported by the state-recognised Rashtriya Mill Mazdoor Sangh as well as by INTUC) is the only such union-sponsored centre in India. Concerned with 'how to achieve industrial harmony', 'how labour can contribute even more effectively to smoothen the process of the country's social and economic development', and 'with such international analogies as appropriate', this institute fits well into the perspectives of Indian management and state, of the ILO and the European-based International Trade (union) Secretariats. It also obtains contracts for specific research projects from these.

All these 'above' and 'outside' linkages would seem likely to interfere with such messages as INTUC might otherwise receive from below. This does not mean that it is deaf to these. At least the AILS officer I met insisted repeatedly on the threat to responsible trade unionism in Bombay represented by 'violent' and 'anarchistic' tendencies (represented, I later discovered, not by the communist unions, but by the populist INTUC leader, Dr Datta Samant). But such recognitions, as with veiled admissions of the success of the independent radical mineworkers' unions (Mehta 1978:37), do seem to come from INTUC elements somewhat further from the Delhi headquarters of INTUC and the international agencies, and somewhat closer to the ground.

Evidence of the limitations of traditional trade unionism was provided by what I found 25 kilometres from the union headquarters in Delhi in the peri-urban district of Mehraulienuka. This is an area that has become well known through the organising work of Primila Lewis (1978), and which has possibly had more attention from reformers, project organisers, the national and international media than any such other. It is an area of small farms, of quarries, brick fields and small factories. Many of the farms are the weekend cottages of the Delhi rich (including Mrs Gandhi), and others are more systematically developed as a second source of income from fruit, flowers, vegetables, chickens, cattle or horse breeding. Despite the efforts of individual organisers or reformers such as Primila Lewis, and despite the claims of Ramesh Gupta, the Delhi advocate who leads the Brick Kiln Labourers Union, it was still possible in 1980 to meet a bonded labourer—a man whose family was being held as security for his return from a wedding since he was indebted to a labour contractor. It was also possible to talk to landless labourers who had been legally granted land, but who had their crop recently destroyed by a village head who was still threatening their land and lives.

That such a situation can exist some 60 minutes by bus from the headquarters of the national trade unions, the national peasant or agricultural labourer's organisation—organisations that are busy with 'rural development projects' or with slogans of 'worker/peasant alliance', speaks more loudly than the developmentalism of the one type or the somewhat routine self-criticism of the other.

Both the brick kiln labourers and the poor peasants were *harijans* (outcasts). In the absence of the traditional trade unions, the kiln workers are dependent on their own meagre capacities, on sympathetic radicals or on such help as they might get from the *harijan* elite that leads the Dalit Panthers (the word *dalit*—oppressed—is the favoured one of *harijan* radicals). In the absence of a union with an ideology of class, they have one with an ideology of caste. As for the farmers and landless labourers, they are in this particular case being protected by a detachment of police, the farmers being accompanied daily to their fields by three armed policemen. But such 'protection' (which does not remove the individul who threatens them nor equip them for self-protection) is in the Mehrauli case probably due to the publicity work and political influence of the middle-class radicals.

Autonomy and Unity

Evidence on the tendency toward political autonomy and united working class action came from a lecture by Michael Fernandes, President of the Indian Telephone Industries Workers' Union in 1980. ITI can perhaps be taken as an example of a modern, large-scale (20,000 employees) state enterprise. Its union was presented as the politically autonomous, united and exclusive representative of ITI workers nationally. Although now a worker-controlled union, Fernandes gave credit to various 'outsiders' (mostly socialist or communist) who had created it, and revealed that he himself had been an executive engineeer within ITI, was on paid leave, was leading 19 other unions, and had been a mmber of the Janata Party for three years. I later discovered that he was also, or had been, elected or appointed to various local governmental positions in Bangalore. Fernandes' account of various battles did suggest a growing breadth of struggle over a 20-year period, including one in 1966 in which other union centres had rejected a joint action committee, a violent conflict during the Emergency (including police gas attacks and arrests of 94 workers), and ending with a nine-day strike in 1979 jointly with other public sector enterprises (which predominate in Bangladore). Less than one year later, Bangladore was rocked by a long, bitter and violent strike which pitted this working class 'elite' against the state and provided stimulus to Mrs Gandhi's strike-ban plans (Anon 1981).

Fernandes showed some consciousness of the manner in which the state sector is directly stimulating small-scale capitalism by subcontracting to its own engineers or to political clients. He claimed that Bharat Heavy Electricals Limited (a gigantic state corporation much criticised recently, as in Ramamurti 1978, 1979; *Business India*, 1980; *Blitz* 1980), was obtaining a considerable percentage of its production externally at Rs. 3-6 per day, rather than at Rs. 500 per month within the enterprise. Such awareness of the role of the state sector in the political economy of India did not seem, however, to lead Fernandes to demans wider than the state sector iself. He concentrated on wages and conditions issues, as well as on the symbols of managerial prestige such as separate toilets and canteens.

Fernandes' critique of management's participation schemes was, however, sharp (compare Basu 3.9.77 and Ramaswamy and Ramaswamy 1981: Ch.9). He expressed an *admiration* for the Yuguslav model. But he only *argued* for the kinds of demands being currently made in *Western* Europe—demands which do not seem to speak to the problems of a primarily agricultural and rural society. When he did speak on company responsibility to those outside the enterprises (a traditional theme in Indian discussion on the role of the state sector: see Vijayendra and Mohan 1981), it was to ridicule current practices, and to suggest that managements should gradually hand over their urban and rural welfare projects to the unions. Other restrictions on at least the ITI model of unionist were either revealed unintentionally by Fernandes, or intentionally by an ITI manager (possibly wishing to punish Fernandes for his threat to managerial toilets). Thus, Fernandes, when discussing the possibility of writing a history of the ITIWU, said it would have to be externally financed because union funds were restricted to the half rupee per month's membership fee. This miniscule fee (0.1% of the minimum ITI wage) contrasts sharply with the Rs2.00 being paid monthly to the worker-led general workers union, the Sarva Shramik Sangh in Bombay. And the ITI manager, commenting on the worker credit co-operatives of which Fernandes had proudly spoken suggested that they were a source of corruption when he stated that workers spent tousands of rupees to get elected to their boards.

The New-Style Leaders

Evidence of a new-style union leadership was found in such widely differing and separated areas as the capitalist textile and engineering centre provided by Bombay, and the nationalised coalmining centre of Dhanbad, Bihar.

I have already mentioned the fear apparently being struck into the heart of institutionalised unionism in Bombay by Dr Datta Samant. The fear was closely allied with a disdain for the workers 'who will follow any leader who offers them something, just like sheep' (The irony of my question was missed when I suggested that we needed to know why such sheeplike workers were just now switching from the RMMS). I unfortunately missed the chance to interview Samant in 1980 just at the point at which INTUC was deciding to disembarass itself of someone they had tried unsuccessfully to digest. I heard more of Samant from a tendency which possibly has almost as much reason to fear him, but which certainly has more appreciation of what he represents (Pendse 1981). This is the independent Marxist tendency which has also been trying to replace the predominant but sclerotic RMMS and the INTUC unions in Bombay. Samant seems to personalise the bitter frustration and aggression of the Bombay workers, as well as their continuing incapacity to create worker-led democratically-run, class-oriented unions. he has cut through the restrictive cobweb of labour legislation, grievance procedure and colelctive bargaining like (to change metaphors in mid-sentence) a hot knife through frozen ghee. He will not reputedly handle individual grievances, treats bargaining procedures and company accounts as—respectively—capitalist tricks and capitalist lies, and organises mass movements for broad, non-negotiable demands. He has even gained rural backing for wage-worker struggles.

Workers in the mood to fight turn to him from their traditionally corrupt and compromising leaderships. This is presumably why INTUC, wishing to have a second string to its bow, was prepared to associate itself with him. The obvious limitation on the Samant model is its personalism. There is no real attempt to create permanent worker-controlled organisations, such democracy as exists being of a plebiscitary style. *Goondas* (thugs) are said to be employed against those of the other unions and managements, and low-level leadership is often assumed by adventurist, aggressive and careerist types. Moreover, it is said that despite his uncompromising public behaviour and activity, Samant is not averse to a very traditional type of closed-door politicking out of sight of his followers. Finally, it should not be forgotten that this is (despite his use of popular language) once again a middle-stratum leader, reinforcing in workers' minds dependence not only on behaviour, but also on one from a higher social stratum.

The leadership of the Dhanbad mineworkers is being provided by an ex-engineer, A.K. Roy, who was expelled from the CPI(M) in 1973 as an 'extremist'. Roy's leadership is clearly a much more advanced phenomenon, although similarities with that of Samant do exist. Roy operates in a much tougher environment, a provincial city now widely recognised as being dominated by a Teamster-style mafia of contrctors-*goondas*-politicians-unionists, affiliated mostly to the Indian Mineworkers Federation, the IN-TUC, the social-democratic-dominated International Mineworkers Federation and ICFTU (Ketkar 1979; Bose 1979; Ghosh 1979). A local officer of the State- and management-approved and INTUC-affiliated union admitted cheerfully to me that union officers were contractors, 'since union members do not pay their leaders enough to live on', but did not even want to talk about the question of who might have gunned down his former boss. In a situation that combines features of 19th century Wales with the Chicago of the 1920s, and in which migrating labourers have been favoured for permanent jobs over the *adivasi* (tribal) population, Roy has managed not only to personally survive but to get himself, together with his Dhanbad rural associate, Sibu Soren, elected as the sole two independent Lok Sabha (parliament) members in the 1980 general elections. How this has been achieved will be dealt with later. But it should here be pointed out that whilst the Bihar Colliery Kamgar Union may make a virtue out of its lack of a formal representative structure and office facilities (it is sited in a poor district and housed in a room the size of the neighbouring teastall, whilst the INTUC union is to be found amongst the government offices, and housed in a three-storey edifice), the effect may be to reproduce the membership-leader dependency of Samant's operation. Sympathetic local informants suggested that low-level leaders were sometimes of the Samant type.

Worker-led Unions

The creation of worker-led unions, independent of either middle-stratum external secretaries or of the middle-stratum dominted parties, must be considered important in the building of working-class self-confidence in a country where this is traditionally lacking. Yet, as the case of the ITI Workers

Union suggests, such unions are not by this token liberated from the ills of the traditional ones. Nor, on the other hand, can we automatically assume that externally-led or affiliated unions are simply subservient to outside forces or classes (this latter point is convincingly argued by Ramaswamy 1979). The three worker-led unions I did meet all had some relations with outside intellectuals and/or parties, and it would require investigation to discover whether their differences from each other were less than their similarities, or whether their similarities with the old type were not more than their differences. Yet, freedom from formal linkages to the inevitably sectarian parties and the self-interest of professional middle-stratum leaders would seem to make them more open to pressures from their own memberships—more representative in the full sense of the word.

Although the Kamani Employees Union is also based on one engineering company of some 4,000 workers, it would appear to be of a more advanced type than the Bata union. Competiton for leadership positions is not on the basis of party lists, and its executive has included supporters of the Marathi communalist Shiv Sena and Congress, as well as the various red flag parties. The union is marked by a high level of participation and internal democracy, with all levels of leadership being directly elected from the base. It has taken part in local struggles outside the enterprise, taken solidarity action in favour of state farm workers, and was in 1980 linked with an all-Maharashtra mass alliance (see below). When marches of landless labourers come into Bombay, Kamani workers have contributed their mid-day meal to them. The union also released its 'Working President' (a post distinguished from that of an external figurehead leader) to work with textile workers in Kanpur, some 800 kilometres or so away. In the face of redundancies due to a bankruptcy provoked by ownership incompetence, the union once offered to purchase the shares of a Kamani plant from the official receivers. Although this offer had been rejected, the union leadership was, when questioned, sympathetic to the idea of worker co-operatives being brought into relationship with rural production and with consumer co-operatives. Conscious of the danger of replicating the capitalist co-operatives that predominate in India, unionists I interviewed declared that they did have access to ouside experts with a pro-worker orientation, and one stated that they were interested in a 'class struggle' co-operative strategy rather than co-ops integrated into capitalist market operations. They were also hoping in the future to release one or two of their officers, on minimum wages, to organise unorganised workers in the surrounding area.

The very structure of the Sarva Shramik Sangh (All Toilers' League) in Bombay would seem to deny it the inward-looking propensity of a plant- or enterprised-based union. As its name suggests, it is a general workers union, and it claims 15,000 members in the bombay area. It is open to both permanent and contract workers, organises many small-scale units (such as are found in the many industrial estates in India), as well as the women saltpan workers in the Bombay peri-urban area. Membership fees are four times higher than those of the ITI workers, at Rs 2 per month, of which 50 Paise is for strike funds. The union was fighting some seven strikes, including a seven-month lockout. It was also involved in an inter-union dispute with followers of Samant! The SSS claimed that the traditional unions were interested neither in organising the small enterprises, nor in solidarity with other oppressed people. Thus, it had been the only one in Bombay to call for a solidarity strike (which not even all its own members had accepted) in protest against a massacre of *harijans*. It had also collaborated with socialist feminists in running a three-day camp (school) for the women saltpan workers.

Both the Sarva Shramik Sangh and the Kamani workers had mentioned to me their affiliation with the Maharashtra Workers, Employees and Rural Toilers' Conference, an organisation set up following a state-wide government workers' strike a couple of years previously (Pendse 1978a). They said 50 unions were affiliated, with a worker membership of 1-200,000. This autonomous body has managed to collect Rs 300,000 to set up what was the only independent workers' daily newspaper in India, *Shramik Vichar (Toilers' Thought)*. This body would appear to provide the highest level of politically-autonomous, class-oriented, mass alliance presently in India. Although the newspaper may have only a precarious existence, and even if the conference should not be able to advance or to preserve its autonomy and unity, it clearly deserves closer examination. I was unable to meet any of its organisers. But I did hear of a previous experience of state-wide popular organisation during the Maharashtra state agitation of the 1950s, a time during which unions did dispatch activists into the rural areas. There are also a number of cases of forceful rural organisation and protest in Maharashtra, some with a long tradition behind them (Da Silva *et al.* 1979a, b; Mies 1976; Upadhyaya 1981). Finally, there does seem to be some kind of political-ideological leadership available, in the form of Maharashtra's Lal Nishan (Red Flag) Party, a party which seems to have assisted the co-ordination mentioned above without monopolising it (a more sceptical view of this party from someone with experience of working wth it is given by Omvedt 1980a, Ch.4 and pp.160-61). All in all, the Bombay-Maharashtra experience of the last five or ten years would seem worthy of closer examinaton by those interested in a new strategy for labour in India (Pendse 1978b; Patankar 1981).

Mass Alliance

We have here inevitably strayed into the last area—that of common action of unions with other labouring and oppressed sectors. But it should not be assumed that *only* the auntonomous and worker-led unions are capable of this. The very considerable distance between top national leaderships (inevitably concerned with party-political compromises, organisational self-interest, electoral alliances, class compromises and international sponsorship) and leaders at city or enterprise level, leaves the latter in a very different situation, open to quite other experiences. Thus, one knows that whilst one of the red flag unions collaborated vociferously with the Emergency (AITUC), and whilst another (CITU) cautiously kept its head down, many of their activists suffered dismissal, blacklisting, arrest, torture and death (Selbourne 1977). Indeed, what is common amongst the leaders of the four organisations I intend to mention here is not their class origin, nor their political affiliations, but their experience of repression during the past. A.K. Roy of the BCKU and Sankar Neogy of the Chhatisgarh Mines Sramik Sangh (CMSS) were both in prison during the Emergency. P.K. Ganguli of the AITUC in Jamshedpur has also been in prison. And Sayeed Waquar ul Ahad of CITU in Jaipur had to hide at a relative's farm near Delhi in order to avoid arrest.

Of the three cases, that of the BCKU is perhaps the most dramatic and best known (Iyer and Maharaj 1977; Das 1978; Rodrigues 1978; Pradeep and Das 1979).

Less a union than a movement, this body appears to overlap with the Jharkand Mukti Morcha (Forests and Mountains Movement). The latter is a peasant and regional autonomy movement based on the Santals and other *adivasis* in the wooded uplands of eastern Bihar and bordering states. The JMM appears, again, to be less tribalist or regionalist than a broad popular protest movement, expressing mass resentment against the particularly crude forms of oppression, exploitation and despoliation exercised in what is India's mineral heartland. The union itself began largely as a protest against the *goonda* unions that represent one face of the company-contractor-political party-state complex of exploitation and oppression. This local ruling bloc naturally exploited every possible division amongst the masses for control purposes Hindu-*adivasi*, Hindu-Muslim, migrant-local, permanent worker, contract worker, etc.). But over time even permanent migrant workers have discovered the support that can be offered them by the rural *adivasi*—who have egalitarian traditions and long history of armed resistance to British and Indian oppressors alike (see the three-part study of Pardesi 1980). Just as the autonomy of the BCKU suggests the failure of the traditional unions to effectively defend the less-industrialised workers, so does the creation of the JMM suggest the failure of the traditional parties to defend the most-oppressed sectors.

The JMM differentiates itself from pervious local autonomy movements on the grounds that it is (1) non-tribal; (2) linked precisely with the workers through the BCKU; (3) Marxist; (4) seeks to create a socialist state within the Indian Union. A distinction is made amongst the *adivasis* between the outsiders who oppress *diku* and those who don't. At the peak of the rural *adivasi* movement some years ago, there was a social renaissance, in which liquor stills were smashed, schools started, land occupied, grain pooled, wife-beaters beaten (by women), women educated and armed. Along with some notion of future collective working of land, there exists also some vague idea of worker

management of the massive state and private mining and engineering enterprises of the region. There also exists a growing consciousness of state and
capitalist despoliation of the delicately-balanced natural environment of this
low-rainfall, poor-soil, rock upland region. The symbol of the JMM in
Singbhum (where the JMM cadidate Devendra Manjhi narrowly missed election in early 1980) was the 'double leaf' of the sal tree, one of the trees on
which the forest-dwellers survive, and which are being felled by the Forest
Department's private contractors. Given that mines are scattered amongst the
villages, and that many miners are local farmers, it might be felt that a worker-
peasant alliance here is 'easy' or 'natural'. But the development of permanent,
democratic and politically stable organisations is certainly not so (A.S. 1980;
Dhar 1980).

It may be true tht the existence of worker-peasants or peasant-worker does
provide a base within individual or family experience for such an alliance.
Thus, whilst the JMM in Singbhum has backed strikes of the peasant-
workers who are forced to supplement agricultural income with *bidi* (cheap
cigarette) making, local workers and railway unions have (with honourable individual exceptions) failed to reciprocate the solidarity they received from
villagers during the repression of the national railway strike of 1974. To see
an alliance here as natural would be to ignore its previous non-existence, and
the work that was required to convert the labour force experience of the
labourers into such a political form as has so far been achieved.

Jaipur, capital of industrially-backward Rajasthan, provides a less obvious
base for the building of such alliances, which is probably why even certain
achievements have received virtually no attention nationally. The most
dramatic achievement is the existence of a squatter settlement of 600-700
families called Mazdoor Nagar (Workers' Town).

This is the most advanced settlement of the Rajasthan-based Kachee Bastee
(Hutment Dwellers) Federation. The Federation is supported by socialists
and communists, yet preserves a non-partisan white flag, a symbol which can
be seen flying over the straw and rag huts of the poorest migrant labourer
camps in Jaipur. Mazdoor Nagar is itself evidently under the control of the
CIP(M) and CITU, one of whose activists took us to it. The very existence of
a permanent and widespread organisation of squatters or slum-dwellers is an
achievement attested to by their virtual non-existence elsewhere in India (but
see Singh 1979). A militant in Bombay admitted to me ruefully that even
when the red flag flies over the factory, the orange flag of the communalist
Shiva Sena flies over the *bastee* (see an account of a Shiva Sena *bastee* by
novelist V.S. Naipaul (1977: Ch.3)). The difficulty of organising labourers at
the place of residence in India (as compared, for example with Latin America)
lies evidently in the tendency to communal concentration according to caste,
language, religion, and even village of origin. Given this general situation, the
development of Mazdoor Nagar, which has existed as a permanent settlement
of *pukka* (brick or cement) houses for five years or more (see Punamia 1978) is

even more exceptional. It is a multi-class area, housing rickshaw-pullers, dairymen, factory workers, government clerks, and even policemen. It has places of worship for at least two or three religions. It has a leadership consisting of both Rajputs (the previously predominant military caste) and *harijans*. Among its most active leaders are women (from these two groups!). Its 1980 elections were reportedly on a non-party basis, and I was present when it was being argued that a certain problem should be settled internally and not by appealing to the CITU and KBF leader present.

The same CITU officer, Waquar ul Ahad, has been trying to organise the artisans in the gem-cutting industry. Gem cutting is one of at least 20 major artisan industries in a city the 18th century walls of which still surround a two-mile square area of largely 18th century crafts and commerce. Outside the old city, employment is dominated by government offices and public services, although some factories do exist and new estates are being developed.

The difficulties of organising artisans are recognised by the CITU officer concerned, and he was not sure whether they should be organised as unions or as co-operatives. Even at the first public meeting of CITU's Gem Manufacturers Union (which title nicely captures the ambiguity of an organisation of artisans), the demands being put forward appeared to be those of petty-producers rather than of wage-labourers. And the aims of the organisation were described to me rather in terms of a co-operative than of a union. It was also interesting to note a division of labour (conscious or not) between the two CITU officers met. Both were educated men, but one was an outsider evidently incorporated into the thought processes of traditional communist parties and unions, whilst the one responsible for the artisans and hutment dwellers was a local man, a muslim (thus belonging to a discriminated minority) had a broad knowledge of Rajasthani history and culture, and was also incorporated into the petty-producer culture of the Jaipur artisans. The creation of a worker-artisan alliance in such a city is evidently a task facing many false turnings and pitfalls, but it is noteworthy that leaders of a traditional red flag union are attempting it.

If it could be argued that the occupational structure of such a city urges such an alliance on the unions, this could hardly be said for Jamshedpur, Bihar, a modern steel and engineering city built around the giant steelworks and heavy motor chassis plants of Tata. The Tata family is one of India's leading industrial capitalist concerns, with interests spread across the board (but see Singh 1979) Jamshedpur, named after the company's founder, was conceived as a capitalist company welfare enclave, possibly on the British Bournville model. It is today a city of some 500,000 with some 100,000 in industrial employment. Although many other large companies and medium-scale estates have developed, and although the city has come to surround the TISCO (steel) and TELCO (vehicle) enclaves, it is still physically dominated by the Tata works and graced by the Tata-planned residential areas, parks, schools, hospitals, welfare centres and libraries. After a stormy union history in the inter-war years, and considerable CPI and AITUC influence in the post-war period (Kannappan 1959) the Tatas have evidently established a symbiotic relationship with the INTUC (Mamkootam 1977, 1978) for which Jamshedpur is some sort of national engineering union headquarters, and in which reside two important INTUC leaders, Gopeshwar and Gopal. That the word 'symbiotic' is not misplaced is evidenced by the manner in which the INTUC here related to the rest of the urban and rural poor. One of the IN-TUC officers criticised TELCO management for presenting its various local welfare projects as if they were the property of the company alone. They were, he said in 1980, a union initiative, and union leaders such as himself sat on the boards that supervised them: 'They were *our* projects', he claimed, 'the company is only the executing agency'. Despite the joint efforts of Tata and INTUC to build in Jamshedpur a model of class and communal harmony, it was the scene in 1979 of one of the most bitter and widespread religious riots to have recently occurred in India (see CPI 1979 and *Trade Union Record* 1979).

Furthermore, on the slagheaps of the iron foundry, women and children can be seen scrabbling for metal remnants in the clinker. A couple of years previously, half a dozen women engaged in such work had been murdered by contractors trying to monopolise even this miserable source of income. Even if the 'citadel image' of modern industrial employment is grossly misleading (as argues Holmstrom 1978) Jamshedpur, with its huge modern factories surrounded by miles of walling, barbed wire and watchtowers, provides the best imaginable evidence for it. The possibilities for joint labourer action in *this* environment would seem limited indeed. Yet an interview with communist union leader P.K. Ganguli in 1980 suggested that some such attempt was being made by the most moderate of the red flag unions—the AITUC. Once again, the very constituency of the unions concerned seemed to encourage a focus on workers beyond the single enterprise, and beyond the securely-employed. The Jamshedpur Mazdoor Union organises across the engineering and steel companies. And the Jamshedpur Contrctor Workers Union attempts to organise temporary labour in the same industries. The AITUC officers (of whom one was a TELCO toolroom worker, the other a blacklisted TELCO worker) claimed to 'usually lead contractor labour' in Jamshedpur. The activity of the communists amongst the unorganised workers was admitted to by an INTUC leader, but criticised for being 'on a political basis'.

The AITUC people said that there were around 20,000 contract labourers in the seven largest companies in Jamshedpur, of whom large proportions were tribals and women. The great majority of the temporary workers were, in fact, continuously employed and—under a 1970 law covering 'perennial work'—should have long ago been given permanent status (for union failures to get this law applied in CIP(M)-ruled in West Bengal, (see Basu, 1977b and 1979)). In early 1980, TELCO was nonetheless still using several hundred casual and contract workers for materials handling and other jobs on the assembly lines or within the plants—not to mention cleaning and loading work outside. It was said that all kinds of manoeuvres were employed by the companies to preserve large pools of temporary workers: the giving out of contracts (with workers being switched from one contractor to another, denying them legal status), the creation of 'co-operatives' of labourers (cf. Basu 1978b), the giving of contracts to certain union officers (thus evidently dampening their ardour with respect to at least casual labourers).

There had been a series of struggles for decasualisation, with certain improvements since 1971. In 1980 the struggle was entering third phase—that of seeking permanent company status for these workers. The recent TELCO agreement on decasualisation had been earlier shown to me by Gopeshwar, Secretary of the TELCO Workers Union (INTUC). It had been signed by himself, by AITUC, a JMM-affiliate, and various other unions. Yet, when I witnessed TELCO contract labourers being informed of decasualisation in 1980, this was being done by a contract worker leader of the JCWU—a man whose own name had been excluded from the decasualisation list accepted by TELCO workers in support of the casual labourers in March 1978. He denied that this had been inspired by the self-interest of the regularly employed assembly line workers (who had to shift their own materials when the casually employed handlers went on strike), and insisted that it was a matter of solidarity and fellow-feeling for men with whom they might have worked for 10 years. It was also claimed that the union had been looking after the interests of the least privileged amongst the temporary workers—contract labour—and those of the women amongst both categories. The women we spoke to were often the main income earners in their families, privileged over their menfolk because sand-loading and sweeping and cleaning jobs at TELCO were reserved for women. They did claim that their husbands were taking on more tasks at home, and agreed (when it was put to them by myself) that it would be nice to have the lighter factory assembly jobs. But this did not seem to be a union demand, nor were either they or their union aware of any danger of their jobs being 'de-feminised' once they had won security and welfare benefits (which Banerjee 1979 shows to have been the historical trend in India). Nor did there appear to be any women in the union leadership. Nonetheless, the Jamshedpur case did seem to show the possibilities for unions to move outside the 'citadel' as well as suggesting that the m~ privileged workers can be moved in the direction of the less so, n~ when the latter stand close by them and themselves take inde

This was my conclusion in 1980. When I returned in ear' the middle of a major movement of the contract workers demonstrations, picketing, and physical violence by cor The contract labourers were getting only clandestine h the permanent workers, and were being forcefully op of the official TISCO Workers' Union and the comr Director of this company (which is directly respon

the surrounding region) claimed that the campaign was a conspiracy to capture the TISCO company area, then Jamshedpur, Ranchi and Dhanbad, in a
bid to establish control of the whole of Bihar (*Times of India,* 3 March 1981)!
Much more effective in isolating the casual workers was the manipulation of
the 'temporary' ones. The temporary workers are relatives of (presumably
diligent and servile) permanent ones, who stand first in line for any permanent jobs going. Despite the fact that the jobs to be decasualised were *un*skilled labouring ones, and that the temporary workers had claim to the *semi*-
skilled factory floor work, management and union were effectively using the
tempoary workers agaisnt the casual ones. There was some discussion
amongst the somewhat dispirited communist union activists over whether
enough work had been done before the strike amongst the permanent and
temporary workers. Here, the need of workers outside the 'citadel' for those
inside becomes apparent.

The Need For a New Labour Strategy

The above evidence from my brief travels cannot be taken as much more
than illustrating the propositions. In the case of Proposition 4, I have not even
provided such illustrations—although one could take the existence of the
Dalit Panthers and of the Jharkand Mukti Morcha as demonstrating the differing forms in which the protests of the 'weaker sections' are currently being
articulated. Nor does it suggest in more than the vaguest manner the way out
of the crisis. For there is no justification in suggesting that the four positive
elements amount to a *movement* in the sense of a series of different protest actions and popular organisations with some kind of agreed direction.

This brings me back to my starting point. For if there is no synthesis of the
past experience of the labour movement, there is no way of settling accounts
with the existing organisations and strategies, of determining what must be
jettisoned, and what in them provides a basis for new strategies. Thus, we
find much intellectual energy—and not only by the 'acadeMarxists' in whom
India is rich—being put into discussions of 'left unity' in India (Panikkar
1979; Pendse December 1978). At another extreme, we find a tendency to
simply write off the traditional organisations and strategies (my initial impression from the voluminous writings of Timir Basu). Another response
is—either in activity or in theory—to bury oneself within one section of the
masses, either ignoring or denying the necessity for linkages with others and
for some kind of overall national or even international strategy.

The model for this is the peasant messianism of Indian Maoism (the tragic
of which is well portrayed in Hiro 1979: Ch.13). *Within* Maoism there
ared another such exceptionalism: the notion that one state or
hical zone would provide the Yenan from which the revolution would
n Bengal, Maharashtra, Bihar, and no doubt other areas of India,

there are powerful social protest movements that seem to see a local concentration as the antidote to the empty all-Indianism of the traditional left. The danger of the caste, regional and sectoral movements becoming casteist, regionalist and sectionalist is evident. It is *precisely* the isolation of the wage-worker movement from those of other sectors of the masses that have disarmed it. The lessons for peasant, caste, women's or regional movements should therefore be clear.

Efforts have, indeed, been made by the present generation of radical intellectual activists to come to terms with the crisis, the new upsurge of popular activity, and their own role within it (Sethi, 1978, 1979; Patankar 1981). Their efforts, however, are running not only behind events but also behind the efforts of India's bourgeoisie. In an article of remarkable prescience, Gail Omvedt (1980b) has revealed how the National Institute of Bank Management is itself analysing the various strategies of the traditional Indian left—and the rural mobilisation work of independent, critically-minded activists.

The Indian (and international) left will have long considered most rural development efforts and co-operative projects to have been functional to capitalist development, but both may be unnerved to discover the sympathetic interest that the NIBM is showing in the quite bitter struggle of the radical and independent Bhoomi Sena movement amongst Maharashtrian *adivasis*. (The Bhoomi Sena movement is, however, not as independent of state and capital as Omvedt's article seems to suggest. Da Silva *et al.* (1979b: 70) makes clear that the NIBM has had previous contact with the movement. And the study itself was supported by the NIBM, as well as that international organ of capital, state, reformist intellectuals and state-oriented unions, the Interntional Labour Organisation).This year, NIBM interest is in co-operatives; next year in workers' self-management?

Now, there is no reason to assume that Indian capitalism's house Marxists will not next year come up with equally sophisticated (or sophistical) strategies for class struggle and 'social ownership' in the urban areas. Provided that these are similarly institutionalised, similarly limited to production or consumer or exchange activity, similarly separated from mass mobilisation elsewhere, and providing that there is similarly no threat to the state. The alternative to such cunning is the mass alliance.

I believe that what many Indian Marxists may still consider as the *'privileged, male chauvinist, middle class wage earner in the enclave economy or within the state bureaucracy, incorporated into capitalism within his bureaucratised trade union'*, has a central role to play in the creation of such a mass alliance directed against capital and state. Whatever the truth in the quoted characterisation, it must be recognised that the Indian working class, on a broad definition, *includes* millions of wage-earners within the state apparatus (that the NIBM requires as an unchanged structure) and the tens of millions of landless agricultural wage earners (whom the NIBM wishes to socialise

292

under control of capital and state). It also includes the womenfolk of workers, even if these are overwhelmingly excluded from wage employment. To state this is not to give back to the working class the messianic role or promethean qualities asserted by the traditional ideologists of labour. Even where Indian captialism has most 'proletarianised' labour, it has tended to leave it with at least peripheral ties to petty-agricultural production, and to greatly encourage petty-entrepreneurial or middle-class aspirations. Without assistance from outside the workplace, proletarianisation produces only job, factory or industy consciousness. This assistance from outside is not to be simply conceived in a traditional way as being provided by the revolutionary intellectuals of the vanguard party—although such intellectuals and parties (plural) will have a role to play. It is rather to be provided by the self-activity of the less-proletarianised, which will remind workers that they stand not one-quarter of the way up a vertical ladder, but at the hub of a horizontal wheel, with spokes running to the periphery of the nation state (and beyond).

I did hear in India of more acts of solidarity by non-workers with workers than *vice versa*. Maybe the non-workers recognise the value to them of worker protest, maybe the immediate cost to them in terms of lost income is lower. On the other hand, I note that it was following a state-wide strike of *government employees* that the Maharashtra Workers and Employees Conference was first created, and that this organisation is apparently now extending its coverage to rural toilers. These may only be straws in the wind. But only those who can interpret the significance of such straws will be able to ride the whirlwind that follows.

Which leads to one last reflection, on the role of the intellectuals with respect to such a mass alliance. It seems to me that the question of who in the India of the 1980s is a revolutionary will be decided neither by the dexterity in the handling of Marxist categories, nor in the energy of organising one section of the exploited and oppressed (in which, on the basis of present performance, the NIBM may well be a front runner), but precisely on the contribution to generalising and linking the rich variety of complex mass struggles constantly occurring in the country.

Bibliography

Abraham, Amrita, 1979. 'Maharashtra Sugar Workers Draw a Blank'; *Economic and Political Weekly* 14(50) pp.2035-7.

Anon. 1981. 'Public Sector Workers' Strike', *Background Papers*, Build Documentation Centre, Bombay. May. pp.48-63.

As (Arun Sinha). 1980. 'New Aspects of Coalfield Politics', *Economic and Political Weekly*, Vol 15, No.49, p.2046.

Banaji, Jairus. 1980. 'Accumulation and Exploitability—Some Notes for a Study of Industrial Capitalism in India'. Paper to UNITAR Conference, New Delhi. March 11-14.

Banerjee, Nirmala. 1979. 'Indian Women and the Urban Labour Market', *Labour Capital and Society*, Vol.12, No.2, pp.123-44.

Basu, Timir. 1977b. 'Futility of Contract Labour Act', *Economic and Political Weekly*, 2 July 1977; pp.1041-2.

Basu, Timir. 1977a. 'Democracy or Collaboration', *Frontier*, September 3.

Basu, Timir. 1978ja. 'Bata Strike', *Frontier*, 18 March 1978, pp.2-3.

Basu, Timir. 1978b. 'Porters of Howrah Goods Shed', *Economic and Political Weekly*, 9 December 1978, pp.1998-9.

Basu, Timir. 1979. 'Plight of Casual Workers in Railways', *Economic and Political Weekly*, 7 July 1979. pp.1115-1116.

Basu, Timir. 1980. 'Calcutta Notebook' *Frontier*, February 2. pp.8-10.

Blitz, 1980. 'PM Halts Witch-Hunt of BHEL Official'. *Blitz*, April 12.

Bose, A. 1979. 'Dhanbad: The City of Terror', *Sunday* (Calcutta), March 3.

Business India, 1980. 'Is BHEL in a Mess?' *Business India*, March 31-April 13.

C.P.I., 1979. *Carnage at Jamshedpur*, Delhi: Communist Party of India, 13.6.79.

Chhachhi, Amrita, 1978. 'Towards a Theory of the Labour Movement: A Critical Review of Studies on the Indian Working Class'. M.Phil Dissertation, Centre for the Study of Social Systems, Jawaharlal Nehru University, New Delhi.

Dandekar, V.M. 1978. 'Nature of Class Conflict in Indian Society', *Artha Vijnan*, 20(2), Pune.

Das, Arvind Narayan, 1978. 'Agrarian Unrest and Socio-Economic Change in Bihar (1930-1970), Ph.D. Thesis, Calcutta University.

Das, Arvind and Peter Waterman. 1981. 'The Labour Movement and Labouring People in India', Paper to Workshop on the Trade Unions and the Labouring Poor, PECCE, New Delhi. 88pp.

Da Silva, G.V.S. *et al.* 1979a. 'Bhoomi Sena: From the Village to the World Order', *National Labour Institute Bulletin*, Vol.5, No.1-2, pp.14-22.

Da Silva, G.V.S. *et al.* 1979b. 'Bhoomi Sena: A Struggle for People's Power', *Development Dialogue (Uppsala)*, No.2 (July), pp.3-70.

Desai, A.R., 1979. *Peasant Struggles in India*. Delhi: Oxford University Press.

Dhar, Hiranmay. 1980. 'Split in Jharkand Mukti Morcha', *Economic and Political Weekly*, Vol.15, No.31, pp.1299-300.

Economic and Political Weekly. 1981. 'Gua Massacre of Tribals', p.1581.

Gerhardt, Paul. 1980. 'Mrs Gandhi's Victory and the Indian Working Class' *Socialist Review*.

Ghosh, T. 1979. 'The Mafia Still rules' *Sunday*, (Calcutta).

G.O. (Gail Omvedt) 1979. 'Maharashtra Sugar Factories Strike: No Attempt at Worker-Rural Poor Alliance', *Economic and Political Weekly*; 14(18), pp.1942-44.

G.O. (Gail Omvedt) 1980. 'Maharashtra Sugar Workers: Round Two', *Economic and Political Weekly;* 15(1), pp.16-18.

Goedhart, Peter. 1981. 'Dutch Aid to the Organisation of the Rural Poor: Is the FNV more Right-wing than a VVD-CDA Government?' (In Dutch), *India Nieuwsbrief,* No.14, pp.2-8.

Hiro Dilip. 1979. *Inside India Today.* New York: Monthly Review Press (revised edition).

Iyer, K.G. and Maharaj, R.N. 1977. 'Agrarian Movement in Dhanbad', National Labour Institute, Ne Delhi. p.141. Mimeo.

Jeuken, Piet. 1978. *Trade Unions and Development Projects in Asia: General, India, Philippines: Report of a work-trip.* (In Dutch). Netherlands Trade Union Federation (FNV), November, 75pp.

Kanappan, S. 'The Tata Steel Strike: some Dilemmas of Industrial Relations in a Developing Country', *Journal of Political Economy,* Vol.47, No.5, pp.489-507.

Ketkar, Kumar. 1979. 'Gangsterism in Dhanbad', *Economic Times,* March 5.

Lewis, Primila, 1978. *Reason Wounded: An Experience of India's Emergency.* New Delhi: Vikas Publications.

Lieten, K. 1981. 'Development Aid from Above—The Harnessing of the FNV' (In Dutch), *India Nieuwsbrief,* No.10. pp.13-19.

Mamkootam, K. 1977. 'Factionalism and Power in Trade Unions: A Case Study', *Indian Journal of Industrial Relations,* Vol.15, No.2.

Mamkootam, K. 1978. 'Industrial Relations in a Steel Plant', in E.A. Ramaswamy (ed.), *Industrial Relations in India,* Macmillan, New Delhi.

Mehta, Kanti. 1978. 'Relevance of Gandhi'. Mazdoor (Mineworker). May Day Issue.

Mies, Maria. 1976. 'The Shahada Movement: A Peasant Movement in Maharashtra', *Journal of Contemporary Asia,* Vol.6, No.2, pp.172-185.

Mukherjee, Kalyan. 1981. 'Dalli-Rajahara Pines for its Hero', *New Delhi,* March 16-29, pp.16-18.

Naipaul, V.S. 1977. *India: A Wounded Civilisation.* London: Penguin.

Nair, P.J. 1980. 'Labour Policy and Organised Working Class', *Indian Worker,* October 27. pp.5-9.

Newsletter of International Labour Studies. 1980. 'Special Theme: Indian Labour Studies', No.8. October. 28pp.

Omvedt, Gail. 1980a. *We will Smash this Prison: Indian Women in Struggle.* London: Zed Press and New Delhi: Orient-Longman.

Omvedt, Gail. 1980b. 'New Strategies of the Bourgeoisie, *Frontier,* Jan. 5, (Reprinted: *Build Documentation Centre Background Papers,* March 1980).

Pannikar, K.N. (ed.). 1979. *Prospects of Left Unity.* New Delhi: Envee Publishers, 1979.

Pardesi, Ghanshyam. 1980. 'Jharkand', *Mainstream,* Vol.18, Nos.47, 48, 50.

Patankar, Bharat. 1981. 'Towards Building a Revolutionary Working Class

Movement: An On-Going Attempt'. Paper to Workshop on the Trade Unions and the Labouring Poor, PECCE, New Delhi, 7pp.

Pendse, Sandeep. 1978a. Maharashtra Government Employees Strike, *Economic and Political Weekly*. Vol 13, No. 9

Pendse, Sandeep. 1978b. 'Working Class Struggles: 1977-8: Bombay'. 29pp. Mimeo.

Pendse, Sandeep. 1981. 'Labour: The Datta Samant Phenomenon', *Economic and Political Weekly*, Vol.16, pp.695-9 and No.17, pp.745-9.

Pradeep, Prem & Das, Arvind Narayan, 1979. 'Organisation of the future? A Case Study of the Bihar Colliery Kamgar Union', *Human Features* (New Delhi); 2(3), pp.240-55.

Punamia, Vidya. 1978. 'Workers Raise a City of Their Own', *Mainstream*, (Annual Number), pp.125-7.

Rajshekar, Shetty. 1980. 'Class-Caste Struggle: Indigenous Marxism?', *Caravan*, March, pp.12-15.

Ramamurti, P. 1978. *Stop BHEL's Dangerous Truck with Siemens*. New Delhi: Centre of Indian Trade Unions.

Ramamurti, P. 1979. *For Whom the BHEL Tolls*. New Delhi: Centre of Indian Trade Unions.

Ramaswamy, E.A. 1979. 'Politics and Organised Labour in India'. In R. Cohen, P. Gutkind and P.P. Brazier (eds.), *Peasants and Proletarians: The Struggles of Third World Workers*. London: Hutchinson and New York: Monthly Review Press.

Ramaswamy, E.A. and Ramaswamy, Uma. 1981. *Industry and Labour: An Introduction*. Delhi: Oxford University Press. pp.284.

Selbourne, David. 1979. *An Eye to India: The Unmasking of a Tyranny;* London: Penguin.

Sengupta, Nirmal. 1981. 'Beyond Marx's "Capital": "Sons of the Soil" in Particular, Ethnic Upsurges in General'. Paper to Workshop on the Trade Unions and the Labouring Poor. PECCE, New Delhi, pp.37.

Sethi, Harsh. 1979. 'Lok Chetna Jagaran' (Popular Consciousness Raising). Unpublished Paper, Indian Council of Social Science Research, New Delhi, February.

Sethi, Harsh. 1979. 'Between Myth and Reality: The Making of a Vision. Report of a Meeting of Activists'. Unpublished Paper, Indian Council of Social Science Research, New Delhi.

Singh, Rajan. 'The Urban Poor and Organisation: Bombay Slum-dwellers Organise', *How*, Vol.2, No.11 (November), pp.3-6.

Trade Union Record. 1979. 'Trade Union Convention against Communalism', *T.U.R.*, Vol.37, No.17, pp.3,9-10.

Upadhyaya, Ashok. 'Peasant Organisations in Thane District—A Critical Overview'. Gokhale Institute, Pune.

Vijayendra, T. and Mohan Mani. 1981. 'Trade Unions and Socially Disad-

296

vantaged Groups in Public Enterprises in India'. Paper to Workshop on the Trade Unions and the Labouring Poor, PECCE, New Delhi, pp.15.

Waterman, Peter, 1981a. 'Smashing the Indian Prison' (Review of Gail Omvedt, 'We will Smash this Prison!: Indian Women in Struggle'), *Book Review*, Vol.VI, No.2, pp.55-60.

Periodicals with radical news, reviews and analysis of Indian labour

Business Standard. Daily. 6 Prafulla Sarkar St., Calcutta 700 001, India.

Economic and Political Weekly. Weekly. Skylark, 284 Shahid Bhagatsingh Rd., Bombay 400 038, India.

Frontier. Fortnightly. Irregular. 61 Mott Lane, Calcutta 700 013, India.

How. Monthly. 6/9 Sarva Priya vihar, New Delhi 110 016, India.

Newsletter of International Labour Studies. Quarterly. Galileistraat 130, 2561 TK, The Hague, Netherlands.

INDIA: TRANSCENDING THE
TRADITIONAL COMMUNIST MOVEMENT

Bharat Patankar

Over the last fifteen years, except for the victory of the Vietnamese revolution and the liberation movements in Southern Africa, the history of communist and working-class movements has been one of the formation of new
groups, their disintegration and attempts at re-formation.

When these groups were formed in the late 1960s and early 1970s, all traditional commmunist and socialist parties started branding them as the expression of petty-bourgeois romanticism, individualism and left sectarianism.
They were not ready to look at this phenomenon as the outcome of the changing objective situation of world imperialism and working peoples'
movements, or why this was happening in the field of the communist movement, simultaneously all over the world.

' India is a good example to examine because it combines modern relations of
production with the problems of a backward society. It has the most advanced
industry of the multinationals and state and private Indian monopolies; it has
areas of sophisticated technology and research, and it has a long tradition of
bourgeois democracy. And, ironically, all this is combined with the most
backward forms of caste oppression, women's confinement in purdah and the
home—even atrocities like bride-burning—and the extreme exploitation of
unorganised workers in small-scale industry, of adivasis in mines, and of
migrant labourers both in urban areas and in the rural areas of the 'green
revolution'. This objective situation poses a combination of problems to the
Indian working peoples' movements, for which they have to appropriate the
experiences of the most advanced workers' movements in Western countries,
as well as those of revolutionary movements in 'Third World' countries.

The break in India from the orthodox communist mould began in 1966-7
with the 'Naxalbari' and the 'Naxalite movement'. Though the Naxalbari and
the Srikakulam uprisings were the most dramatic expressions of the situation,
a more complex reality expressed itself in new movements all over India.
From the beginning, along with the tendencies which split away from CPI(M)
and called themselves 'Marxist-Leninist' and followers of Mao Tse-tung
thought, there were many groupings which remained critical of this dominant
trend. Even in eastern India, the centre of the Naxalite upsurge, such groupings could be found. In the early 1970s, in industrially advanced Maharashtra
state, a new group developed which, while taking its emotional inspiration
from Naxalbari, started out with a critical attitude towards the theoretical-
political approach of the Marxist-Leninist groups—going as far as to say, 'We
will put Marx himself underneath the microscope.' And in Delhi, a new

From Race & Class, *Vol XXVI, No 3, Winter 1985, published by the Institute of Race Relations, London. Reprinted
with permission.*

group emerged from within the Trotskyite tendency which was to evolve a critical approach to Trotskyism and Marxism as a whole. With only one or two exceptions, these groups were not just petty-bourgeois discussion circles, but were immersed in both rural and urban working peoples' movements from the beginning. Thus, the post-1967 political formations were an eclectic combination which emerged out of the social contradictions in India with its two fold character of modernity and backwardness.

Since this early period, that is 1967 to 1971-2, many changes have taken place in the movement. After the early 1970s, the CPI(M-L) suffered a period of demoralisation and splits, as did, subsequently, the groups in that milieu, and then, by the late 1970s, the groups outside it. Though this period was apparently one of disintegration and fraustration, it enabled the whole spectrum of political groups critically to assimilate both their own and other movements' experiences.

In fact, what was emerging can be explained in terms of the upsurge in new forms of peoples' movements from the early 1970s onwards. Because of their interaction with these new forms of popular movement, the communist groups and tendencies began, after a prolonged period of disorganisation and frustration, to have a more advanced consciousness and involvement. Even those groups that still hold fast to their own theories and ideologies have to confront the realities of changing class relations in the backward areas which they usually choose to work in. Unable to make an alliance with 'rich peasants' in the rural areas, unable to evade caste questions and the issue of women's oppression, compelled to confront problems of the forest areas and ecology, they have to attempt to acclimatise themselves to a rapidly changing situation. The time is fast approaching when they will be unable to find a 'backward' area where they can go without confronting these issues and still proceed in a revolutionary manner.

One of the most important new tendencies, which called itself the Dalit* Panthers after the US Black Panthers, emerged in the early 1970s in Maharashtra. Just as racism gave rise to the Black Panthers in the US, it was caste oppression, an issue that the working-class movement led by the communists had never been able to come to grips with, which gave rise to the Dalit Panthers in India. Not that this was the first attempt to fight caste oppression—such struggles went back to the late nineteenth century. In the twentieth century, these struggles were most highly organised in states such as Maharashtra, Kerala and Tamilnadu. With independence, the bourgeoisie, for a time, tried to nullify the struggle by absorbing middle-class dalits. But by the early 1970s, dalit working-class youth, already hit brutally by unemployment, caste discrimination and oppression, came to consciousness, in a most advanced way and at a mass level, in a situation when the process of transformation of their sections in the villages into agricultural labourers was culminating.

★ 'Dalit', meaning 'downtrodden', is becoming the most popular and militant term by which ex-untouchables refer to themselves.

The dalit movement was one which raised questions not only in the economic sphere, but also in the fields of art, culture and social relationships, it dealt a blow to the cultural and social practices even of communists (Why do they do pujas? Why do they have arranged marriages and take big dowries for their daughters?) The dalits emerged with a new form of poetry which was not mechanically stamped with ideology but arose out of their lives—they were not afraid to use obscenity even regarding the Indian flag. The movement also came forward as a fighting force in Bombay against the fascist organisation called Shiv Sena, which was attacking the working class and communists. Along with the Dalit Panthers, there emerged new socialist trends from within the social democrats, who carried, though unwittingly, the ideology (put forward elsewhere by Marcuse) that students and marginalised sections (in India, dalits and, later, women) were the most revolutionary.

At the same time, new things started happening in the field of art. In Calcutta, a peoples' theatre emerged which had its background in the once-strong traditon of the Indian Peoples' Theatre Association (IPTA). It took the form of street-plays and called itself the 'third theatre' (the 'first' being folk drama and art, the 'second' being the traditional western-style stage.) This cultural form, developing in various aspects, spread all over India during the following decade.

The struggles of adivasis (tribal people) have, since colonial times, taken place in isolated pockets all over India. It is a peculiarity of the Indian social formation that there are still many adivasi communities maintaining their cultural milieu to a large extent intact. Following independence, one can see in some of these areas the combination of extreme backwardness with the most technologically advanced industry. Before the late 1960s and the early 1970s, adivasi struggles were mainly against the government attacks on their traditional rights to the forests and forest products. Though this remains a major aspect of their struggles, the problems have become more complex as both adivasis and the forests have become more and more drawn into capitalist relations.

The Jharkhand Mukti Morcha, which was ideolgically and organisationally more modern, emerged in the early 1970s and brought to the fore the issue of adivasis as an oppressed nationality, along with issues centred around forests, ecology and class oppression. This organisation was the first to focus on the forest issue, which had never been brought forward by the communist-led adivasi movement. It fought deforestation; it fought the construction of dams, and it fought World Bank-stimulated replacement of the traditional sal tree by commercial teak plantations. The strong alliance between this movement and the Dhanbad mine workers' union meant that the movement acquired a deeper dimension, in that a relationship was built between the working-class movement and movements of oppressed nationalities. Later, in the mid-1970s, the same issues were focused on by a movement in Madhya Pradesh state, called the Chattisgarh Mukti Morcha.

But things went further than this in the mid-1970s. From 1975 onwards, the women's liberation movement started gaining ground, on the basis of the militant participation of women in urban and rural class struggles. Leaving aside the traditional communist parties, even the most celebrated revolutionary movement of that time, the Marxist-Leninist, had a very conservative attitude towards this question. But Marxist and socialist groups in Maharashrtra and Delhi, and movements like the Dalit Panthers and neo-socialists, along with some traditional splinter communist parties, strongly supported such movements. Almost a decade later, the struggle for women's liberation has become an established fact, and even the traditional parties cannot publicly ignore it or the issues raised by its Marxist-feminist tendency.

In the sciences, there was a significant beginning in the mid-1950s with the establishment of the Kerala Shastriya Sahitya Parishad. But this did not acquire nationwide importance or expand until the late 1970s, becoming the 'peoples' science movement'. Recently, it was successful in stopping the building of a dam in Kerala which would have destroyed a forest called Silent Valley. It was successful in raising mass opposition to the dam with a publicity campaign about the disturbance of the ecological balance and the importance of maintaining vegetation and animal life—and fought both a communist-led and bourgeois state governments successively. Today, there are numerous examples in West Bengal, Kerala, Karnataka and Maharashtra where the peoples' science movement is raising issues related to agriculture, ecology, dams, pollution, etc., and getting more closely united with the overall working peoples' movement.

The field of health has also been touched by the emergence of new trends in the field of science. This began with the formation of the Medico Friends' Circle, by a small group of doctors from various states, and is now on the verge of becoming a wider movement. Marxist doctors are now developing the concept of alternative health not only in published and theoretical work, but also through some forms of mass work. A recent strike of residential and government doctors in Calcutta raised many issues related to alternative health, such as the malpractices of the multinational pharmaceutical companies, the necessity of viewing health care from the standpoint of preventive and social medicine, and the need to oppose the technocratic-mechanical concept of establishing health centres. The strike was against a CPI(M)-led Left Front government in West Bengal, which had to agree that it had not even thought about the socialist reorganisation of health.

Finally, since the mid-1970s, and particularly after the Emergency, the industrial working class, through its trade union movement, has started to show some new characteristics which have enriched all these developments. Asserting its strength through mass struggle rather than fighting through the courts has become more and more the distinctive feature of this working-class movement. The Calcutta working class had shown this same militancy from 1962 to the late 1960s, but since 1976, such an approach has become widespread all over India. The Bombay working class, which is confronted by the most advanced and shrewd bourgeois policy, made a breakthrough in this period. Because the character of exploitation and repression is much more subtle in Bombay and other Maharashtrian industrial cities than in other states, the existence of such a fighting policy shows the depth of militancy in the working class. Not only do Bombay workers face a highly advanced bougeoisie, but in addition, they confront the most modern technology and participate in the most advanced forms of the production process. So here, the working class can forge future strategies for those sections of the working class in more backward industrial areas.

The strength of the new fighting mood was shown in the celebrated strike of the Bombay textile workers, which started in January 1982. By its end, with the struggle continuing even while most workers had returned to the mills, the strike had brought forward much wider problems than those originally raised. These included nationalisation and its effects on the conditions of workers' lives; automation in relation to the reorganisation of agriculture and industry, including the reorganisation of the division of labour in the production process itself; and how to deal with strike-ban acts. Because the workers had gone to their villages during the strike and taken some new forms of struggle there also, the problem of putting forward a common strategy for the rural poor and the industrial working class came sharply into focus. As experience shows, the old strategy of 'addition' of the struggles of the rural poor on their demands and of urban workers on their own issues has exhausted itself.

Besides this, in the last four or five years, isolated struggles in chemical and engineering industries like Philips, Bajaj Auto, Rashtriya Chemical Fertilizers, etc., have shown that the issue before the trade union movement goes deeper than that of gaining economic benefits and wage rises. It increasingly becomes one of formulating alternatives in reorganising the division of labour and organising the modern production process on alternative lines.

The isolation of the struggle of these workers also raised the issue of how to make their problems more relevant to the broad working masses. At present, none of the communist parties and groups are capable of helping workers to develop a new strategy for solving these problems— but the gains achieved in the people's science, anti-caste and cultural movements, women's liberation, etc., can help in formulating such a strategy.

The last fifteen years have brought about the formation of numerous small groups and tendencies as a part of many new movements. Appropriation of all these experiences would necessarily imply the appropriation of the experiences of the European working class and the working class in post-revolutionary societies. This becomes clear if we enumerate the conceptions which are implicit and explicit in the movements that have developed in the last decade and a half.

1 In the late 1960s and the early 1970s, by 'revolution', people meant smashing the state, establishing a new working-class state, taking over the major means of production, reorganising land ownership, going for cooperatives and collectives—and this was all. This whole conception appears so outmoded now as to be laughable to many of those who themselves held it earlier. Now, revolution means not only this, but the beginning of a struggle to implement a new strategy regarding the relationship between men and women and between people of different castes and nationalities. It means alternative ways of organising and managing the production processes, alternative concepts of agriculture, an integrated concept of agriculture/industry/ecology and alternative health care. The second aspect of the new conception is the constitution of a proletarian state which does not stand over the heads of the working class, getting more and more alienated from it, but which is the process through which working people will gain control over reconstructing their lives. The struggle to establish organisational forms for this proletarian state is an inevitable part of the struggle for alternative strategies of organising social relationships and relationships with nature.

2 The concept of an alliance between different sections was limited ten or fifteen years back to the alliance between workers and peasants. Now, it becomes a question of alliances between various movements—cultural, women's liberation, anti-caste, etc.—and also of having a single concept of alternative social practices and an alternative production process. Under the previous conception, which saw social change as being mechanically brought about by changing the ownership of the means of production, the immediate programme could have no direct link with the final outcome.

3 Along with this, the formation of the programme of revolution cannot remain the function of a party or party intellectuals, but has to be a process in which the broad masses of the working people, with all their specificities of caste, nationality, sex, etc., will participate.

4 All this is going to have very crucial effects on the conception of the communist party, 'the vanguard party of the proletariat'. It cannot now be understood as one which trains the working class in it ideology, Marxism, that is, scientific socialism. Now it will be an integrated process of learning, both for those who already consider themselves conscious communists and for the totality of the working people—learning from each other and from the overall practice in the movements. So the party can never remain an organisation which is above the masses and specialises in handing down a blueprint for action. This changes both the conception of the party and the relationship between the party and the masses.

All these changes in understanding the revolutionary process are still in an embryonic form. But the objective situation for their continuing development exists in the changes in the structure of imperialism, as well as in the birth of new movements—changes and movements which will go on deepening. The questions which are raised by the Polish working class, very explicitly and recently, or by dissenting marxist theoreticians in post-revolutionary societies can now be related to the language which is evolving in the movement within both the 'backward' and 'advanced' sections of the capitalist world.

The process, one can note, has started almost all over the world. Not everybody who is involved in it is aware to the same extent of its worldwide character, nor is there any organisational link or dialogue on the basis of all these new concepts. But it is certain that what appears as crisis and disintegration is going to prove a gestation period towards a new working-class and communist movement.

CULTURE, STATE AND THE REDISCOVERY OF INDIAN POLITICS

Ashis Nandy

I

A society can conceptualise the relationship between its culture and its state in two ways. The first way is to look for the means by which culture can be made to contribute to the sustenance and growth of the state. The state here is seen as operating according to certain fixed, universal, sociological rules. Elements of the culture which help strengthen the state are seen as good; those elements of the culture which do not help the proper functioning of the state or hinder its growth are seen as defective. A mature society, in this view, is expected to shed or actively eliminate these defective elements so as to improve both the functioning of the state and the quality of the culture.

The second way of looking at the relationship between culture and the state is to do so from the standpoint of the culture. This approach may regard the state as a protector, an internal critic or a thermostat for the culture but not as the ultimate pace-setter for the society's way of life. The state here is made to meet the needs of survival or enrichment of the culture; it is never allowed to dictate terms to the culture. Even when the state is used as a critic of the culture and the culture is sought to be transformed, the final justification for the criticism and the transformation is not sought in the intrinsic logic of statecraft or in the universal laws of state-formation. That justification is sought in the self-perceived needs of the culture and the people, or in the moral framework used by the people.

This dichotomy between the state- and the culture-oriented views of society, of course, dissolves if one used the older idea of the state-as-part-and-parcel-of-culture (as in many traditional societies) or if one refuses to accept the modern idea of nation-state as the only genuine version of state (as is assumed by most modern political and social analysts today). In most non-modern societies, among people who work with the older concept of the state and not with the modern concept of the nation-state, the culture-oriented approach to state is seen as natural and the state-oriented approach as an imposition.[1] Likewise, in modern societies the nation-state-oriented approach seems natural and rational, and the culture-oriented one looks unnatural, irrational or primitive. The choice, therefore, boils down to one between the culture-oriented and the nation-state-oriented. However, for the sake of simplicity, I shall use here the expression state-oriented or statist to mean the nation-state-oriented.[2]

From Economic and Political Weekly, *December 8, 1984. Reprinted with permission.*

It will be noticed that I am not taking into account in this dichotomy the nature of the state and the nature of culture. These are vital issues and I have briefly discussed them elsewhere.[3] For the moment, however, I want to avoid them because I want to be fair to the culture-oriented approach which believes that a state can destroy the civilisation of which it is a part even when the 'intentions' of the state are 'honourable' and even when it is trying to improve a decaying civilisation. When a state becomes ethnocidal, the culture-oriented approach believes, the remedy does not lie in only capturing the state, since it provides no check against the captured state becoming as ethnocidal in scope as it was before being captured.

II

For the last 150 years, westernised, middle-class Indians have learnt to look at the first approach — the one which orients the needs of the culture to the needs of the state — as the very epitome of political maturity, achievement and development. Since the nation-state system acquired its present global predominance in the last century, most political analysts in the West, too, have forgotten the other alternative. And since a global science of politics became fully operational after the Second World War, the state-oriented attitude to culture has become the only way of looking at culture the world over.[4] Nearly all studies of political development and political culture done in the fifties and sixties have this cultural engineering component built into them. From Talcott Parsons and Edward Shils to Samuel Huntington and Lucian Pye, it is the same story.

This is part of a larger picture. Take for instance, the studies of cultural contexts of economic growth done during the same period. The main function of culture according to these studies was to facilitate economic growth. Aspects of culture which stood in the way of such growth had to be ruthlessly excised. In 'stagnant' cultures, that is, in cultures which did not nurture a thriving modern economy, the engineering challenge was to rediscover or introduce cultural elements which would trigger or sustain economic growth and the spirit of the market which went with it. This was the thrust of the psychological studies of achievement motive done by David McClelland and company and the studies of Protestant-ethics-like elements in non-Western cultures by a drove of social anthropologists. Even the hard, tough-minded economists of the period, who did not believe in the relevance of such woolly psychological or cultural-anthropological work, never faltered in their belief that a society had to give primacy to the needs of the modern economy, howsoever defined, over the needs of culture. So did the mercenaries among them vending the materialist — read economic — interpretation of history to ensure the centrality of their dismal science in the world of social knowledge. In India, at least, I have not come across a single work of any Marxist economist of the period who challenged the basic priority of economics and sought to restore, even as a distant goal, Marx's original vision of a society freed from the bondage of economism.[5]

An exactly similar case can be made about science. Most science-and-culture studies of the fifties and sixties sought to make the society safe for modern science. For this purpose, all non-modern cultures were sought to be retooled and made more rational or modern. Thus, scientific criticisms of culture were encouraged but cultural criticisms of science were dubbed obscurantist. Occasionally shallow criticisms of the social relations of science were allowed — in the sense that the control over science exercised by imperialism or capitalism or by army generals was allowed to be exposed. But this was done as a part of an attempt to protect the text and the core values of modern science which were seen as absolute and as the last word in human rationality. Here, too, culture was always at the receiving end, while science kept the company of modern political and economic institutions.

We however are talking of politics at the moment, not of the witchcraft called economics or the mega-corporation called modern science. And I want to suggest that in India the primacy granted to the needs of the state — seen as a necessary part of a ruthless, global, nation-state system — is not a new idea coined in the late 1940s by the first generation of the post-Independence managers of Indian polity. The primacy of the state was not the discovery of Jawaharlal Nehru or Vallabhbhai Patel, two very different persons who arrived at roughly the same statist ideology through very different personal and intellectual paths. Nor did the primacy-of-the-state theory evolve in the fifties or the sixties when the structural-functional models of political development and positivist-Marxist models of the state endorsed, at two ends of the political spectrum, the primacy of the state. The new model merely relegitimised what had been brewing for more than a hundred years in India and, perhaps, for more than three hundred years in Europe.

The statist model first came to India in the nineteenth century, in the second phase of colonialism, when a more reactive, self-defensive Hinduism began to take shape in response to the consolidation of social theories which saw colonialism as a civilising influence and as a pathway from feudalism to modern statehood.[6] It was towards the middle of the nineteenth century that a series of dedicated Hindu religious and social reformers first mooted the idea that what Hinduism lacked was the primacy which most forms of post-medieval, Western Christianity granted to the state. Even Islam, they felt, had a built-in space for such primacy. The Hindus did not. That was why, they decided, the Hindus were having it so bad. The sorrow of that generation of reformers was that the Hindu was an animal peculiarly hostile and insensitive to the subtleties of the nation-state system; their hope was that the hostility and insensitivity could be corrected through proper cultural and social engineering. This the religious reformers tried to do through a revision of the Hindu personality and way of life. This effort, because it came as part of a defence of Hinduism, hid the fact that this was the first influential indigenous form of the primacy-of-the-state thesis advanced in India. The thesis, for the first time, brought modern statism within Hinduism, in the sense that the Hindu state of the future was not to be the Hindu polity of the past but a centralised, modern nation-state with a Brahmanic idiom.[7]

The earlier generation of reformers, in what can be called the first phase of British colonialism, had pleaded for greater political participation of Indians and also for greater state intervention in the society. But there were externally imposed limits to their enthusiasm; they did not stress the absolute primacy of the state partly because the state was not theirs and partly because even their British rulers had not yet shown any great ideological commitment to the state system they were running.[8] The state for the first generation of British rulers was mainly a means of making money, not a means of cultural engineering. These rulers feared and respected Indian culture which they tried not to disturb as long as it did not stand in the way of their greed. Moreover, the raj occupied a relatively small part of the sub-continent and certainly did not give the impression of being the paramount power in the country. The Indians pressuring their British rulers to intervene in Indian society could not internalise a highly activist or an aweingly grand image of the state.

Nonetheless, the first generation of social reformers had provided the base on which the second generation of reformers built their adoration for the modern idea of the nation-state and their suspicion of all grassroot politics. Certainly, these latter reformers did not put any premium on participatory politics, which they accepted theoretically only as a vague, populist possibility. Even when they spoke of mass politics as desirable, they saw it as something which had to come later — after the Hindu had been morally and educationally uplifted and after he had learnt to take on modern responsibilities.[9] This shielded them from the awareness that they were unwilling or incapable of mobilising the ordinary Indians for basic political changes.

These votaries of a Hindu nation-state, thinking that they were pleading for a Hindu polity, were also mostly unaware that the nation-state system was one of the more recent innovations in human civilisation and that it had come into being only about two hundred years earlier in Europe, in the mid-seventeenth century. They chose to see it as one of the eternal verities of humankind. Naturally, they diagnosed the Hindu inadequacy in state-oriented politics as a result of a major defect in the Hindu personality and culture, which had to be reformed as the first step to political freedom. (The British in India for their own reasons, endorsed this priority of the cultural over the political enthusiastically.). Many of these social reformers, inappropriately called Hindu revivalists, were to later have much sympathy for the anti-British terrorist movements. But that sympathy did not go with any passion for wider political participation of the masses. Indeed, they were always a little afraid of the majoirty of Hindus who lived in the 500,000 Indian villages. *Hindurajya*, yes; but not with the full participation of all the *Hindupraja*; at least not with the *praja* as they were, and certainly not with the participation of all Hindus in the short run. The conspiratorial style of the terrorists came handy in this respect since it automatically restricted mass participation. Even the constant invocation of the Hindu past by the revivalists—the practice which gave them their distinctive name—was a criticism of the living Hindus. It was a compensatory act. It hid the revivalists' admiration for the West and for middle-eastern Islam, seen as martial and valorous, and it hid the desperate search for the same qualitites in the Hindu past. The political consequence of this admiration for the conquerors of the Hindus was the continuous attempt by many to re-educate the 'politically immature', anarchic living Hindus, so that the latter could redisover their lost Western and Islamic values and play their proper role in the global system of nation-states. Swami Vivekananda, when he envisioned a new race of Vedantic Hindus, who would build a Western society in India, was only being true to the primacy-of-the-state thesis.[10]

I am arguing that the nineteenth century characters the modern Indians have learnt to call revivalists were never truly anti-west or anti-Islam. They were only anti-British and anti-Muslim in the Indian context. Their ideal, in important respects, was Western Christianity or middle-eastern Islam. And as for their concept of the state, it was perfectly modern. If anything, they were fundamentally and ferociously anti-Hindu.[11] The only good Hindu to them was the Hindu who was dead, that is, the Hindu who had lived a few thousand years ago. They wanted to enter the world scene with an engineered Hindu who, but for his ideological commitment to classical Hinduism, would be Western man, a man who would accept the rules of the game called the nation-state system and who could not be short-changed either by the Westerner or by the Muslim.

It was this heritage on which both the mainstream liberal and the official Marxist ideologies in India were to later build. Strange though it may sound to many, there *is* a cultural continuity between this early primacy accorded to the state and the strand of consciousness which was to later seek legitimacy in the popular modern theories of the state in India. Both the liberals and the official Marxists like to link themselves to the earlier integrationist tradition of social reform, the one beginning with Rammohun Roy and more or less ending with Rabindranath Tagore (1861-1940) and Gopal Krishna Gokhale (1866-1915). This ignores the checks within the ideological frame of these pioneers. Rammohun Roy, for instance, was a moderniser but he located the origins of the problems of Hindu personality and culture in the colonial situation and not in Hindu traditions. He believed that the pathologies of Hinduism he was fighting could be found only around the structures introduced by British rule and, therefore, his own religious reforms and the new Hindu sect he established were directed only at the exposed Hindus, not to the parts of the soceity untouched by colonialism. In his own crude, unsure way Roy did try to protect the architectonics of Indian culture. He did not want Indian culture to be integrated into the modern world; he wanted modernity to be integrated into Indian culture. His modern admirers have chosen to forget the checks within him—weak though the checks were. They have built him up only as the father of modern India and as a mindless admirer of everything Western.

Thus, as far as the role of nation-state in the Indian civilisation is concerned, Indian modernists as well as radicals have drawn upon the ideological framework first popularised by Hindu nationalism. It was in their model that the modern nation-state first became an absolute value and acquired absolute primacy over the needs of the Indian civilisation.

III

Yet, there has always been in India during the last 150 years another intellectual current which has looked at the needs of the society differently. This current sees state-oriented politics as a means of criticising Indian culture, even as a means of renegotiating traditional social relationships, but it refuses to accept such politics as the *raison d'etre* of Indian civilisation. However, though a majority of Indians may have always lived with such a concept of politics, for modern India, the concept has survived only as a part of an intellectual underground since the middle of the nineteenth century.

It was only under the influence of Gandhi (1869-1948) that this current temporarily acquired a certain self-consciousness and political dominance. Gandhi has been often called an anarchist. To the extent he suspected and fought state power and refused to grant it any important role in guiding or controlling political and social change, he was close to anarchism. Also, while leading a freedom struggle against a foreign power, he could get away with his antipathy to the state. But this situation could not last beyond a point. His very success dug the grave of his ideology; his anti-statist political thought quickly went into recession after Independence. The demands of statecraft in a newly Independent nation were such that the national leaders not only began to look with suspicion at the Gandhian emphasis on cultural traditions, they also began to encourage political interpretations of Gandhi which fitted him into the state-oriented frame of politics, neutralising or ignoring his culture-oriented self as irrelevant saintliness or eccentricity. On this ideological issue, they were in perfect agreement with Gandhi's assassin, Nathuram Godse, and avowed statist. It was not accidental that Godse, though called an ultra-conservative, did not feel threatened by the modernists but by Gandhi.[12]

It is only now that this recessive strain of consciousness is again coming into its own in the works of a number of young and not-so-young scholars—traditionalists, countermodernists, post-Maoist Marxists, anarchists and neo-Gandhians. Evidently, an open polity has its own logic. At the peripheries of the modern Indian polity itself, the demand for fuller democratic participation by people who carry the heavy 'burden' of their non-modern culture is becoming an important component of the Indian political idiom.

This consciousness has been endorsed by a political reality having two facets: (1) an increasingly oppressive state-machine which constantly threatens the survival and the ways of life of those Indians it has marginalised and (2) the growing efforts of this marginalised sections to interpret their predicament in terms alien to the modern world and to the state-centred culture of scholarship.[13] I believe that this strain of consciousness will begin to set the pace of the public consciousness in India in the coming decades and the following section is written as a guide and a warning for those pragmatic spirits and hardboiled modernists of both the right and the left who might have to close ranks to fight this new menace to the modern Indian nation-state. Pre-warned after all is pre-armed.

The first element in this odd strain, the strain which views the needs of a civilisation as primary, is the belief that a civilisation must use the state as an instrument and not become an instrument of the state. This of course also means that the Indian state should be reformed before the Indian civilisation is sought to be reformed. This does not argue out cultural reforms or, even, cultural revolutions. But such interventions are not seen from the viewpoint of the needs of the state. The idea that a civilisation can be destroyed or changed beyond recognition reportedly for its own survival in the jungle of the nation-state system is given up here. At the same time, the culture-oriented approach believes that if there is a need either for a cultural revolution or for modest cultural changes in this society, it should begin in deculturised Anglo-India and then, if necessary, end in its externed parts (to translate into English the concept of *bahiskrit samaj* used by Sunil Shasrabuddhe).[14] Culture, in this approach, is the worldview of the oppressed and it must have precedence over the worldview associated with oppressors, even when the latter claims to represent universal, cumulative rationality and sanctions the latest theories of oppression.

Secondly, this approach believes that a culture, in the sense of traditions, represents the accumulated wisdom of the people—empirical and rational in its architechtonics, though not in every detail. It does not automatically become obsolete as a consequence of the growth of modern science or technology. In fact, a complex culture has its own ethnic science and technology which are sought to be destroyed by modern science and technology with the help of state power and in the name of the obsolescence of traditional knowledge systems and life styles.[15]

The non-statists believe that the traditions are under attack today because the people today are under attack. As classical liberalism and czarist Marxism have both by now shown their bankruptcy, many liberals and Marxists have increasingly fallen upon the use of concepts like cultural lag and false consciousness to explain away all resistance to the oppression which comes in the guise of modern science and development. The primacy-of-culture approach fears that more and more models of social engineering will be generated in the modern sector which would demand from the people greater and greater sacrifices in the name of the state and in the name of state-sponsored development and state-owned science and technology. The culture-oriented approach believes that when the lowest of the low in India are exhorted to shed their 'irrational', 'unscientific', and anti-developmental traditions by the official rationalists, the exhortation is a hidden appeal to them to soften their resistance to the oppressive features of the modern political economy in India.[16]

Third, the culture-oriented approach presumes that culture is a dialectic between the classical and the folk, the past and the present, the dead and the living. Modern states, on the other hand, emphasise the classical and the frozen-in-time, so as to museumise culture and to make it harmless. Here, too, the modernists endorse the revivalists who believe in time-travel to the past, the orientalists to whom culture is a distant object of study, and the deculturised to whom culture is what one sees on the stage. Such attitudes to culture go with a devaluation of the folk which is reduced to the artistic and musical self-expression of tribes or language groups. Ethnic arts and ethnic music then becomes, like ethnic food, new indicators of the cultivation of the rich and the powerful. Correspondingly, new area of expertise open up in the modern sector such as ethnomuseology and ethnomusicology. And cultural anthropology then takes over the responsibility of making this truncated concept of culture communicable in the language of professional anthropology, to give the concept a bogus absolute legitimacy in the name of cultural relativism.

Culture, however, is a way of life and it covers, apart from 'high culture', indigenous knowledge, including indigenous theories of science, education and social change. The defence of culture, according to those who stress cultural survival, is also the defence of these native theories. The defence must challenge the basic hierarchy of cultures, the evolutionist theory of progress, and the historical sense with which the modern mind works.[17] This radical departure from the post Enlightenment Western worldview the modern admirers of native cultures cannot accept.

Fourth, the culture-oriented approach tries to demystify the traditional reason of the state: national security. It does not deny the importance of national security, even though the statists feel that anyone who is not a statist jeopardises such security. However, the culture-oriented approach believes that national security can become disjunctive with people's security and may even establish an inverse relationship with the latter.[18] Some of them fear that India is fast becoming a national security state with an ever-expanding definition of security which threatens democratic governance within the country as well as the security of India's neighbours, who are parts of the Indian civilisation.[19]

In addition, the culture-sensitive approach to Indian politics seeks to demystify the two newer reasons of state: conventional development and mainstream science (including technology). It believes that new forces of oppression have been unleashed in Indian society in the name of these new reasons of the state and the new legitimacies they have created. Those for the primacy of culture believe that these three reasons of state - security, development and modern science - are creating internal colonies, new hierarchies and recipient cultures among the people, so that a small elite can live off both economic and psychosocial surpluses extracted from the people as part of the process of modernisation.[20] Modernisation, the argument goes, has not fallen into wrong hands; it has built into its codes which are opppressive. The concept of the expert or the revolutionary vanguard is a part of the same story or, as it looks to the non-moderns, part of the same conspiracy.[21]

It is the feature of the recipient culture sought to be created through the modern state system that the superstitions of the rich and the powerful are given lesser emphasis than the superstitions of the poor and the lowly. This is the inescapable logic of development and scientific rationality today. Only the young, the 'immature' and the powerless are left to attack the superstition of the powerful. (For instance, the belief of the superpowers that national security requires the capacity to kill all living beings of the world twenty times over, as if once was not good enough; the belief of our rulers that every society will one day reach the level of prosperity of the modern West, as if the earth had that kind of resources; or the faith of our science bosses that the expansion of TV or of nuclear energy in India would strengthen development without setting up a centralised political control system.) The so-called mature scientists, the ultra-rational liberals and the professional progressives are kept busy attacking superstitions such as astrology because they are small-scale enterprises of the ill-bred, native entrepreneurs, not the trillion-dollar enterprises which arms trade, cosmetics and pet food industries are. It is a part of the same game to emphasise the unequal economic exchanges between the East and the West and underemphasise the unequal cultural exchanges between the two which has already made the modern Western man the ideal of the official culture of India. The culture-oriented activists believe that the latter form of unequal exchange is more dangerous because it gives legitimacy to the 'proper' dissenters wanting to lead the masses to a utopia which is but an edited version of the modern West. The first step in the creation of this new set of elites for the future is the destruction of the confidence of the people in their own systems of knowledge and ways of life, so that they become recipients both materially and non-materially.[22]

Fifth, the faith in the primacy of culture over the state does not mean the absence of a theory of state. It means another kind of theory of the state, a theory rooted in the non-modern understanding of modernity and in a worm's-eye-view of the imperial structures and categories which go with modernity. It can also be called an outsider's theory of mainstream politics. (I have already said at the beginning that this approach does give a role to the state as a protector, an internal critic or as a thermostat for the culture.) However, it is an undying superstition of our time that only the modernists can handle the complexities or negotiate the jungle of international politics, ensure internal and external security, maintain national integration and inter-communal peace. It is a part of the superstition to believe that politics is exclusively the politics organised around the state and the prerogative of the self-declared professional politicians.[23]

The theories of the state used by the outsiders—by those who take the cultural approach seriously—differ in important respects from the dominant theories of political modernisation. It is the presence of such alternative theories of the outsiders which accounts for the allegations of irrationality or false consciousness made against these outsiders. These alternative theories look bottom upwards towards the modern sector of India, therefore, they are not palatable to people who rule India or who want to rule it in future after capturing the state from the present rulers. I have explored some aspects of such theories elsewhere.[24] I only need to add here that such non-modern theories of the state have no commitment to the idea of one language, one religion or one culture for India; nor do they think that such linguisitc, religious or cultural unification advances the cause of the Indian people. Unlike the modernists and the Hindu-nationalists, those viewing Indian politics from outside the framework of the nation-state system believe it possible to conceive of a state which represents a confederation of cultures, including a multipliciy of religions and languages. To each of these cultures, other cultures are an internal opposition rather than an external enemy. Thus, for instance, true to the traditions of Hinduism, many of these outsiders believe that all Indians are definitionally Hindus, crypto-Hindus or Hinduis-ed; it sees the modern meaning of the exclusivist concept 'Hindu' as a foreign imposition and as anti-Hindu.

The culture-oriented do have a commitment to India as a single political entity, mainly because it helps the Indian civilisation to resist the suffocating embrace of the global nation-state system and the homogenising thrust of the culture of the modern West. But they are willing to withdraw the commitment if the statist forces begin to dismantle the civilisation to make it a proper modern nation-state and a modern culture, that is, if India is sought to be fully de-Indianised for the sake of a powerful Indian nation-state. This does not imply any innocence about the nature of the global system. It indicates a refusal to accept the games the nations play and an awareness that the problem of internal colonialism in India is a part of a global structure of dominance.

Sixth, it should be obvious from the foregoing that the cultural approach draws a distinction between political participation and participation in state-oriented politics—between *lokniti* and *rajniti*, as some following Jai Prakash Narain put it—and it stresses the former. This is the kind of participation which tries to bring all sections of a society within politics without bringing all aspects of the society within politics. To those stressing such participation, the politics of the nation-state is only a part of the story and democratisation must have priority over system legitimacy. Alas, this also means that the non-statists refuse to see the need for democracy as a secondary to the need for a strong state. In recent years, this approach to politics has spawned a vigorous civil rights movement in India which is trying to make democratic participation more real to the lowest of the low.[25]

To the statists, this other kind of political participation is a danger signal. It looks extra-systemic and noninstitutionalised—the kind of participation which the modern political scientist, if brought up on the likes of Samuel Huntington, has learnt to identify as a sure indicator of political decay—a situation where political participation outstrips system legitimacy.[26] No wonder, many of those militantly allegient to the Indian state would prefer to see the peripheries and the bottom of the society either remain apolitical or, in case the latter are already in politics, be systematically depoliticised.[27]

In other words, the culture-oriented approach takes the concept of open society seriously. It knows how the glib talk of culture often hides third world despostism. Indeed, the approach takes the principles of democratic governance to their logical conclusion by refusing to accept the definition of civic culture vended by the usurpers or controllers of the state. Culture, this approach affirms, lies primarily with the people. Next door in Pakistan, the dumb general with the toothy smile can find no consolation in the new culturist point of view which is emerging in many traditional societies and, particularly, in this sub-continent. Nor can the senile Ayatollah of Iran in his new incarnation as an Islamic Dracula. Their Islam is a state controlled set of slogans and gimmicks; it has little to do with Islamic culture, for such a culture can be identified only through open democratic processes. Hopefully, a culture-sensitive polity in India will not stop at mechanical electoral representation of atomised individuals or secularised classes; it will extend representation also to the myriad ways of life in the hope that in the twentyfirst century Indian democracy will reflect something of the uniqueness of this civilisation, too, and pursue the principle of freedom with dignity as a basic human need.

IV

Finally, I must borrow two terms from contemporary philosophy of science to explain the 'link' between the worldview which swears by the primacy of the state and the one which swears by the primacy of culture. The former thinks it has an explanation of the latter which it sees as a product of the frustrations of those who have been displaced from their traditional moorings by the forces of modernity. More, not less, modernity is seen as the antidote for the insane, anti-scientific worldview of the disgruntled, culture-drunk, uprooted non-moderns. This is the tired crisis-of-change thesis. The latter worldview believes that alternative paradigms of knowledge—whether they come from updated Indian traditions or from more powerful post-modern theories of the state—cannot be legitimised by categories generated by the presently dominant paradigms of political analysis. There is fundamental and irreconcilable incommunicability between the two sets of paradigms. This is one instance, this worldview claims, where no genuine common language or dialogue is possible. However, the non-moderns do believe that it is possible for parts of the modern paradigm to survive in another incarnation, as a subset of another, specifically post-modern, and simultaneously more authentically Indian paradigm—somewhat in the way the Newtonian worldview survives inte post-Einsteinian world. With the growing cultural self-confidence of Indian intellectuals and informed activists, it is possible that the modern West will be seen by a growing number of future Indians the way Gandhi used to see it: as part of a larger native frame—valuable in many ways, but also dangerous by virtue of its ability to become cancerous.

It is known that when the Newtonian worldview is sought to be explained in Einsteinian terms, elements of it such as mass and velocity retard rather than facilitate communication. This is because the concepts common to the two worldviews, even when the same names are being used for them are rooted in different theories and, thus, have different meanings. (This is of course the well known meaning-variation argument in post-Popperian philosophy of science.) In the context of the issues we are discussing, this means that concepts such as rationality, empirical data, mathematisation and experimental verification provide no bridge between the state-oriented and the culture-oriented worldviews. Nor do concepts like history, culture, injustice, patriotism or dissent. No sentiment-laden lecture by the national-security chap on how much he loves his culture is going to appease the activist working among the tribals to protect their lifestyle; and no copious tears shed by the ultramodern, rationalist scientist for the Indian villager is going to cut any ice with the person to whom the superstitions of the rich (such as the billion-dollar con-games involving anti-diarrhoeal drugs or the so-called health-food products like Horlicks and Bournevita) are more dangerous than the pathetic antics of the small-time pavement palmist, being pursued by the urbane rationalists for conning someone out of a couple of rupees (somewhat in the manner in which the village lunatics are pursued by stone-throwing teenagers). If you speak to the culture-oriented Indian about the superstitions of the witch-doctors or *mantravadis,* he wil shrug his shoulders and walk away; he is more concerned about the irrational search for permanent youth which manifests itself in the annual cosmetics bill of American women outstripping the combined annual budget of all the African countries put together; he is more worried about the superstitious fear of being left behind by other nations which prompts the Indian Sixth Plan to invest more than Rs 900 crore in only the R and D for space and nuclear programmes when the corresponding figure for the R and D for education is 1.2.[28] The two sides—the statists and the culturists—speak entirely different languages. It is the unmanageable crisis of one worldview—in this case that of the nation-state-oriented modernity which has prompted some to switch sides. Call this defection another kind of political realism or call it an act of faith. I like to call it the latter; after all, faith *does* move mountains.

NOTES

[1] In traditional India, for instance, the state was clearly expected to be a part of culture and the king was expected to see himself not only as a protector of *dharma* but also as a protector of multiple ways of life and a promoter of ethnic tolerance. The *Arthashastra* may not provide a clue to this but *lokachar* does.

[2] It must be obvious that the word 'statist' does not have, in this context, the meaning it generally has in debates between the socialist thinkers and those believing in a minimal state.

[3] Ashis Nandy, 'The State of the State', *Seminar*, January 1982 (289), pp57-61; and 'Cultural Frames for Social Intervention: A Personal Credo', in J.D. Sethi (ed), *Gandhi and Social Theory* (New Delhi; Vikas, forthcoming).

[4] So much so that when confronted with the hard reality of a successful or unsuccessful culture-oriented approach to the state, as in the case of a Gandhi or a Khomeini, the modern political analysts and journalists fall back on state-oriented analytic categories, even when the categories show poor interpretive powers.

[5] One of the first Marxist thinkers in the third world to expliciitly recognise the primacy of culture was Amilcar Cabral (1924-1974). See his *Return to the Source: Selected Speeches* (New York, Monthly Review Press, 1973). He, of course, drew upon the works of Aime Cesaire and Leopold Senghor. One suspects that the African heritage of all three had something to do with this sensitivity. The disintegrating native cultures they saw around them were more threatened than threatening, something which even a Mao Zedong could not say abut China. In India, unfortunately, even the Marxism of classical scholars like D.D. Kosambi has remained in essence another version of Western orientalism and colonial anthropology.

[6] For a dicussion of the political consciousness which characterised this phase of colonial politics, and its persistence within the culture of Indian politics as an important strain, see my 'Making and Unmaking of Political Cultures of India' *At the Edge of Psychology: Essays in Politics and Culture* (New Delhi: Oxford University Press, 1980), pp47-69.

[7] Probably Bankim Chandra Chatterjee (1838-1894) was the first well-known theoretician of the state-oriented approach in India. I say 'probably' because he stated his position indirectly, often through his literary and theological works or commentaries on the works of others.

[8] The limits were partly internal, too. For instance the ambivalence of Rammohun Roy (1772-1833), who aggressively worked for the abolition of the practice of *sati* but also doubted the wisdom of a state-imposed ban on *sati*.

[9] Aurobindo Ghose (1872-1950) in his revolutionary years was a good example of such romantic populism. The revolutionary hero of Sarat Chandra Chatterji's novel *Pather Dabi*, Sabyasachi, is a faithful idealisation of this attitude to political participation.

[10] It was the same vision of India which explains Sister Nivedita's (1867-1911) discomfort with Ananda Commaraswamy (1877-1947) whom she considered too conservative.

[11] This has been discussed in Ashis Nandy, *The Intimate Enemy: Loss and Recovery of Self Under Colonialism* (New Delhi: Oxford University Press, 1983).

[12] Ashis Nandy, 'Godse Killed Gandhi', *Resurgency*, January-February 1983, (96) pp28-29.

[13]It is the attempt to grapple with this reality which has revived Gandhian social theory in India, mostly among people who will not be accepted as even admirers of Gandhi by the orthodox Gandhians. This revival has as little to do with the personal life and the personal successes or failures of Gandhi as Marx's life and his successes and failures have to do with Marxist thought today. The modern Indians naturally like to give the credit for this revival to either 'Hindu woolly-headedness' or to the false consciousness generated by 'romantic propagandists' like Richard Attenborough.

[14]Sunil Sahasrabuddhe, 'Towards a New Theory', *Seminar*, May 1982 (273), pp19-23; and 'On Alien Political Categories', *Gandhi Marg*, February 1983, 4 (11), pp896-901. Sahasrabuddhe is one of the few serious Marxists in India who have self-consciously built into thier models indigenous cultural categories.

[15]In the context of Indian traditions of science and technology, this point has been made indirectly and painstakingly by Dharmapal, *Indian Science and Technology in the Eighteenth Century: Some Contemporary European Accounts* (New Delhi: Impex India, 1971); and directly and passionately by Claude Alvares, *Home Faber: Technology and Culture in India, China and West 1500 to the Present Day* (New Delhi: Allied, 1979).

[16]On development, as it is seen by the wretched of the earth, from outside the modern worldview, the clearest statement is in Claude Alvares, 'Deadly Development', *Development Forum*, 9(7), October, 1983. See also Ashis Nandy, 'The Idea of Development: The Experience of Psychology as a Cautionary Tale', *The Times of India*, July 5 and 6, 1983.

[17]In the Indian context such a point of view was aggressively advanced by Gandhi. See the pioneering essay of A.K. Saran, 'Gandhi and the Concept of Politics', *Gandhi Marg*, 1980, 1(1) pp675-726. Also Ashis Nandy, 'From Outside the Imperium; Gandhi's Cultural Critique of the "West" ', *Alternatives*, 1981, 7(2), pp171-194; and Thomas Pantham, 'Thinking with Mahatma Gandhi: Beyond Liberal Democracy', *Political Theory*, 1983, 2(2), pp165-188.

[18]For instance, Giri Deshingkar, 'Civilisation Concerns', *Seminar*, December 1980, (256), pp12-17; and 'People's Security *versus* National Security', *Seminar*, December 1982, (280), pp28-30.

[19]This point has been sharply made by Bharat Wariavwallah, 'Indira's India: A National Security State?' *Round Table*, July 1983, pp274-285. Also, Deshingkar, 'National Security *versus* People's Security'.

[20]For some culture-sensitive Indian intellectuals, the definition of conventional development given by Eghbal Afsaneh, in the context of Africa, is the only valid one: 'Development is a structure in which a centralised power, in the form of a young sovereign state, formally negotiates international funds for rural populations representing ethnicity ... no external aid, in the field of development, can relate directly to ethnic groups caught in the problematique of survival. All aid is first absorbed and often plundered by state power.'
Eghbal Afsaneh, 'Ethnicity, State and Development Strategy in Africa', *Alternatives*, forthcoming. The Indian critic of development will however further generalise the principle and affirm that it holds for internal resources, too. An excellent description on the process of development in India from this point of view is in Alvares, 'Deadly Development'. For a theoretically alert description of the political context within which such developmental pathologies emerge, see Rajni Kothari, 'The Crisis of the Moderate State and the Decline of Democracy', in Peter Lyon and James Manor (eds) *Transfer and Transformation: Political Institutions in the New Commonwealth* (Leicester: Leicester University Press, 1983), pp29-47.

[21]A proper critique of the rhetoric of revolution has not yet developed in India. Revolution could be considered *in certain contexts*, a reason of a shadow state, the state which would come into being after the present one will have been captured by middle-class, urbane, modern revolutionaries. The sacrifices which revolutionaries demand subserve, therefore, the class interests of the shadow rulers of a shadow state. However, a critique of statism and a non-modern awareness of culture has just begun to take shape at the peripheries of the Marxist movements in India. See for instance some of the works of the Patriotic People Oriented Science and Technology group, published in the various issues of the *PPST Bulletin*.

[22]Ashis Nandy, 'A Counter-Statement on Humanistic Temper', *Mainstream*, October 10, 1981, and *Deccan Herald*, October 18, 1981.

[23]I must again emphasise that the culture-oriented approach to the state stands for greater democratic participation and, thus, for more politics, not less. It wants to pursue the logic of an open polity to its end, to widen the compass of democratic politics. On the other hand, state-oriented politics, in societies where there are living non-modern traditions, have often shown the tendency to throttle democratic institutions the moment participation by the underprivileged crosses a certain threshold.

I should also emphasise that non-statist politics is not the same as non-party politics. However, the two can sometimes overlap. The new interest in non-party politics is not the same which inspired some of the earlier writers on the subject such as M.N. Roy and J.P. Narayan. The new interest, however, builds upon the old. For a sample of recent writings on the non-party political processes in India, see D.L. Sheth, 'Grass-Roots Stirrings and the Future of Politics', *Alternatives*, 1983 9(1), pp1-24; and some of the papers in Harsh Sethi and Smitu Kothari (eds), *The Non-Party Political Process: Uncertain Alternatives* (Delhi: UNRISD and Lokayan, 1983), pp18-46, mimeographed. On the issue of culture and authoritarianism in India, particularly on how authoritarianism often rears its head in such societies as a part of the effort to contain the non-modern political cultures of the peripheries. 'Adorno in India: Revisiting the Psychology of Fascism', in *At the Edge of Psychology*, op.cit, pp99-111; and 'Political Consciousness', *Seminar*, 1980 (248), pp18-21.

[24]Nandy, 'State of the State', op.cit; and 'The New Idiom in Indian Politics', forthcoming.

[25]See the various issues of the *PUCL Bulletin* for an idea of the scope and concerns of various such groups, the best-known of which are, of course, the People's Union of Civil Liberties and People's Union of Democratic Rights.

[26]Evidently, liberal democracy in a multi-ethnic society has built-in limits on its own commitment to democracy. See Kothari, 'The Crisis of the Moderate State and the Decline of Democracy'.

[27]Such depoliticisation may come through increasing criminalisation of politics or from apathy structured by the failure of political opposition to tackle basic social problems. Both can be found in India today.

[28]Dhirendra Sharma, 'India's Nuclear Estate' (New Delhi: Lancers, 1983) p141.

CONTRIBUTORS

Javed Alam teaches Political Science at Himachal Pradesh University, Simla (India).

Kaiser Bengali and **Khalid Nadvi** are Pakistani economists.

K. R. Bombwall teaches at the University of Punjab (India).

Akmal Hussain teaches at the University of Punjab (Pakistan).

P. C. Joshi is Professor at The Institute of Economic Growth, Delhi (India).

Shahid Kardar is a Pakistani economist.

Rajni Kothari is Director of The Centre for the Study of Developing Societies (New Delhi) and editor of *Alternatives*.

Ashis Nandy is a Fellow of The Centre for the Study of Developing Societies and author of *At the Edge of Psychology*.

Gail Omvedt is the author of *We Will Smash This Prison* and a leading political activist on the radical left in India.

Bharat Patankar is a leader of Shramik Mukti Dal, Maharashtra (India).

Richard Reeves is a journalist with *Washington Post* and the *New Yorker*.

Sumit Sarkar is Professor of History at the University of Delhi (India).

Amartya K. Sen is Professor of Economics at the University of Oxford (U.K)

Peter Waterman teaches at the Institute of Social Studies, The Hague.

Editor

Iqbal Khan was until recently Lecturer at College of the Bahamas in the Bahamas. He is now working on a thesis on Marxist aesthetics.